The Urban Scene

THE
URBAN SCENE

HUMAN ECOLOGY AND DEMOGRAPHY

Leo F. Schnore

 THE FREE PRESS, *New York*
COLLIER-MACMILLAN LIMITED, *London*

Library of Congress Catalog Card Number: 65-15727

Second Printing August 1965

FOR *Elinor, Carol,* AND *Barbara*

Preface

The papers gathered in this volume represent some of the results of a ten-year search for rational patterns in the urban scene. I hope that they demonstrate that there is a considerable amount of order in a setting that is too often portrayed as entirely chaotic.

I would like to thank the publishers of the following journals for their generous permission to reprint articles: *Administrative Science Quarterly, American Journal of Sociology, American Sociological Review, Demography, Journal of the American Institute of Planners, Journal of the American Statistical Association, Land Economics, Social Forces, Sociological Inquiry, Sociological Quarterly*, and *Traffic Quarterly*. I am grateful to Robert R. Alford, J. John Palen, and Harry Sharp, who co-authored various chapters. The assistance of Bryna Silverman and Janice Deneen was also invaluable.

The preparation of this book was greatly facilitated by the receipt of an unrestricted Auxiliary Research Award from the Social Science Research Council.

Leo F. Schnore

Madison, Wisconsin
August, 1964

Contents

Part One

Human Ecology and Demography: Scope and Limits

THE FIRST CHAPTER in this volume traces some interesting links between human ecology, as it was developed in this country, and the approach known as "social morphology" as it was developed in France by Émile Durkheim and his followers. This essay first appeared in the *American Journal of Sociology*, Volume 63 (May, 1958), pp. 620–34. In one sense, it represents an attempt to establish a "legitimate" sociological heritage for a point of view that has often been regarded as peripheral or marginal to the main body of sociology.

This theme is continued in Chapter 2, which first appeared in *Sociological Inquiry*, Volume 31 (Spring, 1961), pp. 128–39. An effort is made to show that human ecology is a variety of "macro-sociology" in which variable properties or attributes of whole populations are related one to another. As such, human ecology can be readily contrasted with other sociological approaches.

Having roughly circumscribed the field of human ecology in the first two chapters, we turn to the field of demography in Chapter 3. Like those that precede it, this essay is a kind of exercise in elaborating a definition, wherein the scope and limits of an approach are set out. It first appeared in the *American Sociological Review*, Volume 26 (June, 1961), pp. 407–23. The main thrust of the argument is that demography must be regarded as an approach that is broader than the simple analysis of fertility, mortality, and migration. Changes in status are also amenable to demographic analysis, so that the narrow confines of the field as it is traditionally conceived must be extended considerably. When dealing with advanced urban–industrial civilizations, in particular, demographers are frequently dealing with one or another form of social mobility.

Chapter 1

Social Morphology
and Human Ecology

INTRODUCTION

ÉMILE DURKHEIM, of course, was not himself a human ecologist. The ecological viewpoint did not develop within sociology until near the end of Durkheim's life, and then in America.[1] There is no evidence that this new approach to social phenomena exerted any profound influence upon his thought, despite the fact that he regarded "social morphology" as one of the major branches of sociology. In Durkheim's scheme, this field was to be devoted to two major inquiries: (1) the study of the environmental basis of social organization and (2) the study of population phenomena, especially size, density, and spatial distribution.[2] These areas of interest obviously converge with those of human ecology as it was originally formulated.

This paper consists of an exegesis and a critique of one of his major theoretical contributions and a consideration of the broad implications of his "morphological" analysis for contemporary human ecology. It is concerned, for the most part, with Durkheim's doctoral dissertation, *De la division du travail social: étude sur l' organisation des sociétés supérieures*, first

[3]

published in 1893.[3] More particularly, the discussion is largely limited to Book II, where he dealt with the "causes" of division of labor and where the morphological approach was most explicitly used. The brief exegesis is based on a selective restructuring of his main argument, which is unfortunately scattered through many pages. We trust that taking up the crucial elements in his thought in somewhat different order does no violence to the essential logic of his position. This procedure has been adopted in order to point up the contrasts between his morphological theory of differentiation and the alternative explanations that were available at the time that he wrote.

EXEGESIS

First, it must be emphasized that Durkheim's intention in Book II of *Division* was to account for differentiation and its obvious increase in Western societies. The very subtitle is the key: "A Study of the Organization of Advanced Societies." Second, it is necessary to preserve the historical context of his work. The division of labor had long interested social philosophers, especially in the West. As early as 1776, Adam Smith had pointed to division as the main source of "the wealth of nations," and the concept itself can be traced at least to the Greeks. Unfortunately, these earlier writers gave scant attention to the determinants of differentiation, contenting themselves with analyses of its nature and its implications for economic efficiency and productivity.

In the latter half of the nineteenth century, however, increasing effort was given to explaining the process, with special reference to the "advanced" societies of the time. Comte dealt with the matter at some length, discussing the nature of differentiation as a generic social phenomenon.[4] Tönnies and Simmel also examined the problem in publications that preceded Durkheim's by only a few years.[5] By the time that Durkheim began his work, however, the dominant views in intellectual circles were still a peculiar admixture of utilitarian and evolutionary "explanations," both best represented in the works of Herbert Spencer. In large part, Durkheim's analysis must be seen as a reaction against the Spencerian view.

Durkheim's own analysis actually began in Book I, with a distinction between two forms of organization somewhat similar to the types sketched by Maine and Tönnies. The first type ("mechanical") was used by Durkheim to describe the relatively undifferentiated or "segmented" mode of organization characteristic of small and isolated aggregates, in which little control has been achieved over the local environment. The basis of social unity is likeness or similarity. There is minimal differentiation, chiefly along age and sex lines, and most members are engaged most of the time in the same activity—collecting, hunting, fishing, herding, or subsistence agriculture. The "social segments" of the community (families and kinship units) are held together by what they have in common, and they derive mutual support from their very likeness. Unity is that of simple "mechanical" cohesion, as in rock forms, and homogeneity prevails.[6]

Durkheim was fully aware that structural differentiation is a variable characteristic of aggregates, for he recognized another and fundamentally different mode of organization. He saw that modern Western society was based increasingly upon differentiation, and his concept of the "organic" type of organization was designed to describe the complex and highly differentiated structural arrangements of his own time. According to Durkheim, a complex and heterogeneous society, like all but the most rudimentary organisms, is based on an intricate interdependence of specialized parts. Labor is divided; all men do not engage in the same activities, but they produce and exchange different goods and services. Moreover, not only are individuals and groups differentiated with respect to functions, but whole communities and nations also engage in specialized activities. In short, there has been a breakdown of internal "segmentation" *within* communities and societies and a reduction of isolation *between* them, although mechanical solidarity never completely disappears.[7]

With this distinction between major types of organization in mind, Durkheim's task in Book II was to explain the conditions under which "mechanical" organization is superseded by the "organic" form. According to the mode of analysis that prevailed at the time that he wrote, Durkheim viewed this change in social organization as comprising a kind of "evolutionary" sequence, and much of his theory was cast in these terms. However, it would be extremely misleading to portray his work as that of an uncritical evolutionist, for Durkheim possessed a sensitive, critical mind and he considered and rejected a number of alternative hypotheses that had been widely accepted as explanations of increasing differentiation.[8]

With respect to the popular utilitarian version, Durkheim vigorously attacked the idea that differentiation was somehow the product of man's rational desire to increase his own happiness. In fact, he rejected all individualistic interpretations. The notion that social structure is merely the product of the motivated actions of individuals was apparently almost repugnant to him. It ran directly counter to his conception of society as an entity *sui generis*, and it obviously violated his most famous principle: that "the determining cause of a social fact should be sought among the social facts preceding it and not among the states of the individual consciousness."[9]

Durkheim then turned his attention to the evolutionary portion of the Spencerian argument. The organismic analogy, of course, was in vogue at the time, and Spencer had used it brilliantly. As to the division of labor in society, Spencer had held that "along with increase of size in societies goes increase of structure. . . . It is also a characteristic of social bodies, as of living bodies, that while they increase in size they increase in structure. . . . The social aggregate, homogeneous when minute, habitually gains in heterogeneity along with each increment of growth; and to reach great size must acquire great complexity."[10] In other words, Spencer's theory of differentiation—despite its cosmic overtones and utilitarian underpinnings—reduced to an explanation based on sheer population size. At the very least he pointed to a universal association between size and differentiation.

Durkheim recognized the potential role of population increase in bringing about further differentiation. Along with

Adam Smith, he was aware of the permissive effect of sheer size.[11] Large aggregates allow greater differentiation to emerge, but Durkheim concluded that the population-size factor was a necessary, but not a sufficient, cause. His reasons for this conclusion are particularly instructive. In contrast to Spencer, who exemplified the deductive method of proceeding from first principles, Durkheim was very much the inductive analyst. In fact, he showed the underlying weakness of Spencer's theory by pointing to "deviant cases." Concretely, he called attention to large, densely settled areas in China and Russia clearly characterized, not by extreme differentiation (organic solidarity), but by homogeneity (mechanical solidarity).[12]

Having thus rejected the Spencerian argument on empirical grounds, Durkheim tried to explain the absence of any marked differentiation in these places in the face of great size and density. It is at this point that Durkheim introduced a series of essentially sociological concepts, the first of which must be seen as an "intervening variable." First, he noted that social segmentation had not broken down (i.e., that there was minimal contact between the constituent parts of Chinese and Russian society). In the face of limited contact, these parts remained homogeneous, very much like each other with respect to structure and functions, representing a proliferation of essentially similar village units. Durkheim asserted that this "segmentation" disappears and that division increases only with an increase in "moral" or "dynamic density." In contrast to physical density—the number of people per unit of space— "dynamic density" refers to the density of social intercourse or contact or, more simply, to the rate of interaction—the number of interactions per unit of time. Until this rate of interaction reaches a high (although unspecified) level, the constituent social segments or parts remain essentially alike. According to Durkheim: "The division of labor develops . . . as there are more individuals sufficiently in contact to be able to act and react upon one another. If we agree to call this relation and the active commerce resulting from it dynamic or moral density, we can say that the progress of the division of labor is in direct ratio to the moral or dynamic density of society."[13] In other words, differentiation tends to increase as the rate of social interaction increases.

Durkheim then asked the next logical question: Under what conditions does this rate of interaction increase? In answer, he first observed that dynamic density "can only produce its effect if the real distance between individuals has itself diminished in some way."[14] He then pointed to two general ways in which this might come about: (1) by the concentration of population, especially in cities, i.e., via increases in *physical density;* (2) by the development of more rapid and numerous means of transportation and communication. These innovations, "by suppressing or diminishing the gaps separating social segments . . . increase the [dynamic] density of society."[15]

Thus, to demographic factors (essentially the Spencerian explanation), Durkheim added a technological emphasis. An increase in population size and density *plus* more rapid transportation and communication bring about a higher rate of interaction. However, the crucial questions still remain: what brings about differentiation? Why should a simple increase in the rate of interaction produce greater division of labor? If social units (whether individuals or collectivities) are brought into more frequent contact, why should they be obliged to specialize and divide their labor? A simple identification of "factors" obviously was not enough; Durkheim was also compelled to indicate the mechanism that would produce further differentiation under the prescribed circumstances. As it turns out, he had in mind a particular type of interaction, viz., competition.

It is in his identification of competition as the vital mechanism that Durkheim borrowed most heavily upon Darwinian thought, and it is this part of his theory that has been most widely distorted. Durkheim's argument was based on Darwin's observation that, in a situation of scarcity, increased contact between like units sharing a common territory leads to increased competition. Being alike, they make similar demands on the environment. Inspired by the Malthusian account of population pressure on limited resources, Darwin had been led to stress the resultant "struggle for existence" as the essential condition underlying the differentiation of species. In the human realm, Durkheim reasoned in turn, individuals or aggregates offering the same array of goods or services are potential, if not active, competitors. Thus, according to Durkheim,

> If work becomes divided more as societies become more voluminous [i.e., larger in size] and denser, it is not because external circumstances are more varied, but because struggle for existence is more acute. Darwin justly observed that the struggle between two organisms is as active as they are analogous. . . . Men submit to the same law. In the same city, different occupations can co-exist without being mutually obliged to destroy each other, for they pursue different objects. . . . The division of labor is, then, a result of the struggle for existence, but it is a mellowed dénouement. Thanks to it, opponents are not obliged to fight to a finish, but can exist one beside the other. Also, in proportion to its development, it furnishes the means of maintenance and survival to a greater number of individuals who, in more homogeneous societies, would be condemned to extinction.[16]

The division of labor is thus seen by Durkheim as essentially a mode of resolving competition and as an alternative both to Darwinian "natural selection" and to Malthusian "checks."

CRITIQUE

One might conclude from the foregoing that Durkheim merely substituted one variety of evolutionism for another, by pointing to a Darwinian struggle for existence between competitors as the mainspring of differentiation, rather than Spencerian cosmic forces leading inexorably to increased division. Indeed, the common interpretation of *Division* has been along these lines. Consider, for example, Benoit-Smullyan's remarks:

> Having disposed of the psychologistic and individualistic explanations of the division of labor, Durkheim now turns to his own morphological explanation. . . . Division of labor is due to changes in social structure arising out of an increase in

material and moral density. The increase in population intensi-
fies competition and thus forces individuals to specialize, in
order to survive. Thus Durkheim, rather reluctantly, comes to
rest his entire explanation upon the factor of an assumed natural
increase in population. This is obviously a biologistic rather
than a sociologistic type of explanation.[17]

On the contrary, Durkheim tried to spell out the conditions
under which one variety of "social evolution" would occur, by
pointing to the factors underlying increased structural complexity. Far from assuming natural increase and then using
population growth as the explanation (à la Spencer), Durkheim
clearly asserted that differentiation will accompany growth
only if interaction increases concomitantly; moreover, he suggested that this intensification of interaction ordinarily occurs
as a result of technological changes that facilitate contact, exchange and communication.[18] Thus Durkheim rejected a single-
factor explanation—whether it be the individual's desire for
happiness, cosmic evolutionary force, or population size—and
proceeded to construct a multiple-factor theory.

But what of the charge that Durkheim disobeyed his own
rules and thus became guilty of "biological reductionism"?
This question can be answered best by recalling the explanatory concepts that he employed (i.e., dynamic density and
competition). Both refer to interaction and can hardly be called
intrinsically biological constructs without stretching the meaning of "biological" to the point where it loses all discriminatory
value. If anything, these are clearly sociological concepts.
Moreover, Durkheim's technological emphasis—his stress upon
the role of improvements in transportation and communication
—cannot properly be called "biological" reasoning.

As to the dependence of the theory upon an assumed natural increase, Durkheim's critics have again fallen into error.
An increase in effective population size can obviously occur in
several ways, of which natural increase is only one. Following
out the implications of Durkheim's thought, is is readily apparent that improvements in transportation and communication
can bring into sustained contact previously separate areas and
populations. Historically, such "growth by merger" has fre-

quently involved political merger, whether by violent subjuga-
tion or peaceful assimilation, and often has witnessed an
extension of the area of regular economic exchange. These
political and economic changes can be subsumed under the
"biological" rubric only with difficulty, if at all.[19]

Although Merton is also inclined to view parts of Durkheim's explanation as biological, he has pinpointed the truly
sociological character of Durkheim's analysis in the following
passage:

> It is true that he finds the "determining cause" of increased
> division of labor in the growth and heightened density of popu-
> lations, which is primarily a biological factor, but it is only in
> so far as this demographic change is associated with increased
> social interaction and its concomitant, enhanced competition,
> that the stipulated change will occur. *It is this social factor—
> the "dynamic density" as he terms it—which Durkheim finds
> actually determinant.* . . . To the extent that this differentiation
> is generalizable as a social process it may be said to be asso-
> ciated with competition between individuals and between
> groups, whatever the factors leading to such competition.[20]

Even Durkheim's "evolutionism" is not really biological in
orientation. Although he did use the language of evolutionary
thought, he clearly rejected most of the prevailing evolutionist
views on the nature of social change. There is no idea here of
unilinear, irreversible development in a fixed sequence of stages,
no suggestion of "progress" as a necessary consequence of
greater complexity, no hint of blind cosmic forces animating
the whole process, as in Spencer's thought.[21] Durkheim simply
attempted to specify the social conditions under which a particular change in social organization tends to occur. In addition,
he attempted to identify the general mechanism by which like
units become unlike, through the resolution of competition.
Unfortunately, the process is not described in any detail.
Presumably the unsuccessful competitors (individuals, groups,
or territorial aggregates) take up new functions and somehow
become integrated in a more inclusive and complex system.

At any rate, it should be evident by this point that most
criticisms of Durkheim's theory of differentiation have been

misplaced. As they have been stated, they might better be aimed at Spencer—the theorist against whom Durkheim was contending throughout his entire analysis. The unfortunate effect of these errors of interpretation is plain: to the extent that these secondary sources are read in place of the original work, a whole generation of American sociologists has been given an essentially incorrect image of one of Durkheim's most important theoretical contributions. American sociology is probably the poorer for it. Durkheim clearly viewed "the origin of social species" as the product of social and not biological forces. If his analysis were not so clear on this issue, the apparent unanimity of his critics would be more compelling.

To say that most of the prevailing criticisms of Durkheim's theory are themselves unsound, however, is not to say that the theory is entirely satisfactory as it was originally stated. The major difficulty stems from his treatment of competition. In view of the great importance that he attached to it, his discussion is surprisingly brief. If differentiation is the resolution of competition that does occur and if a more complex organizational pattern does emerge to integrate the new specialties, it may be correct to view these developments as due to increases in effective size and improvements in the facilities for movement. However, a number of writers have suggested that differentiation is not the only resolution of competition.[22]

"Competition" occurs whenever the number of individuals or units with similar demands exceeds the supply, whether it be food, raw materials, markets, or occupational positions. As Durkheim suggested, differentiation represents a less harsh resolution of competition than that stressed by Darwin and Malthus. But in the case of human populations, the competition resulting from an increase in demand (population) theoretically can be resolved in a number of ways. Among them are the following:

Demographic changes—(1) As Durkheim recognized, following Darwin and Malthus, an increase in the death rate can bring population into line with resources. (2) Similarly, a decrease in the birth rate can have the same effect, although not so immediately. (3) Migration may remove excess numbers at least temporarily and thus reduce demand.

Technological changes—A number of possible developments may redefine and expand the effective environment, thus altering the supply. (4) Previously unused local resources may be brought into use via technological innovation or diffusion; the result is a more intensive use of environmental elements already present but unexploited. (5) Technological changes in transportation and communication, whether indigenous or borrowed, can make new areas and new resources available; such changes may also improve the internal distribution of commodities. (6) The substitution of mechanical for human energy may increase production and release manpower for other pursuits, including new occupations; thus the shift in the energy base of modern societies can be viewed as a process of displacement of the affected sectors of the population.

Organizational changes—As noted above, previously isolated areas, resources, and peoples can be absorbed by conquest or assimilation. However, internal reorganization of a given population can also result in supporting increased numbers. (7) "Revolutionary" changes may occur; the surplus formerly held by the few may be distributed among the many, and increased numbers can be supported, with perhaps an even higher average level of living. (8) The converse can also occur; for a variety of specific reasons, the average level of living may be lowered, permitting a given area and its resources to support even greater numbers. (9) Finally, as Durkheim suggested, occupational and territorial differentiation may occur.

This list of "alternatives" is probably not exhaustive, but it suggests that further differentiation is only one of a number of ways to resolve competition. It is also clear that these alternatives are not mutually exclusive, for a number of them have occurred simultaneously in the Western world.[23] This observation suggests that the changes that have occurred are concomitants of differentiation itself. Indeed, closer analysis reveals that each of these "alternatives" involves either (1) elimination of excess numbers, (2) expansion of the resource base, or (*3*) functional differentiation, or some combination of these changes.

In view of the importance that Durkheim attached to competition, however, it is unfortunate that he did not present a more explicit and systematic treatment of its resolution. He was inclined to invoke competition and to let it go at that. In passing, he remarked that "Spencer ably explains in what manner evolution will be produced, if it does take place, but he does not tell us the source producing it."[24] Durkheim, on the other hand, pointed to the sources of differentiation but offered little in the way of a detailed account of the manner in which it is to be produced. In fairness, of course, it must be said that such a statement has yet to appear.

A more serious weakness in Durkheim's theory is the inadequate attention accorded the physical environment. He apparently was reluctant to give such factors as climate and topography any major role in his analysis. In part, this probably is due to the restrictive character of his own rules, adherence to which obliged him to seek the explanation of social facts in other social facts. He tended to dismiss the physical environment as a relevant variable and to regard the "social environment" as the ultimate source of differentiation. But this procedure has its own blind alleys; for one thing, the analyst does not get "outside the system" in his search for relevant variables.

To accept Durkheim's view of the limited role of environmental variability is to ignore two key considerations, the first of which is implicit in his own thought. (*1*) As suggested above, the effective environment can be altered by technological and organizational changes. These changes redefine the environment by bringing new resources into use—local resources already "there" but unexploited or resources found at sites that were previously inaccessible because of limited transportation facilities and exchange mechanisms. Although the initial impetus may not be the environment itself, it may become an important condition with respect to further organizational change. (*2*) Environmental variability must be viewed in static as well as dynamic terms. The plain fact of the matter is that the physical environment confronting mankind is almost infinitely variable, in the sense that there are enormous geographical differences from place to place. Some of these differences may favor organizational change. Long before Durkheim's time, Adam Smith perceived the significance of this factor, pointing to the greater likelihood of differentiated units appearing at the water's edge.[25] Since Durkheim wrote, the role of a favorable geographic position has been stressed frequently in discussions of the sites of early civilizations and of the deep-water orientation of most great cities throughout history. This emphasis also appears in Cooley's famous "break-in-transportation" theory, and it can be easily merged with Durkheim's own views on the crucial role of transportation and communication technology.[26]

Nonetheless, Durkheim's own theory clearly minimizes the potential relevance for organization of variations in physical environment. The corrective probably lies in adopting the modern geographer's concept of the environment as a vital permissive factor with respect to human activities. This approach is best summed up in the view known as *possibilisme*, wherein the environment is viewed as a set of limiting conditions, which may be narrow or broad, depending upon the technological devices and modes of organization that prevail in a given population.[27]

Despite these minor shortcomings, Durkheim provided a highly useful framework for the analysis of social structure and particularly for the examination of changes in structure. From the ecological standpoint, *Division*'s major contribution is its stress upon the significance of technological advances for the development of a more elaborate division of labor. As Durkheim correctly pointed out, the efficiency of transportation and communication affects the degree to which spatially separate and functionally dissimilar activities may be interrelated. This is especially evident in the case of territorial differentiation, in which whole areas are devoted to specialized functions. Such a development clearly depends upon the loss of isolation and the establishment and maintenance of sustained contact.

Division provides, though only in outline, a framework for studying one of the most salient aspects of social organization, viz., the degree of structural differentiation. It can be applied to static, cross-sectional analysis as well as to dynamic, longitudinal study. Although it stands in need of certain modifications, his morphological theory seems particularly useful in approaching the problem of structural differentiation within and between areally based aggregates, i.e., communities. It is to this contention that the following section is addressed.

IMPLICATIONS FOR HUMAN ECOLOGY

The very first point to be made is that ecologists concern themselves with precisely the same problem as that attacked by Durkheim in Book II of *Division*. Just as he tried to explain one aspect of social structure, contemporary ecologists try to identify the factors determining variations in structure. Hawley, for example, defines human ecology as the study of the form and development of the community. At one point, he adopts Durkheim's exact phraseology and describes the ecologist's objective as the elucidation of "the morphology of collective life in both its static and dynamic aspects."[28] Although he represents a more traditional ecological viewpoint, Quinn also declares that the logic of ecological inquiry points to the study of "the occupational pyramid" as essential subject matter, despite the unfortunate preoccupation of some ecologists with spatial distributions.[29] Thus modern human ecology deals with the Durkheimian problem of "morphology" and takes the same dependent variable (structure) as its *explanandum*. This is despite the fact that ecologists of Hawley's persuasion frequently limit themselves to discussing community structure, avoiding Durkheim's broader concern with society.

Second, once the environment is brought into the picture, modern ecology can be regarded as working with essentially the same array of *independent* variables—most broadly, population, technology, and the environment. Building on Hawley's theory, Duncan has labeled the resulting scheme "the ecological complex."[30] Although it tends to be implicit rather than explicit, Hawley's own effort seems to consist of treating community structure as the product of the interaction of these broad factors. The structure of a given community is viewed as a collective adaptation on the part of the population to its total environment (including other organized populations, as well as physical features), an adaptation that is strongly modified by the technological equipment in use and by certain "purely" demographic attributes of the population itself, notably its size, rate of growth, and biological (age-sex) composition.[31]

Thus the general relevance of Durkheim's thought to modern ecology is clear. He worked with essentially the same broad factors, taking one of them (structure) as his dependent variable. Moreover, his general mode of analysis is highly similar to that employed in current ecological theory. This becomes particularly apparent when one considers Hawley's treatment of differentiation, which clearly follows Durkheim in its major outlines.[32] Moreover, there are obvious formal parallels between Durkheim's *mechanical-organic* typology and the concepts of *commensalism* and *symbiosis, categoric* and *corporate groups,* and *independent* and *dependent communities* in Hawley's work.[33] Both writers point to (*1*) two modes of relationship, or forms of interaction, between like and unlike unit parts and to (*2*) two major forms of organization, depending upon which type of relationship is most prominent. Also deserving stress here is their common search for the factors that explain the progressive breakdown of isolation, the welding-together of larger and more inclusive functional units, and the emergence of a more complex structure.

An even more recent variety of ecological thought—Julian Steward's "cultural ecology"—is amenable to interpretation along the lines suggested here. In other words, the "ecological complex" appears to be in use throughout much of Steward's work, despite the fact that he does not consciously focus upon organization as the *explanandum,* preferring to work with "culture," a much broader dependent variable, and despite the fact that he gives a much larger role to the physical environment than either Durkheim or Hawley.[34] Durkheim's influence on

Steward is apparently more indirect, via Durkheim's contribution to the development of "functional anthropology."

But we need not confine ourselves to the most recent statements of ecological thought. A Durkheimian approach has informed human ecology since its inception. In one of his most influential essays—"The Urban Community as a Spatial Pattern and a Moral Order"—Robert E. Park identified the subject matter of human ecology as "what Durkheim and his school call the morphological aspect of society."[35] It has probably also occurred to the reader that the use of the concept of competition in Durkheim's work is highly similar to Park's. To quote Park: "Competition determines the distribution of population territorially and vocationally. The division of labor and all the vast organized economic interdependence of individuals and groups of individuals characteristic of modern life are a product of competition."[36] Thus both Durkheim and Park saw structure as ultimately emerging out of competition in a context of scarcity, although Park was no more helpful than Durkheim in providing a detailed account of the process as a whole.[37]

In addition, it should be pointed out that Durkheim anticipated much of McKenzie's theoretical work, especially the latter's treatment of the rise of "metropolitan" communities. In Durkheim's analysis, we have seen that great stress is given to advances in transportation and communication technology, which lessen isolation and break down "social segmentation." McKenzie showed that this theory can be readily given an areal referent, since formerly isolated and territorially distinct populations are frequently brought into more intimate contact by virtue of improvements in transportation and communication. McKenzie saw the key feature of metropolitan development as the emergence of an intricate territorial division of labor between communities that were formerly almost self-sufficient, and he viewed the whole process as mainly due to technological improvements. In fact, McKenzie went so far as to characterize the metropolitan community as "the child of modern facilities for transportation and communication."[38]

Although Durkheim's analysis was largely at the societal level and dealt mainly with occupational differentiation, Mc-

Kenzie used an essentially similar model in treating communities and regions, analyzing the problem of territorial differentiation. The process of differentiation is presumably the same in each case. Units that are brought into contact via technological improvements become competitors; such units necessarily compete to the extent that they offer the same goods and services to the same population. In the communal or regional context, the resolution of this competitive situation is frequently effected by territorial differentiation. Certain areal units, including whole communities, then give up certain functions and turn to new specialties. A case in point is the historical "flight" of certain specialties, particularly infrequently purchased goods and services, from nearby smaller cities to the metropolis, following the development of the automobile. In the process, formerly semi-independent centers, which once offered a rather full range of services, came to take up more narrowly specialized roles in a larger and more complex division of labor—the metropolitan community as a whole.[39]

At any rate, whether we examine earlier or more recent versions of human ecology, Durkheim's stamp is clearly imprinted.[40] In order to provide maximum utility in ecological analysis, Durkheim's theory needs certain modifications, particularly along the lines of bringing the environment into the schema as a factor worthy of recognition. As a result of its conceptual heritage from biology, human ecology has a rather full appreciation of the role of the physical environment as it affects social structure. This is not to say, however, that the ecologist is an environmental determinist; rather, he points to the relevance of the environment as it is modified and redefined by the organized use of technology. To paraphrase a recent compendium of valuable ecological data, man has a key role in changing the face of the earth.[41] Although the human ecologist's initial concern may be with the interaction between "man and his total environment," as a sociologist he inevitably turns to a study of the organized relations between man and man in the environmental setting, i.e., to morphological considerations. As Park said for ecology, it is "not man's relation to the earth which he inhabits, but his relations to other men, that concerns us most."[42] And in following out the interaction of a given aggregate with other organized populations, the ecologist necessarily concerns himself with what Durkheim called "the social environment."

CONCLUSIONS

The only American sociologists to make any intensive use of Durkheim's earliest and most ambitious work are those who have adopted the ecological perspective. Very little attention has been given to Durkheim's "social morphology," and his theory of differentiation has been widely misunderstood. Most American writers who have discussed *Division* have drawn upon Book I, where Durkheim treated the effects of division with his customary insight. His later works, especially those dealing with suicide and religion, have been much more influential in this country. In these later studies Durkheim was more frequently dealing with individual behavior, especially as it is "normatively defined" and modified by group ties.

This selective emphasis by American writers is probably related to the main drift of American sociology in this century (i.e., toward increasing concern with social-psychological considerations). Instead of taking social structure as the phenomenon to be explained—the dependent variable—most American sociologists habitually deal with social structure as an independent variable with respect to individual behavior. More particularly, structure is usually treated as it is perceived by the individual.

Now it must be made very clear that this procedure is an entirely legitimate enterprise; the variables with which one works and their analytical status depend upon the problem to be investigated. Moreover, this approach has vastly illuminated the human situation. Since the individual is somehow regarded as a less abstract unit than the organized aggregate and as a more interesting subject for study, social psychology has grown rapidly and has made giant strides toward acceptance in the scientific community. Witness the present status of "behavioral science." For all its past progress and future promise, however, the social-psychological sector of sociology still deals with some of the consequences of structural arrangements, leaving the determinants of structure to someone else.

In the light of these considerations, Durkheim's conception of *collective representations*—"shared norms and values" in the contemporary lexicon—provides an interesting sidelight on the position of social psychology within sociology. Durkheim regarded these social phenomena as mere "emanations" of underlying social morphology or structure.[43] If one accepts this position, then he holds that the social psychologist be concerned with little more than the derivative manifestations or passive reflections of underlying structural arrangements. Such a view clearly poses the analysis of structure itself as a logically prior problem. However, if current sociological output is any measure, few of us are inclined to grant any kind of priority to a morphological approach.

It is true that Durkheim himself turned more and more to the analysis of individual behavior in his later years, but he rarely departed from his original position regarding the undesirability of attempting to explain "social facts" by reference to individual characteristics.[44] This is in dramatic contrast to the direction taken in American sociology: toward the view that has been labeled "voluntaristic nominalism." As the most significant characteristic of American sociology, our fundamental postulates have recently been identified as follows: "The feeling, knowing, and willing of individuals—though limited by cultural prescriptions and social controls—are taken to be the ultimate source of human interaction, social structure, and social change. . . . Social behavior is interpreted voluntaristically. Social structures are real only as they are products of individuals in interaction."[45] One must be impressed by the fact that so many American theorists now acknowledge a heavy indebtedness to Durkheim. If this voluntaristic position is actually dominant, however, we have only succeeded in turning Durkheim upside down.

Be that as it may, Durkheim's conception of "social morphology" suggests that one of the most promising areas of structural analysis lies in the development of a general taxonomy of aggregates and collectivities. Few sociologists seem to have addressed themselves to this task in recent years. To the extent that "types of society" are used today, they represent minor variants of the dichotomies presented long ago by Tönnies, Durkheim, and other writers of the nineteenth century. More important, most of the refinements and reformulations of these typologies in recent years have been left to writers like Redfield and Steward. In other words, a genuinely sociological tradition is being kept alive by the efforts of anthropologists.

With respect to "types of community," the initiative has been taken taken by economists and geographers, despite the fact that many areas of current sociological interest absolutely require close attention to the community context. To choose only the most obvious example, community studies of stratification would probably be enormously improved if the overall structure and functions of the selected research sites were indicated with some precision according to their taxonomic types. For one thing, the overgeneralizations that seem to emerge from many such studies might be far less frequent.[46] It is probably unfortunate that the few sociologists currently attempting to develop a systematic taxonomy of communities appear to be those who employ an ecological framework.[47]

As for types of groups within communities and societies, we have not advanced very far beyond the rather rudimentary notions of "in-" and "out-groups" and "primary" versus "secondary" groups. Both of these dichotomies, of course, tend to be employed within a social-psychological context. The only notable recent addition to this limited array of group types is the notion of "membership" versus "reference" groups. However, the latter turn out not to be groups at all, for the distinction rests not upon structural or functional attributes of aggregates but upon the identifications and aspirations of individuals. It would be difficult to find a better index of just how far we have gone in bartering our sociological heritage for a mess of psychological pottage.

Morphological problems, including the development of fundamental structural taxonomies, deserve far greater attention than they have received in recent years. These are the tasks that have been largely ignored since Durkheim's day. Moreover, Durkheim's earliest work offers a challenge to those interested in the most neglected area of sociology—the analysis of the determinants of structure. As we have tried to suggest, Durkheim also provided a fascinating view of the problematics of social psychology. Given the current division of labor within American sociology, Durkheim's morphological theory of structural differentiation is probably of greatest value to ecologists, although not without relevance to other students of social organization. In this age of specialization, that he saw developing so rapidly, the sheer breadth and scope of Durkheim's achievement becomes all the more impressive with the years.

NOTES

1. Durkheim died in 1917, and the first use among sociologists of the term "human ecology" did not appear until 1921, in Robert E. Park and Ernest W. Burgess (eds.), *Introduction to the Science of Society* (Chicago: University of Chicago Press, 1921), pp. 161–216. However, Durkheim was familiar with the work of Ernst Haeckel, who coined the word "ecology" in 1868 and who is often described as the father of plant ecology.

2. Taken from Durkheim's essay, "Sociologie et sciences sociales" (1909); cited in Harry Alpert, *Émile Durkheim and His Sociology* (New York: Columbia University Press, 1939), p. 51. Durkheim's own discussion of social morphology appears in scattered essays and reviews in *L'Année sociologique* (old series), e.g., "Note sur la morphologie sociale," 2 (1897–98), 520–21.

3. Paris: Alcan, 1893; translated by George Simpson as *The Division of Labor in Society* (New York: Macmillan Co., 1933; Glencoe, Ill.: Free Press, 1947). All citations to *Division* hereafter refer to the 1947 edition. Occasional reference will also be made to *Les Règles de la méthode sociologique* (Paris: Alcan, 1895), a collection of essays that had appeared in *Revue philosophique* in 1894. *Les Règles* was translated by Sarah A. Solovay and John H. Mueller and edited by George E. G. Catlin as *The Rules of Sociological Method* (Chicago: University of Chicago Press, 1938; Glencoe, Ill.: Free Press, 1950). All subsequent citations to *The Rules* refer to the 1950 edition.

4. August Comte, *The Positive Philosophy*, translated and edited by Harriet Martineau (New York: D. Appleton, 1853).

5. Ferdinand Tönnies, *Gemeinschaft und Gesellschaft* (1887), translated and edited by Charles P. Loomis as *Fundamental Concepts of Sociology* (New York: American Book Co., 1940). Although it is not cited in *Division*, Durkheim had previously reviewed *Gemeinschaft und Ge-*

sellschaft in highly favorable terms (see *Revue philosophique*, 27 [1889], 416–22). Georg Simmel's *Über soziale Differenzierung* appeared in 1890, but Durkheim indicated that he did not see it until after 1893, when *Division* first appeared. For a general critique of Simmel see Durkheim's "La Sociologia ed il suo dominio scientifico," *Rivista Italiana di sociologia*, 4 (1900), 127–48.

6. "We say of these societies that they are segmental in order to indicate their formation by the repetition of like aggregates in them" (*Division*, p. 175). This type is not to be understood as somehow lacking any differentiation whatsoever (see pp. 129, 173, 177, 180). As Redfield has suggested, homogeneity in simpler societies is more than merely "occupational," extending to biological characteristics and even to outlook. Small size and extreme isolation appear to be crucial factors in the development of both genetic and cultural homogeneity (see Robert Redfield, "The Folk Society," *American Journal of Sociology*, 52 [1947], 292–308).

7. See *Division*, p. 229, and Durkheim's assertion that "mechanical solidarity persists even in the most elevated societies" (p. 186). Some critics erroneously accuse him of failing to see that both forms of integration can be found in every society.

8. Durkheim usually tried to dispose of competing hypotheses before setting out his own views. *Division* contains a perfect example of his didactic style, which Alpert calls the method of "argumentum per eliminationem" (*op. cit.*, pp. 84–87).

9. *The Rules*, p. 110. In the course of his argument, Durkheim cited comparative suicide rates as "proof" to the contrary. Whatever the merits of this argument, it is interesting to note that Durkheim here anticipated his later work in this area. At another point, he dealt with religious phenomena (Book I). A number of writers have observed that *Division* contained the seeds of all his later work.

10. Herbert Spencer, *Principles of Sociology* (London, 1876; New York: D. Appleton & Co., 1884 and 1892), I, 459 (1892 ed.).

11. See Smith's famous aphorism to the effect that "the division of labor is limited by the extent of the market" (*The Wealth of Nations* [New York: Modern Library], p. 17).

12. *Division*, p. 261. This thought is further developed in *The Rules*, p. 115.

13. *Division*, p. 257. Later, Durkheim graciously credited Comte with this basic idea (see *ibid.*, pp. 262–63). In the quoted passage and elsewhere, Durkheim spoke as if the individual were the referent. However, the treatment of change that he applied to interindividual relations appears to be even more appropriate in the analysis of the changing relations between areal units or whole aggregates in the process of differentiation.

14. *Ibid.*, p. 257.

15. *Ibid.*, pp. 259–60. Durkheim went on to say that one can usually substitute physical density ("this visible and measurable symbol" or index) for dynamic density, but that they are not inevitably correlated (see n. 11, p. 260). The point apparently troubled Durkheim, for in *The Rules* he repeats this idea in the form of an apology for having confused the two types of density (see *The Rules*, p. 115).

16. *Division*, pp. 266–70.

17. Émile Benoit-Smullyan, "The Sociologism of Émile Durkheim and His School," in Harry Elmer Barnes (ed.), *An Introduction to the History of Sociology* (Chicago: University of Chicago Press, 1948), p. 508. This point has been widely misunderstood. Sorokin, for example, says that "as soon as Durkheim puts this problem, he has to recognize at once its dependence on the factor of procreation and multiplication of the people—a factor essentially biological. Increase of labor division is principally the result of an increase of population. Such is his answer" (Pitirim Sorokin, *Contemporary Sociological Theories* [New York and London: Harper & Bros., 1928], p. 480). In a similar vein, Parsons says: "What he ends up with is population pressure, not in any analytical sense a social element at all, but essentially biological. In so far as this is Durkheim's main line of thought it is a familiar one here; it is the breakdown of utilitarianism into radical positivism, in this case the 'biologizing' of social theory" (Talcott Parsons, *The Structure of Social Action* [New York: McGraw-Hill Book Co., 1937; Glencoe, Ill.: Free Press, 1949], p. 323). Regarding Durkheim's explanation, Alpert has written: "If we accept this statement at face value, we must conclude that Durkheim's causal explanation of the division of labor is couched, contrary to his own methodological postulate that social facts must be explained socially, in biological, or, more exactly, in demographical terms. It is no wonder, then, that his book has been qualified as Malthusian" (*op. cit.*, p. 91).

18. It is true that he did not go on to "explain" growth or technological innovation. The task that he had set for himself was the explanation of differentiation, and to confine his discussion to the implications of increase in size and density—whatever their sources—was an entirely legitimate scientific procedure.

19. The critics cited above do not seem to appreciate the fact that changes in effective population size need not depend upon natural increase or decrease. Demographers have long been aware that the organizational response to population pressure in a given area has frequently taken the form of a splitting-off process, in which a whole segment of a local community moves off to establish a new colony. This process, to which biblical reference may be found, apparently had a large role in the spread of mankind over the earth; it may be labeled "fission." Growth by merger, however, presents a contrasting phenomenon. Although it often generates substantial migratory streams, migration is not intrinsic to the process, nor is natural increase or decrease necessarily involved. To preserve the metaphor, this form of increase may be called growth by "fusion." Both processes, of course, refer to sociological (organizational) changes and not to biological changes.

20. Robert K. Merton, "Durkheim's Division of Labor in Society," *American Journal of Sociology*, 40 (1934), 325–26; italics added. In addition to calling population change "biological," Merton is in error regarding the implied universality of the association between competition and differentiation.

21. See *Division*, pp. 141–42. Merton has erroneously identified Durkheim as a unilinear evolutionist (*op. cit.*, pp. 324–25). Marjolin provides a more accurate view of Durkheim's position: "For him there does not exist any single general human society, but only particular societies which follow diverse evolutions, and it is not possible to consider the conditions

which they have reached as stages in a single developmental sequence" (see Robert Marjolin, "French Sociology—Comte and Durkheim," *American Journal of Sociology*, 42 [1937], 694).

22. As Parsons has noted, Durkheim "recognizes the fact that there is more than one possible outcome of this intensification [of competition]. It might lead simply to the elimination by natural selection of a larger proportion of those born" (*op. cit.*, p. 322). Benoit-Smullyan indicates emigration or war as additional alternatives (*op. cit.*, p. 530). Alpert extends the list: "Of course, there are many other ways out, such as migration, suicide, civil war, crime, etc." (*op. cit.*, p. 94).

23. When they occur, it is clear that these changes need not "run in the same direction." The modern nations of the West have lowered their birth rates, extended the environment in breadth and in depth, substituted machines for men, and have become more highly differentiated at the same time that gigantic streams of migration were set loose. Meanwhile, death rates did not rise but declined, and the level of living did not fall but rose dramatically. Whether or not these other changes are intrinsic to differentiation, Durkheim took a rather over-simplified view of the entire process. It must be noted that he clearly recognized the first alternative listed above and that others (especially the fifth) are implicit in his analysis. It will be seen that alternatives 1, 2, 3, 7, and 8 have their primary effect upon the population, or "demand" side of the competitive equation, while alternatives 4, 5, and 6 have their major impact upon the resource, or "supply" side. Interestingly enough, alternative 9 (differentiation) has important effects upon *both* supply and demand; not only is the number of competitors effectively reduced, but the efficiency of differentiation presumably increases the supply.

24. *Division*, p. 265.

25. Smith, *op. cit.*, chap. i.

26. Charles Horton Cooley, "The Theory of Transportation," *Publications of the American Economic Association*, 9 (May, 1894), entire issue; reprinted in Robert Cooley Angell (ed.), *Sociological Theory and Social Research* (New York: Henry Holt & Co., 1930). In fairness, it should be pointed out that Spencer appreciated the role of environmental variation, although his thinking on this issue is not easily reconciled with his general theory of differentiation. Spencer observed that all physical resources are not perfectly ubiquitous and that some areas are better suited to specialization in a narrow range of production (Spencer, *First Principles*, p. 381; cited in Durkheim, *Division*, p. 263). Durkheim's rejection of the environment as a significant factor in differentiation led him away from a potentially fruitful line of analysis—the study of territorial division of labor. He did note that "since the 14th century, the interregional division of labor has been developing" (*ibid.*, p. 188). In addition, his most detailed example involves an instance of territorial differentiation (*ibid.*, pp. 268–69).

27. This view is commonly associated with the names of Jean Brunhes and Paul Vidal de la Blache. For a recent statement along these lines see Robert S. Platt, "Environmentalism versus Geography," *American Journal of Sociology*, 53 (1948), 351–58.

28. Amos H. Hawley, *Human Ecology: A Theory of Community Structure* (New York: Ronald Press, 1950), p. 67.

29. James A. Quinn, *Human Ecology* (New York: Prentice-Hall, 1950), p. 14.

30. Otis Dudley Duncan, "Human Ecology and Population Studies," in Philip M. Hauser and Otis Dudley Duncan (eds.), *The Study of Population* (Chicago: University of Chicago Press, 1959).

31. In contrast to earlier ecological emphases, spatial distributions of population and human activities enter into Hawley's thinking only as convenient indexes of organizational form; in this view, space is of interest only to the extent that it reflects structure. The same thing can be said for temporal patterns, which also have value as indexes of organization (see Amos H. Hawley, "The Approach of Human Ecology to Urban Areal Research," *Scientific Monthly*, 73 [1951], 48–49).

32. Hawley, *Human Ecology*, chap. xi.

33. *Ibid.*, chap. xii.

34. Steward criticizes Hawley as "uncertain in his position regarding the effect of environmental adaptations on culture" and indicates that he prefers to give this factor a larger causal role (Julian H. Steward, *Theory of Culture Change* [Urbana: University of Illinois Press, 1955], p. 34). This greater stress on physical-environmental factors is undoubtedly related to the fact that ethnologists are more frequently concerned with simpler societies, where the physical environment is literally a more fundamental determinant, pressing upon small and stable local populations that survive by means of relatively simple and unchanging technology and organization. To use Duncan's "ecological complex" once again, where technology and population are relatively constant, the environment assumes the position of the dynamic causal variable with respect to organization.

35. Originally published in 1925 as "The Concept of Position in Sociology" (see Robert E. Park, *Human Communities: The City and Human Ecology* [Glencoe, Ill.: Free Press, 1952], p. 166).

36. Park and Burgess, *op. cit.*, p. 506.

37. On the use of competition as an all-explanatory concept in the earlier ecological literature see Amos H. Hawley, "Ecology and Human Ecology," *Social Forces*, 23 (1944), 398–405.

38. See R. D. McKenzie, *The Metropolitan Community* (New York: McGraw-Hill Book Co., 1933); see also Leslie Kish, "Differentiation in Metropolitan Areas," *American Sociological Review*, 19 (1954), 388–98.

39. That differentiation is not the only mode of resolution of competition is again dramatically demonstrated by the experience of many rural service centers and hamlets after the coming of the automobile. With their markets usurped by larger centers now within easy access, a great number of these smaller places literally disappeared.

40. This review has been confined to American developments. In France, Durkheim's morphological interests were carried on by his students, especially Maurice Halbwachs. In addition to extending Durkheim's analysis of suicide and "collective representations," Halbwachs' *Morphologie sociale* (Paris: Armand Colin, 1938) drew heavily upon his mentor's views and—at the same time—incorporated an ecological perspective that is often strikingly similar to Park's. Halbwachs visited the United States and taught at the University of Chicago in 1930 (see his

"Chicago, expérience ethnique," *Annals d'histoire économique et sociale,* 4 [1932], 11–49).

41. William L. Thomas, Jr. (ed.), *Man's Role in Changing the Face of the Earth* (Chicago: University of Chicago Press, 1956).

42. Park, *Human Communities,* p. 165.

43. See Durkheim's "Représentations individuelles et représentations collectives," *Revue de métaphysique et de morale,* 6 (1898), 273–302.

44. Durkheim's shifting interests are mirrored not only in the subjects of his later books but also in his writings in the old series of *L'Année sociologique.* Although references to "social morphology" are less frequent after about 1905, it should be noted that it was maintained as a major caption as long as Durkheim himself held the editorship.

45. Roscoe C. Hinkle, Jr., and Gisela J. Hinkle, *The Development of Modern Sociology* (New York: Doubleday, 1954), p. 73.

46. See Seymour M. Lipset and Reinhard Bendix, "Social Status and Social Structure: A Re-examination of Data and Interpretations," *British Journal of Sociology,* 2 (1951), 150–68 and 230–54; Harold W. Pfautz and Otis Dudley Duncan, "A Critical Evaluation of Warner's Work in Community Stratification," *American Sociological Review,* 15 (1950), 205–15; and Ruth Kornhauser, "Warner's Approach to Stratification," in Reinhard Bendix and Seymour M. Lipset (eds.), *Class Status and Power* (Glencoe, Ill.: Free Press, 1953), pp. 224–55.

47. See Otis Dudley Duncan and Albert J. Reiss, Jr., *Social Characteristics of Urban and Rural Communities, 1950* (New York: John Wiley & Sons, 1956), pp. 215–370; for a more limited set of sub-community types see Leo F. Schnore, "Satellites and Suburbs," *Social Forces,* 36 (1957), 121–27.

Chapter 2

The Myth of

Human Ecology

WE HAVE BEEN MOTIVATED to give some thought to the matter of ecology's place in sociology by Kingsley Davis's recent discussion of "The Myth of Functional Analysis". We were struck, for example, by his reference to the fact that "Characteristics that the functionalists themselves regard as either accidental faults or as totally alien to their point of view . . . critics often regard as the essence of the approach."[1] Davis also observes that "so-called functionalists and professed enemies of functionalism are often *doing* the same kind of analysis."[2] Both of these remarks, of course, could be applied to human ecology and ecologists with some justification, and one could list examples at some length. An ecologist is not inclined to claim that his approach is the only mode of analysis that deserves recognition as distinctively sociological, but if we agree from the start that human ecology does not represent the sum and substance of sociology, where does it fit? How does it articulate with the main body of sociological analysis? In my opinion, the prevailing *"myth"* of human ecology is that ecology is somehow *"marginal"* to sociology.

A paper presented at a student-faculty Colloquium, Department of Sociology, University of Michigan, Ann Arbor, Michigan, April 13, 1960.

One finds ecology represented as marginal, for example, in introductory textbooks, as when Arnold Rose states that sociology, as a discipline, "has historically come to include the study of two sets of phenomena which are not logically part of their central subject matter, any more than economics and political science are part of sociology. These two subdisciplines are demography . . . and human ecology."[3] A more extreme version is to be found in Boskoff's assertion that "In seeking a distinctive set of phenomena, orthodox human ecology has not only seceded from modern sociology—it has largely withdrawn from science."[4] However, advocates as well as critics are numbered among those who regard ecology as marginal to sociology. Thus we find one of the acknowledged founders of human ecology—Ernest W. Burgess—contending that "human ecology, logically, is a separate discipline from sociology. Like population studies, it has become attached to sociology because it provides the substructure for the study of social factors in human behavior."[5]

In the following sections, we intend to argue that human ecology—rather than being marginal to sociology—represents one effort to deal with *the central problem of sociological analysis*. Further, we shall argue that the ecologist's efforts appear to be marginal only in the light of certain *tendencies within American sociology*—tendencies which are themselves to be explained in large part by methodological developments. Finally, we shall argue that ecology's real potential lies in its *contributions to a macro as over against a microsociology*. We shall take up these points in somewhat different order, and then proceed to identify ecology's distinctive attack upon the central problem of sociology.

THE NEED

One key task confronting anyone who advocates a particular approach is the obligation to demonstrate that it has emerged naturally as an extension of prior work. In the chapter concerned with Durkheim's "social morphology," we tried to show that ecology has a legitimate *sociological* ancestry, and that it is something more than a simple attempt to "apply" some rudimentary biological concepts to social phenomena; the latter is one of the older and lesser myths of human ecology.[6] A more critical task is to show that the approach one advocates is fruitful, i.e., that it yields distinctive hypotheses for research. This stipulation amounts to saying that one must demonstrate the existence of a genuine *need*. While we cannot pretend that there is a great popular clamor on behalf of the ecological perspective, we are convinced that there is a widespread and barely hidden dissatisfaction with certain salient features of contemporary American sociology.

First of all, several writers, including representatives of radically different schools of thought, have commented upon the microsociological—and even psychological—drift of American sociology in recent decades. Some of these writers adopt a neutral stance, expressing no explicit preference for the macroscopic as over against the microscopic approach. Others, however, have expressed varying degrees of dissatisfaction with the current state of the field. Thus Bellah has observed that "Since the generation of Weber and Durkheim macroscopic problems involving comparative and historical research have been somewhat slighted as microscopic research based on new methods and instruments has come to the fore. Not only general sociology, but microsociology itself, would suffer if this imbalance were to go too far."[7]

The technical–methodological basis of this drift toward the microscopic has ben noted elsewhere. Perhaps the most sweeping indictment of all is to be found in the charges levelled by James S. Coleman: "Social theory has, I think, allowed itself to be sidetracked off its main task, which is to develop theories for social systems—whether they be total social systems or systems of behavior in small groups. Our attention is too often drawn away from the system itself to the individuals within it, so that we construct theories to account for some individual's behavior."[8] Coleman agrees that our techniques have led us in the direction of microsociology:

> Two things have happened: the complexity of these [data-gathering] techniques has shifted our focus from substantive problems to the techniques themselves; and secondly, this very

move down to the individual level has kept us fascinated there, unable to get back up to the social level. Survey research has continued to be a kind of aggregate psychology, rather than sociology; it has continued to study the opinions of a population sample rather than public opinion, to study buyers rather than the market, to study individuals rather than the community. . . .

The second problem, the psychologizing of sociology through survey research, has already shown signs of solution. Techniques are being devised, and studies are being designed and carried out, which pervert the survey into a truly sociological instrument. Structural effects analysis, comparing several social contexts, relational analysis, using sociometric techniques, and more traditional survey methods, using variables like social class and sibling position in the family, or status in an organization, and so on, are beginning to allow the study of sociological problems rather than purely psychological ones. . . . Yet in most of these techniques, the individual behavior or attitude is still the dependent variable, though social structure or norms are the independent variables. The functioning of a social system is seldom analyzed by quantitative techniques—as it has been by qualitative observational studies.[9]

With respect to the difficulties attending the microscopic interpretation of macroscopic problems, C. Wright Mills has presented an equally forceful statement:

The idea of social structure cannot be built up only from ideas or facts about a specific series of individuals and their reactions to their milieux. Attempts to explain social and historical events on the basis of psychological theories about "the individual" often rest upon the assumption that society is nothing but a great scatter of individuals and that, accordingly, if we know all about these "atoms" we can in some way add up the information and thus know about society. It is not a fruitful assumption.[10]

But enough of appeals to authority. Each of these eminent writers would very probably prescribe different solutions to the same problem. We are not trying to persuade anyone that these antimicroscopic views have suddenly become dominant;

far from it, for these are the words of "critics of the existing order". Nor are we advocating an ecological approach as the sole solution—or even the "best" solution—to the problems they have raised. Certainly human ecology is not widely regarded as a strong intellectual force in contemporary American sociology, if one may judge (1) from the fact that only 100 out of 4200 members of our professional association select it as a major interest, and (2) from the extremely limited attention given it in three recent evaluations of the current status and future prospects of the field as a whole. Ecology receives only brief treatment in the chapters devoted to urban sociology in the volumes entitled *Sociology in the United States of America, Review of Sociology: Analysis of a Decade*, and *Sociology Today: Problems and Prospects*.[11] In the last two, in fact, emphasis is placed upon the rash of criticisms of the ecological approach that appeared in the late 'forties and early 'fifties. But some of us are persuaded that human ecology—despite its possible defects and imperfections—has a great deal to offer contemporary sociology, and that its signal contribution might be toward a genuine *macrosociology*.

We can start with the proposition that the study of *social organization* is the central focus of the entire sociological enterprise.[12] In Rossi's words, "The proper study of sociology is social organization. On this perspective there is probably the greatest degree of agreement in our discipline."[13] The logical status of the concept "organization," however, varies significantly according to its *analytical position* in the frame of reference that is employed. At risk of oversimplification, it can be said that aspects of organization—or, more generally, structural properties of whole populations—appear in two quite separate guises in sociological analysis: as independent and as dependent variables. Similarly, properties of individual organisms have these dual analytical positions. The logically possible frames of reference are four in number, and we may first of all distinguish two general modes of analysis directed to the explanation of the behavior of the individual organism: *individual* psychology and *social* psychology.

INDIVIDUAL PSYCHOLOGY

"Individual psychology" largely seeks its explanatory variables among properties of individual organisms other than that which is the *explanandum* at the moment. Thus a psychologist setting out to account for variations in learning or perception tends to confine himself to properties of the organism in his search for independent variables. Because sociology is our subject, a universally acceptable definition of individual psychology is not essential to our purposes, but we might pause to consider the following statement by Tolman: "The final dependent variable in which, as a psychologist, I am interested is behavior. It is the behavior of organisms, human and subhuman, which I wish to predict and control." He goes on to identify "the five independent variables of (*1*) *environmental stimuli*, (*2*) *psychological drive*, (*3*) *heredity*, (*4*) *previous training*, and (*5*) *maturity*."[14]

The last four of these are clearly properties of individual organisms, but "environmental stimuli" are clearly external to the organism. However, it seems to be commonly accepted as axiomatic that it is only as these stimuli are experienced by the organism that behavioral reactions ensue. Thus, there is justification for asserting that individual psychologists tend generally to predict from one property of an individual organism to another, or to another set of behaviors. If this effort is pursued self-consciously and consistently at the individual level of analysis, the result is a kind of biological or physiological inquiry; it seeks a universalistic explanation of a particular psychological process, an account that holds for all men everywhere, without respect to social position, group membership, allegiance to particular norms, etc.

SOCIAL PSYCHOLOGY

As soon as these last-named variables enter the analysis, however, the analyst leaves the domain of individual psychology *per se*—psychology unadorned by qualifying adjectives—and enters the realm of "social psychology."

This view is distinctive in that it seems to represent an

attempt to move between two levels of analysis, with certain group properties (e.g., size) serving as independent variables, and certain individual properties (e.g., cognitive processes) taken as dependent variables. Much of the work in "small group" research is of this nature, but this mode of analysis is by no means confined to situations in which face–to–face inter-action is possible. (In addition, we shall see that not all small-group research is social psychological in orientation.) The use of "social" explanations of "psychological" processes can also be found in analyses of society in the large, especially within that portion of the literature that focusses upon "cultural" dif-ferences in behavior.

In general, it may be said that any effort to explain in-dividual behavior by reference to group membership or posi-tion, real or imagined, makes use of a social-psychological hypothesis. Social psychology tends to ignore what is common to all men (this is left to individual psychology) and to ignore what is unique to particular individuals (this is left to the bi-ographer); it deals with what is common to classes of individu-als in a particular culture, a particular stratum, a particular role. (This point sometimes leads to needless confusion. Some social psychologists firmly deny that they deal with "individual be-havior". What they mean is that they eschew any concern with the actions of particular, named individuals. However, the conduct of classes of individuals or "actors"—or classes of in-dividual behavior—is precisely central to their interests.)

Now the treatment of "social organization" is not inevit-ably the same in all social–psychological inquiries. The ex-planation ordinarily proceeds by predicting from population to individual properties. An example is Wirth's famous analysis of "urbanism as a way of life," in which variations in popula-tion size, density, and heterogeneity are employed in an attempt to account for variations in individual behavior and outlook in the urban setting.[15] In addition to appearing as attributes of populations, however, certain aspects of social organization may be transmuted into individual properties for analytical purposes. Examples of social–psychological analysis strictly confined to the individual level are to be found in most of the work subsumed under "role analysis," almost all of contemporary survey research, and in the analysis of "reference groups". Here the individual's position in the social structure is essentially regarded as a *personal* attribute, analytically speaking, and it is employed to explain his behavior *vis-a-vis* other persons playing complementary roles, or in particular areas of conduct that are amenable to a survey approach, such as voting or fertility. The "reference group," too, is an individual attribute, in that it designates an individual's sense of allegiance to or affiliation with a group or category, without respect to actual membership; in some instances, in fact, it refers to little more than a stereotype in the mind of an individual, while in others it specifies a specific position or a broad social category to which he aspires.

Organization has a different meaning in these various inquiries, sometimes appearing as the "social environment" which is perceived by the actor, sometimes as a set of normative constraints, sometimes as a congeries of cultural values. In all of them, however, the common stamp is an effort to explain individual behavior by reference to organizational attributes of populations or to real or imagined positions within the social structure. In summary, we may identify the major mode of social–psychological inquiry as a broad-scale research strategy that attempts to predict—if only contextually—from some aspect of social organization to some individual behavior or conduct. Thus Newcomb has specified "the characteristic point of view of social psychology" as follows:

> We may say that social psychology deals with the association of variations in the behavior of one or more individuals with variations in social environment. . . . Secondly, differences in social environment and the way in which they are experienced are very largely determined by the way in which the individual's society is organized.[16]

PSYCHOLOGICAL SOCIOLOGY

In contrast to "social psychology" is an approach that we prefer to call "psychological sociology." The positions of the adjective and the noun designate the independent and de-

pendent variables respectively. "Psychological sociology" sub-
sumes all efforts to explain properties of populations by
reference to the properties of the individuals who—from one
perspective—may be said to compose these populations. One of
the most succinct expressions of this point of view is to be
found in a plea by Swanson, who asks

> that we take seriously the dictum of Thomas, Znaniecki, and a
> host of others that, in theorizing about the causes of *any* be-
> havior, *individual or collective*, we conceive of our independent
> variables in terms of the environment as experienced by those
> behaving, and that we assume that their acts are efforts to deal
> with the world as they perceive it. This has many implications.
> The only one stressed here is the suggestion that, assuming
> human biology to be constant for purposes of theory-building,
> *one may predict variations in the organization of a group* from
> variations in environmental problems as its members experience
> them.[17]

Many other examples are to be found in the literature on
"culture and personality," at least in that phase of this work
which attempts to account for such macroscopic features as
forms of political organization in terms of individual experience
with child–rearing practices, etc. Particular analyses, of course,
are likely to slip into the social–psychological mode of reasoning from time to time. Moreover, certain population attributes
appear sometimes as no more than "intervening variables,"
where individual properties are said to give rise to certain
group properties, and the latter—in their turn—are viewed as
influencing individual behavior. One of the best–known examples is to be found in Kardiner's discussion of "primary" and
"secondary" institutions and their mutual relations to individual
behavior.[18]

In any event, most efforts to explain macroscopic social
phenomena in terms of "basic personality structure" or "national character" partake of the assumptions identified here as
those of psychological sociology. To a strict and doctrinaire
Durkheimian, these efforts are almost doomed to defeat, since
they patently violate his famous methodological stricture:

"The determining cause of a social fact should be sought among the social facts preceding it and not among the states of the individual consciousness."[19] However, to the extent that these efforts are ultimately directed, no matter how circuitously, toward the explanation of individual behavior, they may be regarded as entirely legitimate, even from the standpoint of one who insists upon viewing society as a phenomenon *sui generis*.

It is evident here that one's assumptions concerning levels of "emergence" are crucial to the development of his position on these matters. Some writers assume that "only the individual is real," and that social structure is either a kind of convenient fiction or a shorthand designation for summarizing individual behavior in aggregative terms; these "social nominalists" are inclined to the view here labelled "psychological sociology," although they eclectically adopt certain aspects of social–psychological thought as it suits their analytical needs. In contrast, "social realists" assert that social structure represents something other than the simple sum of individual actions, and they are much more likely to confine themselves to social psychology, as defined here, or else to adopt an ecological perspective.[20] They tend to be Durkheimian in orientation, rejecting the easy reductionism that underlies psychological sociology. Needless to say, it is difficult to place individual writers in one or another of these convenient categories; different portions of the work of particular authors, however, can be readily identified in these terms. One might even say that a sure index of an analyst's theoretical sophistication is the extent to which he gives evidence that he is aware of a shift in the direction of his analysis when it does occur.

MACROSOCIOLOGY

The first of the two modes of analysis identified here as "macrosociological" has one feature in common with "psychological sociology" as defined above. Both approaches take organization, or some particular aspect of it, as the *explanandum*. Aside from a common interest in the same type of dependent variable, however, there are few other similarities. This is most clear with respect to human ecology, especially as it has been developed by Amos H. Hawley.[21] For one thing, the ecological mode of analysis remains at one level with respect to the variables it employs; it seeks its independent variables among other "attributes of organized populations," such as their demographic features. (It should be added, of course, that there is nothing to prevent the use of other organizational features in the effort to explain a given facet of organization. Durkheim's use of increasing "dynamic density" and competition to explain mounting structural differentiation is a case in point. In fact, this is the only one of the perspectives discussed so far that conforms strictly to Durkheim's rule regarding the explanations of "social facts.")

There is, however, another macrosociological mode of analysis that can be identified, and it is one that ecologists are inclined to use from time to time. Here organization appears—not as the dependent variable—but as one of the *independent* variables. In point of fact, human ecology represents a broad *type* of analysis, within which more specific types can be identified, with their designation depending upon the nature of the dependent variable. Within the ecological framework, effort can be directed to the explanation of technological, organizational, or demographic features, so that several "ecologies" might be identified. Just as different varieties of individual psychology are designated by subclassification according to the analytical purposes at hand (e.g., the various "psychologies" of perception, learning, memory, etc.) one can similarly identify "population ecology" and "organizational ecology."[22]

Now both of the "macrosociological" approaches we have identified can be applied to populations of any size and degree of complexity; that is why we label them "macrosociological" rather than "ecological." Human ecology is only one of a *variety* of conceivable macrosociological modes of analysis. In fact, one of the major themes in "small group" research and theory is directed toward the analysis of group properties *per se*. For example, the analysis of the interrelations of group size and patterns of internal communication can be conducted from either of these last two perspectives. In addition, of course, sociometric techniques are adaptable to these modes of inquiry; rather than utilizing sociometric observations to identify individuals (as "stars," "isolates," etc.), one simply characterizes whole networks of interaction according to patterns, and then proceeds to deal with these patterns *as properties of aggregates.*[23]

CONCLUSIONS

The four modes of analysis identified here are broad indeed; they cross–cut much of social science. For one thing, a single "discipline" may employ all of them at one point or another, and we have already noted that a particular investigator may use all of them in different parts of his work. Even a single study—particularly a comprehensive effort—may employ these different approaches in rapid succession; an outstanding example is the recent study of *Union Democracy* by Lipset, Trow, and Coleman.[24] Community studies are particularly prone to make use of all of these devices at one point or another in the analysis. Perhaps there is danger in undisciplined eclecticism, for the analyst may not be aware that he is shifting perspectives, or moving to another level of analysis. Burgess has sounded a clear warning against this hazard:

> It is possible to inquire how ecological processes work, without the necessity of doing research on the social–psychological processes. It is also possible to inquire about the social–psychological processes, without doing research on the ecological aspects. These are two different ways of looking at human behavior . . . While it is true that both approaches can be brought together to produce significant findings on particular problems, their joint use should be conscious and deliberate. Many research workers unwittingly mix the two; as a consequence, they make a mess of their studies.[25]

Despite these reservations, however, a single "subject matter" may be greatly illuminated by the use of all four perspectives. To take an area with which we have some acquaintance—

population analysis—valuable examples of each type of inquiry can be readily cited. First, there is a substantial literature dealing with the individual physiology and psychology of reproduction, aging, and death; contributions can be found in disciplines located throughout the full range of biology. Secondly, the social–psychological approach is employed with increasing frequency, particularly by students of migration and fertility. There is even an occasional effort to apply the approach that we have labelled "psychological sociology," for some writers have tried to explain certain aspects of the reorganization and redistribution of metropolitan populations by reference to assumed individual propensities.[26] Lastly, there are numerous instances of the "macrosociological"—and particularly the ecological—modes of analysis. For example, substantial literature has accumulated in which the organizational consequences of variations in population size are examined; a recent and detailed illustration may be found in the work of Duncan and Reiss.[27] Organizational variables are also frequently utilized as explanatory factors in demographic analysis, as in various efforts to account for variations in population composition in terms of the economic base and functional organization of communities.

In summary, we have attempted to identify four more–or–less distinctive modes of analysis to be found in social science, one of which is the "macrosociological." We have indicated some of the ways in which we see this mode as different from two other major types of inquiry within sociology, and we have suggested that *"human ecology" might be best regarded as a type of "macrosociology."* Its most distinctive feature can perhaps be seen in its adherence to a single level of analysis, in which properties of whole populations are at issue. Although other approaches also take social organization as an independent or dependent variable, this adherence to a consistent level of analysis makes the perspective of human ecology somewhat unusual in the analytical *armamentarium* of the discipline. At the same time, the central role given to organization—as dependent or independent variable—places ecology clearly within the sphere of activities in which sociologists claim distinctive competence, i.e., the analysis of social organization. If human ecology is "marginal" to sociology, what is central?

NOTES

1. Kingsley Davis, "The Myth of Functional Analysis as a Special Method in Sociology and Anthropology," *American Sociological Review*, 24 (1959), p. 758.

2. *Ibid.*, p. 771.

3. Arnold M. Rose, *Sociology: The Study of Human Relations* (New York: Alfred A. Knopf, 1956), p. 366.

4. Alvin Boskoff, "An Ecological Approach to Rural Society," *Rural Sociology*, 14 (1949), p. 308.

5. Quoted in Howard W. Odum, *American Sociology* (New York: Longmans, Green & Co., 1951), p. 353.

6. Leo F. Schnore, "Social Morphology and Human Ecology," *American Journal of Sociology*, 63 (1958), pp. 620–34.

7. Robert N. Bellah, "Durkheim and History," *American Sociological Review*, 24 (1959), p. 461.

8. James S. Coleman, "The Future of Sociology," a paper presented at the 36th Annual Institute of the Society for Social Research, University of Chicago, May 23, 1959, p. 10.

9. *Ibid.*, pp. 19–20.

10. C. Wright Mills, *The Sociological Imagination* (New York: Oxford University Press, 1959), p. 163.

11. Hans H. Zetterberg (editor), *Sociology in the United States of America* (Paris: UNESCO, 1956); Joseph B. Gittler (editor), *Review of Sociology: Analysis of a Decade* (New York: John Wiley and Sons, 1957); Robert K. Merton, Leonard Broom, and Leonard S. Cottrell (editors), *Sociology Today: Problems and Prospects* (New York: Basic Books, 1959).

12. Jack P. Gibbs and Walter T. Martin, "Toward a Theoretical System of Human Ecology," *Pacific Sociological Review*, 2 (1959), pp. 29–36.

13. Peter H. Rossi, "Comment," *American Journal of Sociology*, 65 (1959), p. 146.

14. Edward C. Tolman, "The Intervening Variable," in Melvin N. Marx (editor), *Psychological Theory* (New York: Macmillan Co., 1951), pp. 88–89.

15. Louis Wirth, "Urbanism as a Way of Life," *American Journal of Sociology*, 44 (1938), pp. 1–24.

16. Theodore Newcomb, *Social Psychology* (New York: Dryden Press, 1950), p. 25.

17. G. E. Swanson, "A Preliminary Laboratory Study of the Acting Crowd," *American Sociological Review*, 18 (1953), p. 522; italics added.

18. Abram Kardiner, *The Individual and His Society* (New York: Columbia University Press, 1939).

19. Emile Durkheim, *The Rules of Sociological Method* (Glencoe: Free Press, 1950), p. 110.

20. For a recent use of the distinction between realism and nominalism, see Kurt H. Wolff, "The Sociology of Knowledge and Sociological Theory," in Llewellyn Gross (editor), *Symposium on Sociological Theory* (Evanston: Row, Peterson, 1959), pp. 557–602.

21. Amos H. Hawley, *Human Ecology: A Theory of Community Structure* (New York: Ronald Press, 1950).

22. Jack P. Gibbs and Walter T. Martin, "Urbanization and Natural Resources: A Study in Organizational Ecology," *American Sociological Review*, 23 (1958), pp. 266–77.

23. One would hesitate to call such sociometric inquiries "ecological," and to regard small–group interests as "macrosociological," but the fundamental similarity in approach is noteworthy, despite the strain placed on the language. Perhaps "holistic" versus "atomistic" would provide a more clearcut set of alternatives; this possibility was suggested by Professor Duncan in a private communication. With him, we are inclined to reserve the term "human ecology" for efforts to understand the interconnections between variations in population, organization, environment and technology in the context of such macroscopic *units* as communities, regions and societies. See Otis Dudley Duncan, "Human Ecology and Population Studies," in Philip M. Hauser and Otis Dudley Duncan (editors), *The Study of Population* (Chicago: University of Chicago Press, 1959), pp. 678–716; and Otis Dudley Duncan and Leo F. Schnore, "Cultural, Behavioral, and Ecological Perspectives in the Study of Social Organization," *American Journal of Sociology*, 65 (1959), pp. 132–46.

24. S. M. Lipset, Martin A. Trow, and James S. Coleman, *Union Democracy* (Glencoe: Free Press, 1957).

25. Ernest W. Burgess, "The Ecology and Social Psychology of the City," in Donald J. Bogue (editor), *Needed Urban and Metropolitan Research* (Oxford, Ohio and Chicago: Scripps Foundation for Research in Population Problems, and Population Research and Training Center, University of Chicago, 1953), p. 80.

26. Wendell Bell, "Familism and Suburbanization: One Test of the Social Choice Hypothesis," *Rural Sociology*, 21 (1956), pp. 276–83; Sylvia Fleis Fava, "Suburbanism as a Way of Life," *American Sociological Review*, 21 (1956), pp. 34–37.

27. Otis Dudley Duncan and Albert J. Reiss, Jr., *Social Characteristics of Urban and Rural Communities, 1950* (New York: John Wiley and Sons, 1956).

Chapter 3

Social Mobility in Demographic Perspective

THE SCOPE OF DEMOGRAPHY

ALTHOUGH ITS PLACE in demographic analysis is not fully appreciated, the topic of social mobility can be easily shown to lie within the province of demography when the field is realistically defined. All that is required is an awareness of the demographer's interest in population composition. The concept of "population composition" refers to any view of an aggregate that recognizes differences within it. In theory, the criteria and cutting points employed and the categories utilized could cover an unlimited range of quantitative and qualitative characteristics amenable to being distinguished and counted; the fact that they do not do so is a matter of convention.[1]

Failure to recognize the place of social mobility in the field is not surprising, for demography has presented definitional difficulties since the term was coined in 1855.[2] In fact, it appears that there was no clear-cut conception of demography as a

Prepared for the Workshop on Methodology and Systems Formulation, Social Systems Research Institute, University of Wisconsin.

discipline with distinguishable boundaries until the present century. One widely quoted definition was set out by Wolfe in 1931, wherein demography was described as, "The numerical analysis of the state and movement of human population inclusive of census enumeration and registration of vital processes."[3] This definition has the virtue of specifying the basic sources of demographic data, but its broad reference to the "state and movement" of population is unnecessarily ambiguous. As we shall see, only certain aspects of the "state" of a population come under demographic purview, while the "movements" to which demographers attend—social as well as physical—are quite readily specified.

Sources of data—The "state" of a population is ordinarily ascertained by means of a *census*—an enumeration, whether complete or partial (via sampling), of the number and characteristics of a given population at a given point in time. The cross-sectional element in this definition is critical; a census offers a snapshot, or an essentially static portrait of a population. However, only three facets are of demographic interest: (*1*) size, (*2*) spatial distribution, and (*3*) composition. This last aspect—the "make-up" of a population—represents the subdivision of a population into significant biological, social or economic categories.

In sharp contrast with the census stands the *registration* system, designed to record and compile the incidence of certain events at or near the time of their occurrence. Note that "events" and not persons are the units employed; more important, recording occurs more or less continuously, rather than at arbitrary points in time, so that the census "snapshot" may be augmented by a "moving picture" of closely spaced observations. Now "registration," as a system of data collection, is not to be confused with "vital statistics," which typically include only births, adoptions, marriages, separations, annulments, divorces, and deaths.[4] Other events that are amenable to registration are migration and various types of mobility. Movements between modern nation-states, or "international migrations," are commonly registered. In contrast, "internal migration," or change of residence within a country, is less frequently a subject of registration. Registration is also logically applicable to other types of mobility, in the sense of movements in the social system, or status changes. For example, occupational changes may be recorded in a registration system; they are analogous to changes in marital status, and may be registered just like marriages and divorces, albeit at great expense.[5]

In any event, the two major sources of demographic data—census and registration systems—must be seen as complementary devices, and they are particularly informative when their products are combined. The mutual relevance of the two types of demographic data is readily appreciated as soon as it is recognized that the "movements" of population that are of interest to demographers include all those events that bring about alterations in a population's size, distribution, or composition.[6]

The demographic equation—The demographer is obviously interested in such phenomena as fertility and mortality, the "vital processes" by means of which the size of the world's population is determined. Here is also the basis of the demographer's concern with migration, or physical movement through space. Even in the absence of significant variations in fertility and mortality, substantial changes in distribution, and in the size of local populations, can be readily effected by migratory movements.

Recognition of the fundamental role of the vital processes (fertility and mortality) in producing changes in population size has given rise to definitions of the field phrased solely in terms of vital statistics.[7] This emphasis has survived in more recent definitions, although migration is typically added. As an example, consider Davis's delineation of the province of demography:

> The primary tasks of demography are (*1*) to ascertain the number of people in a given area, (*2*) to determine what change—what growth or decline—this number represents; (*3*) to explain the change, and (*4*) to estimate on this basis the future trend. In explaining a change in numbers the populationist begins with three variables: births, deaths, and migration. He subtracts the deaths from the births to get "natural in-

crease" and he subtracts the emigrants from the immigrants to get "net migration" . . . It is clear that any factor influencing the number of people must operate through one or more of the variables mentioned. *In no other way can a population be changed.* For this reason we may call the four variables [fertility, mortality, immigration, and emigration] "the primary demographic processes." They represent the core of population analysis.[8]

More recently, Davis has identified these four variables as "the strictly demographic realm [containing] the first-order variables—those through which, and only through which, any other factor can influence population change."[9] While it is an adequate representation of demographic interest in population size and distribution, we shall see that this view contains a serious deficiency as a characterization of demography as it has actually developed in the course of the past century. What it fails to include is an explicit recognition of the demographer's interest in population *composition*, and his complementary concern with *social mobility*.

Compositional change occurs in the absence of vital events, and in the absence of any migratory movement whatsoever. Consider a population composed of persons in various marital statuses. The marital composition of the population in any short time interval can obviously be altered without any births, deaths, or migrations if a substantial number of persons marry or secure a divorce, i.e., change their marital status. Although not ordinarily so labelled, these movements are forms of "social mobility" in the generic sense that we want to develop here.

Another, more complicated example will serve to show that many compositional changes are the effects of variations in fertility, mortality, migration, *and* social mobility operating in combination. Consider the problem of the changing "social class" composition of a purely hypothetical nation. In this imaginary country, *fertility* is inversely related to social class— i.e., the higher classes exhibit significantly lower fertility. Similarly, *mortality* and social class are negatively associated, so that substantially higher death rates occur in the lowest strata. Let us suppose, however, that the net effect of these tendencies favors the lower classes, whose fertility rates are high enough to compensate for their higher mortality rates, so that their rates of natural increase consistently remain above replacement requirements. Let us further assume that the higher strata are reproducing themselves at levels so low that even their low mortality rates cannot prevent net deficits from being sustained year after year. With respect to *migration* into and out of this hypothetical country, moreover, let us imagine that immigrants typically arrive with occupational skills that fit them for unskilled and menial labor; immigrants thus tend to enter the national class structure at the bottom. At the same time, emigration from the country—much smaller in volume—is not occupationally selective, so that neither upper nor lower strata lose disproportionate numbers from their ranks.

Now the combined effect of all these class-contingent demographic processes, operating over a period of time, would yield a class structure exhibiting a progressively greater bulge at the bottom, accompanied by a radical shrinkage at the top. The lower strata, constantly replenished by the numbers represented by the "gap" between the vital rates, and further swollen by net immigration, would expand rapidly. At the same time, the upper strata would be suffering the numerical decimation of an unfavorable balance between the vital rates, and— unable to depend upon immigration to compensate for the "natural" deficits—would exhibit absolute losses.

Up to this point we have considered only certain simple relations between social class, vital rates, and migration. What of the implications of this situation for class composition and social mobility? Let us suppose that a series of censuses over the period of observation disclosed no noticeable change in class composition, as indexed by the proportions in various occupations. Despite the implications of immobility or class equilibrium suggested by these data, we would actually have to infer considerable net upward *social mobility*. In other words, substantial numbers of persons would have to experience occupational changes—either intergenerationally or in individual career terms—from lower to higher positions, in order to preserve the same over-all class composition. This is because the remaining demographic variables are behaving in such fashion as to yield surpluses at the bottom and deficits at the top. If the successive censuses revealed changes in class composition representing an occupational "up-grading" of the entire population, by means of expansions at the top and contractions at the base, then even more net upward mobility would have to be inferred. Note that we specify "net" upward mobility, in recognition of the fact that changes may occur in either direction as far as individuals are concerned.

We may summarize the foregoing argument in more abstract terms. If one is exclusively interested in changes in population size and/or distribution in a given time interval, then the four "first-order variables" specified by Davis are sufficient for demographic analysis. As he has pointed out,

If "r" is the rate of growth, then the following equation holds:
$$r = (b - d) + (i - e)$$
where "b" is the birth rate, "d" the death rate, "i" the immigration rate, and "e" the emigration rate for a given period. If the population in question is that of the whole world, migration drops out of the picture, leaving only natural increase.[10]

By strictly analogous reasoning, changes in population distribution can be disaggregated or separated into their demographic components, and appropriate weights can be assigned to the responsible processes according to their actual contributions.

If one is concerned with changes in composition, however, the "demographic equation" must be modified accordingly, in order to take account of the possible role of social mobility. Thus for the changes in the size of a particular occupational stratum or marital status category, the proper expression would read:
$$(B - D) + (I - E) + (X - Y)$$
where "B," "D," "I," and "E" refer to the *absolute* numbers of births, deaths, immigrants and emigrants respectively, and where "X" signifies movement into, and "Y" denotes movement out of, the stratum or category.

Thus social mobility is a subject of vital interest to demographers. The concern may be direct and for its own sake, as in the analysis of accessions to and departures from the labor force. More frequently, certain kinds of mobility are of interest for the bearing they may have upon vital rates, as exemplified by the concern shown by students of fertility over the marriage rate, which reflects the relative frequency of one kind of change in status. Demographers frequently analyze changes in composition into their "components," as portrayed in the expression given immediately above. Whatever the motivation behind the work, however, and whatever the practical or theoretical ends that are served, the study of various kinds of social mobility is an important part of the demographer's stock in trade.

Defining the field—The most serviceable definition of demography—one that is neither unmanageably broad nor unduly restrictive, and one that gives due attention to the actual activities of professional demographers—has recently appeared in a formulation by Hauser and Duncan:

> Demography is the study of the size, territorial distribution, and composition of population, changes therein, and the components of such changes, which may be identified as natality, mortality, territorial movement (migration), and social mobility (change of status).[11]

These writers distinguish rather sharply between "demography" and what they choose to call "population studies," reserving the former term for the more technical and descriptive aspects of demographic inquiry. Under the rubric of "population studies" they refer to any analysis, undertaken from any of a wide variety of disciplinary viewpoints, that focusses upon demographic phenomena as either independent or dependent variables. This distinction gives formal recognition to the many points of contact between demography and a host of scientific specialties, both biological and social, and these links deserve a few brief remarks.

It should be obvious that demography is not the exclusive property of any one discipline. Demographic study is informed by any body of theory or research that bears upon the questions of human birth, death, and movement, whether through social or physical space. Many subfields of biology thus qualify

as conducting "population studies," although there is some disposition among social scientists to pre-empt the field, as when
Davis asserts that "whenever the demographer pushes his inquiry to the point of asking why the demographic processes
behave as they do, he enters the social field."[12] Moreover, it is
futile to try to link demography to any one of the special social
sciences. The fact that most demographers in the United States
are trained as sociologists is as fortuitous as that most representatives of the profession in Europe are trained as economists,
actuaries, public health statisticians, or anthropologists.[13] Nevertheless, we will attempt to show that demography has immediate relevance for sociology, in that (1) a *compositional* view
of population inevitably provides a proximate description of
social structure, and (2) a demographic treatment of *changes
in status* yields invaluable data on *social mobility*. Nothing that
is said here should suggest that similar arguments could not be
made for the special relevance of demography for (say) economics or geography.[14] The author writes as a sociologist, and
as one especially concerned with macroscopic aspects of social
structure and social mobility as major foci of that discipline. In
general, he subscribes to the view that

> Demography may be considered as a service discipline to
> the other branches of social science. Its data and findings are
> basic to every other social science because of their immediate
> descriptive value and, what is even more important, because of
> their use in suggesting problems for research in other disci-
> plines.[15]

These preliminary remarks should serve to establish the relevance of social mobility for demography. Our next task is to
focus more closely upon mobility, to distinguish subtypes of
mobility, and to specify the manner in which they are treated
demographically.

TYPES OF MOBILITY AND THEIR MEASUREMENT

Up to this point, we have been content to speak of mobility
as change in status. Satisfactory as this may be for preliminary
purposes, closer analysis must begin by classifying statuses, and

then proceed to subdivide them according to the manner in which they may be altered. As it happens, our initial distinction derives, not from demography, but from the literature of anthropology and sociology. It is the widely recognized distinction between *"ascribed"* and *"achieved"* statuses usually credited to Linton.[16]

Ascribed statuses—Commonly cited examples of universally "ascribed" statuses are age, sex, and certain kinship statuses; these share a nonvolitional quality, in that no amount of effort on the part of the individual can alter them. An equally apt example is one's place of birth; although one may lie about it, one's birthplace cannot be changed. By contrast, "achieved" statuses are more clearly subject to change, and as the term itself suggests, effort and volition frequently have a role. In addition, one's educational or marital status, his occupation, and his place of residence are not immutably fixed. Even if they cannot be changed at will (since the norms of many societies treat them in ways as fully deterministic as those governing age and sex) they have the common quality of *potential* for change. The basis of the distinction, however, does not turn upon the presence or absence of a capacity for change *per se;* we shall see that at least one ascribed status changes automatically, and that the forms of change taken by various achieved statuses do not reduce to a single type. Nor does the distinction rest, at bottom, upon the capacity for volition to be exercised. As it turns out, this dimension of status—ascription versus achievement—hinges upon whether or not the status can be determined at birth.[17]

As concrete examples, let us consider the universally "ascribed" statuses first. These include age, sex, place of birth, and kinship within the family of orientation.[18] Among these, age stands out distinctly as a changeable status; while all of the others are immutable, one's age is constantly changing from the instant of birth, for aging is a biological fact to be reckoned with continuously. Equally vital for our purposes is the fact that this change has the quality of irreversibility. Trivial as it may seem at first blush, the fact that one's age changes in only one direction turns out to be of critical significance, conceptually and in terms of measurement.[19]

Achieved statuses—Upon superficial examination, it may seem that "achieved" statuses are simply those that are changeable, since it is difficult to conceive of any that are absolutely resistant to change.[20] Why then utilize the ascribed-achieved dichotomy at all? We shall deal with this issue below; it is more profitable, for the moment, to consider some concrete instances of changeable statuses that fall under the "achieved" rubric. Among the important achieved statuses that are commonly recognized are the following: education, occupation, income, religion, marital status, and kinship in the family of procreation. Each of these could serve as the subject for detailed discussion, but two or three of them merit special attention.

First of all, when educational status is defined in terms of school years completed (as in our census system), it has a more or less unique quality. One may add to, but never subtract from, the number of years of attendance.[21] Another interesting case illustrates the importance of the definitions of the categories employed. If one is concerned with marital status, one is likely to work with a set of categories similar to those used in the United States census, viz., single, married, separated, divorced, and widowed. If so, some of the statuses are clearly reversible, in the sense that a person can be divorced or widowed and he may subsequently remarry, at which time he reassumes a status previously held. For some purposes, however, demographers find it profitable to work with only a crude dichotomy: "never-married" (single) and "ever-married" (including the currently married, separated, divorced, and widowed). In this case, the only possible status change is irreversible.

The other achieved statuses are chiefly marked by the fact of reversibility. Adherents of a particular religion may enter and leave, they may join another church or sect, rejoin their original faith, or forswear allegiance to any religious group. Similarly, an individual may move through a whole series of occupations, from time to time reassuming a position that had been previously abandoned. Finally, one can alter his place of residence, with the obvious option of returning to a place previously occupied. Although we prefer to discuss changes in place of residence as "migration," it is important to recognize the fundamental parallel between such changes and those that may ensue between other statuses; they are cognate processes, and offer a number of interesting problems when they are jointly considered.[22]

Status changes—It remains only to identify the traditional interest of sociologists in "social mobility" in these terms. This task will be facilitated, however, if we summarize the foregoing discussion in graphic form. Table 1 encompasses all of the concrete cases discussed above; note that the "unchangeable reversible" cells are empty by definition, since reversal is a form of change. It is undoubtedly the irreversible and unchangeable quality of most ascribed statuses, together with the changeable and reversible character of most achieved statuses, that have tempted most writers to emphasize the matter of volition. Our analysis, however, has demonstrated that this is not the crucial basis of distinction; rather, it is the extent to which a status is amenable to assignment at birth.

Table 1—Types of Status Change, with Examples

	Type of Status Change			
	CHANGEABLE		UNCHANGEABLE	
Type of Status	Reversible	Irreversible	Reversible	Irreversible
Ascribed	"Citizen"	Age		Sex Place of birth Kinship in family of orientation "Race"
Achieved	Occupation Income Religion Marital status Place of residence Kinship in family of procreation	Education		"Veteran"

Sociological interest in statuses has taken a number of directions. Perhaps the most popular approach starts from the image of the individual as simultaneously occupying a number of statuses, each of which constitutes a membership in some group or social category. This line of thought leads naturally to a statistical consideration of the co-occupancy of statuses, as in the work of Lenski, Gibbs and Martin,[23] or (more frequently) into a nonstatistical analysis of the compatibility of statuses. Concern with "role conflicts" and "marginality" are typical problems here. Both of these approaches may derive from a simple cross-sectional consideration of statuses held at a given point in time. But still another direction of sociological effort begins with the observation that individuals pass through a series of statuses in sequence during the course of a lifetime. Thus some writers are concerned with modal sequences and with the appropriateness of one status for its probable *sequelae* (e.g., youth for adulthood).[24] Allied concepts that have grown out of this area of discussion include "anticipatory socialization" and "resocialization," and the general interest is longitudinal or developmental, with the individual career at issue.

All of these theoretical and empirical efforts bear the common stamp of an individualistic emphasis, although degrees of status crystallization or integration can be properly regarded as variable properties of populations in certain applications. Quite different facets of the problem come into view, however, if we assume another posture and consider statuses from the standpoint of social structure in the large. As Gutman has observed, "Many population characteristics about which information is collected in census tabulations are relevant also to the analysis of social structure."[25] Social structure, in other words, is amenable to study in terms of population composition. The United Nations has recommended the following items for inclusion in all censuses: sex, age, marital status, place of birth, citizenship, mother tongue, educational characteristics, fertility data, economic characteristics, household data (including the relationship of the individual to the head of the household), and urban and rural place of residence.[26] Such data would comprise a rich mine, indeed, for the student of comparative social structure, for they include all of the specific statuses discussed above, and census cross-tabulations permit an elaborate description of a society's gross morphology. Unfortunately, very few countries compile and publish data on all of these subjects, and the amount of cross-tabular detail is even more limited. Truly comparative structural analysis of more than a small and biased sample of countries will have to await the implementation of these recommendations by nations and territories outside the Western sphere. This fact notwithstanding, it is important to take note of the potential for structural analysis that resides in a compositional view of population.

Sociological views—Our final task in this section is to locate the traditional interest of sociologists in "social mobility" within the framework that we have developed here. Sociological effort has been focussed almost exclusively upon the cluster of statuses in the lower left-hand corner of Table 1, or more explicitly, on the "reversible achieved" statuses. Not all of these, however, have been the subject of scrutiny in terms of mobility. Studies of changes in marital status are ordinarily taken up in the context of family studies. Changes in place of residence and religion have been somewhat slighted in the mobility literature in favor of emphasis upon occupation, income and education, and "social mobility," in the sociological lexicon, has primary reference to changes in these statuses.[27]

Now these three statuses—education, occupation, and income—have seemingly come into analytical prominence because of two facts: (*1*) social mobility, as a subject of sociological inquiry, has been absorbed into a more general content area, i.e., "stratification;" (*2*) much of the theoretical and empirical literature in this latter area treats statuses unidimensionally. It ranks them along a single scale, e.g., in accordance with the differential evaluation accorded various statuses. These three statuses have the common feature of being more or less readily ranked; for contrast, one need only to think of marital statuses, the "ranking" of which is difficult. Of all the achieved statuses listed in Table 1, only educational, income, or occupational movements can be meaningfully labelled as "upward" or "downward." Indeed, two of them (income and education) are almost intrinsically quantitative, and can be easily represented as relatively unambiguous scales. It might also be added that a whole host of studies have shown the utility of these variables in predicting a wide variety of behavior of sociological interest—including consumer decisions, voting performance, fertility preferences, and life styles in general. Our intention is not to deny or minimize the value of these inquiries. Rather, it is to point to the rather narrow canvas upon which mobility has been portrayed, and to point to some possible advantages that might derive from a generic conception of "social mobility."

To take one example, sociologists concerned with mobility are in the habit of dealing only with occupational movements *between* broadly defined strata, ignoring movements *within* the stratum. (Such movements have come to be labelled shifts within a "situs" by a few writers.)[28] There is also a tendency to regard only changes across a particular occupational line—such as those between manual and non-manual jobs—as "true" mobility. Although sometimes dictated by the small number of cases under analysis, and by the demand for imposing comparability upon data derived from different sources, such procedures harbor grave methodological hazards if one is setting out to assess the total amount of occupational mobility in a system wherein the strata consist of assemblages of occupations. Finally, there is the vexing problem of the disposition of agricultural occupations, which do not fit nicely into the usual ranking schemes; what constitutes "upward" versus "downward" mobility is sometimes difficult to determine in rural to urban shifts. Some of these problems are clarified by the adoption of a demographic perspective. Toward this end, we will turn to a review of some demographic contributions to the study of social mobility, viewed in the larger sense to which we have alluded.

DEMOGRAPHIC CONTRIBUTIONS TO THE STUDY OF SOCIAL MOBILITY

Demographers, of course, are likely to work with all of the variables enumerated in Figure 1, at least in simple combination. For the most part, however, their empirical efforts have been confined to cross-sectional examinations of co-occupancy patterns among the various statuses. Thus differences between various age grades in education, occupation, income, marital status, place of residence, etc., are rather well known for countries possessing modern census systems. Still, it must be recognized that these materials do not furnish *direct* evidence concerning mobility between statuses. The cross-sectional emphasis stems from the fact that censuses are typically far more inclusive, with respect to the list of statuses treated, than are registration systems.[29]

Items that are widely registered include the following: births, adoptions, marriages, separations, annulments, divorces, and deaths. Certain countries maintaining "continuous registration" systems add data on changes in place of residence; these record-linkage systems, however, are expensive to maintain, and they tend to be rather fragile, in the sense that they are easily subject to error.[30] Direct demographic evidence is thus effectively confined to changes in marital and familial statuses. Marriage and divorce statistics are especially favored by demographers because of the fundamental bearing of nuptiality upon fertility. These materials are probably of limited interest to most sociologists concerned with social mobility.

There are other changes in status that have not been adequately treated in demographic terms. One of these concerns religious affiliation. In the United States, this item is not even enumerated in the decennial census, and though religion is recorded in some state vital registration systems, actual changes in religious affiliation are not registered as such. Still, this topic is of considerable interest from the standpoint of mobility, when it is regarded in prestige terms. Moore has observed that "Protestant religious denominations in the United States have differential prestige, at least at the community level, and there is some indication of changes in affiliation with career success," and he goes on to suggest the desirability of measuring the more general relation "between income-and-occupational mobility and changes in number and types of associational memberships."[31]

As we have indicated, sociologists evince considerable interest in the relationship between education and social mobility. Although relatively little demographic effort has gone into this subject in the United States, it is perhaps significant that the most intensive investigation thus far conducted in a Western country was carried out under the general direction of a demographer, and that it makes effective use of a variety of demographic techniques.[32] As in the case of religion, this represents another instance in which American demography has not contributed its full potential to the study of mobility.

American demographers, like their sociological counterparts, have been much more concerned with occupational mobility. They have become increasingly involved in various types of "labor force analysis," and this is one area in which occupational mobility is approached more or less directly. Combining data from censuses, sample surveys, and a variety of statistical sources, a large amount of information has been assembled on such matters as rates of entry into and separation from the work force; labor force participation rates by sex, age, and other characteristics; migration and labor mobility; and the length of working life.[33] A number of contact points between this work and various specialties within sociology—including social stratification and social mobility—are concisely enumerated in an essay by Philip M. Hauser on "The Labor Force as a Field of Interest for the Sociologist."[34]

The demographic analysis of social mobility is typically focussed on the relationship between mobility and the "traditional" demographic variables, particularly migration and fertility. The literature on rural-urban migration contains a wealth of indirect evidence on occupational mobility, since this shift in place of residence typically involves occupational changes from agricultural to nonagricultural pursuits; selectivity of migration, or the characteristics of movers versus non-movers, has been frequently studied. However, more direct inquiries into the relationship between migration and occupational mobility have been conducted by Goldstein, Bogue, and Freedman and Hawley.[35] Each of these studies, although conducted by a professional demographer, made use of data from other than the traditional demographic sources (nation-wide censuses and registration systems). Goldstein employed data from a series of city directories, Bogue used quarterly reports from the Bureau of Old Age and Survivors Insurance for two states, and Freedman and Hawley utilized materials from a special state census of unemployment in which complete work histories were collected. (The latter data are not gathered in the typical census.) It is also important to note that all of these studies conceive mobility in career terms, i.e., as taking place within the individual's own working life, rather than inter-generationally. Both of these features—"nondemographic" data and a career definition of mobility—also characterize another recent demographic study of mobility, that by Jaffe and Carleton, in which the results of a six-city sample survey are utilized.[36]

Demographers have also displayed some interest in mobility in the course of studying fertility. In the empirical work that has been accomplished, mobility has ordinarily entered the analysis as an independent variable, both inter-generational and career measures have been employed, and income changes as well as occupational shifts have sometimes been considered.[37] These sources are perhaps of less direct interest to sociologists concerned with mobility because they offer little in the way of an explanation of the phenomenon, rich as they are in suggesting some behavioral consequences of mobility.

Of greater general interest to the sociologist is the demographic perspective on social mobility provided in Elbridge Sibley's well-known essay, "Some Demographic Clues to Stratification." Sibley succeeded in integrating differential fertility, immigration, and technological progress, considered as factors contributing to a long-term net upward mobility in the United States, and offered a cogent discussion of the potential role of education in continuing the process. He concluded that, "Together, immigration and differential fertility have contributed more than technological progress to the upward movement of individuals in America."[38] Although he made no effort to demonstrate this thesis statistically, his discussion remains one of the most lucid analyses of the ways in which the demographic processes bear upon each other, and the ways in which they combine to effect changes in population composition.

Freedman and Freedman have more recently been able to show that rural-to-urban migrants in the United States tend to be found near the bottom of the urban class structure, when their status is measured by income, education, and occupation.[39] Though this may result from excessive downward mobility on the part of migrants (since the survey materials do not identify the point of entrance), the Freedmans infer that rural-urban migrants tend to enter the urban class structure at the bottom. Building upon this basic finding, Goldberg has recently argued that this disproportionate representation of rural migrants in the lower urban strata accounts for the usually observed inverse relationship between social class and fertility in urban populations. Goldberg finds insignificant differences in the fertility of "two-generation urbanites" in the various class levels. The usual inverse pattern is observed only in the farm-reared segment of the urban population. The relevance of his argument at this point should be clear: if the farm-reared typically enter the urban class structure at or near the bottom, it is apparently the upwardly mobile farm-reared migrants who limit their child-bearing most severely.[40] An additional possibility worthy of investigation is that many of the traits and behaviors found to be related to social class standing in urban areas (a) are products of the heavier representation of rural migrants in the lower strata, and/or (b) result from selective upward mobility of farm-reared elements in the urban class structure. In any event, Goldberg's work represents another instance of a demographer working simultaneously with three broad variables—fertility, migration, and mobility. It is out of such detailed investigations that the empirical dimensions of social mobility will be filled in with greater precision.

All of the foregoing studies exemplify ways in which demographic techniques and a demographic perspective throw light upon a subject that is rarely viewed as lying within the province of the discipline. With his repertoire of sophisticated techniques, the demographer seems particularly well qualified to aid the sociologist in the task of measuring the volume, direction, and characteristics of the mobile portion of the population. By virtue of his awareness of certain methodological dangers, such as those attending the use of inter-generational measures of mobility, the demographer is also able to provide warning against incomplete treatment of the subject. (Since the demographer employs the concept of a closed system in working with the demographic equation, he is inclined to be sensitive to various "leaks" that characterize sample survey data, as illustrated in our earlier discussion of inter-generational mobility in footnote 36.) The fact that more demographic research on mobility has not been accomplished to date can probably be attributed to the absence of systematic registration of most status changes. The increasing use of sample survey materials by demographers should fill in these lacunae in the traditional sources of demographic data, and they can learn a great deal from those sociologists who have already acquired the methodological sophistication required for handling these materials. Equally important, however, is an awareness on the part of both sociologists and demographers that the latter are well equipped, both technically and conceptually, to tackle the problem of social mobility.

CONTRIBUTIONS OF SOCIOLOGISTS TO THE DEMOGRAPHIC ANALYSIS OF MOBILITY

With its tradition of descriptive research, it might be thought that the greatest single deficiency characterizing the treatment of social mobility in demography is in regard to conceptualization. Indeed, demographers have been criticized as being inclined to describe without explaining, and as if they were at least averse to theory-building if not actually debilitated by a trained incapacity to theorize.[41] This view represents a gross over-simplification, although students of population have no cause for complacency; their methodological assurance and the somewhat restricted scope of their specialty should have permitted the construction of far more elegant theory than is currently available. In actual fact, however, demographers have much to learn from sociological students of mobility in matters other than concept manipulation at the verbal level.

First of all, there are a number of empirical investigations by nondemographers that merit attention on methodological grounds.[42] The most familiar study is probably the one by Rogoff, in which data from marriage license applications in a single county in Indiana were employed in order to assess the amount, direction and character of occupational mobility in two different time periods.[43] Aside from the substantive results, the main interest of this study lies in Rogoff's effort to distinguish between "individual mobility," as it is ordinarily conceived in inter-generational terms, and "structurally-induced mobility." The latter type of mobility derives from alterations in the occupational structure wrought by technological and organizational changes; different time periods may thus offer different probabilities of mobility for the individuals concerned. By means of an ingenious variant on familiar contingency methods, Rogoff attempted to control structurally-induced mobility and to observe changes in individual mobility. She was unable, of course, to separate the latter from the mobility resulting from differential fertility and mortality, as well as from other sources, but the possible application of her general method to other areas of demographic interest has yet to be attempted; it appears to be appropriate to the study of rural-urban migration in periods and in areas (e.g., nations) characterized by different distributions of population according to size of place.

In a similar vein, Kahl's work on the sources of social mobility merits close attention by demographers.[44] First of all, Kahl distinguished "technological mobility" (roughly synonymous with the "structurally-induced mobility" discussed above) from "immigration mobility" and "reproductive mobility," with the latter types referring to the differential demographic behavior of the various social strata. By comparing occupational distributions in the United States in 1920 and 1950, by employing estimates of the occupational distribution of net immigration in the same period, and by the use of occupational net reproduction rates, Kahl attempted to estimate the amount of occupational mobility attributable to these sources. Drawing upon data from a national sample survey, in order to estimate total inter-generational mobility, he then proceeded to subtract the foregoing "component" estimates from this total, and thus to derive the amount of "individual" mobility. Although necessarily rough and inexact, Kahl's effort deserves attention, if only as an attempt to give statistical substance to Sibley's discussion.

Another study that stems from a sociological concern with stratification and mobility is the recent comparative study by Seymour Martin Lipset and Reinhard Bendix.[45] Although it has been properly heralded as the first general theoretical treatment of the subject since Sorokin's classic appeared some thirty years earlier,[46] the major interest in the work attaches to the data presented. Most of these derive from two sources: (1) a study of career mobility in a sample of Oakland, California workers; (2) a large number of sample surveys from various nations, dealing mainly with inter-generational mobility. There are few innovations in the career-mobility materials, and the analysis of the international data is marred by several minor technical deficiencies caused by the nature of the data. For one thing, attention is focussed upon the inter-generational crossing of the "manual-nonmanual" line, despite evidence that such a dichotomous treatment obscures the total volume of mobility; indirect evidence to this effect, in fact, is to be found in the author's own Oakland data. Secondly, the study fails satisfactorily to resolve the problem of rural-to-urban occupational mobility, the significance of which varies from country to country, depending upon levels of urbanization. Despite these methodological defects, the volume warrants close attention by reason of the sheer scope of its comparative coverage, which is certainly the most ambitious to be found in the literature.

Lest it be inferred from earlier remarks that demographers have little to learn from sociologists in the way of theoretical insights, attention must be called to the analysis of social mobility by Sorokin, mentioned above. After thirty-odd years, this volume remains the most rewarding general treatment of the topic in the sociological literature, and it deserves perusal by any demographer who undertakes work in the area. Examination of the Lipset-Bendix volume also yields large dividends. Yet there are gaps in the sociologists' discussion of the topic, and some of them are surprising in view of the discipline's presumed interest in explaining variations in mobility at the macroscopic level. By and large, a great deal of attention has been devoted to such matters as motivations for mobility, the emotional consequences of mobility, the stresses and strains that impinge upon the mobile person, and the individual behavioral correlates of mobility. Few sociologists appear to have grappled with the broad issue of *the determinants of variations in mobility at the societal level.* Sorokin, Sibley, Kahl, Lipset and Bendix are certainly prominent exceptions, but there have been only occasional efforts by other sociologists.

The determinants of mobility—One little-known discussion of the sources of mobility that deserves some attention has been offered by Havighurst. The major portion of this paper is devoted to an effort at comparing mobility in the United States, England, Australia, and Brazil by reference to sample survey data; unfortunately, some of the methodological difficulties that characterize the Lipset-Bendix comparative materials are even more in evidence here. In the course of his discussion, however, Havighurst attempts to identify the conditions that make for net upward mobility in a society. First, although he neglects class-selective migration, Havighurst correctly identifies a demographic factor by pointing to the role of differential reproduction; in this respect, his analysis is similar to that of Sibley and Kahl. Havighurst goes on, however, to specify in detail another general condition—the one variously identified as "structurally-induced mobility" by Rogoff, and as "technological mobility" by Sibley and Kahl. In Havighurst's words, this condition is

A shift in occupational distribution so as to increase the proportion of middle and higher status occupational positions. This could result from:

a. Change in technology of production which increases the proportion of more technical and highly-skilled jobs. For instance, automation does this.

b. Change in type of industry from those with many unskilled jobs to those with more jobs requiring technical training. The change from agriculture to manufacturing industry usually does this; and so does a change from farming with human labor to farming with machinery.

c. Introduction of new industries which require a high proportion of technically-trained and well-paid workers.

d. Increase of industrial productivity with resultant increase in wages and salaries, which allows people to spend more of their income on services provided by professional people, thus increasing the proportion of such people.

e. Free or easy access to valuable natural resources, such as good land, gold, diamonds, oil, uranium. This creates people with wealth who take the status positions of owners of wealth.[47]

The principal merit of this brief discussion is that it attempts to move beyond the simple recognition of the possibility of changes in occupational structure—changes that may affect the individual's chances for moving within that structure—to a specification of some sources of structural change *per se*. Although the list he presents is probably not exhaustive, and though it is clearly not made up of mutually exclusive "factors," it serves as a starting point for further analysis.

An ecological approach—The sources of change in occupational structure enumerated by Havighurst appear to be amenable to reformulation in terms of the "ecological complex," a heuristic device that seems particularly appropriate to this problem.[48] From the ecological standpoint, mobility may be treated as a demographic variable, with sources of change in that variable to be sought in four general areas, i.e., among other demographic, organizational, technological, and environmental factors. Let us specify social mobility as the *explanandum*, or dependent variable, in an analysis that takes the nation-state as the unit of observation. The independent variables may then be said to include the following:

A. *Other demographic factors:*
   1. Differential replacement, according to social strata, brought about by differential fertility and mortality.
   2. Class-selective net immigration.

B. *Technological factors:*
   1. Innovations in the technology of production (see Havighurst's item "a");
   2. Innovations in the technology of distribution, and especially in transportation and communication, that yield

changes analogous to B-1 above, or to C-4, C-5, or D-3 below.

C. *Organizational factors:*

1. Change in type of industry (see Havighurst's item "b");
2. Introduction of new industries (see Havighurst's item "c");
3. Increases in the size of firms, in order to realize "internal economies," which tend to increase employment in white-collar jobs;
4. A redistribution of wealth resulting from increased productivity, leading to increased demand for certain services (see Havighurst's item "d");
5. A redistribution of wealth by political means, involving either a more or less equitable allocation among the various strata, leading to changes in demand for certain services;
6. A reorganization of external relationships with other nation-states, leading to the creation or expansion of certain occupations (e.g., those in trade and military activities).

D. *Environmental changes:*

1. Bringing new elements of the physical environment under control by technological changes, leading to new industries (see C-2 above) or redistribution of wealth (see C1-4 above);
2. Bringing new natural resources into use by discovery or conquest, leading to results similar to those suggested in D-1 above;
3. Bringing new natural resources into use via organizational changes (see C-6 above) or by increased ease of distribution (see B-2 above).
4. The exhaustion of non-replaceable resources, by depletion, erosion, desiccation, etc.

Although this scheme undoubtedly remains incomplete, it suggests a new direction for research and analysis that would push our understanding of the sources of social mobility beyond its present point. For one thing, this ecological treatment—based upon an extension and reorientation of Havighurst's reasoning—suggests that we should not be content to point to changes in occupational structure as a prime source of mobility; rather, we should be encouraged to press our analysis one step further, in the direction of a consideration of the *sources* of alterations in occupational structure *per se*. Secondly, this brief effort should indicate how complex and ramified a question is posed when we consider the sources of upward mobility; it should be evident that we cannot be satisfied to point to "industrialization" and leave it at that. Finally, this discussion should serve to demonstrate the potential utility of viewing social mobility from a demographic perspective. Although the adoption of an ecological framework—or any other analytical scheme—obliges the analyst to work with other variables as well, nothing appears to be lost and much might be gained when mobility is treated as a demographic variable.

SUMMARY AND IMPLICATIONS

This paper has attempted to show the relevance of a demographic approach to the study of social mobility. Starting with a brief consideration of demography's actual scope, we have tried to show that certain salient aspects of the subject are within the province of demography, and that, in fact, it is a frequent subject for demographic study. Working with a typology of statuses and status changes, we then proceeded to review some demographic contributions to the study of mobility in the large, and as it is more narrowly conceived by sociologists. Reversing the procedure, we then reviewed a number of works by sociologists that recommend themselves to demographers on either methodological or conceptual grounds. In conclusion, we sketched an ecological approach to the problem, in order to illustrate the mutual relevance of a demographic conception of mobility and at least one sociological point of view.

In general, there appear to be three potential contributions —theoretical, technical, and empirical—that would serve to facilitate interchange between sociology and demography in the study of social mobility:

1. Conceptually, it appears that there is much to be gained from a rigorous exploration of the formal analogies between migration and mobility. It is a commonplace that territorial movement and movement through "social space" possess more than a few commonalities, but the potential utility of such a theoretical undertaking appears to be substantial. First of all, the sociologist studying mobility and the demographer studying migration share an obvious interest in the volume and direction of these movements, as well as in the characteristics of movers versus non-movers. Starting with the conceptual apparatus currently employed in migration analysis, it seems that certain concepts and hypotheses recommend themselves for use in the study of mobility; among them are the following: the concepts of migratory pushes, pulls, and opportunities; the intervening-opportunities hypothesis; the concept of migratory backflow, or return migration; the concept of selective migration; the problem of the exhaustion of "pools" of potential migrants; and the distinction between "migration" and "residential mobility."[49]

2. Technically, the major task confronting both sociologists and demographers is the creation of better classificatory systems. Comparatively speaking, the problem of metrics seems to be a minor one in the case of income and education. Hierarchical classification of occupations, however, constitutes an extremely difficult issue. Representatives of both disciplines in this country are prone to use either the census classification developed by Edwards or a modification of the Hatt-North scale, although recognizing the severe limitations of both schemes.[50] Among other difficulties, the lack of an adequate taxonomy has prevented intensive demographic research into occupational and class differentials in mortality in the United States;[51] this deficiency renders equivocal some of the findings on differential fertility. With respect to mobility, the problem is clear: the very volume of mobility observed is partially dependent upon the number of strata distinguished in the analysis. A reclassification of occupations might proceed along the lines taken by Edwards in his effort to validate his original scheme, i.e., by exploring the educational and income levels achieved by the various occupations, but employing age controls and more

up-to-date techniques.[52] Ideally, such a reclassification would take account of census practices in other countries, so that comparative analyses would be facilitated.

3. Empirically, the great need is for further comparative study. We should not be satisfied with the type of material reviewed by Lipset and Bendix, suggestive as it is, but we should exploit other existing sources of data. One such source is represented by census statistics on occupation. Comparisons of successive censuses in a number of countries, and the computation of simple coefficients of redistribution,[53] would serve to test the major conclusions of the Hollingshead and Lipset-Bendix reviews: that rates of social mobility are substantially the same in all industrialized nations. The ecological approach to mobility sketched here also contained the implicit hypothesis that societal rates of mobility are linked to levels of economic development and urbanization. If these census-based tests tended to confirm these hypotheses, we would be enabled to pursue more extensive comparative investigations, utilizing data for many nations in which sample survey studies of mobility *per se* have yet to be conducted; all that would be required would be two or three successive censuses. Demographers profess pride in the comparative heritage of their discipline, while American sociologists are frequently accused of an ethnocentric preoccupation with their own culture. Be that as it may, the cross-cultural study of social mobility offers still another logical contact point between the interests of demographers and sociologists.

NOTES

1. See Joseph J. Spengler and Otis Dudley Duncan, editors, *Demographic Analysis* (Glencoe: Free Press, 1956), p. 439; George Lundberg, *Foundations of Sociology* (New York: Macmillan, 1939), pp. 459–60; and Kingsley Davis, *Human Society* (New York: Macmillan, 1949), p. 552.

2. Achille Guillard, *Eléments de statistique humaine; ou démographie comparée* (Paris: Guillaumin et cie., 1855).

3. A. B. Wolfe, "Demography," *Encyclopaedia of the Social Sciences* (New York: Macmillan & Co., 1931), 5, pp. 85–86.

4. Although sometimes discussed as the means of entering or leaving

a particular population, closer examination reveals that vital statistics refer to ways of entering or leaving a given family. This fact is undoubtedly related to the legal basis of these data collection systems.

5. A census may provide surrogate data on mobility. See Donald J. Bogue, "The Quantitative Study of Social Dynamics and Social Change," *American Journal of Sociology*, 57 (May, 1952), pp. 565–568; Bogue describes "mobility statistics" as census data referring to a "change in some status during an arbitrarily selected interval of time," and "tenure statistics," wherein "each person is asked when he entered his present status."

6. For more detailed accounts, see George W. Barclay, *Techniques of Population Analysis* (New York: John Wiley and Sons, 1958); Mortimer Spiegelman, *Introduction to Demography* (Chicago: The Society of Actuaries, 1955); Peter R. Cox, *Demography* (Cambridge: At the University Press, 1950); Hugh H. Wolfenden, *Population Statistics and Their Compilation* (Chicago: University of Chicago Press, 1954, rev. ed.).

7. See, for example, George Chandler Whipple, *Vital Statistics* (New York: John Wiley and Sons, 1919), p. 1.

8. *Op. cit.*, pp. 551–52; italics added.

9. Kingsley Davis, "The Demographic Consequences of Changes in Productive Technology: An Essay on the Problem of Measurement," in *Social, Economic and Technological Change* (Paris: UNESCO, 1958), p. 197.

10. *Ibid.*, p. 197.

11. Philip M. Hauser and Otis Dudley Duncan, "Overview and Conclusions," in Hauser and Duncan, editors, *The Study of Population* (Chicago: University of Chicago Press, 1959), p. 2.

12. Davis, *Human Society*, *op. cit.*, p. 552.

13. David V. Glass, editor, *The University Teaching of Social Sciences: Demography* (Paris: UNESCO, 1957).

14. See Glenn T. Trewartha, "A Case for Population Geography," *Annals of the Association of American Geographers*, 43 (June, 1953), pp. 71–97, and the essays concerned with the various disciplines in Hauser and Duncan, *op. cit.*, Part IV.

15. Amos H. Hawley, *Human Ecology: A Theory of Community Structure* (New York: Ronald Press, 1950), p. 70. See also Philip M. Hauser, "Demography in Relation to Sociology," *American Journal of Sociology*, 65 (September, 1959), pp. 169–73.

16. Ralph Linton, *The Study of Man* (New York: Appleton-Century-Crofts, Inc., 1936), p. 115.

17. The fact that they can be ascertained at birth may tempt one to call them "biological" characteristics, but the inclusion of kinship and birthplace as important subtypes stretches the meaning of the terms to a point of diminishing utility. Moreover, age and sex are socially defined statuses in every society.

18. This type of family refers to the kin group into which one is born; it is to be contrasted with the "family of procreation," created when one marries. Adoption into another family of orientation is possible, of course, and it has actually served as an avenue of social mobility in some societies; the existence of the practice makes for a certain degree of ambiguity in classification.

19. Viewed more broadly, "age" can be conceived in a manner that makes it reversible: one begins life in a state of dependence, moves to a stage of relative independence, and then ages into dependency with respect to a wide range of social responsibilities. The status of "citizen" is also an interesting one, typologically speaking. Determined at birth, at least in the United States, it can be legally lost and regained, as by inmates of certain custodial institutions; in this sense it is changeable and reversible, albeit technically ascribed. The status is also open to achievement, by naturalization. We are ignoring here those cases of changes in sex that occur from time to time. For a distinction between "population structure" (referring to "unalterable characteristics") and "population composition" (referring to "changeable features") see John V. Grauman, "Population Estimates and Projections," in Hauser and Duncan, *op. cit.*, pp. 565–69.

20. Perhaps "veteran" is one such status; it is clearly not reversible. This example, by the way, should be enlightening to those who persist in attaching particular significance to the exercise of will in "achieved" statuses, for volition may or may not operate.

21. If educational status is defined in terms of simple literacy, the possibility of forgetting acquired skills of reading and writing would make this a potentially "reversible" attribute.

22. One example will serve. Residence rules (e.g., matrilocal, patrilocal, neolocal) require migration of one or both spouses at the time of change in marital status.

23. Gerhard Lenski, "Status Crystallization: A Nonvertical Dimension of Social Status." *American Sociological Review*, 19 (August, 1954), pp. 405–413; Jack P. Gibbs and Walter T. Martin, "A Theory of Status Integration and Its Relationship to Suicide," *American Sociological Review*, 23 (April, 1958), pp. 140–47.

24. See, for example, Talcott Parsons, "Age and Sex in the Social Structure of the United States," *American Sociological Review*, 7 (October, 1942), pp. 604–16.

25. Robert Gutman, "In Defense of Population Theory," *American Sociological Review*, 25 (June, 1960), p. 328.

26. United Nations, *Population Census Methods* (New York: United Nations, 1949).

27. The related topics of "race" and ethnic membership constitute difficult problems of conceptualization and measurement, and they have been practically ignored in this presentation. At first glance, they are obviously ascribed, unchangeable, and irreversible. Such a classification, however, reckons without such phenomena as "race passing" and "assimilation," and evades a whole series of problems arising out of "race mixtures"—problems which render the subject somewhat resistant to systematic treatment. Moreover, an entire racial group may experience upward or downward mobility. The space required to deal with these complex issues can be better devoted to other matters.

28. See Émile Benoit-Smullyan, "Status, Status Types, and Status Interrelations," *American Sociological Review*, 9 (April, 1944), pp. 151–61; Paul K. Hatt, "Occupations and Social Stratification," *American Journal of Sociology*, 45 (May, 1950), pp. 533–43; Richard T. Morris and Ray-

mond J. Murphy, "The Situs Dimension in Occupational Structure," *American Sociological Review*, 24 (April, 1959), pp. 231-39.

29. See the recommendations listed in United Nations, *Principles for a Vital Statistics System* (New York: United Nations, 1953) and the review of actual registration practices summarized in United Nations, *Handbook of Vital Statistics* (New York: United Nations, 1955), pp. 114-19.

30. Such systems are described in some detail by Dorothy S. Thomas in Appendix C, National Resources Committee, *Problems of a Changing Population* (Washington: U. S. Government Printing Office, 1938).

31. Wilbert E. Moore, "Measurement of Organizational and Institutional Implications of Changes in Productive Technology," in *Social, Economic and Technological Change, op. cit.,* p. 245.

32. David V. Glass, editor, *Social Mobility in Britain* (London: Routledge and Kegan Paul, 1954).

33. The best general introduction to this area is still A. J. Jaffe and Charles D. Stewart, *Manpower Resources and Utilization* (New York: John Wiley and Sons, 1951).

34. *American Sociological Review*, 16 (August, 1951), pp. 530-38.

35. Sidney Goldstein, "Migration and Occupational Mobility in Norristown, Pennsylvania," *American Sociological Review*, 20 (August, 1955), pp. 402-08; Donald J. Bogue, *An Exploratory Study of Migration and Labor Mobility Using Social Security Data* (Oxford, Ohio: Scripps Foundation for Research in Population Problems, 1950); Ronald Freedman and Amos H. Hawley, "Migration and Occupational Mobility in the Depression," *American Journal of Sociology*, 55 (September, 1945), pp. 170-77.

36. A. J. Jaffe and R. O. Carleton, *Occupational Mobility in the United States, 1930-1960* (New York: King's Crown Press, 1954). Strictly speaking, a "career" definition of mobility is the only one that conforms to the demographic model elaborated above, in that it yields (together with data on migration, mortality, and fertility) a complete accounting for compositional change in a population. An inter-generational approach to mobility, although somewhat more convenient from the standpoint of data collection, provides only an indirect and incomplete accounting. Comparison of an individual's occupation with that of his father, for example, is roughly analogous to a comparison of population distribution at two points in time. Net shifts can be approximately inferred, but there are numerous gaps, including the omission of losses through mortality. Methodological pitfalls include the difficulty of specifying one occupation for the father, when he may have actually held many in the course of his career. (See Richard Centers, "Occupational Mobility of Urban Occupational Strata," *American Sociological Review*, 12 [April, 1948], pp. 197-203). A third type of mobility measurement—relating occupations of newly married men to those of their wives, or to those of the fathers of the spouse—has even more severe methodological restrictions, and is without a direct demographic analogue. Some studies of assortative mating and homogamy have used demographic techniques, but not the "demographic equation." Inter-generational and inter-marriage measures of mobility are discussed in Ruth Shonle Cavan, *The American Family* (New York: Thomas Y. Crowell Co., 1953), pp. 226-33. For other prob-

lems of measurement, see Melvin M. Tumin and Arnold S. Feldman, "Theory and Measurement of Occupational Mobility," *American Sociological Review*, 22 (June, 1957), pp. 281–88.

37. For general statements, see Jerzy Berent, "Fertility and Social Mobility," *Population Studies*, 5 (March, 1952), pp. 244–60; Charles F. Westoff, "The Changing Focus of Differential Fertility Research: The Social Mobility Hypothesis," *Milbank Memorial Fund Quarterly*, 32 (January, 1954), pp. 69–103; and Ruth Riemer and Clyde V. Kiser, "Economic Tension and Social Mobility in Relation to Fertility Planning and Size of Planned Family," *ibid.*, 32 (April, 1954), pp. 167–231. Both of these latter reports are from the Indianapolis Study.

38. *American Sociological Review*, 7 (June, 1942), pp. 322–30.

39. Ronald and Deborah Freedman, "Farm-Reared Elements in the Nonfarm Population," *Rural Sociology*, 21 (March, 1956), pp. 50–61. This study was based on data from a national sample survey; unfortunately, native and foreign-born migrants were not distinguished in the analysis. Similar findings from a survey of a single city are reported in Seymour Martin Lipset, "Social Mobility and Urbanization," *Rural Sociology*, 20 (September–December, 1955), pp. 220–28. See also Howard W. Beers and Catherine Heflin, "The Urban Status of Rural Migrants," *Social Forces*, 23 (October, 1944), pp. 32–37.

40. David Goldberg, "The Fertility of Two-Generation Urbanites," *Population Studies*, 12 (March, 1959), pp. 214–22. Goldberg questions the relevance of mobility in explaining differentials in fertility, and presents data showing no systematic variation among various (inter-generational) mobility categories. See also David Goldberg, "Another Look at the Indianapolis Fertility Data," *Milbank Memorial Fund Quarterly*, 38 (January, 1960), pp. 23–36. For an earlier study, see Clyde V. Kiser, "Birth Rates Among Rural Migrants to Cities," *Milbank Memorial Fund Quarterly*, 26 (October, 1938), pp. 369–81.

41. See Rupert B. Vance, "Is Theory for Demographers?" *Social Forces*, 31 (October, 1952), pp. 9–13; George A. Hillery, Jr., "Toward a Conceptualization of Demography," *Social Forces*, 37 (October, 1958), pp. 45–51; and Leighton van Nort, "On Values in Population Theory," *Milbank Memorial Fund Quarterly*, 38 (October, 1960), pp. 387–95. For effective contradictions of this view, see Kingsley Davis, "The Sociology of Demographic Behavior," in Robert K. Merton, *et al.*, editors, *Sociology Today* (New York: Basic Books, 1959), pp. 309–33, and Robert Gutman, *op. cit.* If general sociology offers a more elegant "middle-range" theory than the stable population model developed by A. J. Lotka, the author is unaware of it. Even the theory of demographic transition fares well in comparison with many sociological efforts.

42. Our identification of "non-demographers" is according to apparent major interest and affiliation with professional societies. Actually, no sharp boundary can or should be drawn; it is the problem, the technique, and the conceptual perspective that counts. Some relevant efforts, however, seem to escape the attention of sociologists and demographers by reason of title or place of publication, so that this rough classification may be useful to the reader. We cannot possibly review all of the relevant sociological contributions here. Useful bibliographies are to be found in Kurt B. Mayer, *Class and Society* (Garden City: Doubleday and Co.,

1955); and Raymond W. Mack, Linton Freeman, and Seymour Yellin, *Social Mobility: Thirty Years of Research and Theory* (Syracuse: Syracuse University Press, 1957). A rich literature from other countries has been ignored; see, for example, Theodore Geiger, "Mobilité sociale dans les sociétés européennes de notre temps," in *Problèmes de population* (Strasbourg: Centre Universitaire de Hautes Études Européennes, 1951), pp. 123–34.

43. Natalie Rogoff, *Recent Trends in Occupational Mobility* (Glencoe: Free Press, 1953). A useful summary of the main facts for the nation, together with a discussion of their implications for social mobility may be found in Albert J. Reiss, Jr., "Change in the Occupational Structure of the United States, 1910 to 1950," in Paul K. Hatt and Albert J. Reiss, Jr., editors, *Cities and Society* (Glencoe: Free Press, 1957), pp. 424–31.

44. Joseph A. Kahl, *The American Class Structure* (New York: Rinehart & Co., 1957), Chapter IX.

45. *Social Mobility in Industrial Society* (Berkeley: University of California Press, 1959).

46. Pitirim Sorokin, *Social Mobility* (New York: Harper and Brothers, 1927), republished as *Social and Cultural Mobility* (Glencoe: Free Press, 1960).

47. Robert J. Havighurst, "Education and Social Mobility in Four Countries," *Human Development Bulletin*, University of Chicago, Committee on Human Development, 1958, pp. 35–6; italics added.

48. For brief discussions and analytical uses of the ecological complex, see Otis Dudley Duncan, "Population Distribution and Community Structure," *Cold Spring Harbor Symposia on Quantitative Biology*, 22 (1957), pp. 357–71; Leo F. Schnore, "Social Morphology and Human Ecology," *American Journal of Sociology*, 63 (May, 1958), pp. 620–34; Otis Dudley Duncan "Human Ecology and Population Studies," in Hauser and Duncan, *op. cit.*, pp. 678–716; and Otis Dudley Duncan and Leo F. Schnore, "Cultural, Behavioral, and Ecological Perspectives in the Study of Social Organization," *American Journal of Sociology*, 65 (September, 1959), pp. 132–46.

49. See Otis Dudley Duncan, "Human Ecology and Population Studies," *op. cit.*, pp. 699–700. Migration is defined as *inter*-community movement, residential mobility as *intra*-community movement; the mobility analogue of the latter may be movement within a "situs." (See the previous references in Footnote 28.) An interesting taxonomic treatment of migration that has no counterpart in the mobility literature is to be found in William Petersen, "A General Typology of Migration," *American Sociological Review*, 23 (June, 1958), pp. 256–66. One might even seek the mobility analogues of such recurrent physical movements as commuting, for the latter involves temporary shifts in status, i.e., between familial or domestic and occupational roles. See Talcott Parsons, "The Principal Structures of Community," in his *Structure and Process in Modern Societies* (Glencoe: Free Press, 1960), pp. 250–79; and Leo F. Schnore, "Transportation Systems, Socioeconomic Systems, and the Individual," in *Transportation Design Considerations*, Washington: National Academy of Sciences—National Research Council, 1961, pp. 201–12.

50. See Alba M. Edwards, *A Social-Economic Grouping of the Gainful Workers in the United States* (Washington: U. S. Government Print-

ing Office, 1938); Paul K. Hatt and Cecil C. North, "Jobs and Occupations: A Popular Evaluation," *Opinion News*, 9 (September 1, 1947), pp. 3–13.

51. See Iwao M. Moriyama and L. Guralnick, "Occupational and Social Class Differentials in Mortality," in *Trends and Differentials in Mortality* (New York: Milbank Memorial Fund, 1956), pp. 61–73.

52. See Alba M. Edwards, *Comparative Occupation Statistics for the United States, 1870–1940* (Washington: U. S. Government Printing Office, 1943). For a modern approach, see Otis Dudley Duncan, "A Socioeconomic Index for All Occupations," in Albert J. Reiss, Jr., *Occupations and Social Status* (New York: Free Press, 1963), pp. 109–138.

53. The coefficient is equal to the sum of the plus or minus percentage-point differences between two distributions, when the data are arrayed according to the same categories. The latter stipulation renders comparison between countries difficult in some instances, but exploratory work with a number of censuses suggests that the problem is not insurmountable. For an illustrative use of the coefficient of redistribution, see Edgar M. Hoover, "The Interstate Redistribution of Population, 1850–1940," *Journal of Economic History*, 1 (May, 1941), pp. 199–205. Since this procedure ignores differential reproduction and immigration, the results yield inexact estimates of total mobility, but precise assessments of the net shifts. The use of Kahl's method would be preferable, but the requisite data are not at hand for most countries. A large-scale study under the direction of Simon Kuznets and Dorothy S. Thomas has already yielded a rich body of historical statistics on the redistribution of the labor force, manufacturing activity, and residential population; see *Population Redistribution and Economic Growth, United States, 1870–1950*, Volumes I and II (Philadelphia: American Philosophical Society, 1957 and 1960).

Part Two

Metropolitan Growth
and Decentralization

IN CHAPTER 1, it was observed in passing that much of ecological research effort has gone into delineating the phenomenon of the "metropolitan" form of urban community organization. At least since the work of R. D. McKenzie, ecologists have devoted a considerable fraction of their attention to the metropolis and its environs. Population growth and its areal spread over the landscape have fascinated ecologists for at least thirty years.

Opening this section, Chapter 4 attempts to provide a brief recapitulation of metropolitan development. This historical essay first appeared in the *American Journal of Sociology*, Volume 63 (September, 1957), pp. 171–80. It underscores the importance of modern technology, and especially new forms of transportation and communication, in bringing about the rise of this new form of urban "super–community," and goes on to outline a program of relevant research on the topic.

The second chapter in this section first appeared in the *Journal of the American Institute of Planners*, Volume 25 (November, 1959), pp. 200–206. Chapter 5 is also historical in

[77]

orientation, and represents an effort to document the emergence of "decentralization" or "suburbanization" in empirical terms. It is shown that the sheer age of the community, as crudely measured by the number of decades that have passed since a certain point in size was reached, is a critical variable in understanding the phenomenon of decentralization.

Finally, Chapter 6 brings the story of "decentralization" up to date, at least to the point made possible by the most recently available census statistics. First published in the *American Journal of Sociology*, Volume 67 (January, 1962), pp. 406–17, this study stresses the importance of taking account of changes in political boundaries when one is attempting to assess the extent of population redistribution.

Chapter 4

Metropolitan Growth
and Decentralization

A GREAT DEAL of effort has been devoted to research in metropolitan growth and decentralization in recent years. In particular, the detailed statistical studies by Thompson, Bogue, and
Hawley have provided a clear image of the main demographic
facts. However, a search of the literature reveals two important
omissions: nowhere is there available a succinct historical recapitulation that provides a summary description of metropolitan development from its beginning to the present time;
and, as a probable consequence, the literature contains very few
explicitly developmental hypotheses regarding metropolitan
growth and decentralization. This chapter is addressed to these
two broad problems. First, a brief narrative account of metropolitan growth and development is offered. Second, a number
of implications derived from the review are set out in the form
of concrete problems for research. In each problem the focus
is upon process, in a frank effort to offset the static orientation
of the available literature. Moreover, a number of the hypotheses refer specifically to the influence of transportation, a
factor frequently mentioned but rarely studied in the metro-

politan context. The historical treatment is deliberately phrased in very general terms. Most of the statements are well established, although diverse in origin; others rest upon more limited evidence; and a few, while frankly speculative, are phrased as questions for empirical research and not as final answers.[1]

A HALF-CENTURY OF METROPOLITAN GROWTH

Metropolitan development can best be conceived as a new form of urban growth especially characteristic of twentieth-century America.[2] It must be recognized, of course, that a large increase in urban population antedated this century. Cities have grown faster than rural areas since 1820. The first decade of this century, however, marked the end of one important phase of urban development, being the last decade in which migration from other countries contributed large numbers to the growth of American cities. The decade from 1910 to 1920, including

Table 1—Rates of Increase in Population, by Metropolitan Status, 1900–1950

METROPOLITAN STATUS	1940–50	1930–40	1920–30	1910–20	1900–1910
A. Interdecade Rates of Population Increase					
Total United States	14.5	7.2	16.1	14.9	21.0
Nonmetropolitan	6.1	6.5	6.0	6.7	13.6
Metropolitan	22.0	8.4	27.5	25.9	32.5
Central cities	13.8	5.5	24.2	27.9	37.1
Rings	34.2	13.4	33.2	22.4	25.6
Urban	26.0	8.0	42.6	35.9	49.2
Rural	45.2	21.3	22.0	9.4	8.4
Incorporated	34.1	13.2	28.6	24.1	45.0
Unincorporated	46.5	22.3	21.2	7.8	5.6
B. Ratios of Total National Increase					
Nonmetropolitan	0.43	0.90	0.37	0.45	0.65
Metropolitan	1.52	1.17	1.71	1.74	1.55
Central cities	0.95	0.76	1.50	1.87	1.77
Rings	2.36	1.86	2.06	1.50	1.22
Urban	1.79	1.11	2.65	2.41	2.34
Rural	3.12	2.96	1.37	0.63	0.40
Incorporated	2.35	1.83	1.78	1.62	2.14
Unincorporated	3.21	3.10	1.32	0.52	0.27

Source: Leo F. Schnore, "Patterns of Decentralization" (unpublished doctoral dissertation, University of Michigan, 1955), Table 101, p. 214.

as it did World War I, witnessed the stemming of the great
streams of migrants from overseas, and over-all urban growth
was slowed as a result.[3]

Restrictive legislation in the 1920's, including a rigid system
of quotas, prevented the resumption of international migration
on a prewar scale, but the national population continued to
increase, and cities grew rapidly, but now, however, largely by
internal migration. The attenuated growth of cities in the
1930–40 decade was also the result of a decline in migration,
but in this instance it consisted of a lessened flow of internal
(i.e., rural-to-urban) migrants. Job opportunities in urban
areas, drastically reduced during the depression, multiplied
during the early 1940's, largely due to wartime demands. Urban
employment was maintained at fairly high levels in the years
immediately following World War II as the nation returned to
a peacetime economy, and it was further stimulated by the
outbreak of hostilities in Korea.

What have been the metropolitan concomitants of twentieth-century urban growth? Part A of Table 1 shows interdecade rates of increase within the entire continental United
States. In this table the total land area of the nation is represented according to metropolitan status. The first distinction is
that between metropolitan and non-metropolitan parts. The
next subdivision in the table distinguishes between the metropolitan central cities and their surrounding "rings." Growth
rates for urban and rural parts of the ring are then shown
separately. Finally, within the "rural" portion of the ring,
separate growth rates are given for incorporated and unincorporated areas. Part B expresses all these rates as ratios of the
national increase, providing a control over variation in over-all
growth between decades.[4]

Table 1 shows that the presently defined metropolitan areas
have captured a disproportionately large share of the total
national increase in population throughout the entire fifty-year
period. Within metropolitan areas, however, central city
growth has become progressively slower, while the ring has
tended to grow more and more rapidly. It is this over-all pattern of differential growth in favor of the peripheral area that

is usually labeled "decentralization," although these rates reflect only *net* changes arising from a variety of sources.

A part of the slowed city growth is the result of the cities' failure or inability to annex the surrounding densely settled areas. Probably more significant, however, are two complementary trends in migration and residential mobility: a tendency for residents of the central city to move in increasing numbers to various parts of the adjacent ring area and a tendency for migrants from outside the metropolitan area to move directly to the ring rather than to the city itself. The total effect is a *relative* decentralization or net peripheral growth in excess of that of the center. As far as migration and mobility are concerned, decentralization has two sources—outward *relocation* from the center and growth via *accretion* at the periphery. As yet, however, the relative contributions of these two distinct types of movement have not been firmly established.[5]

Despite our inadequate answers to these basic questions, however, recent studies have established some important relationships between the extent of decentralization and certain structural and functional characteristics of metropolitan areas. One way to present these is to take a deliberately oversimplified view of metropolitan development as a more or less continuous process and to introduce the findings of recent research in historical sequence.

At the turn of the century most urban centers were still rather compact and self-contained entities. Most of the larger cities were at deep-water sites, although a few had begun to develop inland at railway intersections. The residents were concentrated near the principal workplaces, living in tenements and row houses, and most of them walked to work or rode on public vehicles. The horsecar was still very much in evidence on the city streets, although it was being replaced by the electric streetcar. However, the automobile was still a novelty, and its price was beyond the means of all but the wealthy. Some of the latter who could afford the time and the cost of the trip had already begun to live outside the congested city and to

travel to their places of business by automobile or by interurban railway.[6]

These railways—powered by steam or electricity—spread
out from the largest cities in radial strings, and along their lines
began to appear clusters of dwellings. In the interstices lay
wide areas of open country, much of it in farms. Small villages
scattered throughout this open country served the immediate
needs of the farm population. These subcenters lay at intersections of rural roads and near the railway lines, and through
them were distributed the processed goods required by the
agricultural population. They also served as the primary collection points for the produce of the agricultural hinterland.

Larger urban subcenters within the orbit of the central
city provided the hinterland with less frequently needed goods.
In addition to serving as collection and distribution points,
these larger places were frequently engaged in the processing
of goods, particularly if water power was immediately available. Most industry, however, was still concentrated in the
large city, where the economies of steam power could be best
realized.[7] As a rule the larger subcenters had direct railway
service to the central city; over these lines flowed the overwhelming bulk of interurban freight. At any rate, the whole
arrangement of urban and village agglomerations came to resemble a planet and its satellites.

The larger cities were still growing more rapidly than the
smaller places, chiefly through migration, and the rural population was suffering continued losses as more and more efficient
methods of farming were put into use and as smaller subsistence farms were consolidated into larger holdings. The surplus
agricultural population flowed toward the city, probably in a
series of intermediate moves, to be joined there by migrants
from foreign countries.[8]

Metropolitan areas during the early years of the century
were thus characterized by an axiate or star-shaped form of
settlement. Most urban places beyond 10 or 15 miles remained
largely independent of the center. Within that zone, however,
interurban railways were gradually able to provide more regular service; as time passed, more and more people working in

the city found it possible to live outside its formal boundaries. These early suburbanites lived in new residential developments within walking distance of the railway commuter stations. In Hoyt's words, "as these communities gradually coalesced in solid bands, the settled area maps of the New York and Chicago metropolitan areas showed long finger-like appendages extending out, with large vacant areas lying in between. This was the result of the faster travel time on the suburban railroads than on other means of transportation."[9]

An appreciation of the importance of the railroad during the early part of this century can be gained from a review of historical statistics (Table 2). At the turn of the century, there were more than four times as many railway locomotives as motor vehicles in operation. As late as 1910, there were more miles of railroad track than miles of surfaced highways in use. After 1920, however, the number of motor vehicles increased significantly, while the number of locomotives began to decline. Similar trends can be discerned when the two types of route are compared.

Table 2—Railroad and Motor Vehicle Routes and Carriers, 1900–1950

Year	Railroad Trackage (Miles)	Surfaced Highways (Miles)	Railroad Locomotives (No.)	Motor Vehicles (No.)
1950	223,779	1,714,000	42,951	48,566,984
1940	223,670	1,367,000	44,333	32,035,424
1930	249,052	694,000	60,189	26,531,999
1920	252,845	369,000	68,942	9,239,161
1910	240,293	204,000	60,019	468,500
1900	193,348	128,500	37,663	8,000

Source: U.S. Bureau of the Census, *Historical Statistics of the United States, 1789–1945* (Washington: Government Printing Office, 1949), Tables K-29, K-34, K-175, K-182, and K-229, and *Continuation to 1952 of Historical Statistics of the United States, 1789–1945* (Washington: Government Printing Office, 1954), same tables.

World War I brought two particularly significant developments. First, migration from abroad, which had provided a large share of the city's manpower needs, was practically cut off. The demands of war, however, compelled urban manufacturing centers to increase their output. To staff the mills and plants, they had to depend on attracting people from other parts of the nation, and for the first time the migrant streams began to include large numbers of Negroes, particularly from the South.[10]

The second crucial development occasioned by the war was the rapid increase in the number of motor vehicles. Burdened to their capacity, the railroads were simply unable to carry all the freight that had to be shipped. Motor trucks, which had been used primarily for local hauling within the city, were pressed into service to move less bulky goods between urban areas. An extensive program of highway improvement on all levels of government was put into effect, and hard-surfaced roads began to crisscross the areas surrounding the largest centers. In effect, truck transportation was subsidized by governmental funds, for highways were publicly financed. In addition, some of the methods learned under the pressure of the wartime demand for motor transport were applied to the production of private automobiles. Many of the techniques of modern mass production—later adopted in almost every sector of the economy—were first developed in the automobile industry.

The years immediately following World War I, although marked by a few minor fluctuations, ushered in a period of expansion. Enormous strides were made in industrial productivity, and, as national production increased, significant advances occurred in real wages. The techniques of mass production and increased mechanization reduced the manpower required in industry. Since a similar trend was continuing in agriculture as an effect of the introduction of power machinery, the surplus population from both agriculture and industry gradually shifted into occupations providing for the distribution of goods and services.[11]

Spatial changes followed from these technological innovations. At the same time that these fundamental transitions were taking place in the national economy, the physical pattern of the large city and its surrounding area began to undergo crucial alterations. Decentralization, which had occurred first in only the largest centers, became a significant aspect of the growth of many smaller cities in the 1920's; both industry and population were scattering as a response to the development of the motor vehicle. The hard-surfaced route, of course, was adaptable to the movement of the people as well as to the carrying of goods. The elaborate networks of main arteries and feeder routes around large and middle-sized cities permitted a number of the functional components of the community to break away from the center. Most of them located at intersections in the highway network. Urban subcenters appeared in increasing numbers and grew at rates in excess of that of the center. New construction was started in volume in the periphery of both large and middle-sized cities. As residential population gathered in sufficient densities, retail and service establishments arose to provide the suburbanites with urban conveniences.

With the increased ease of travel, however, some of the larger subcenters underwent a significant transition. They lost their high degree of independence and fell under the dominating influence of the metropolis. For example, many establishments devoted to the provision of luxury goods abandoned operations in the subcenters, being unable to compete with the metropolis, which was now easily accessible to a wide market. At the same time, the principles of mass production were increasingly adapted to distribution, and chains of retail outlets began to appear, particularly in the convenience-goods lines. Such units, under a single ownership and directed from a site in the central city, could take advantage of the economies of mass buying and standardization. During the same period, significant changes in communication came about with the development of the radio and the telephone. Instantaneous contact with a broad area now became possible, and the independence of subcenters was diminished accordingly.

At the same time, industry became increasingly free to locate away from the city itself, as cheap electrical power replaced steam.[12] The telephone permitted peripheral location of production facilities while the functions of management and control could remain in the center. In addition, the widespread ownership of the automobile meant a more mobile labor force. Heavy industry, which tends to operate more efficiently in one-story buildings occupying large areas, apparently was particularly attracted by the lower costs of land in the ring, where the competition of alternative uses was less intense.

However, not all elements of the community were equally free to participate in this outward movement: during the early phase of decentralization, many activities were bound to the center as securely as in previous years. The retailing of luxury goods and the provision of infrequently needed services were particularly obliged to remain in central locations, in order to maintain maximum access to a large potential market. The functions of management and direction also appeared to cling to the metropolis, apparently in order to facilitate contact with other units engaged in communication, finance, and marketing.

At any rate, the depression of the 1930's appears to have accentuated the trends of differential growth incipient in many areas in previous years. With decreased job opportunities to offer, central city growth dropped to a low level, with many cities sustaining net losses. The growth of the residential population of the metropolitan ring, although reduced from the levels of the previous decades in many instances, tended to remain above that of the center and of the nation as a whole. Although there is little evidence of a genuine "back-to-the farm" movement during this decade, it appears that there was considerable piling-up of potential migrants in the outlying areas.

It is clear, however, that, within metropolitan rings, "rural" growth exceeded urban during the depression decade, and the growth of unincorporated rural areas was in excess of that of small incorporated places.[13] The threat of war and the subsequent armament drive in the last years of the decade probably pushed the interdecade growth rates of many central cities to higher levels than would otherwise have been realized. In spite of the probable resumption of heavy cityward migration toward the end of the 'thirties, ring growth tended to exceed the growth of even the smaller metropolitan cities. A distinct majority of the cities of 50,000 and over were now exhibiting the pattern of relative decentralization formerly seen around only the larger cities.[14]

Finally, the most recent intercensal decade (1940–50) has witnessed a progressive diffusion of the patterns that had begun years earlier in the largest centers. Not only metropolitan centers but the larger satellites within the metropolitan orbit are decentralizing. The growth of "rural" and unincorporated area continues to outstrip that of the urban and incorporated places. The physical form of the metropolitan area, which had been axiate in pattern, is filling in, and the area resembles a great amorphous mass, although outlines of the older star-shaped pattern can still be discerned. More important, the functional boundaries of the metropolitan area, as indicated by the outward shift of the high growth rates, appear to have shifted from a ring of approximately 10 miles to one of 20–25 miles in diameter.[15]

Throughout these fifty years of transition, a number of structural and functional circumstances appear to have been related to centrifugal growth, the most important of which is sheer size of population. In fact, most of the other factors associated with centrifugal growth are themselves associated with metropolitan size. Regional location also appears to be a factor of real significance. Other variables associated with size and regional location, however, show associations with decentralization that remain when these two variables are controlled.

In addition to the primary variables, recent research has indicated that the areas in which decentralization occurred first and proceeded furthest tend to have densely populated central cities, in which growth has been slow during the last fifty years. They are most frequently older coastal cities. Manufacturing activity within the area has been decentralizing throughout most of the period.[16] All these findings, when taken together, suggest the importance of what might be termed the "maturity" of metropolitan areas. Those areas which have exhibited the earliest and most extreme evidence of decentralization appear to have reached an advanced stage of maturity that is merely reflected in the structural and functional characteristics enumerated here. In a rough sense, in fact, decentralization is an index of the maturity of metropolitan areas.

SOME RESEARCH IMPLICATIONS

In addition to the research needs touched upon previously, a number of other problems present themselves for empirical scrutiny. A whole category of research problems can be subsumed under the rubric of the sources of differential growth within metropolitan areas. In addition to the relative contributions of natural increase and net migration, we need to know the origins of migrants by areal and functional types. Another whole range of empirical questions emerges when we consider the demographic and functional composition of the various parts of the metropolitan area and the migrant streams that flow between them. Imposing as these problems are, however, they relate only to the residential population of metropolitan areas.[17]

In addition to a concern with the redistribution of residential population, of course, a full description of the changing organization of the metropolitan area must treat the other sociological units that constitute the total community. It appears that all the typical urban activities—the so-called "secondary" and "tertiary" functions of fabrication, distribution, and control[18]—have been subjected in some degree to the same forces of decentralization that have so dramatically altered the residential settlement pattern within local areas. The reduction of the friction imposed by distance has had noticeable effects in almost every sphere of life.

With respect to secondary (manufacturing) activities, there is obviously increasing freedom to locate at the margins of the community. As Bogue points out, "economists and industrialists have discovered that under modern conditions of transport it is no longer necessary for great industries to be located within the limits of the central city. There is a broad zone of indifference, probably several miles in diameter, which is locationally suitable."[19] Tertiary activities (trade, services, etc.) are probably affected similarly by changes in locational tolerance, but they have been less carefully studied. The decentralization of functions such as wholesaling, storage, and distribution deserves more research. These activities have been traditionally viewed as centrally oriented, but recent developments in metropolitan organization warrant a reconsideration of this assumption. Faster and more frequent transportation, for example, may have decreased the need for central warehouse facilities. The handling of freight since the development of the motor truck has become a much more flexible operation, and a great deal of storage is apparently effected en route, without the necessity for maintaining large stockpiles and inventories immediately at hand.

Many administrative functions may also be increasingly free to leave the center and locate at the periphery of the metropolitan community. For example, the central offices of large insurance companies, whose chief contacts are with agents scattered throughout the nation, may represent a type of administration that can be as efficiently managed in the ring as in the center. The control and direction of other industries, however, which require frequent contacts with lawyers, brokers, news media, advertising agencies, and out-of-town buyers, may continue to require central location. Further research should identify the other units with which a given function is in most frequent contact—via both transportation and communication facilities—in addition to its requirements for space, in both amount and kind. These facts would provide valuable clues to the amount of decentralization to be anticipated among various functions.

Functional differences between suburban and satellite places still remain to be explored, and detailed knowledge of them is necessary for a full description of the social and economic organization of the expanded community.[20] In addition, more should be learned of the growth tendencies of different types of subnuclei in the metropolitan ring. Employing satellites, for example, show patterns of growth notably different from those of exclusively residential suburbs.[21] The growth of more specialized areas, including educational and recreational centers, may show divergent patterns in keeping with their narrowly specialized roles in the whole metropolitan area.

Trends in population growth within the central city itself

are worthy of further exploration. Physical congestion in the center has frequently been advanced as a cause of decentralization. Most large cities have high proportions of habitable land that remains vacant,[22] but a substantial portion of it is in small parcels held for speculation, forcing prices beyond the limits possible for residential development.

At the same time, a more accurate description of the role of congestion can probably be gained by turning attention to traffic, itself a product of the separation of land uses seen in residential decentralization.[23] Traffic densities probably exert a greater influence than the more frequently measured densities of residential population. The daily massing of great volumes of people and vehicles in central areas may inhibit movement to such an extent that the center loses its traditionally favored position as the point of maximum accessibility to the entire metropolitan area.

A closely related area of metropolitan research offers great promise for cross–cultural comparisons. A number of studies of the daily journey to work have been conducted in both Europe and the United States.[24] The studies in this country have been based primarily upon by-product data from traffic research, and being limited to areas with particularly serious traffic problems, the American investigations probably represent a biased sample of all urban areas. Many of the European studies, however, have been based upon census materials, for the census schedules of most European nations include at least one question regarding the place of work of members of the employed labor force.[25] This is one of the rare instances in which the United States census lags behind data-collection in other nations of the world. Information on place of work in future censuses in this country would permit a much more complete description of the functional organization of the entire metropolitan area; the daily circulations and exchanges—centrifugal, centripetal, and lateral—between the various sub-parts of the area could then be accurately determined.[26]

Previous remarks imply that long-distance commuting is restricted to upper-income groups. However, the rapid increase in automobile ownership in all social strata in our society has made suburbs and satellites, as well as the unincorporated places in the ring, accessible to those with moderate incomes and even to some with lower incomes. Wherever zoning regulations are not in effect, cheap housing can be built on cheap land. Scattered research has suggested that the European pattern of part-time farming by urban workers may become established in the vicinity of many American industrial cities, particularly near those in which factory work is seasonal.[27] Ride-sharing arrangements between urban workers who live in the ring are still another device permitting peripheral residential location of families which otherwise could not afford the high cost of transportation to the center.[28] More generally, trends in housing have had an important place in this entire development, but here research is seriously deficient. With the passage of the years, the techniques of mass production have been adapted to the construction of dwellings. We need to know the dynamic causal factors operating to bring about areal differentials in construction of various types within the metropolitan community. Such knowledge would throw light upon the problem of the redistribution of residential population, as well as other functional components, such as industrial and commercial establishments.[29]

In this connection, some research should be directed toward delineating more carefully some of the differences in socio-economic level between suburban and satellite places within the metropolitan ring. Rental and income data are now available for at least the larger incorporated places in the ring, and these can be easily supplemented by statistics on education and occupational and ethnic composition. Many observers have suggested the emergence of rigid segregation in the suburbs along social and economic lines. Indeed, it is said that the mass production of suburban housing attracts persons of similar status,[30] an economic compulsion toward segregated living which seems to be further implemented by zoning. Whether these trends are any more coercive, however, than the forces that have long made for segregation *within* the city is a matter for future research.

The foregoing discussion has made extensive use of the

concept of the Standard Metropolitan Area. Every use in research of such a statistical reporting unit, of course, constitutes
something of a test of its validity. There is some evidence that
the Standard Metropolitan Area encompasses only the zone of
most rapid growth in recent years, but both Bogue and Hawley
have shown that the influence of the metropolis is reflected in
the growth rates of areas many miles beyond the commuting
zone. Beyond this zone of primary interchange, of course, lies
a much broader hinterland in which integration with the center
is expressed through indirect contacts. Thus research cannot
be confined to the Standard Metropolitan Area alone. The area
of direct contact with the center, however, appears to be well
delineated by the definition. At any rate, the utility of these
areas as reporting units is enhanced by the vast amount of data
assembled on a county basis by many governmental and private
agencies. Fuller use of the data will permit at least tentative
answers to many current questions.

Conclusions

Many problems of administration and planning arise out of
our ignorance of the details of change in the form of the community. The provision of accurate descriptions of community
structure is the responsibility of sociological research, but the
task is far from complete. If we are ever to solve the host of
practical problems so rapidly developing in the wake of decentralization, we still have to assemble more and more facts.
But, even more important, we shall have to provide conceptual
schemes with which to interpret these facts.

The problems in this paper point to the fact that we need
a complete theory, subsuming both structural and functional
aspects of all the constituent units of the community. Moreover, such a theory should be capable of generating testable
hypotheses referring to both static and dynamic relationships
between variables. Technological innovation, land-use conversion, segregation, population growth and redistribution—
all these are terms referring to *processes*. Any sound conceptual
approach must be phrased in dynamic terms such as these, if

for no other reason than that the modern metropolitan community is constantly changing.

The construction of such a theory will be no mere intellectual exercise. As one demographer has recently asserted:

> One of the reasons for such strong disagreements and conflicting recommendations about so-called "decentralization" is that specialists in the field of urban population and human ecology have failed to produce a theory of urban growth that is valid for the mid-20th century. Perhaps we have been overly concerned with perfecting a static theory of city structure. . . . Our study of structure needs to be accompanied by a rigorous program of research into growth and change. Research in urbanism and metropolitanism should have dynamic as well as static aspects.[31]

One can only agree with these ambitious goals and hope that the discussion contained in this chapter will contribute to their ultimate achievement.[32]

NOTES

1. Both the historical narrative and the derived outline of research problems are based on the premise that the general pattern of metropolitan development should be established before individual variations are examined in detail. This is not to derogate case studies of individual areas, an extremely valuable source of hypotheses. However, an excessive concern with apparent exceptions appears to be premature at this point; a more fruitful approach is the documentation of major trends. Once the broad set of relationships has been firmly established, the exceptions become variations around these central tendencies, which are themselves subject to explanation.

2. See N. S. B. Gras, *An Introduction to Economic History* (New York: Harper & Bros., 1922); and R. D. McKenzie, *The Metropolitan Community* (New York: McGraw-Hill Book Co., 1933).

3. Natural increase was apparently not a compensating factor of any consequence during this period, for city dwellers failed to reproduce at replacement levels. There is evidence, however, that this long-established fact did not hold during the most recent intercensal decade (see Donald J. Bogue and Emerson Seim, "Components of Population Change in Suburban and Central City Populations of Standard Metropolitan Areas, 1940 to 1950," *Rural Sociology*, 21 [September–December, 1956], 265–75).

4. Official definitions of the 168 Standard Metropolitan Areas, recognized by the Census Bureau, have been retrojected to 1900, so that area is held constant. The "old" (1940) census definition of "urban" is used

throughout. Because of differences in areal definition, these rates differ in minor detail from those given in Donald J. Bogue, *Population Growth in Standard Metropolitan Areas, 1900–1950* (Washington: Government Printing Office, 1953), Table 1. Bogue's data refer to 162 metropolitan areas with "county-equivalent" areas used in New England in place of the town-based areas defined by the Census Bureau. Because the official definitions of the Standard Metropolitan Areas are used here, the data are not directly comparable with those reported in Warren S. Thompson, *The Growth of Metropolitan Districts in the United States, 1900–1940* (Washington: Government Printing Office, 1947).

5. The relative importance of these two migrant streams are known for only a few areas and for a limited and probably atypical time period. Migration data from the 1940 Census can be examined in terms of the 1935 places of residence of migrants living in metropolitan central cities and rings in 1940 (see Warren S. Thompson, *Migration within Ohio, 1935–1940* [Oxford, Ohio: Scripps Foundation for Research in Population Problems, 1951]), and Amos H. Hawley, *Intrastate Migration in Michigan, 1935–1940* [Ann Arbor: University of Michigan Institute of Public Administration, 1953]).

6. Adna F. Weber, *The Growth of Cities in the Nineteenth Century* (New York: Macmillan, 1899).

7. National Resources Committee, *Our Cities: Their Role in the National Economy* (Washington: Government Printing Office, 1937), pp. 29–30.

8. Early urban research, of course, concentrated on the clusters of ethnic settlements within large cities. However, comparative data on segregation are notably deficient for more recent periods.

9. Homer Hoyt, "The Influence of Highways and Transportation on the Structure and Growth of Cities and Urban Land Values," in Jean Labatut and Wheaton J. Lane (eds.), *Highways in Our National Life* (Princeton: Princeton University Press, 1950), p. 202.

10. Thus began a South-to-North movement that continues unabated. Most Negro migrants continue to move directly to the central city rather than to the metropolitan ring. Racial differentials in the various migrant streams involved in decentralization have yet to be fully reported.

11. For the original distinction between "primary," "secondary," and "tertiary" industries and occupations see Colin Clark, *The Conditions of Economic Progress* (2d ed.; London: Macmillan Co., 1951).

12. National Resources Committee, *op. cit.*

13. The old (1940) definitions of "urban" and "rural" used here tend seriously to overstate the rural component; many people classified as rural are actually urbanites by any reasonable functional definition.

14. Donald J. Bogue, *Metropolitan Decentralization: A Study of Differential Growth* (Oxford, Ohio: Scripps Foundation for Research in Population Problems, 1950).

15. Amos H. Hawley, *The Changing Shape of Metropolitan America: Deconcentration Since 1920* (Glencoe: Free Press, 1956).

16. *Ibid.* In each instance the direction of association between a given variable and centrifugal growth tends to be the same as that found between the variable in question and metropolitan size. The direction of these relationships remains the same, although reduced in extent, within

size classes. Although no single area can be found to possess every one of the characteristics, they tend to be associated with one another.

17. Albert J. Reiss, Jr. has recently suggested a number of excellent topics for research in this area (see "Research Problems in Metropolitan Population Redistribution," *American Sociological Review*, 21 [October, 1956], 571–77). A number of his topics, however, are static in orientation. Another valuable discussion is contained in Henry S. Shryock, Jr., "Population Redistribution within Metropolitan Areas: Evaluation of Research," *Social Forces*, 35 (December, 1956), 154–59.

18. Clark, *op. cit.*

19. Donald J. Bogue (ed.), *Needed Urban and Metropolitan Research* (Oxford, Ohio: Scripps Foundation for Research in Population Problems, 1953), p. 40.

20. See Sanford M. Dornbusch, *A Typology of Suburban Communities: Chicago Metropolitan District 1940* ("Urban Analysis Reports," No. 10 [Chicago: Chicago Community Inventory, May, 1952]), and Leo F. Schnore, "The Functions of Metropolitan Suburbs," *American Journal of Sociology*, 61 (March, 1956), 453–58.

21. Leo F. Schnore, "The Growth of Metropolitan Suburbs," *American Sociological Review*, 22 (April, 1957), 165–73.

22. Harland Bartholomew, *Land Uses in American Cities* (Cambridge: Harvard University Press, 1955).

23. Donald L. Foley, "Urban Day-Time Population: A Field for Demographic-Ecological Analysis," *Social Forces*, 32 (May, 1954), 323–30.

24. *Ibid.*; and Kate K. Liepmann, *The Journey to Work* (New York: Oxford University Press, 1944).

25. Foley, *op. cit.*

26. The rapid advances made in sampling techniques should permit this valuable addition to the 1960 Census. Technical problems can be solved by experimentation with alternative methods in the Current Population Survey and in special state and local censuses prior to adoption in the federal decennial census.

27. Nathan L. Whetten and R. F. Field, *Studies of Suburbanization in Connecticut*, No. 2: *Norwich: An Industrial Part-Time Farming Area* (Storrs: Connecticut State College Agricultural Experiment Station Bull. 226 [1938]); W. R. Gordon, *Satellite Acres* (Kingston: Rhode Island State College Agricultural Experiment Station Bull. 282 [1942]); Walter Firey, *Social Aspects of Land Use Planning in the Country-City Fringe* (East Lansing: Michigan State College Agricultural Experiment Station Bull. 339 [1946]); Glenn H. Beyer, *Housing and Journey to Work* (Ithaca: Cornell University Agricultural Experiment Station Bull. 877 [1951]).

28. Leo F. Schnore, "The Separation of Home and Work: A Problem for Human Ecology," *Social Forces*, 32 (May, 1954), 336–43. The so-called "marginal labor force" appears to be physically marginal to industrial cities. This suggests that the "rural-urban fringe" is amenable to identification in functional (occupational) as well as areal terms. The latter conception, in fact, may be extremely misleading in many instances.

29. Dorothy K. Newman, "Metropolitan Area Structure and Growth as Shown by Building-Permit Statistics," *Business Topics*, 4 (November, 1956), 1–7. Within metropolitan areas, new housing construction is espe-

cially rapid in the ring. Although Newman presents data for only a small number of areas, all but 8 of the 168 currently recognized Standard Metropolitan Areas have higher proportions of newly constructed dwelling units in the ring than in the central city.

30. Leslie Kish, "Differentiation in Metropolitan Areas," *American Sociological Review*, 19 (August, 1954), 388–98.

31. Bogue, *Needed Urban and Metropolitan Research*, p. 38.

32. The author has recently attempted to summarize modern ecological thinking about some of these problems. See Leo F. Schnore, "Urban Form: The Case of the Metropolitan Community," in Werner Z. Hirsch (ed.), *Urban Life and Form* (New York: Holt, Rinehart and Winston, Inc., 1963), pp. 167–97.

Chapter 5

The Timing of Metropolitan Decentralization: A Contribution to the Debate

METROPOLITAN DECENTRALIZATION is one of the most thoroughly explored areas of investigation in the study of population distribution in the United States.[1] However, little explicit attention has been directed toward differences in the timing of the outward shift of residential population in individual areas. Yet it can be argued that variations in the timing of decentralization around individual cities are facts of crucial importance in acquiring an understanding of the whole phenomenon. For one thing, analysis of these differences among cities might provide some clues to the causal factors involved, particularly if it should be found that cities experiencing relatively early decentralization reveal systematic differences in other characteristics from those undergoing decentralization more recently. Perhaps even more fundamental is the fact that "decentralization"—however it may be defined in operational terms—is ordinarily conceived as a *process*, so that temporal considerations are necessary in the very nature of the case.

THE DEBATE OVER TIMING

Unfortunately, the American literature exhibits little agreement upon the simple issue of when the movement got under way. One of the most thorough of the American studies bears the subtitle "Deconcentration Since 1920," suggesting a rather recent phenomenon.[2] Closer examination, however, reveals that this phrase is clearly intended to characterize a whole aggregate of cities and is not to be taken as a description of the experience of individual places. Still, this characterization makes intuitive sense, in view of the presumed importance of the private automobile—which became widely used only after World War I—in permitting wider residential dispersion without loss of contact with the center.

Other portions of the American literature suggest that viewing decentralization as a recent phenomenon can be seriously misleading. After all, the Census Bureau was led to assemble data for large cities and their adjacent areas as early as the thirteenth census of 1910. Rapid peripheral growth must have been clearly evident well before that date; in fact, official discussions in various census sources make this abundantly clear. In addition, of course, Adna F. Weber had clearly perceived an outward shift of residential population around certain larger cities in the last quarter of the nineteenth century.[3] The view that decentralization is a process of long standing has been most vigorously stated by Robert Schmitt.

> There is nothing new about suburbanization. For at least a century, large American cities have grown chiefly by peripheral accretion. Population has always increased more rapidly on the outskirts than close to the central business district. . . . Suburbanization is old stuff.[4]

PROBLEMS OF MEASUREMENT

One major difficulty is immediately encountered in any attempt to approach the question of the timing of decentralization empirically. The data are assembled in terms of politically defined areal units, and we are without any precise standards or criteria for the very definition of decentralization. The

Table 1—The Timing of Urban Growth and Decentralization in the United States: 99 Metropolitan Areas with Central Cities of 100,000 or More Inhabitants

Census Year in Which the Central City First Reached 50,000	DECADE IN WHICH "DECENTRALIZATION" BEGAN:										Continued "Centralization"	Total Number of Areas
	1850's	1860's	1870's	1880's	1890's	1900's	1910's	1920's	1930's	1940's		
1800	—	—	1	—	—	—	—	—	—	—	—	1
1810	—	—	1	—	—	—	—	—	—	—	—	1
1820	—	—	1	—	—	—	—	—	—	—	—	1
1830	—	—	—	1	—	—	—	—	—	—	—	1
1840	—	—	—	1	—	—	—	—	—	—	—	1
1850	—	—	—	—	1	1	1	—	—	—	—	3
1860	—	—	—	—	1	4	1	—	—	—	—	6
1870	—	—	—	—	1	2	1	3	—	—	—	7
1880	—	—	—	—	1	2	1	3	—	—	—	7
1890	—	—	—	—	—	1	4	5	7	—	—	17
1900	—	—	—	—	—	—	5	7	1	—	—	13
1910	—	—	—	—	—	—	—	6	12	—	—	18
1920	—	—	—	—	—	—	—	4	9	—	—	13
1930	—	—	—	—	—	—	—	—	3	—	4	7
1940	—	—	—	—	—	—	—	—	—	2	—	2
1950	—	—	—	—	—	—	—	—	—	—	1	1
Total no. of areas	0	0	3	2	4	10	13	28	32	2	5	99

resulting lack of conceptual precision can be indicated in the form of a question: at what point does "normal" city growth —which almost inevitably occurs at the periphery of existing settlement—become "decentralization"? This is more than merely a matter of quibbling over definitions. Most of that which has been labelled "decentralization" may simply represent the exhaustion of space for residential development within city boundaries. If a growing city is unable, for whatever reason, to annex surrounding territory, little else can be expected than relatively high rates of growth at the periphery. In fact, sheer availability of space for residential development may be so significant as to make most hypothetical "determinants" of decentralization redundant in any real explanatory sense.[5]

At any rate, the data presented here have been assembled in order to throw light upon these fundamental and interlocking questions: (1) When did decentralization, as commonly measured, begin in individual cities of the United States? (2) What are some of the characteristics of cities that have undergone decentralization at different time periods? (3) What is the theoretical link between "decentralization" and "metropolitanism"?

A review of the literature on decentralization yields a long list of "factors" said to be causally operative; these range from rather gross attributes of cities themselves (e.g., sheer size) to the most subtle psychological motivations of persons. To reconcile these "explanations" in some orderly theoretical fashion would be an imposing task indeed. Our intention here is not to undertake such an exercise in codification, but merely to provide some base-line descriptive data with respect to the timing of decentralization as it is frequently measured, and to discuss some of the implications of our findings for theory and further research.

DATA AND PROCEDURES

The empirical materials presented here are based upon the observed growth of the 99 metropolitan central cities that have had a population of at least 100,000 at some point in their development. For comparative purposes, official areal definitions of Standard Metropolitan Areas in the 1950 census were retrojected to the earliest possible date; this procedure affords at least a rough control over total area and permits the observation of the relative redistribution of population within these areas for a series of decades. Growth rates for the individual cities and their respective "rings" were then compared.

Especially close attention had to be given to annexations and detachments of area by the central cities. Since annexations far outnumber detachments of territory, the over-all effect of these areal changes has been to understate decentralization as measured by comparison of city-versus-ring growth rates. With respect to timing, the effect has been to delay decentralization as narrowly defined here. Many cities have maintained higher growth rates by almost continuous areal expansion at the expense of the ring. In this study, annexation imparts a bias in the direction of classifying cities as "decentralizing" *later* than they would actually appear to be if city area were truly held constant. However, careful attention was given to the annexation history of each city throughout the entire period under review, so this bias is minimized although not entirely eliminated.[6]

At any rate, following a review of city and ring growth and of annexations, each city was classified according to the *earliest* decade in which relative decentralization became evident, that is, the earliest decade in which ring growth began *systematically* to exceed that of the city. At least three consecutive decades of higher ring growth had to be registered before a city was classified as decentralizing.[7]

FINDINGS

Peripheral growth in excess of that of the center is clearly not a unique product of the 'twenties—nor of the twentieth century, for that matter. Table 1 contains our basic data with respect to the timing of decentralization. It can be seen that one city (New York) was "decentralizing" as early as the 1850's and that it was joined by nine others before the turn of the century.[8] (See the "total" row at the bottom of the table.) However, it is equally clear that it was not until the 'twenties that the majority of these cities began to exhibit lower growth rates than their own rings. Fully 60 cities began to decentralize within the space of twenty years—between 1920 and 1940. It appears that decentralization occurred with a rush following World War I; thus Hawley's reference to "deconcentration since 1920" is confirmed as a summary description of a majority of large cities in the United States.

Table 1 also contains basic information on the history of urban development in this country (see the "total" column at the extreme right.) Although at least one city of 50,000 population (again, New York) could be found as early as 1800, the forty-year interval between 1880 and 1920 appears to have been the most intensive "city-building" period in the history of the United States. Over 60 places achieved a size of 50,000 during this interval.

The five places reaching 50,000 prior to 1850 (New York, Philadelphia, Baltimore, Boston, and New Orleans, in that order) show no clear-cut pattern; the first large cities apparently began to decentralize at widely separated dates, and in no particular sequence. Those reaching 50,000 in 1850 or later, however, show a rather clear pattern. Among these 94 cities, only three (Duluth, Beaumont-Port Arthur, and Baton Rouge) began to decentralize before reaching this minimum size. It is perhaps more important that only one of these cities (Washington, D.C.) failed to begin decentralization within five decades after reaching this minimum size, and most cities began within four decades. As a result, there is a rather clear correlation between the timing of decentralization and sheer age of settlement, as these characteristics are measured here; in general, the older places tended to decentralize earlier. But what other features are associated with early or late decentralization?

Certain selected characteristics of this same universe of American cities are set out in Table 2. It should be noted that these characteristics are among those previously investigated by Thompson, Bogue, and Hawley in their studies of metropolitan decentralization, in which these items were revealed to be important differentiating factors. Table 2 indicates that each of these variables shows a rather clear pattern with respect to the timing of decentralization. To summarize the findings, the *earliest* decentralization was exhibited by cities that are currently largest, and located in the Northeast, at deep water sites, relatively close to other metropolitan centers. However, all these characteristics are themselves related to age of settlement, for this description would also serve to characterize the oldest cities. These facts suggest that a notion of "metropolitan maturity" might be usefully applied. Age certainly appears to be important, but age *per se* can hardly be decisive. As we shall

Table 2—The Timing of Decentralization and Selected Characteristics of 99 Metropolitan Areas with Central Cities of 100,000 or More Inhabitants

Selected Characteristics	NUMBER OF AREAS IN WHICH DECENTRALIZATION BEGAN IN: 1910's or Earlier	1920's	1930's or 1940's	Number of Areas Showing Continued Centralization	Total Number of Areas
Central city size, 1950					
1,000,000 or over	5	1	0	0	6
500,000–1,000,000	8	3	1	0	12
250,000–500,000	5	8	6	0	19
100,000–250,000	15	16	26	5	62
Census region					
Northeast	16	6	5	0	27
North Central	6	11	9	0	26
South	6	8	15	5	34
West	5	3	4	0	12
Distance to nearest metropolis[a]					
Less than 50 miles	19	12	12	0	43
50 to 100 miles	9	13	11	3	36
Over 100 miles	5	3	10	2	20
Geographic site features[a]					
Sea or lake coast	20	6	5	1	32
Navigable river	10	14	7	0	31
Other (land-locked)	3	8	21	4	36
Total	33	28	33	5	99

a. See Amos H. Hawley, *The Changing Shape of Metropolitan America;* these classifications are used with the kind permission of the author.

argue in the following section, the organizational concomitants of long-term settlement may be the factors deserving further study.

What are we to infer from these findings? Certain conclusions are immediately evident. Just as the designation "metropolitan" loses specificity when applied wholesale to all cities of 50,000 or over, the label "decentralization" appears to be robbed of much of its denotative value when it is applied to all these places in which city growth rates have fallen below those of immediately surrounding areas, without any regard for the precise period in which this shift occurred. To call a city of 50,000 a "metropolis"—thereby implying that it is somehow equivalent to places inhabited by millions—may be highly gratifying to the residents of the smaller city, but it hardly enhances our knowledge of metropolitanism. By the same token, we may do well to devise different labels for the outward shifts of higher growth rates of the 1850's as against the 1950's, for they may be qualitatively different phenomena. However, this raises the whole question of definition to which we have alluded above, and we must return again to the conceptual considerations that gave rise to this study.

THE THEORY OF METROPOLITAN DECENTRALIZATION

We have already commented upon the difficulties stemming from a lack of base-line comparisons between "normal" city growth and decentralization. But there is another major flaw in current approaches to metropolitan development. The bulk of the research literature on decentralization, including the material contained here, exhibits one striking feature. The statistical and other data assembled only rarely include elements that can be viewed as structural, despite the fact that the theoretical literature has treated the rise of metropolitanism as essentially an organizational change, in which whole areas and their constituent units (manufacturing establishments, commercial enterprises, private households, etc.) are brought into a new kind of relationship. Despite this clear theoretical emphasis, the data assembled by researchers have only tangential bearing upon the crucial structural features of metropolitan areas as conceived by the major theorists.

Yet, to point to this wide gap between current research and existing theory is perhaps to point to a way out of the dilemma. What is obviously required at this point is a great deal of exploratory effort aimed at specifying the critical organizational features of both (1) "metropolitanism" and (2) "decentralization." Both concepts have an obvious demographic component of a very simple type. For "metropolitan" areas, a minimum population-size criterion is certainly to be desired— although the limit may turn out to be well above that in current census usage. At the same time, any reasonable definition of "decentralization" will probably *include* the existence of peripheral rates of growth in excess of the rates for the centers themselves.

However, failure to move beyond these minimal definitions is to invite continued confusion. In common usage, a "metropolitan" area is more than merely a large assemblage of people concentrated in a relatively limited space. Large and dense agglomerations have been known throughout history. The added element in any reasonable conception of "metropolitan" is a matter of social and economic organization—some unique structural configuration that is lacking in the densely settled alluvial plains of contemporary agrarian societies and in the large preindustrial cities of the past.

TRADITIONAL THEORY

Judging from the general tenor of the American theoretical literature, the key structural feature of the metropolitan area is an extremely high degree of *interdependence* that is reflected in an intricate *territorial division of labor*. To quote N. S. B. Gras, the economic historian,

> We may think of metropolitan economy as an organization of people having a large city as a nucleus. . . . Mere agglomeration of individuals, important as that is, does not constitute a me-

tropolis. . . . What counts most is commercial dominance over a wide area . . .⁹

Yet Gras went on to qualify the notion of "dominance" as some kind of one-way street. It is true that the outlying area is dependent upon the city, but the center is also dependent upon the hinterland. In Gras' own words, "Interdependence of the parts is really the key to the whole thing."¹⁰ Working with a highly similar conception, R. D. McKenzie described the modern metropolitan community as a "new type of super-community organized around a dominant focal point and comprising a multiple of differentiated centers of activity."¹¹

These writers make it abundantly clear that we cannot profitably conceive the metropolitan area as a simple two-part arrangement of center and ring, a large city with its adjacent territory. To the extent that this oversimplified model has found its way into the literature on metropolitan areas, it constitutes a theoretical retrogression from the pioneering work of Gras and McKenzie. The metropolitan community must be viewed—in organizational terms throughout—as a highly specialized mosaic of subareas tied together into a new functional unity. Moreover, it is to be viewed as a multinucleated territorial system. Within these broad areas, the large centers are marked by functional diversity, while the smaller places, many of them formerly independent cities in their own right, tend to be narrowly specialized. At the same time, however, the main centers are specialized in the coordinating functions of administration and control. It is a striking fact that the very best empirical work that has been conducted in terms of this conception of metropolitan structure, the research by Bogue, Kish, and Isard and Whitney, has been essentially static in orientation, so very little light is shed upon such "processes" as decentralization.¹²

By the same token, "decentralization" requires further specification in structural terms. The existing literature is less helpful here, but something more than rapid peripheral growth is implied in much of the theoretical literature. Aside from attempts to characterize living outside city boundaries as "a way of life," the underlying theme in these accounts, implicit as it may be, is best identified as organizational *complexity*, a functional unity that is achieved over a broader area of interdependence by virtue of movement and exchange.

MOVEMENT AND METROPOLITANISM

One of the key features distinguishing the true metropolis from the large cities of past history (and other high-density assemblages of people) is the ease and rapidity of exchange or movement, whether of persons, commodities, or information. However, even the smaller cities of the Western world, which also enjoy the advanced transportation and communication facilities of the metropolis, share this ease of movement. The *unique* features distinguishing movement in the metropolitan area appear merely to reflect the enhanced complexity associated with a system of interdependent nuclei.

Physical movement in the metropolitan area is much less simple with respect to direction and over-all orientation. In contrast with the simple in-and-out movement between center and periphery of the smaller city, the metropolitan area appears to have a very high proportion of *lateral movements*, in complicated crosscurrents and eddies. Commuting, in particular, is not merely a matter of centripetal and centrifugal flows morning and evening, but a confusing and asymmetrical compound of variously oriented threads of traffic, overlaying the older (and perhaps rudimentary) center-oriented pattern.

This greater complexity of movement, of course, is related to the structural feature that we have identified as typologically essential to metropolitanism—interdependence reflected in an extreme territorial division of labor. Organizational interdependence between the constituent segments of the whole metropolitan area is only achieved via specialization of land use, and areal specialization requires complex movement systems.[13] It is obvious that the functional fragmentation of space requires movement, and that as the underlying patterns of interdependence become more complex, the manifest patterns of movement will become progressively less simple.[14]

In fact, "*decentralization*," defined in terms of organizational complexity and measured by patterns of movement between subareas, *may even serve as a rather readily observed index of "metropolitanism."* Complex movement systems may be assumed to arise out of the decentralization of many of the constituent functional units of the total area, including places of employment as well as households. Such a complex movement system would necessarily represent a high degree of interdependence of parts, the very feature which we have previously identified as the major organizational element in theoretical discussions of metropolitan phenomena.[15]

IMPLICATIONS FOR FURTHER STUDY

The problem of availability of data for observation cannot be ignored. Some attention must necessarily be given the construction of indexes to stand for these rather vague and abstract terms—"complexity," "interdependence," etc. As a beginning in this direction, we might suggest the use of direct observations of movement. Ratios of lateral to centripetal-centrifugal trips can be assembled on a comparative basis (e.g., for a range of various-sized cities). Hypothetically, the "true" metropolitan areas would show very high proportions of lateral movement, while smaller areas (non-metropolitan cities) would exhibit high proportions of simple in-and-out movement.

Available traffic data, however, are rather scattered and they refer to different dates. Moreover, they cover a biased sample of cities—those experiencing particularly severe problems of congestion. It is at this point that the "place of work" question on the 1960 census should be most useful. Present plans call for the identification of work sites on a county basis, with separate identification of cities of 50,000 or more inhabitants. With somewhat more detailed areal codes, reliable ratios of lateral to centripetal-centrifugal movement could be computed for metropolitan areas. Work-trips having their origins *and* destinations within different parts of the ring could be treated as lateral, while exchanges *between* city and ring could be treated (separately) as centripetal and centrifugal.

One of the most significant by-products of this work would be the provision of a standardized and rigorous test of the current delineations of the individual metropolitan areas. Any doubts concerning the inclusion or exclusion of particular outlying counties could be resolved in a systematic fashion with these commuting data. It must be remembered that commuting is one of the criteria that the federal government attempts to use in its current delineation procedures. In the absence of adequate data, however, commuting patterns must be estimated. The result of these suggestions would be a reconceptualization of metropolitan areas as essentially "commuting areas." However, there is nothing to prevent the use of additional criteria, newspaper circulation, telephone traffic, etc. But at least one of the defining criteria would be available on a comparable basis, if only after the census was completed.

In any event, the judicious use of movement data should enhance our understanding of the structure of today's metropolitan area. Decentralization is too often conceived in oversimplified terms. The central city is thought to remain the major work site for a dispersed labor force, while surrounding municipalities are considered to be little more than "dormitories" or "bedroom towns." However, indirect evidence reveals that outlying centers in many areas regularly attract significant numbers of workers who live elsewhere. Many of these "satellites," or employing subcenters, like some residential suburbs, were formerly semi-independent centers that were drawn into the orbit of the larger central city with the development of faster means of transportation and communication, while others appear to have developed as appendages of the metropolis. Whatever their past history, however, they are now involved in the territorial division of labor of the metropolitan area as a whole, and movement data are most appropriate for showing the vital links that have been forged between them and other parts of the metropolitan area.

RESEARCH ALTERNATIVES

Assuming more intensive research along these lines, the prospects are excellent for increased knowledge of the structure and dynamics of contemporary metropolitan areas. We have far fewer opportunities to reconstruct the history of metropolitan decentralization, except for case studies of individual areas.[16] Historical-statistical investigations of any scope are obviously limited to a few pieces of data available for the period under review. Such items are usually very simple, either those "static" attributes that do not change (e.g., location) or those less complex "dynamic" variables that are readily accessible in such sources as the census (e.g., size and rate of growth). However, much remains to be done even within the narrow limits imposed by the available data. To a certain extent, imaginative research design can offset the disadvantages encountered in longitudinal study. One such suggestion has been put forward by Otis Dudley Duncan:

> Extensive attempts to measure the [suburban] trend and efforts to isolate its determinants are prominent in the literature. This is a field of research with more than ordinary difficulties of conceptualization and measurement. All too often researchers . . . have somewhat naively accepted findings of differential growth rates between central and peripheral portions of urban communities as evidence of a specific process of "suburbanization" or "decentralization," without attempting an operational distinction between these alleged processes and the normal tendency for expansion to occur on the periphery of the community area. One may hazard a guess as to the approach needed to clarify this problem. Comparative studies in considerable longitudinal depth should match a city of a given size at a recent date with one of the same size at a remote date, and note whether the recent pattern of growth is a more dispersed or "suburban" one than that occurring at the earlier period. An adequate comparison would require detailed examination of patterns and changes of population density.[17]

Thus the foregoing suggestions regarding the use of movement data represent only one of many possible approaches toward the fusion of research and theory on metropolitanism and decentralization. Whatever its merits, however, we would underscore the desirability of incorporating *organizational* variables in the study of metropolitan areas and population redistribution, whether the approach is longitudinal or cross-sectional. Perhaps the fact that a very large share of the research on these topics is carried on by sociologists and economists, who have a theoretical heritage of concepts of structure and change, will soon yield happier results. At any rate, we can hopefully expect new insights to emerge soon from the new research which is increasingly oriented to expanding the body of theory.

NOTES

1. For example, Warren S. Thompson, *The Growth of Metropolitan Districts in the United States, 1900–1940* (Washington: Government Printing Office, 1947); Donald J. Bogue, *Population Growth in Standard Metropolitan Areas, 1900–1950* (Washington: Government Printing Office, 1953).

2. Amos H. Hawley, *The Changing Shape of Metropolitan America* (Glencoe: Free Press, 1956).

3. *The Growth of Cities in the Nineteenth Century* (New York: Macmillan Co., 1899), especially pp. 458–75.

4. "Suburbanization: Statistical Fallacy?" *Land Economics*, 32 (Feb., 1956) pp. 85–87. See, however, the comment following Schmitt's by Amos H. Hawley, "A Further Note on Suburbanization," *ibid.*, pp. 87–89.

5. Leo F. Schnore, "Metropolitan Growth and Decentralization," *American Journal of Sociology*, 63 (September, 1957), pp. 171–80.

6. These areal changes are ignored or obscured in almost all the available studies of decentralization, including previous work by the writer, with the notable exception of a recent study by Donald J. Bogue, *Components of Population Change, 1940–1950: Estimates of Net Migration and Natural Increase for Each Standard Metropolitan Area and State Economic Area* (Oxford [Ohio] and Chicago: Scripps Foundation for Research in Population Problems and Population Research and Training Center, 1957); for a summary, see Donald J. Bogue and Emerson Seim, "Components of Population Change in Suburban and Central City Populations of Standard Metropolitan Areas: 1940–to–1950," *Rural Sociology*, 21 (September–December, 1956), pp. 267–75. In the present study, areas (in square miles) of each city at each census date were examined in order to determine whether or not territorial changes had taken place in the intervening decades.

7. Since an element of judgment is necessarily involved—especially in view of the frequency of annexation—a complete list of the cities has been prepared, with all relevant data clearly indicated. This list is available from the author upon request.

8. The other cities that apparently began to decentralize before 1900 are: Cincinnati, San Francisco, New Haven, Boston, Albany, Baltimore, St. Louis, Scranton, and Duluth.

9. *An Introduction to Economic History* (New York: Harper and Brothers, 1922), p. 184.

10. *Ibid.*, p. 187.

11. *The Metropolitan Community* (New York: McGraw-Hill Book Co., 1933), pp. 6–7.

12. Donald J. Bogue, *The Structure of the Metropolitan Community* (Ann Arbor: University of Michigan Press, 1949); Leslie Kish, "Differentiation in Metropolitan Areas," *American Sociological Review,* 19 (August, 1954), pp. 388–398; Walter Isard and Vincent H. Whitney, "Metropolitan Site Selection," *Social Forces,* 27 (March, 1949), pp. 263–69. All these are based upon the 1940 census data.

13. Donald L. Foley, "Urban Day-Time Population: A Field for Demographic-Ecological Analysis," *Social Forces,* 32 (May, 1954), pp. 323–30.

14. Still another aspect of this complexity to be noted is the increasingly *indirect* (and decreasingly observable) nature of the relationships between the constituent units of the metropolitan area as a whole. Metropolitan organization appears to ramify into patterns so intricate as to defy description. In this connection, it is interesting to note that the sociological and anthropological literature on community organization is almost entirely confined, in an empirical sense, to much smaller places.

15. Decentralization is too often conceived as involving only the outward shift of residential population. Complete understanding of the phenomenon will come only when all the constituent functional units in the community have been systematically examined with respect to their physical dispersion. The most valuable material that is currently available is to be found in the series of studies in population distribution sponsored by the Scripps Foundation for Research in Population Problems, especially those by Cuzzort, Kitagawa, and Bogue on the suburbanization of services and manufacturing.

16. See Hans Blumenfeld, "The Tidal Wave of Metropolitan Expansion," *Journal of the American Institute of Planners,* 20 (Winter, 1954), pp. 3–14.

17. "Human Ecology and Population Studies," in Philip M. Hauser and Otis Dudley Duncan (editors), *The Study of Population* (Chicago: University of Chicago Press, 1959), p. 697.

Chapter 6

Municipal Annexations and

Decentralization, 1950-1960

THE GROWTH of metropolitan suburbs in the United States has captured the attention of everyone concerned with the description and understanding of the changing American scene. Anyone who lives in or near a large American city—and that describes a majority of us—is at least partially aware of the sheer scale of this massive movement. As Dudley Kirk has observed:

> Everywhere we see the growing place of the metropolis and suburbia in our national life. Perhaps the single most significant demographic series in the whole armamentarium of American population statistics is represented by the following: two generations ago, in 1900, the median American lived in the countryside; by 1930 he lived in a small town of 5,000–10,000 population. Today he lives in a metropolitan area, increasingly in the suburbs, and the country-dweller today is as much in touch with world events and cultural innovation as the city-

Revised version of a paper delivered at the annual meeting of the Population Association of America, New York City, May 5–6, 1961. The study was supported by the research phase of the University of Wisconsin Urban Program under a grant from the Ford Foundation. Jean Smith served capably as a research assistant on this project.

dweller of yesterday. It is difficult to overstate the revolution this has meant in the average American's way of life.[1]

It is the task of the demographer to supply some of the basic facts concerning this wholesale redistribution of our population; the major trends for the first half of this century have been well described in a series of historical-statistical studies by Thompson, Bogue, and Hawley.[2] Now the availability of data from the 1960 Census of Population permits us to sketch the outlines of the latest chapter in this epic—one that seems almost certain to be continued for some time to come.

The study reported here makes use of final population counts for the 212 Standard Metropolitan Statistical Areas (SMSA's) delineated by the Bureau of the Budget with the advice of a federal committee composed of representatives of the major federal statistical agencies.[3] We must stress the fact that the results are not directly comparable with earlier studies employing the Standard Metropolitan Areas (SMA's) delineated prior to the 1950 Census; not only have a large number of new areas been recognized, but a substantial number of preexisting SMA's have been altered. This study takes the 1960 SMSA's as given and examines their experience within the last intercensal decade.

Table 1 provides a summary of the major facts concerning recent metropolitan growth in the United States. The 212 metropolitan areas grew almost four times as fast as the rest of the country, and they captured almost 85 per cent of the total national increase. The areas characterized as "metropolitan" in the 1960 Census contained 63 per cent of the country's population, while these same areas held only 59 per cent ten years earlier. Table 1 also summarizes some important aspects of the redistribution of population within broad regions and divisions. A few facts are worth pointing up: (1) The Northeast is the only region in which nonmetropolitan areas grew faster than SMSA's; in divisional terms, New England is the only one showing this aberrant pattern. (2) Though all four regions experienced growth in both metropolitan and nonmetropolitan sectors, three divisions (the West North Central,

Table 1—Indexes of Metropolitan and Nonmetropolitan Growth, United States 1950–60, by Regions and Divisions

Census Region and Division	PER CENT CHANGE 1950–60			SHARES OF TOTAL GROWTH		PER CENT OF TOTAL POPULATION IN SMSA's		
	Total	In SMSA's	Outside SMSA's	In SMSA's	Outside SMSA's	1960	1950	Difference
United States	18.5	26.4	7.1	84.2	15.8	63.0	59.0	4.0
Region:								
Northeast	13.2	13.1	13.5	78.5	21.5	79.0	79.0	0.0
North Central	16.1	23.5	6.5	82.4	17.6	60.1	56.5	3.6
South	16.5	36.2	2.7	90.4	9.6	48.1	41.2	6.9
West	38.9	48.5	19.4	83.6	16.4	71.8	67.1	4.7
Division:								
New England	12.8	12.3	14.2	67.6	32.4	70.3	70.7	−0.4
Middle Atlantic	13.3	13.3	13.1	81.8	18.2	81.6	81.6	0.0
East North Central	19.2	23.5	11.7	77.4	22.6	65.3	63.0	2.3
West North Central	9.5	23.4	−0.8	104.7	−4.7	47.7	42.3	5.4
South Atlantic	22.6	39.7	8.8	78.5	21.5	50.9	44.7	6.2
East South Central	5.0	22.6	−2.4	133.8	−33.8	34.6	29.6	5.0
West South Central	16.6	38.1	−1.1	103.6	−3.6	53.5	45.1	8.4
Mountain	35.1	63.9	15.7	73.3	26.7	48.8	40.3	8.5
Pacific	40.2	45.8	22.6	86.6	13.4	79.2	76.2	3.0

East South Central, and West South Central) sustained losses in their nonmetropolitan parts. (*3*) If one regards the per-centage-point difference between the proportions in SMSA's at the two dates as an index of the speed of metropolitaniza-tion, the process is proceeding most rapidly in the South and West, particularly in the West South Central and Mountain divisions.

So much for background. Our major objective is an assess-ment of differential growth *within* these areas. For present pur-poses, "suburbs" are represented by metropolitan "rings"—those parts of the SMSA's that lie outside the central cities. As Shryock has observed, this is one operational definition of "suburb" that has been used from time to time, although there is still no standardized meaning attached to the term. "In the literature," he remarks, "*suburb* is used almost as loosely by the social scientist as by the layman."[4] Given the peculiarities of political boundaries, metropolitan rings are manifestly heter-ogeneous units, and their use can only be defended on the grounds of expediency; subsequent investigations will neces-sarily employ alternative definitions.[5]

Comparisons of population change within cities and their rings yield only gross results, but they do provide an overview of major shifts in population distribution. One problem that has always proved embarrassing in such comparisons, however, has been the possibility of boundary changes; in particular, annexations by central cities are likely to overstate their growth, and to understate the growth of outlying rings. For-tunately, the 1960 Census of Population yields data that permit an adjustment for this factor: the 1960 populations residing in the 1950 areas are shown for all incorporated places having 2,500 or more inhabitants in 1950.[6] For the first time, then, we are able to take account of the effect of annexation, and we can see the actual extent to which the expansion of city boundaries tends to mask the amount of "decentralization" or "suburbani-zation" that has been taking place. For this reason, all of the materials presented in this report are shown in two forms—*before* and *after* adjustment for annexations by central cities. Comments on the two series will be made in passing. The fact that 160 out of the 212 areas—or over 75 per cent—were affected by such annexations makes an assessment of the impact of boundary changes almost mandatory.[7]

Measures of Suburban Growth

Within the limits of city-ring comparisons, there are three principal indexes of growth that can be employed. All three are affected by annexations on the part of the central city.

1. *Growth rates of metropolitan centers and rings*—The most common approach to the question of suburban growth involves a simple comparison of rates of population change in the two parts between the beginning and the end of the period of observation. This simple measure—percentage increase or decrease—will be employed here for metropolitan areas aggregated in various ways. A disadvantage of this measure is the fact that it is seriously affected by the size of the base population at the beginning of the period of observation. A modest absolute increase over a small base, for example, will yield a high rate of increase. Its principal advantage is its familiarity.

2. *Shares of metropolitan growth going to centers and rings*—Another aspect of metropolitan population change is measured by determining the proportions of total metropolitan growth that have been captured by centers and rings respectively during the period of observation. This measure is less useful than the others employed here, especially in the examination of individual SMSA's, which may be losing population. Though it is affected by the proportions found in centers and rings at the beginning of the period of observation, which are, in turn, influenced by the extensiveness of city boundaries, it does make some intuitive sense. It has also become fairly familiar; the Bureau of the Census employs it from time to time, and Bogue has made use of a slight variant in his analyses.[8]

3. *Shifts in the proportion contained in metropolitan rings*—A third measure is based upon a comparison of the proportions found in metropolitan rings (*a*) at the beginning and (*b*) at the end of the period of observation. Examination of the resulting percentage-point differences permits one to assess the

rate of redistribution within metropolitan areas. After review-ing the characteristics of a number of possible measures, Bogue and Harris concluded that this is "the best index for measuring the speed of suburbanization."[9] A negative shift in the propor-tion found in the ring indicates relative "centralization," while a positive difference indicates "decentralization" or "suburban-ization."

GENERAL FINDINGS

Table 2 provides some basic descriptive data on recent sub-urbanization in the United States. Considering the nation as a whole, the unadjusted data in the lower panel indicate that metropolitan rings grew about four and a half times as fast as the cities they surround and that these outlying parts of SMSA's captured just over three-fourths of the total increase going to metropolitan areas. When adjusted for annexation by central cities, however, the upper panel reveals that the rings grew over forty times as fast as the cities as these were bounded in 1950, and that they captured almost 97 per cent of the total metropolitan increase.

Table 2 also shows variations in city and ring growth within the four census regions and the nine census divisions.

Regions—Even before adjustment, it can be seen that the metropolitan cities of the Northeast were losing population in the aggregate, while those of the North Central region grew only slightly. In the South and West, rings grew twice as rapidly as cities, but cities captured almost half the increase going to southern metropolitan areas, and almost one-third of the growth in western SMSA's—at least before the effect of annexation is removed. After adjustment, however, cities of the North Central region are also seen to be losing numbers in the aggregate, and city growth in the South and West is much less marked. Southern and western rings also claim overwhelming shares of total metropolitan growth.

Divisions—In Table 2, the same indexes of city and ring growth are also shown for the nine census divisions. The note-worthy features of the lower panel—where the unadjusted data

Table 2—Indexes of Metropolitan City and Ring Growth, United States 1950–60, by Regions and Divisions

Census Region and Division	PER CENT CHANGE, 1950–60 SMSA's	Cities	Rings	SHARES OF TOTAL GROWTH Cities	Rings	PER CENT OF SMSA POPULATION IN RINGS 1960	1950	Differences
After Adjustment								
United States	26.4	1.5	61.6	3.3	96.7	53.0	41.4	11.6
Northeast[a]	13.1	-3.3	35.0	-14.2	114.2	51.0	42.7	8.3
New England	12.3	-3.7	28.9	-15.5	115.5	56.3	49.0	7.3
Middle Atlantic	13.3	-3.1	37.0	-13.9	113.9	49.6	41.0	8.6
North Central[a]	23.5	-1.6	66.5	-4.3	104.3	49.7	36.9	12.8
East North Central	23.5	-1.4	66.4	-3.8	103.8	49.5	36.8	12.7
West North Central	23.4	-2.2	66.9	-5.8	105.8	50.2	37.1	13.1
South[a]	36.2	5.3	82.1	8.7	91.3	53.8	40.2	13.6
South Atlantic	39.7	2.8	82.0	3.8	96.2	60.7	46.6	14.1
East South Central	22.6	1.0	54.6	2.5	97.5	50.8	40.3	10.5
West South Central	38.1	10.0	101.1	18.1	81.9	45.0	30.9	14.1
West[a]	48.5	14.5	84.1	15.3	84.7	60.6	48.9	11.7
Mountain	63.9	16.6	128.4	15.0	85.0	58.9	42.3	16.6
Pacific	45.8	14.0	77.4	15.3	84.7	60.9	50.0	10.9
Before Adjustment								
United States	26.4	10.7	48.6	23.7	76.3	48.7	41.4	7.3
Northeast[a]	13.1	-3.1	34.9	-13.8	113.8	50.9	42.7	8.2
New England	12.3	-3.3	28.4	-13.6	113.6	56.1	49.0	7.1
Middle Atlantic	13.3	-3.1	37.0	-13.8	113.8	49.5	41.0	8.5
North Central[a]	23.5	4.3	56.4	11.5	88.5	46.7	36.9	9.8
East North Central	23.5	3.7	57.6	9.8	90.2	46.9	36.8	10.1
West North Central	23.4	6.3	52.5	16.8	83.2	45.9	37.1	8.8
South[a]	36.2	28.4	47.7	47.0	53.0	43.6	40.2	3.4
South Atlantic	39.7	20.9	61.3	28.0	72.0	53.8	46.6	7.2
East South Central	22.6	17.3	30.4	45.8	54.2	42.8	40.3	2.5
West South Central	38.1	41.8	29.9	75.8	24.2	29.0	30.9	-1.9
West[a]	48.5	31.4	66.3	33.2	66.8	54.7	48.9	5.8
Mountain	63.9	73.6	50.6	66.5	33.5	38.9	42.3	-3.4
Pacific	45.8	22.8	68.7	24.9	75.1	57.9	50.9	7.9

a. Census region.

are shown—concern the experience of metropolitan areas in the West South Central and Mountain divisions. Unlike the other divisions, these two show city growth outstripping that of the ring. Adjustment for annexation dramatically reverses these patterns. While the metropolitan cities of the Mountain division appeared to have captured two-thirds of the total increase in SMSA's, growth within the 1950 city boundaries amounted to only 15 per cent of that increase. Similarly, holding city areas constant in the West South Central division shows that cities captured not three-fourths but less than one-fifth of the total metropolitan growth in the entire division. Finally, the very last column shows that metropolitan areas in these two divisions were not centralizing but decentralizing, and at very rapid rates.

All of the results shown so far have simply documented the fact of gross variations from one part of the country to another. The regions and divisions utilized here are those that have been employed for many years by the Bureau of Census. As such, they offer comparability with other census-based materials, but little else. They are not offered as a set of analytical categories, though they do serve some useful purpose in description. We turn now, however, to two variables which do present some analytical possibilities—size and age.

Size of SMSA—Table 3 shows the indexes of city and ring growth for metropolitan areas classified by their size in 1960. There is no systematic variation in over-all metropolitan growth with size, but it can be seen in the lower panel that the larger the area, the lower the rate of city growth. Similarly, the larger the area, the higher the rate of ring growth.[10] With respect to shares of metropolitan growth, central cities in the larger areas captured very little of the total increase, most of it going to their suburban rings; the opposite pattern held for the smaller SMSA's, and there is a fairly regular progression in the columns devoted to shares of growth. In the unadjusted data, the last column in the lower panel suggests that suburbanization was proceeding most rapidly in the very largest areas, while the smaller areas were undergoing "centralization," and again there is a systematic progression from one size class to the next.

Table 3—Indexes of Metropolitan City and Ring Growth, United States 1950–60, by Size of SMSA in 1960

Size of SMSA in 1960	PER CENT CHANGE, 1950–60			SHARES OF TOTAL GROWTH		PER CENT OF SMSA POPULATION IN RINGS		
	SMSA's	Cities	Rings	Cities	Rings	1960	1950	Differences
After Adjustment								
3,000,000 or more	23.2	0.6	72.2	1.7	98.3	44.1	31.5	12.6
1,000,000–3,000,000	25.0	−2.3	52.7	−4.5	104.5	60.5	49.5	11.0
500,000–1,000,000	36.1	4.8	80.0	7.8	92.2	54.9	41.5	13.4
250,000– 500,000	25.6	2.2	52.0	4.5	95.5	56.9	47.0	9.9
150,000– 250,000	26.7	4.5	53.7	9.3	90.7	54.6	45.0	9.6
100,000– 150,000	24.7	5.3	56.2	13.2	86.8	47.8	38.2	9.6
Under 100,000	24.5	8.6	69.9	26.1	73.9	35.3	25.9	9.4
Before Adjustment								
3,000,000 or more	23.2	1.0	71.3	2.9	97.1	43.9	31.5	12.4
1,000,000–3,000,000	25.0	5.6	44.7	11.3	88.7	57.4	49.5	7.9
500,000–1,000,000	36.1	21.2	57.0	34.4	65.6	47.9	41.5	6.4
250,000– 500,000	25.6	16.1	36.2	33.4	66.6	51.0	47.0	4.0
150,000– 250,000	26.7	25.0	28.6	51.7	48.3	45.7	45.0	0.7
100,000– 150,000	24.7	23.5	26.6	58.9	41.1	38.8	38.2	0.6
Under 100,000	24.5	29.2	10.8	88.5	11.5	23.0	25.9	−2.9

Nevertheless, the adjusted data in the upper panel reveal no such clear-cut patterns. The *general* tendencies described above can still be discerned in every case, but the associations are much less clearly manifested.

Age of central city—The literature dealing with metropolitan areas contains occasional reference to a concept of "metropolitan maturity." Older and well-established areas presumably reveal different patterns from those observable in newer areas; indeed, these age differences may lie behind some of the patterns to be seen in data organized by size and regional location.[11] In an effort to get at this matter more directly, we have classified SMSA's according to the census year in which their central cities first reached 50,000 in size; in the case of areas with more than one central city, we used the largest city for this purpose. ("Age," of course, is not entirely independent of size.)[12]

Table 4 shows the results. It is worth noting in passing that the areas with older central cities had notably lower rates of over-all growth and that those with newer cities exhibited progressively higher rates of over-all increase between 1950 and 1960. In addition, the lower panel suggests that the older cities themselves have been losing population, while the newer cities have been growing even more rapidly than their own rings. These differences also appear in the columns devoted to the shares of metropolitan growth going to cities and rings. Finally, suburbanization appears to be proceeding most rapidly in the areas with "older" central cities. All of these patterns, however, emerge only in the unadjusted data. Adjustment for annexation again sharply modifies the regularities that were previously observed.

INDIVIDUAL GROWTH PATTERNS

Up to this point, we have provided no more than a generalized description of suburban growth. The data were highly aggregated, and variations from area to area have been almost completely ignored. Only selected features of metropolitan areas have been examined—size, location, and "age"—and the

Table 4—Indexes of Metropolitan City and Ring Growth, United States 1950–60, by "Age" of (Principal) Central City

Census Year in Which (Principal) Central City First Contained 50,000 Inhabitants	PER CENT CHANGE, 1950–60			SHARES OF TOTAL GROWTH		PER CENT OF SMSA POPULATION IN RINGS		
	SMSA's	Cities	Rings	Cities	Rings	1960	1950	Differences
After Adjustment								
1800–1840	14.1	−1.9	50.2	−9.5	109.5	40.4	30.7	9.7
1850–1860	20.9	−5.2	54.2	−14.0	114.0	56.1	44.0	12.1
1870–1880	20.3	−5.2	51.8	−14.3	114.3	56.5	44.8	11.7
1890–1900	32.1	5.2	68.0	9.2	90.8	54.5	42.9	11.6
1910–1920	32.8	8.4	66.4	14.7	85.3	52.8	42.1	10.7
1930–1940	42.2	5.7	84.1	7.3	92.7	60.2	46.5	13.7
1950 or later	46.3	17.8	76.4	19.7	80.3	58.6	48.6	10.0
Before Adjustment								
1800–1840	14.1	−1.9	50.2	−9.5	109.5	40.4	30.7	9.7
1850–1860	20.9	−4.3	53.1	−11.6	111.6	55.7	44.0	11.7
1870–1880	20.3	−1.2	46.8	−3.2	103.2	54.6	44.8	9.8
1890–1900	32.1	13.3	57.2	23.6	76.4	51.0	42.9	8.1
1910–1920	32.8	27.2	40.6	47.9	52.1	44.6	42.1	2.5
1930–1940	42.2	43.9	40.2	55.7	44.3	45.9	46.5	−0.6
1950 or later	46.3	50.2	42.1	55.7	44.3	47.2	48.6	−1.4

major objective has been to identify broad patterns of population change in cities and their rings. Treatment of the substantial variations around the weighted averages shown for regions, divisions, size classes, and age groups will have to await further analysis, and explanation of the differences that can be observed would obviously require a more sophisticated research design than that used here. "In the last analysis," Davis has observed, "the pattern of metropolitan expansion differs for each metropolitan area and has to be studied on an individual basis, although, for predictive purposes, it is necessary to use comparative techniques in order to determine the main variables that affect the rate of suburbanization."[13] As an intermediate step, we can provide some information on the patterns of growth experienced by individual areas.

We have identified each area according to the general *pattern* of population change that it experienced between 1950 and 1960. Once growth rates have been computed for individual metropolitan centers and their rings, one can readily characterize their experience according to the broad patterns exhibited. There are six possibilities, three of which involve relative *centralization,* and three of which involve relative *decentralization.*

Centralizing patterns—There are three patterns of metropolitan population change that result in relative gains by *centers:*

   I. The center gains numbers while the ring loses;
  II. Both center and ring gain numbers, but the center gains at a faster rate;
 III. Both center and ring lose numbers, but the center loses them at a slower rate;

Decentralizing patterns—Similarly, there are three patterns that yield relative gains by *rings:*

  IV. Both center and ring gain numbers, but the ring gains at a faster rate;
   V. The ring gains numbers while the center loses;
 VI. Both center and ring lose numbers, but the ring loses them at a slower rate.

Table 5—Growth Patterns, Metropolitan Cities and Rings, United States 1950–60, by Regions and Divisions

Census Region and Division	After Adjustment for Annexations					Before Adjustment for Annexations					No. of SMSA's
	"CENTRALIZING"		"DECENTRALIZING"			"CENTRALIZING"		"DECENTRALIZING"			
	City Gained, Ring Lost	Both Gained, City Faster	Both Gained, Ring Faster	City Lost, Ring Gained	Both Lost, City Faster	City Gained, Ring Lost	Both Gained, City Faster	Both Gained, Ring Faster	City Lost, Ring Gained	Both Lost, City Faster	
United States	4	4	109	90	4	28	36	91	51	5	211ᵃ
Region:											
Northeast	0	0	15	27	4	0	0	15	27	4	46
North Central	1	0	33	25	0	6	7	36	10	0	59
South	3	2	41	31	0	20	21	23	12	1	77
West	0	2	20	7	0	2	8	17	2	0	29
Division:											
New England	0	0	11	11	0	0	0	11	11	0	22
Middle Atlantic	0	0	4	16	4	0	0	4	16	4	24
East North Central	1	0	22	19	0	2	3	28	8	0	41
West North Central	0	0	11	6	0	4	4	8	2	0	18
South Atlantic	0	0	15	18	0	3	10	10	9	1	33
East South Central	3	1	6	6	0	3	3	4	3	0	13
West South Central	0	1	20	7	0	14	8	9	0	0	31
Mountain	0	2	9	2	0	2	5	6	0	0	13
Pacific	0	0	11	5	0	0	3	11	2	0	16

a. Meriden, Connecticut, is excluded from table because it has no metropolitan ring.

(In point of fact, Pattern III is not found among the 211 SMSA's for which this comparison can be made, either before or after annexation is taken into account. The remaining five patterns, in the order described, represent a hypothetical developmental sequence through which an area might progress over time.)

In the nation as a whole, Table 5 shows that 64 of the 211 areas (or more than 30 per cent) were "centralizing" before annexation was taken into consideration. This number is reduced to eight areas—or less than 4 per cent—when city boundaries are held constant. Table 5 also shows the number of SMSA's in each region and division that may be found in each of the identifiable growth classes. Again the Northeast region (and its New England and Middle Atlantic divisions) stands out; not one of the 46 Northeast SMSA's experienced "centralization" in the past decade. And, after adjustment for the effects of annexation, the same thing can be said for three additional divisions—the East North Central, the South Atlantic, and the Pacific.

Table 6 provides a concrete illustration of each of the patterns described, and indicates the type of growth manifested before and after adjustment for annexation. It is worth noting that more than one-third of all SMSA's (75 out of 211) must be reclassified after correction for annexation.

Within the size and age classes, Table 7 shows the number of SMSA's experiencing each of the growth patterns described above. Even before adjustment for annexations by central cities, it is noteworthy that very few of the larger areas exhibit the patterns labeled "centralizing," and that all of the thirty-two areas whose central cities reached 50,000 before 1880 are "decentralizing." The adjusted data reveal even more clearly the tendency for "centralizing" areas to be smaller and newer.

Conclusions

If it has contributed nothing else to the understanding of recent suburban growth, this chapter has forcefully demonstrated the need for taking territorial changes into account when one is examining growth differentials within metropolitan areas. As Shryock has noted, "One of the most prominent

Table 6—Types of City Growth before and after Adjustment for Annexation

Area	BEFORE ADJUSTMENT PER CENT CHANGE, 1950-60			AFTER ADJUSTMENT PER CENT CHANGE, 1950-60			No. of Areas Exemplified[a]
	City	Ring	Type	Type	City	Ring	
Sioux City, Iowa	6.2	-6.2	I	I	5.7	-4.2	4
Huntsville, Alabama	340.3	-20.3	I	II	111.7	46.2	2
Tucson, Arizona	368.4	-44.9	I	IV	0.7	129.6	12
Evansville, Indiana	10.1	-7.6	II	V	-9.8	33.3	10
Albuquerque, New Mexico	107.8	24.9	II	II	83.4	73.3	2
Ann Arbor, Michigan	39.6	21.7	II	IV	5.0	41.0	22
Billings, Montana	66.0	8.8	II	V	-8.9	108.1	12
Akron, Ohio	5.7	64.8	IV	IV	5.5	65.2	75
Milwaukee, Wisconsin	16.3	41.7	IV	V	-3.1	80.5	16
Macon, Georgia	-0.7	70.8	V	V	-7.3	77.9	51
Wheeling, West Virginia	-9.3	-0.3	VI	V	-10.7	0.2	1
Johnstown, Pennsylvania	-14.7	-0.6	VI	VI	-14.8	-0.6	4

a. Total number of areas, 211.

trends in municipal development during the 1950's has been the greatly increased number of annexations to incorporated places. No account of urbanization during the period could be complete that overlooks this process, and measurement of the population involved seems to be called for."[14] The metropolitan central cities annexed territory containing 4.8 million people at the end of the decade. If so many central cities had not pursued vigorous annexation programs, almost all of the considerable metropolitan growth during the decade would have gone to the outlying suburban rings, for growth within the 1950 city boundaries was extremely limited.

There is no particular mystery here, for cities regularly exhibit peripheral growth. A clear statement of the salient facts is contained in the census bulletin cited above:

> If there is a considerable area within the city limits which is suitable and profitable for residential development, it is probable that a large part of the population growth will occur within the city limits and that the census will register a population gain for the central city.
>
> If, however, at the beginning of the decade, there is only a limited space within the corporate limits suitable for residential development, and if these limits are not extended, the population of the central city is likely to remain stationary or decline. The growth of urban aggregates tends to be greatest in their periphery, and, as the area of dense settlement spreads outward, it overflows the boundaries of the legal city. At the same time, the growth of the entire aggregate increases the need for non-residential uses of land in its central part to accommodate increased business activity—commercial establishments, office buildings, parking areas, freeways, and the like. Thus, if the city limits remain fixed, there comes a time when the economic growth of the entire metropolitan area may be accompanied by a decline in the populations of the central city or cities.[15]

We have shown that city-ring comparisons unadjusted for annexations substantially understate the amount of "suburbanization" that has occurred in the most recent intercensal decade. This is not to deny the possibility of a significant countermovement on the part of a selected minority (e.g., those older suburbanites whose children have grown and married) that may lead in time to a "recentralization" of substantial numbers

Table 7—Growth Patterns, Metropolitan Cities and Rings, United States, 1950–60 by Size of SMSA in 1960 and by "Age" of (Principal) Central City[a]

| | After Adjustment for Annexations | | | | | Before Adjustment for Annexations | | | | | |
| | "CENTRALIZING" | | "DECENTRALIZING" | | | "CENTRALIZING" | | "DECENTRALIZING" | | | |
Size and Age	City Gained, Ring Lost	Both Gained, City Faster	Both Gained, Ring Faster	City Lost, Ring Gained	Both Lost, City Faster	City Gained, Ring Lost	Both Gained, City Faster	Both Gained, Ring Faster	City Lost, Ring Gained	Both Lost, City Faster	No. of SMSA's
Size of SMSA in 1960:											
3,000,000 or more	0	0	1	4	0	0	0	1	4	0	5
1,000,000–3,000,000	0	0	5	14	0	0	3	5	11	0	19
500,000–1,000,000	0	0	19	9	1	1	4	17	6	1	29
250,000–500,000	0	0	23	22	2	1	7	21	16	2	48
150,000–250,000	0	1	29	16	1	8	10	19	8	2	47
100,000–150,000	1	2	19	20	0	10	4	22	6	0	42
Under 100,000	3	0	13	5	0	7	8	6	0	0	21
Census year in which (principal) central city first contained 50,000 inhabitants:											
1800–1840	0	0	1	4	0	0	0	1	4	0	5
1850–1860	0	0	0	10	0	0	0	1	9	0	10
1870–1880	0	0	3	13	1	0	0	6	10	1	17
1890–1900	0	0	15	18	2	2	3	14	14	2	35
1910–1920	1	0	33	18	1	4	8	28	11	2	53
1930–1940	0	0	18	14	0	8	9	14	1	0	32
1950 or later	3	4	39	13	0	14	16	27	2	0	59

a. Meriden, Connecticut, is excluded from table because it has no metropolitan ring.

of people.[16] It merely dramatizes the extent to which a "decentralized" pattern now characterizes an overwhelming majority of metropolitan areas.

The task that now remains for demographers is to undertake more detailed analyses of these outward shifts in residential population, viewing them in the context of the changing structure and functions of the metropolitan community, and relating them to the larger trends in the American economy and society. The difficulties should not be underestimated. Duncan has pointed out:

> This is a field of research with more than ordinary difficulties of conceptualization and measurement. All too often researchers . . . have naïvely accepted findings of differential growth rates between central and peripheral portions of urban communities as evidence of a specific process of "suburbanization" or "decentralization," without attempting an operational distinction between these alleged processes and the normal tendency for expansion to occur on the periphery of the community area.[17]

Such an operational distinction was not attempted in this paper, for we were primarily concerned with assessing the impact of annexation on "suburbanization" as it is commonly understood. One must always be aware, however, of the fact that cities grow horizontally, extending their areas at the periphery of settlement.[18] What we need now are methods that are adequate to deal with the physical growth of cities, as well as with changes in the size of their populations. Ours is a metropolitan society whose study increasingly requires attention to these massive agglomerations of population, and to the changes occurring therein.

NOTES

1. Dudley Kirk, "Some Reflections on American Demography in the Nineteen Sixties," *Population Index*, 26 (October, 1960), 306.

2. Warren S. Thompson, *The Growth of Metropolitan Districts in the United States, 1900–1940* (Washington, D.C.: Government Printing Office, 1947); Donald J. Bogue, *Population Growth in Standard Metro-*

politan Areas, 1900–1950 (Washington, D.C.: Housing and Home Finance Agency, 1953); Amos H. Hawley, *The Changing Shape of Metropolitan America* (Glencoe, Ill.: Free Press, 1956).

3. See Office of Statistical Standards, Executive Office of the President, Bureau of the Budget, *Standard Metropolitan Statistical Areas* (Washington, D.C.: Government Printing Office, 1959), and the subsequent list of areas released in September, 1960, together with errata and addenda dated September 26, 1960, and November 2, 1960.

4. Henry S. Shryock, Jr., "Population Redistribution within Metropolitan Areas: Evaluation of Research," *Social Forces*, 35 (December, 1956), 155.

5. In "The Growth of Metropolitan Suburbs," *American Sociological Review*, 22 (April, 1957), 165–73, I defined metropolitan suburbs operationally as incorporated places of 10,000 or more inhabitants lying within metropolitan rings, and I have also advocated a functional distinction between "Satellites and Suburbs," in *Social Forces*, 36 (December, 1957), 121–27. See also Richard A. Kurtz and Joanne B. Eicher, "Fringe and Suburb: A Confusion of Concepts," *Social Forces*, 37 (October, 1958), 32–37.

6. These data are shown in Table 9 in the series of state reports PC (1), chap. "A." I am very grateful to the Population Division, United States Bureau of the Census, for the provision of photocopies of these tables for all of the state reports that were still being processed for publication at the time that this paper was in preparation (March, 1961), and I am especially indebted to Henry D. Sheldon and Gordon F. Sutton of the Bureau staff.

7. In an October, 1960, report based on preliminary counts compiled in the 1960 Census field offices, and covering 209 SMSA's, it was stated that "there is evidence that annexation has, in many instances, materially increased the rate of growth of many central cities," but it was noted that "information on the size of the population involved in annexations is not yet available, and therefore the exact effects of this process cannot be determined" (United States Bureau of the Census, "Population of Standard Metropolitan Statistical Areas 1960 and 1950," *U.S. Census of Population: 1960, Preliminary Reports, Population Summaries*, PC (P3)-4 [Washington, D.C.: Government Printing Office, October, 1960], p. 4).

8. See, e.g., Donald J. Bogue, "Urbanism in the United States, 1950," *American Journal of Sociology*, 60 (March, 1955), 471–86, esp. p. 480, Table 5, and Bogue, *Population Growth in Standard Metropolitan Areas, 1900–1950*, p. 14, Table 3.

9. Donald J. Bogue and Dorothy L. Harris, *Comparative Population and Urban Research via Multiple Regression and Covariance Analysis: A Methodological Experiment, with an Illustrative Application to the Study of Factors in the Growth and Suburbanization of Metropolitan Population* (Oxford, Ohio: Scripps Foundation for Research in Population Problems, Miami University; Chicago: Population Research and Training Center, University of Chicago, 1954), p. 45.

10. Similar relationships, observable in advance census data, were shown in a table in *Population Index*, 26 (October, 1960), 310. These materials were used as the basis for that issue's cover chart.

11. One need not postulate an evolutionary sequence or a "life cycle"

through which entire areas pass in order to expect such differences, for cities have developed in dissimilar technological eras. "Because Southern cities have had their greatest growth during the automobile age," T. Stanton Dietrich has observed, "residential areas tend to be dispersed over the countryside, and the extent of this dispersal is probably greater in the South than elsewhere" (see his "Nature and Directions of Suburbanization in the South," *Social Forces,* 39 [December, 1960], 182).

12. The zero-order correlation between (*a*) the number of decades that the 1950 SMA has had a central city of 50,000 or more and (*b*) size of SMA in 1940 was reported to be + .596 by Bogue and Harris, *Comparative Population* . . . , p. 75, Appendix Table II. This measure was also used in Leo F. Schnore, "The Timing of Metropolitan Decentralization: A Contribution to the Debate," *Journal of the American Institute of Planners,* 25 (November, 1959), 200–206. It is far from perfect, since some cities have "grown" into this size class by annexing territory.

13. Kingsley Davis, "Urban Demography and Ecology," *Alpha Kappa Deltan,* 28 (Winter, 1958), 14.

14. Henry S. Shryock, Jr., "What Is New in Our Eighteenth Decennial Census of the Population?" *Proceedings of the Social Statistics Section, American Statistical Association, 1958* (Washington, D.C.: American Statistical Association, 1958), p. 26. In the nation as a whole, "the incorporated urban places of 1950 [lying inside and outside metropolitan areas] annexed territory containing 8.8 million persons at the end of the decade" (Shryock, "Some Results of the 1960 Census of the United States," *Population Index,* 27 [July, 1961], 219).

15. United States Bureau of the Census, "Population of Standard Metropolitan Statistical Areas 1960 and 1950," *op. cit.,* p. 4.

16. Using housing and school data for New York City, A. F. Parrott has argued that "The Flight to the Suburbs Slackens," in *Proceedings of the Social Statistics Section, American Statistical Association, 1960* (Washington, D.C.: American Statistical Association, 1960), pp. 152–58 (see also Philip M. Hauser, *Population Perspectives* [New Brunswick, N.J.: Rutgers University Press, 1960], p. 115).

17. Otis Dudley Duncan, "Human Ecology and Population Studies," in Philip M. Hauser and Otis Dudley Duncan (eds.), *The Study of Population* (Chicago: University of Chicago Press, 1959), p. 697.

18. In an oral discussion of this paper, Kingsley Davis pointed out that growth by political annexation represents an approximation of the actual spread of the physical city and that the demographer's proclivity for holding area constant tends to ignore this fact. Cities grow outward (in area) as well as upward (in density), but there is still no satisfactory model that accommodates both types of increase (see Edward Gross, "The Role of Density as a Factor in Metropolitan Growth in the United States of America," *Population Studies,* 8 [November, 1954], 113–20).

Part Three

The Functions and Growth of Suburbs

CHAPTER 7, which first appeared in *Social Forces*, Volume 36 (December, 1957), pp. 121–27, attempts to revive an ecological distinction between types of suburb that can be found in the earlier literature dealing with the subject. It advances a distinction between "satellites," or subcenters devoted to employment, and "suburbs" as they are more commonly conceived, i.e., as subcenters devoted more narrowly to residence.

Chapter 8 is a study which documents the importance of maintaining a clear distinction between employing and residential suburbs when one considers the simple demographic phenomenon of population growth. It was first published in the *American Sociological Review*, Volume 22 (April, 1957), pp. 165–73. The growth differentials observed between these two types of suburb—even in the face of a number of controls—offer rather clear evidence of the fact that growth experience was markedly influenced by function. The ecological base of the suburb, then, had a great deal to do with its demographic experience during the 1940's.

Chapter 9 brings this matter up to date through the use of 1960 census materials. It is shown that suburban population growth in the 1950's continued to be influenced by the functional bases of the suburbs themselves. This study first appeared in *Sociological Quarterly*, Volume 4 (Spring, 1963), pp. 122–34. It also uses other census materials to construct distinctive "profiles" of satellites and suburbs as of 1960.

Finally, Chapter 10 introduces another dimension of suburban morphology—the political. It shows a systematic series of differences between suburbs governed under different forms. Co-authored by Robert R. Alford, Chapter 10 was originally published in the *Administrative Science Quarterly*, Volume 8 (June, 1963), pp. 1–17.

Chapter 7

Satellites
and Suburbs

INTRODUCTION

THE PURPOSES of this paper are threefold: (*1*) to set forth an explicit distinction between two types of metropolitan subcenter—suburbs and satellites; (*2*) to summarize presently available information on these two basic types; and (*3*) to suggest some important and immediate implications for research that seem to follow from these considerations.

SUBURBS VERSUS SATELLITES

The distinction made here cannot be claimed as original. In a book published over forty years ago, Taylor discussed the unique functional position of "satellite cities." Such places were recognized by Taylor as basically subordinate to larger centers, yet retaining a high degree of independence stemming from their importance as production and employment centers.[1] It was Douglass, however, who first made this distinction in clearcut terms when he discussed two broad types labelled "suburbs of production" and "suburbs of consumption."[2]

By "suburbs of production," Douglass referred to the type of subcenter discussed by Taylor—the satellite offering employment for at least its own residents, and frequently for other commuting workers as well. By "suburbs of consumption," Douglass referred to the suburb as it is described in its popular connotation, i.e., as a "dormitory town" or "bedroom city." The key functions of such subcenters are not production or employment, but rather the provision of residential amenities. They serve, in a sense, as reservoirs of the manpower required to staff the productive enterprises in the central city, in satellite employing places, and elsewhere.

In one form or another, this distinction has gained some currency. In a 1943 article on "Suburbs," Chauncy Harris claimed that "the commonest types of suburb are housing or dormitory suburbs and manufacturing or industrial suburbs."[3] More recently, Reiss has noted that "suburbs often are polarized as 'residential' and 'industrial suburbs,' the residential suburb being considered the modal type."[4] Despite this seeming agreement, a careful and systematic definition has yet to become established among sociologists. As Shryock has indicated, "in the literature, *suburb* is used almost as loosely by the social scientist as by the layman. . . . We badly need some basic concepts here to guide our operational definitions."[5]

The most logically conceived set of definitions appears to be the one recently outlined by Walter T. Martin. To quote Martin at length,

> In general, the term "suburb" refers to the relatively small but formally structured community adjacent to and dependent upon a large central city . . . Certain features of suburban communities may be designated as definitive characteristics. These are the characteristics essential to suburban status. In combination they differentiate invariably between suburban and non-suburban communities. The two definitive characteristics treated first are a unique ecological position in relation to a larger city and a high rate of commuting to that city. . . .
>
> *Ecological position*—By definition *suburban areas,* however sub-categorized, are *primarily residential areas* having a peculiar location; that is, they are farther away from the center of the

major city than urban neighborhoods but closer than rural
neighborhoods. They lie outside the limits of the central city
but remain dependent upon the city as a source of necessary
goods and services. The ecological position thus differs from
both urban and rural positions. . . .

Commuting—Commuting to work, the second definitive
characteristic of suburbs, is a direct outgrowth of the ecological
position. Thus communities located adjacent to larger urban
centers but *providing jobs for their own residents as well as
others* are classified as *satellite cities* rather than suburbs. . . .[6]

Taking Martin's core definitions as a basis, it seems desirable
to make explicit some of the outstanding structural and functional differences between the two types.

Structure. In *spatial* terms, both suburbs and satellites are
often physically indistinguishable from adjacent areas, hemmed
in on all sides by other municipalities. Many of these subcenters, of course, were originally independent and self-contained cities in their own right; now engulfed by the expanding
metropolis, they have somehow resisted annexation and have re-
tained at least political autonomy. Other suburbs and satellites
apparently had their origin in the exhaustion of space in the
nearby central city, developing as the metropolis spilled over
its former boundaries. Yet they are treated as separate legal
entities.[7] Whatever their past history, however, *all* suburbs and
satellites have one structural feature in common. Although
they are treated as separate units for a limited range of purposes, including the reporting of data, *they are themselves
merely constituent parts of a larger urban complex*—the metropolitan structure as a whole.

The structure of suburbs and satellites can also be treated
in *temporal* terms.[8] Like other parts of the entire metropolitan
area, they represent *sources* and *destinations* of the internal circulation of commodities and people that makes up the daily
rhythm of community activity. It is at this point, however,
that the two types can be distinguished most clearly. We can
say that *goods and services* tend to flow out of the *employing
satellites* to other areas (both local and non-local), while *persons* are attracted into these areas for employment. On the

other hand, *residential suburbs* send out *workers* and tend to receive an influx of *goods and services* for consumption by their inhabitants. These are the major components of the daily ebb and flow of movement that gives the whole metropolitan community its temporal organization.

Functions—The general functions of the two types of subcenter can thus be conceived as polar in nature. Stated in most succinct terms, (*1*) *residential suburbs are suppliers of labor and consumers of commodities.* Conversely, (*2*) *employing satellites are consumers of labor and suppliers of commodities.* This conception is in accord with Douglass' original idea that manufacturing subcenters represent the decentralization of production, while residential suburbs manifest the decentralization of consumption.

CHARACTERISTICS OF SUBURBS AND SATELLITES

Assuming the validity of this simple dichotomy, the first question that occurs is the sheer number of subcenters of each type that may be found within metropolitan areas. Here we are able to draw upon two studies using essentially similar methodology. Kneedler presented an "economic base" classification of all of the incorporated places of 10,000 or more inhabitants lying within the Metropolitan Districts defined in the 1940 census.[9] In this study, 160 "dormitory" suburbs were identified, together with 173 satellite subcenters, with the latter classified according to their major economic functions (manufacturing, retail trade, wholesale trade, mining, education, and government). The same general economic types were recognized in a follow-up study by Jones, who classified 183 suburbs and 180 satellites lying within the Standard Metropolitan Areas identified in the 1950 census.[10]

Despite minor differences in the operational definitions used by Kneedler and Jones, the two studies yield the same general picture. First of all, the relative balance between the two types appears to have been similar at both dates, with satellites slightly outnumbering suburbs at the earlier date. However, it must be remembered that these data refer only to incorporated places of 10,000 and over; other data (to be presented below) suggest that satellites tend to be larger in size than suburbs. Thus if the data were available for the full size range of subcenters, it is probable that residential suburbs would predominate numerically,

Secondly, with respect to the *economic bases* of satellites, both studies reveal that the overwhelming majority (81 percent in 1940 and 77 percent in 1950) are manufacturing subcenters. The next most frequent major activity is retail trade (12 percent in 1940 and 18 percent in 1950). Mining is the major function of only a few metropolitan satellites, while areas in which wholesale trade, education, and government predominate are even more infrequent.[11]

In general, then, employing satellites are typically industrial subcenters, so that their characterization as producing places seems most appropriate. Unfortunately, these studies give us no detailed information on the economic activities predominating in residential suburbs. However, it can be generally stated that the bulk of employment that does occur in this type of subcenter lies in the general categories of retail trade and services—particularly in the lines that are relatively inexpensive and frequently needed by a residential population.

The economic characteristics of these subcenters serve to document the basic distinction under discussion. But what of the other characteristics of the two major types? Are there any other general features that serve to distinguish between them? Fortunately, the use of Jones' classification of 1950 metropolitan subcenters allowed the present writer to make a summary comparison of the two basic types. At the risk of oversimplification, the results of that study can be summarized very briefly.[12]

In general, *employing satellites* tend to be concentrated in the heavily industrialized areas of the Northeastern and North Central regions. They appear relatively more frequently in the metropolitan areas with smaller central cities, but they tend themselves to be larger than residential suburbs. Satellites also tend to be older than suburbs. Although satellites appear throughout the metropolitan area, they are more frequently found beyond the limits of the densely settled urban core. As distance from the central city increases, in fact, satellites are found with relatively greater frequency. Finally, these employing satellites are typically characterized by low rent levels.

In contrast, *residential suburbs* are distinctly different, although they are found in the metropolitan areas of all the major regions. They tend to appear with increasing relative frequency near larger central cities, but they are themselves smaller than satellites. Residential suburbs predominate among the more recently incorporated subcenters. Very few of them lie either outside the densely occupied urbanized area or farther than 30 miles from the central city. Finally, rents are higher than average in these residential suburbs.

These data throw further light on the nature of satellites and suburbs, and they also serve to underscore the utility of the distinction. Still further insights can be gained, however, by a closer look at more detailed data on *the characteristics of the populations* occupying these two types of place. At this point we can draw upon a case study of the Chicago Metropolitan District (1940) by Dornbusch.[13] Dornbusch used the basic dichotomy discussed here, further subdividing residential suburbs according to rent level. However, rather than discuss the detailed comparisons between the three resulting types, we will continue to confine our attention to the major differences between satellites and suburbs in general.

Dornbusch's research shows that residents of Chicago satellites tend to have lower average education, and they contain higher proportions of foreign-born whites. In the matter of housing, these employing satellites exhibit lower average rent levels, they have higher proportions of tenant-occupied dwellings, and they have higher proportions of crowded dwellings. The satellites appear to have slightly higher fertility than residential suburbs. In fact, the satellites contain somewhat younger populations. In terms of occupational make-up, roughly two out of three of the employed residents of satellites are found in the "blue-collar" categories, as contrasted with one out of three in the suburban population. At the same time, a somewhat smaller percentage of persons is found to be employed in satellites.

In general, the images that emerge from Dornbusch's results are those of two rather clearly contrasting types: (1) *employing satellites containing younger populations of lower than average socioeconomic status*—as measured by educational, ethnic, residential, and occupational variables; and (2) *residential suburbs containing slightly older populations of higher than average socioeconomic status*. Suggestive as these data may be, it must be remembered that they refer to the suburbs and satellites of only one Metropolitan District in 1940. However, the conceptual significance of the results—together with the relative simplicity of the methodology employed— would seem to recommend replication for other areas and more recent periods.

SATELLITE AND SUBURBAN GROWTH

Having reviewed the relative numbers of satellites and suburbs, as well as some of their more distinctive characteristics, we may now turn to the matter of their relative rates of growth in recent years.

A study by Harris provides information for the 1930–1940 decade. On the basis of an examination of growth rates in all places of 10,000 and over in 11 Metropolitan Districts, Harris reported that the growth rates of residential suburbs (average 11.7 percent) were well in excess of the rates found in industrial satellites (average 1.7 percent).[14]

A more recent study by the present writer revealed that the same general tendency persisted in the 1940–1950 decade. Suburban growth (average 31.9 percent) was well in excess of that of satellites (average 17.0 percent). This study covered all of the suburbs and satellites of 10,000 and over in all of the Standard Metropolitan Areas of the United States, and the relatively large number of cases (416) permitted the successive control of a number of relevant variables.

On the average, suburbs grew faster than satellites in all

regions, in all central city size classes, in all satellite and sub-urban size classes, in all concentric distance zones, and in metro-politan areas of every major type of economic activity. One minor exception appeared when rent level was controlled, for the prevailing differential was reversed in the high-rent cate-gory. The only major reversal was found when suburbs were classified according to their dates of incorporation; the differ-ential in favor of residential suburbs was found to characterize only the older places, i.e., those incorporated before 1900. Thus the control of six out of seven relevant factors did not alter the over-all pattern of growth differentials in any significant re-spect. Suburban growth appears to have continued well in ex-cess of that of satellites in the most recent intercensal decade.

These findings may be viewed as reflections of a funda-mental alteration of metropolitan organization in the direction of greater functional and territorial complexity. In many re-spects, it can be argued that these growth differentials simply mirror the changing distribution of housing opportunities emerging as a result of new patterns of building activity in these areas.

Residential suburbs appear to be growing more rapidly be-cause they are becoming even more residential in character, by means of large increments in housing construction. At the same time, employing satellites appear to be growing less rapidly because they—like the central cities themselves—are becoming more *exclusively* devoted to industry and other em-ployment-producing activities. In these employing satellites, the process of land-use conversion—from residential to indus-trial, commercial, and transportation uses—is apparently (*1*) driving out pre-existent residential uses of land and (*2*) dis-couraging new construction of housing.[15]

RESEARCH IMPLICATIONS

The first research question that presents itself concerns the *source* of these growth differentials. However, "source" can be taken to mean either of two things. First of all, we can pose the question in broad demographic terms, by asking "what are the relative contributions of natural increase and net migration to these observed differentials?" In addition, we can ask about the areal or geographic sources of the migrants contributing to the growth of suburbs and satellites. The question then becomes "what are the relative sizes of migrant streams from (1) the central city, (2) other suburbs, satellites, and nearby fringe areas, and areas outside the metropolitan community in question?" Both of these detailed questions are in need of answers. Moreover, the basic distinction between suburbs and satellites should be kept in the forefront of the analysis, for these two types appear to differ with respect to the relative importance of natural increase and net migration, and they may also differ with respect to the geographic sources of persons migrating to them.

Demographic sources of growth—The data from Dornbusch's study of Chicago suburbs and satellites might suggest that natural increase contributes more importantly to the growth of satellites than to suburbs. After all, his data indicate that satellites have higher fertility ratios. In addition, satellites tend to have lower proportions of persons over 65 years of age, so that they might be expected to have lower death rates.

However, the apparent trends in population growth and residential construction in metropolitan areas suggest that this hypothesis be given more elaboration. On the basis of a preliminary analysis of the growth of satellites and suburbs between 1940 and 1950, it appears that natural increase may indeed be especially important to the typical satellite because it offsets net losses of migrants. In other words, satellites may be able to exhibit growth only because of recent high rates of natural increase. Suburbs, on the other hand, appear to be growing more rapidly from *both* demographic sources—natural increase and net in-migration. Thus it appears that employing satellites—which are *functionally* similar to the central city, in that they draw workers from other areas—are also highly similar to the metropolis in their sources of growth.[16]

Geographic sources of growth—Unfortunately, available census data do not permit investigation of the detailed geographic sources of recent migrants to satellites and suburbs.

The 1950 census data on migrants are coded in categories (based on county units) that are inappropriate to the type of study needed here. For the moment, we will have to be content with inferences drawn from scattered case studies and older census data.

Case studies of outlying areas indicate that the popular notion of "decentralization" as simply a "flight from the city" is a gross oversimplification.[17] In addition, studies by Thompson and Hawley, based upon 1935–1940 migration data, show that a substantial component of metropolitan ring growth comes from other areas.[18] Much of this growth—which may be labelled "accretion at the periphery" in contrast to outward relocation from the city—must have taken place in satellites and suburbs, as well as in the "fringe" and open country.

It seems feasible to use the sample survey technique in studies focussed *specifically* upon the geographic sources of migrants to suburbs and satellites. In view of the lack of appropriate census data on this question, such case studies will probably remain the major source of our information for some time.

The question of classification—We need more data on daily commuting (recurrent movements) as well as migration (nonrecurrent movements). In fact, a major research question concerns the very basis of the distinction between these two functional types of area. Up to this time, we have had to depend upon manipulation of census data in order to classify subcenters in these terms. The work of Harris, Kneedler, and Jones has been particularly ingenious, but deficiencies in the basic data reduce the potential value of their contributions.

In *theory*, the types developed by these writers depend essentially upon a comparison of (1) the number of employed people *living* in a given area with (2) the number of people *working* in that area. This is basically a question of "day-time" versus "night-time" population, for suburbs and satellites are dispersing and attracting areas in the daily ebb and flow of movement. Subordinate centers that attract more workers every day than the number of people who sleep there every night are labelled satellites, while those having substantially more residents than jobs are classified as suburbs.

In *practice*, however, many difficulties are encountered in the use of census data in classifying particular areas in these terms. For one thing, the requisite data on employment (the number of jobs in a given area) are not generally available for smaller places—those under 10,000 inhabitants. Moreover, the data for larger places are inadequate in many respects. The employment data have been derived from the Censuses of Business and Manufacturing, while the numbers of employed residents have been drawn from the Population Census. The discrepancy in the very dates of these censuses (e.g., 1947, 1948, and 1950), means that inaccuracies enter the final results. Annexation comprises a major source of difficulties. In addition, any substantial change in employment opportunities or in available housing between these dates can seriously distort the basic "employment-residence ratio." The statistics for the numerator and the denominator of this ratio refer to different time periods, and changes in either element can artificially raise or lower the true value of the ratio. Still another weakness is the fact that all job categories have not been included in the computation of the ratio.

Many of these difficulties may be surmounted in the forthcoming population census. It seems almost a certainty that the 1960 census will contain a question on the individual's place of work. It remains to be seen, however, whether the Census Bureau will be able to present tabulations in sufficient detail to permit the accurate classification of individual suburbs and satellites in these terms. Considerations of cost will undoubtedly prohibit full detail for smaller places, and other priorities will inevitably compete for the funds available. In view of these considerations—and mindful of the additional fact that published census data are at least five years away—we might do better to consider alternative sources of data.

Because the fundamental distinction between satellites and suburbs is essentially a question of commuting flows, our attention is immediately drawn to traffic data as a possible source of information. "Origin-and-destination" data available from sample studies permit the identification of satellites and sub-urbs in a number of metropolitan areas. Punchcards for individual workers contain information on place of employment and place of residence, together with other characteristics. All work-trips to a given satellite or suburb can simply be tabulated by the place of residence of the workers. The simple balance between residents and job opportunities yields an identification of the two main types of subcenter discussed here. In addition, detailed information can be gained on main streams of commuters, and the direction of these streams throughout the entire area—centripetal, centrifugal, and lateral. Furthermore, the characteristics of the workers in these various commuting streams can be compared.

In summary, these detailed commuting data can be used to identify individual suburbs and satellites according to their basic type in many metropolitan areas. Comparison of such results with those derived from analysis of census data should be particularly interesting. In addition, these commuting data will yield information that is not presently available from census sources.

CONCLUSION

As Woodbury has observed, "dormitory towns are only one species of suburb."[19] This paper calls attention to the available evidence supporting a fundamental distinction between satellites (employing sub-centers) and suburbs (residential sub-centers). However, it may well be that these two types are too broadly defined for many research purposes. Dornbusch's study indicates that rent level is another variable of real significance, while Martin suggests population size and density as additional criteria. The demographic source of growth may even be an important distinguishing characteristic. On the face of it, it seems that a place growing or maintaining its size by natural increase might be significantly different from one expanding mainly via net migration.

Whetten has argued that "there is need for further identification and classification of suburban populations into meaningful groupings or community types."[20] The present writer can only agree—hoping that this chapter will help to fill this gap in our knowledge of metropolitan areas. But there are other gaps to be closed. A single example will suffice. One closely related concept that has been ignored in this presentation is that of the "fringe." Although it is used with increasing frequency, there is still little agreement on the fundamental meaning that should be assigned to the term. However, if we are careful to build upon the theoretical and research foundations already established, it should not be too long before we have a much more complete understanding of the structure and functions of the metropolitan area and *all* of its constituent parts.

NOTES

1. Graham R. Taylor, *Satellite Cities* (New York and London: D. Appleton and Co., 1915).

2. Harlan Paul Douglass, *The Suburban Trend* (New York and London: The Century Co., 1925), pp. 74–92. See also his article, "Suburbs," in *The Encyclopaedia of the Social Sciences* (New York: The Macmillan Co., 1934), XIV, pp. 433–35. This distinction can also be found in Louis Wirth, "Urbanism as a Way of Life," *American Journal of Sociology*, 44 (July 1938), pp. 1–24, and in C. D. Harris and E. L. Ullman, "The Nature of Cities," *The Annals*, 242 (November 1945), pp. 7–17.

3. C. D. Harris, "Suburbs," *American Journal of Sociology*, 49 (May 1943), p. 6.

4. Albert J. Reiss, Jr., "Research Problems in Metropolitan Population Redistribution," *American Sociological Review*, 21 (October 1956), p. 575.

5. Henry S. Shryock, Jr., "Population Redistribution within Metropolitan Areas: Evaluation of Research," *Social Forces*, 35 (December 1956), pp. 155–56.

6. Walter T. Martin, "The Structuring of Social Relationships Engendered by Suburban Residence," *American Sociological Review*, 21 (August 1956), pp. 447–48; italics added. A highly similar—though less detailed—distinction was previously outlined by Harris and Ullman, as follows: "Satellites differ from suburbs in that they are separated from the central city by many miles and in general have little daily commuting to or from the central city, although economic activities of the satellite are closely geared to those of the central city." Chauncy D. Harris and Edward L. Ullman, "The Nature of Cities," *The Annals*, 242 (November 1945), pp. 7–17.

7. These diverse historical origins comprise a key dimension in an interesting typology of suburbs developed by Stuart A. Queen and David

B. Carpenter. See *The American City* (New York: McGraw-Hill Book Co., 1953), pp. 116–31.

8. For a complete discussion of the temporal aspect of community structure, see Amos H. Hawley, *Human Ecology* (New York: The Ronald Press, 1950), pp. 288–316.

9. Grace M. Kneedler, "Functional Types of Cities," *Public Management*, 27 (July 1945), pp. 197–203; reprinted in Paul K. Hatt and Albert J. Reiss, Jr. (eds.), *Reader in Urban Sociology* (Glencoe: The Free Press, 1951), pp. 49–57.

10. Victor Jones, "Economic Classification of Cities and Metropolitan Areas," in *The Municipal Year Book 1953* (Chicago: The International City Managers' Association, 1953), pp. 49–57.

11. It is rather interesting to note the specialties in which few satellites are represented—transportation, and resort, retirement, and recreational services. These functions are more likely to be found in independent cities, far from metropolitan centers.

12. Leo F. Schnore, "The Functions of Metropolitan Suburbs," *American Journal of Sociology*, 61 (March 1956), pp. 453–58.

13. Sanford M. Dornbusch, "A Typology of Suburban Communities: Chicago Metropolitan District, 1940," Urban Analysis Report No. 10 (University of Chicago: Chicago Community Inventory, May 1952). Wirth long ago presented the notion that "A one-industry city will present *different sets of social characteristics* from a multi-industry city, as will . . . *a suburb from a satellite, a residential suburb from an industrial suburb* . . ." See Louis Wirth, "Urbanism as a Way of Life," *American Journal of Sociology*, 44 (July 1938), pp. 1–24; italics added.

14. C. D. Harris, *op. cit.*

15. See Leo F. Schnore, "The Growth of Metropolitan Suburbs," *American Sociological Review*, 22 (April 1957), pp. 165–73. It might also be noted here that this general process of land-use conversion has yet to run its course. See Dorothy K. Newman, "Metropolitan Area Structure and Growth as Shown by Building-Permit Statistics," *Business Topics*, 4 (November 1956), pp. 1–7.

16. This analysis was confined to the suburbs and satellites of 10,000 and over in the five largest Standard Metropolitan Areas (New York, Chicago, Los Angeles, Philadelphia, and Detroit), and utilized the general method described in detail in Donald J. Bogue and Emerson Seim, "Components of Population Change in Suburban and Central City Populations of Standard Metropolitan Areas: 1940 to 1950," *Rural Sociology*, 21 (September-December 1956), pp. 267–75. In this study, Bogue and Seim present compelling evidence to the effect that recent central city growth was largely a function of natural increase, high enough to offset migration losses. This reverses the long-term situation, in which net in-migration offset extremely low rates of natural increase or even natural decrease. Ideally, of course, suburbs and satellites should be compared with *parts* of the central city, rather than with the central city as a whole. (See Reiss, *op. cit.*) It should also be noted that *individual* suburbs and satellites exhibit considerable variation within each of these types. Much of this variation may be due to variations in size, age, location, and other characteristics that were not controlled here. One major difficulty that has yet to be surmounted in studies of suburban growth stems from

a lack of appropriate data; there are no reliable statistics on the amount of vacant land available for residential development in sub-centers throughout the nation.

17. See Myles W. Rodehaver, "Fringe Settlement as a Two-Directional Movement," *Rural Sociology*, 12 (March 1947), pp. 49–57; Walter T. Martin, *The Rural-Urban Fringe* (Eugene: University of Oregon Press, 1953), pp. 60–63; Wendell Bell, "Familism and Suburbanization," *Rural Sociology*, 21 (September-December 1956), pp. 276–83.

18. Warren S. Thompson, *Migration Within Ohio, 1935–40* (Oxford, Ohio: Scripps Foundation for Research in Population Problems, 1951); Amos H. Hawley, *Intrastate Migration in Michigan, 1935–40* (Ann Arbor: Institute of Public Administration, University of Michigan, 1953).

19. Coleman Woodbury, "Suburbanization and Suburbia," *American Journal of Public Health*, 45 (January 1955), p. 2.

20. Nathan L. Whetten, "Suburbanization as a Field for Sociological Research," *Rural Sociology*, 16 (December 1951), p. 325.

Chapter 8

The Growth of
Metropolitan Suburbs

DECENTRALIZATION is clearly one of the most significant movements in the long history of urban communities. In the United States the shift to the suburbs began around a few large cities toward the close of the nineteenth century,[1] but it is no longer confined to a mere handful of super–cities. As time has passed, the outward thrust of urban population has become characteristic of smaller and smaller places, and there is no indication that the movement is abating.

Fortunately, social scientists have charted the major trends involved in this suburban revolution during recent decades. The careful historical studies by Thompson, Bogue, and Hawley have described the outstanding population shifts from the turn of the century to the most recent census.[2] They show the principal patterns of growth in the major geographic com-

Revised version of paper read at the annual meeting of the American Sociological Society, September, 1956. The data presented in this report were initially assembled while the writer held a Research Training Fellowship from the Social Science Research Council.

ponents of the metropolitan area as a whole, and though they concentrate on comparisons *between* the central city and its surrounding ring, they also show patterns of re-distribution *within* these broad areas.

Within the framework provided by these extensive studies of decentralization, two major tasks remain: (1) intensive research filling in the *descriptive* details of the suburban movement, and (2) refinement of a general theory making greater *analytical* sense out of the facts assembled. This report is part of a larger study undertaken in accordance with these broad objectives.

On the descriptive side, this report has a narrow focus. Growth rates for a single decade (1940–1950) are shown for only the larger incorporated places (10,000 and over) lying within the the rings of the Standard Metropolitan Areas of the United States.[3] On the conceptual side, the paper has broader scope, exploring the relationship between the growth and the functions of these larger suburbs.

The Functions of Urban Areas—Theoretically, urban areas are usually conceived as large and dense concentrations of people engaged in nonagricultural functions. Since they cannot be self-sufficient, they must produce some goods and/or services for exchange, i.e., for consumption by another population. Urban areas differ widely in the major functions that they discharge, and the literature contains a large number of urban typologies in which places are classified according to their "basic" functions.[4] Internally, however, every urban place must maintain a substantial complement of persons employed in the ancillary activities that provide for the requirements of the inhabitants directly engaged in its major industries. Thus no matter what the principal export it produces, every urban area must allocate a certain portion of its activities to "nonbasic" maintenance functions.[5]

Urban Population Growth—Existing urban theory holds that population growth and the major functions of a given area are definitely related. Urban population is assumed to have a functional base, for the very support of the population of a particular place is thought to depend upon its participation in an extensive set of exchange relationships. Population growth requires an increase in this participation, with a corresponding expansion of economic opportunities. Relative differences in the spatial distribution of these opportunities are thought to be the major influences operating to bring about changes in population distribution by determining the size and the direction of migrant streams.[6]

In this theoretical context, a number of writers have recently spoken of a so-called "multiplier principle" to describe the dynamics of urban population growth. Stated in simplified form, the principle is that (1) increasing economic opportunities in "basic" industries cause population growth; (2) population growth, in turn, causes further increases in employment opportunities—this time in the "nonbasic" industries—so that (3) still further increments are added to the total population of the area.[7]

On the whole, available theory offers a coherent set of hypotheses regarding urban population growth. Urban growth is related to urban functions in a remarkably clear-cut fashion. Moreover, empirical studies of large areal units have indicated a high degree of predictive power for this conceptual approach.[8]

Suburbs, however, pose a different population-growth problem. The relationships between growth and function, as stated for urban areas in general, are not immediately evident when suburbs are examined.

The Functions of Suburbs—Suburbs obviously differ widely in the functions that they discharge. In the traditional popular image, the suburb is little more than the dwelling place of people who work in the central city. While it is correct to characterize many suburbs as literally "dormitory towns" and "bedroom cities," a true picture of metropolitan suburbs must not ignore the fact that many of them are far from exclusively residential areas. Some are primarily devoted to the fabrication of manufactured goods. At the present time, for example, both light and heavy industries are the dominant elements in the functioning of some suburbs in every part of the country. Industrial suburbs, in fact, have a long history.[9] Still other suburbs are basically given over to the provision of specialized services of one kind or another—notably education and recreation—and it is even possible to find suburbs primarily dependent upon extractive industries, such as mining and oil production. In an economic sense, then, the range of specialties found among suburbs approaches that discoverable in other cities.

Despite this wide variation in specific functions, however, a strong case has been made in the literature for the recognition of only two major types of suburb—*industrial* and *residential*. Douglass, an observer of an earlier phase of suburban development, saw these as the two types most apparent in the 'twenties.[10] Moreover, this view was also adopted by Harris, despite the fact that he developed a detailed six-part suburban typology. "The commonest types of suburb," he wrote in 1943, "are housing or dormitory suburbs and manufacturing or industrial suburbs."[11]

More generally, suburbs can be identified as *residential* and *employing*. Centers of employment mainly devoted to education, mining, recreation, etc. may be combined with those concentrating in manufacturing. Such places may be called *employing suburbs*, no matter what their specific products may be. They can be contrasted with *residential suburbs*, which employ relatively few people within their own boundaries. The basis for this distinction is whether or not the suburb draws more workers to its confines every day than the number of working people who sleep there every night. These two types of suburb are "attracting" and "dispersing" areas, reflecting the shift between day-time and night-time population.[12]

Suburban Population Growth—Existing theory tends to assume that both types of suburb, like other urban areas, grow primarily in response to an expansion of employment opportunities, particularly in the so-called "basic" industries. On theoretical grounds, however, they would not be expected to grow equally. Since the employing suburb has a net excess of jobs, it offers more economic opportunities, and it should logically exhibit higher rates of growth than the residential suburb. The only immediately relevant findings from prior research are to be found in a study by Harris, in which growth rates between 1930 and 1940 were reported for the suburbs in eleven large Metropolitan Districts. "Among individual suburbs of more than 10,000 population," according to Harris, "those classified as residential averaged 11.7 per cent increase in population, compared to 1.7 per cent for those classified as industrial."[13]

In the present study, a similar differential was found for the 1940–1950 decade. The rate for all residential suburbs (31.9 per cent) was almost twice that for all employing suburbs (17.0 per cent). Although this differential is not so large as that reported by Harris, it is in the same direction, i.e., in favor of the residential suburbs.

Moreover, this differential tends to persist when other relevant factors are held constant. The limited number of cases prohibits simultaneous control in a cross-tabular format, but successive controls can be applied.[14]

Horizontal examination of Table 1 shows that residential suburbs tended to grow faster than employing suburbs in all regions (*Panel A*), in all central city size classes (*Panel B*), in all suburban size classes (*Panel C*), in all concentric distance zones (*Panel D*), and in metropolitan areas of every major type of economic activity (*Panel E*).

Only one exception appears in *Panel F*, where the prevailing differential is reversed in one of the three rental classes, i.e., among high-rent suburbs. The only major reversal is found in *Panel G*, where suburbs are classified according to their dates of incorporation. The differential in favor of residential suburbs is seen to characterize only the older suburbs, i.e., those incorporated before 1900.[15]

These data are difficult to interpret in terms of economic opportunities. On first examination, the growth rates of *employing* suburbs in the past two decades might appear to support the theory. The very low average rate of growth between 1930 and 1940 can be viewed as nothing more than the result of the severe limitations on manufacturing activity that occurred during this depression decade. In turn, the resumption of substantial industrial activity between 1940 and 1950 might seem to account for the ten-fold increase in growth rates in this type of suburb.

By definition, the employing suburb does offer economic opportunities, since it provides jobs for more than the number of local residents who are employed. Still, the subordinate status of many employing suburbs prevents them from enjoying full autonomy with respect to growth. For example, employing suburbs that provide goods and services primarily for the central city are necessarily sensitive to events occurring there, such as changes in the number of inhabitants of the metropolis, or changes in its income level. At best, then, the theory offers an incomplete explanation of growth in employing suburbs.

However, if the existing theory of urban growth meets resistance in the case of employing suburbs, *residential* suburbs are even less amenable to it. The higher average rates of growth in these suburbs during both of the last two decades can hardly be attributed to an expansion of economic opportunities within their own boundaries. It must be remembered that the residential suburb itself employs relatively few people within its own confines, and these chiefly in such "nonbasic" activities as retail trade and services. As indicated above, increases in these "nonbasic" employment opportunities are commonly treated, within the very framework of the theory, as themselves dependent upon local population growth.

More important, residential suburbs are intrinsically dependent upon other areas. With respect to population growth, almost nothing that can occur within the boundaries of such a suburb is potentially as significant as changes that may occur in the other areas that employ its residents. In the light of these considerations, existing theory falls far short of explaining overall suburban growth, and it fails entirely to account for growth differentials between types of suburb.

Limitations of Existing Theory—Why should the available theory offer so much in explaining growth differentials between large areas (e.g. regions) and fail to explain growth differentials between suburbs? The first major difficulty encountered by the theory in the case of suburbs stems from the fact

Table 1—Growth Rates in Metropolitan Suburbs of 10,000 or More Inhabitants, by Functional Type and Other Characteristics

Selected Characteristics of Metropolitan Suburbs	PER CENT INCREASE IN POPULATION, 1940–50			NUMBER OF SUBURBS		
	Residential	Employing	All Suburbs	Residential	Employing	All Suburbs
A. Regional location						
Northeast	13.3	6.1	8.1	65	110	175
North Central	30.0	17.1	22.8	65	57	122
West	63.6	47.1	53.1	37	43	80
South	77.4	47.4	60.4	20	19	39
B. Central city size						
500,000 or more	27.8	12.4	18.2	136	142	278
100,000–500,000	36.1	13.8	21.6	32	40	72
Less than 100,000	79.5	36.9	42.9	19	47	66
C. Suburban cize						
50,000 or more	15.1	10.0	11.5	17	31	48
25,000–50,000	18.8	14.9	15.8	18	55	73
10,000–25,000	30.9	19.1	24.4	90	102	192
Less than 10,000	104.1	92.6	99.3	62	41	103
D. Distance from central city						
0–10 miles	27.2	16.4	20.8	112	92	204
10–20 miles	40.8	18.2	25.3	61	84	145
20 miles or more	29.4	15.9	18.1	14	53	67

E. Metropolitan area economic base						
Manufacturing	23.6	12.2	16.1	79	105	184
Diversified	33.0	19.3	23.9	89	98	187
Retail	68.9	23.4	39.2	17	23	40
Other	412.7	64.8	103.4	2	3	5
F. Suburban rent level						
Low	31.7	12.8	15.9	7	26	33
Average	29.0	15.1	18.8	91	173	264
High	36.3	44.1	38.4	89	30	119
G. Age of suburb						
More than 50 years	21.8	12.2	15.0	102	178	280
40–50 years	33.1	36.2	34.6	35	31	66
30–40 years	51.8	66.2	57.5	25	12	37
Less than 30 years	116.6	168.5	126.6	25	8	33
All suburbs	31.9	17.0	22.1	187	229	416

that these places are only parts of a larger functional entity, the metropolitan community. The theory of economic opportunities contains a hidden assumption with respect to functional self-containment. As a result, the theory can be valid only for areal units that possess a rather high degree of self-sufficiency. This is apparently the reason for the theory's great explanatory utility in the studies of whole regions and even nations.

Moreover, the theory does not take full account of the increasing flexibility of local transportation in recent decades. Innovations in transportation and communication have permitted community functions to be diffused over a wider territory without loss of contact, and this spatial spread involves an increasing flow of persons between the sites of their various activities. The significance of commuting for population growth is that it may supplant migration as an adjustment on the part of the local labor force to shifting or declining opportunities for employment.[16] As a consequence, residential areas may continue to grow as long as employment opportunities continue to expand anywhere within an extremely broad commuting radius.

It can hardly be said that transportation improvements have been ignored in urban theory. They have received some attention in most discussions of decentralization to be found in the literature. These innovations, however, have been conceived as little more than permissive factors. They are generally said to have set the conditions under which suburban growth could occur. Other factors are undoubtedly at work, but these other factors are increasingly sought in a rather narrow sphere.

Most analysts who have devoted attention to the subject of suburbanization have apparently assumed that the causes of the centrifugal shift are ultimately to be found in the motives of the individuals involved in the movement. Even the human ecologists, who are often thought to be "anti-psychological," are prone to shift to motivational explanations when it comes to suburbanization. In keeping with a general tendency within our discipline, social psychology is coming to supplant the sociological approach in this problem area.

Thus while stressing the key role of economic opportunities

for larger units, such as regions, most writers turn to an analysis of the motives of individual migrants in dealing with decentralization within local areas. Such a procedure rests upon the tacit assumption that explanations of growth in areas of different size must somehow require entirely different approaches, involving different units of analysis and a different range of variables.

It might appear that the evidence presented here offers additional support for such a procedure. After all, the theory—as it has been stated for urban areas in general—clearly fails to account for the observed growth differential in favor of residential suburbs. The results might seem to call for an immediate shift to a social-psychological approach. Indeed, the ultimate explanation may very well lie in the attitudes, motives, values, etc. of the individual involved in this movement. However, there is a theoretical alternative at least worthy of exploration. The admitted weaknesses of the existing theory might better be resolved not by its abandonment but by modification of certain basic concepts.

A Proposed Modification of the Theory

The first step in this direction is to state the conditions under which factors other than narrowly defined economic opportunities might be important in the determination of growth differentials. Rather than to abandon the concept of opportunities, a logical alternative is to expand it to subsume more than employment.

One consideration so fundamental that it is easily overlooked is that the population of any area must have housing and the related amenities of life. Our attention is drawn to the housing factor for a very simple reason: dwelling units must exist in a given area before people can be enumerated there on a *de jure basis*, and before population growth can be recorded in U.S. census statistics.

If the concept of opportunities is broadened to include opportunities for housing, we can propose the following general hypothesis. Within local areas of the metropolitan community, differential population growth is primarily determined by the distribution of differential housing opportunities, and especially by the different patterns of building activity evidenced in various subareas.[17] Within this theoretical context, in which emphasis is placed upon *housing opportunities*, it is possible to develop specific subhypotheses regarding growth differentials between types of suburb. (*1*) Residential suburbs are growing rapidly because they are becoming even more residential in character, by means of large increments in housing construction. (*2*) At the same time, employing suburbs are growing less rapidly because they are becoming more exclusively devoted to industry and other employment-providing activities. In these employing places, the net effect of this increased specialization in production and employment is (*a*) to drive out pre-existent residential uses of land, and (*b*) to discourage new construction of housing.

Indirect evidence in support of these hypotheses can be adduced by considering central cities themselves. The typical central city is obviously undergoing a conversion to a different range of land uses. Formerly the principal place of residence of its own labor force, it is now being turned over to other urban uses—commerce, industry, and transportation. The concomitant of this trend in land-use conversion is the outward shift of population that is reflected in the growth differentials in favor of the metropolitan ring.[18]

The established employing suburbs appear to be undergoing the very same process of land-use conversion. Thus the oldest employing suburbs themselves are evidently decentralizing at a fairly rapid pace, with only their rates of natural increase preventing most of them from suffering absolute losses in population. In fact, the older employing suburbs are probably losing large numbers directly to the residential suburbs via migration.[19]

The Role of Housing—The hypotheses stated above assert that differential housing opportunities are the major determinants of growth differentials between subareas of the metropolitan community. In the interest of complete analysis, we must go on to ask *why* new housing construction is occurring *where* it is, since we are dealing with growth in different types of area.

Here again a social-psychological approach might seem to be in order, since it is obviously individuals who occupy dwellings and who change residences. But it should be pointed out that relatively few people in a metropolitan area choose a site and then have a house "built to order." On the contrary, the typical purchase is "ready-made" in a large development. Very few urban home owners have a hand in the selection of sites where residential construction will take place and control over location is even more limited in the case of renters.

In a complex economy, the choices of building sites are made by contractors, real estate operators, and others, notably those involved in the initial capitalization of new developments. Families and individuals are not decisive agents in the process of land-use conversion.[20] When asked about their residential movements, the "reasons" they offer to an interviewer may be misleading in the extreme.

Like other "choices" the housing decisions of individuals are strictly limited by objective conditions. Among these conditions, which include the timing and placing of available housing facilities, the *location* of dwelling units will continue to receive emphasis here, since we are dealing with growth differentials between types of area. Once again it will be instructive to consider the case of the metropolis itself.[21]

The existing literature contains a number of hypotheses that attempt to account for the rapid expansion of residential construction in the metropolitan ring as a whole, and the limited building activity within the central city. First, high rates of construction at the periphery may simply be a consequence of *the exhaustion of space for residential development* in the central city. There is undoubtedly some merit to this view, but sheer space alone is hardly decisive, since the percentage of vacant land in most large cities is strikingly high.[22] However, a large proportion of this area is unsuitable for residential development for reasons of cost, location, or prohibitive zoning laws. Among these limitations, it seems probable that *the high cost of land* in the central city is particularly significant, acting as a deterrent to residential use.

Less frequently mentioned, but a matter of increasing importance, is the fact that great economies are made possible by *the mass production of housing*. While vacant land within the city itself is considerable in the aggregate, it tends to be split into a multitude of small parcels. The increasing use of mass production methods in constructing dozens or even hundreds of dwelling units at the same time and in the same contiguous area permits large savings to be made by the builders, with mass buying of materials adding still further savings.[23]

However, purely "spatial" or "economic" considerations are not the only factors operating to determine the sites of housing construction. There is also an important sociological factor. It appears that the locations of the *dominant units in the community* set the broad pattern of land use for smaller and less powerful units, such as households. In one sense, this is nothing more than another expression of the relationships already observed between (1) "basic" industries, (2) residential population, and (3) "nonbasic" industries.[24] The re-distribution of residential population must be viewed in a context that recognizes the vital influence of these other factors.

CONCLUSIONS AND IMPLICATIONS

If the hypotheses set forth here have any validity, one important theoretical conclusion is in order. The metropolitan community must be undergoing a process of increasingly specialized land use, in which subareas of the community are devoted more and more exclusively to a limited range of functions. The result of this mounting "territorial differentiation" is increasing segregation, with similar units and similar functions clustering together.[25] At the very least, there is a bifurcation between the broad functions of consumption and production, i.e., between residence and employment,[26] and the real significance of transportation improvements for the local re-distribution of population is in creating a new scale of distance. In this context, the growth differentials discussed here may be interpreted as mere reflections of a fundamental alteration of community organization in the direction of greater functional and territorial complexity.

Technological and organizational changes are apparently crucial in determining both numerical and distributional changes in population. The outward shift of residential population measured in recent studies can be viewed as one aspect of an important modification in the internal organization of the modern urban community. Under the impetus of technological advances in transportation and communication, the compact city is a thing of the past. Increasing territorial differentiation has been made possible by the increasing flexibility of movement within the total community. Urban functions and urban populations are now spread over a greatly expanded area. Such a radical change in the spatial distribution of urban functions and of urban people apparently represents an adaptive response to the changing conditions of modern urban life. In long-range terms, decentralization can be conceived as a shift toward a new equilibrium that was initiated by the development of new facilities for the movement of persons, commodities, and information.

NOTES

1. Adna F. Weber, *The Growth of Cities in the Nineteenth Century*, New York: Macmillan, 1899.

2. Warren S. Thompson, *The Growth of Metropolitan Districts in the United States, 1900–1940*, Washington: Government Printing Office, 1947; Donald J. Bogue, *Population Growth in Standard Metropolitan Areas, 1900–1950*, Washington: Government Printing Office, 1953; Amos H. Hawley, *The Changing Shape of Metropolitan America*, Glencoe: Free Press, 1956.

3. Among the 168 Standard Metropolitan Areas defined in the 1950 Census only 66 contain incorporated suburbs of 10,000 or more inhabitants. Among those with more than one officially-designated central city, only the largest is treated as the central city in this study, with all other places classified as suburbs. Exceptions to this procedure were made in three areas (Allentown-Bethlehem, Pa., Minneapolis-St. Paul, Minn., and Springfield-Holyoke, Mass.) where twin central cities were recognized.

4. See the references cited in Leo F. Schnore, "The Functions of Metropolitan Suburbs," *American Journal of Sociology*, 61 (March, 1956), p. 453.

5. See Otis Dudley Duncan and Albert J. Reiss, Jr., Part IV, "Functional Specialization of Communities," in their *Social Characteristics of Urban and Rural Communities, 1950,* New York: John Wiley, 1956; and John W. Alexander, "The Basic-Nonbasic Concept of Urban Economic Functions," *Economic Geography,* 30 (July, 1954), pp. 246–61.

6. See Amos H. Hawley, *Human Ecology,* New York: Ronald Press, 1950. Population can grow by either natural increase or net migration, but the latter component has served as the major source of over-all urban growth in the past. As a result, the literature on urban growth has understandably stressed migration.

7. For a detailed discussion and further references see John R. P. Friedmann, *The Spatial Structure of Economic Development in the Tennessee Valley,* Chicago: University of Chicago Program of Education and Research in Planning, Research Paper No. 1, 1955.

8. See Harry Jerome, *Migration and Business Cycles,* New York: National Bureau of Economic Research, 1926, and Dorothy S. Thomas, *Social and Economic Aspects of Swedish Population Movements, 1750–1933,* New York: Macmillan Company, 1941.

9. Graham R. Taylor, *Satellite Cities,* New York and London: D. Appleton and Company, 1915.

10. Harlan Paul Douglass, *The Suburban Trend,* New York and London: Century Company, 1925, and "Suburbs," in *The Encyclopaedia of the Social Sciences,* New York: Macmillan Company, 1934, 14, pp. 433–35.

11. Chauncy D. Harris, "Suburbs," *American Journal of Sociology,* 49 (July, 1943), p. 6.

12. This dichotomy is based upon the "employment-residence ratio" computed by Jones for all places of 10,000 or more inhabitants in 1950. It is simply the ratio of (*1*) *the number of people employed in the suburb* in (*a*) manufacturing, (*b*) retail trade, (*c*) wholesale trade, and (*d*) personal, business, and repair services to (*2*) *the number of employed residents of the suburb,* and it is computed by the formula (1) ÷ (2) × 100. The suburbs identified as *employing* centers in this study have a ratio of 85 or above, with all suburbs having a lower ratio classified as *residential* centers. Source: Victor Jones, "Economic Classification of Cities and Metropolitan Areas," in *The Municipal Year Book, 1953,* Chicago: International City Managers' Association, 1953, pp. 49–57. These and the other data from the same source are used here with the kind permission of the publisher.

13. Harris, *op. cit.,* pp. 10–11.

14. The definitions of the control variables are as follows: (*A*) The *regional* delineation used here is the one developed by the U.S. Bureau of the Census. (*B–C*) *size* classifications are according to the number of inhabitants in 1940, the beginning of the decade under study. (*D*) Each suburb's *distance* classification is based upon radial measurement between its approximate geographic center and the site of the city hall in the central city. (*E*) Each suburb is classified according to the *economic base* of the metropolitan area as a whole in 1950. The areas Jones has designated as "Mm" (manufacturing centers) are treated as *manufacturing* areas in this study. Areas classified by Jones as "M" (industrial centers) and "Mr" (diversified centers with manufacturing predominant) are here combined under the heading of *diversified* areas. Jones' types "Rm" (di-

versified centers with retail trade predominant) and "Rr" (retail trade centers) are here labelled *retail* areas. All of the other types identified by Jones (mining, education, wholesale trade, government, transportation, and resort or retirement centers) are here combined in the residual *other* category. Space limitations preclude a listing of the detailed definitions of each type, which may be found in Jones, *op. cit.* (F) Median *rent levels* for the suburbs in 1950 are classified as follows: *low*—five dollars or more below the median for the entire metropolitan area in which the suburb is located; *average*—within a range of five dollars below to ten dollars above the median for the entire area; *high*—more than ten dollars above the median for the entire area. (Source: Jones, *ibid.*) (G) the *age* of the suburb is approximated by its date of incorporation.

15. A vertical examination of Table 1 suggests that growth rates are related to six of the seven variables taken separately, for both types of suburb. These relationships merely serve here as *prima facie* evidence of the need for controlling these variables in the examination of growth differentials according to functional type.

16. See Hawley, *Human Ecology, op. cit.;* and Kate K. Liepmann, *The Journey to Work,* New York: Oxford University Press, 1944.

17. Housing opportunities, of course, represented the operational definition used in Samuel Stouffer's well-known study, "Intervening Opportunities: A Theory Relating Mobility and Distance," *American Sociological Review,* 5 (December, 1940), pp. 845–57.

18. These statements are documented in Dorothy K. Newman, "Metropolitan Area Structure and Growth as Shown by Building-Permit Statistics," *Business Topics,* 4 (November, 1956), pp. 1–7.

19. Space limitations preclude the discussion of fertility and mortality differentials between types of suburb that may contribute to the observed growth differentials.

20. See William H. Form, "The Place of Social Structure in the Determination of Land Use," *Social Forces,* 32 (May, 1954), pp. 317–23. In addition, the historical context must be kept in mind. Available housing data indicate that the typical metropolitan area comprised a seller's market between 1940 and 1950. In other words, aggregate demand was usually well in excess of the supply of housing available.

21. It may be objected that this presentation ignores the decision-making process among contractors and others who actually initiate housing construction. It is true that discussion of the social-psychological aspect of residential mobility and population re-distribution is deliberately avoided in this paper. Those who are interested in motivational aspects of decentralization might do well to explore the motives of contractors, real estate operators, and financiers, rather than concern themselves exclusively with those of individual householders.

22. Harland Bartholomew, *Land Uses in American Cities,* Cambridge: Harvard University Press, 1955.

23. The importance of large tracts of vacant and cheap land is itself suggested by the fact that the very highest rates of growth in the metropolitan area between 1940 and 1950 were registered in unincorporated rural territory. See Chapter 4, Table 1.

24. Hawley, *Human Ecology, op. cit.,* pp. 276–286. "Basic" industries locate at particular sites, with the residential population taking up posi-

tions with reference to these centers of production and employment. The distribution of residential population, in turn, is the prime determinant of the location of such "nonbasic" activities as retail trade and services.

25. The clearest statement of this development is to be found in R. D. McKenzie, *The Metropolitan Community*, New York: McGraw-Hill Book Company, 1933. For more recent empirical evidence, see Leslie Kish, "Differentiation in Metropolitan Areas," *American Sociological Review*, 19 (August, 1954), pp. 388–98.

26. See Leo F. Schnore, "The Separation of Home and Work: A Problem for Human Ecology," *Social Forces*, 32 (May, 1954), pp. 336–43.

Chapter 9

The Social and Economic Characteristics of American Suburbs

IN THE TRADITIONAL POPULAR IMAGE, "the suburb" is nothing more than the dwelling place of commuters who work in the near-by central city. While it is certainly correct to characterize many outlying subcenters as little more than "bedroom cities," a realistic portrayal must reflect the fact that "dormitory towns are only one species of suburb."[1] Some suburbs are literally manufacturing centers, devoted to light or heavy industry, while others are given over to the provision of such specialized services as education or recreation; as such, they represent significant centers of employment, drawing workers from other subcenters and even from the central city itself. Indeed, the range of economic specialization that can be discerned among suburbs is virtually as wide as that observable among other cities.

This study was supported by the research phase of the University of Wisconsin Urban Program, under the terms of a grant from the Ford Foundation.

[169]

Despite the great variety of suburban functions, however, it has proved useful to distinguish two main types of suburb—employing and residential. This distinction made an early appearance in the literature of urban sociology, notably in the work of Taylor and that of Douglass.[2] Subsequent research has demonstrated the utility of this simple dichotomy. Harris has shown that "the commonest types of suburb are housing or dormitory suburbs and manufacturing or industrial suburbs,"[3] and it has been further shown that these two basic types differ with respect to a number of important social, economic, and demographic characteristics, including their rates of population growth.[4] It is the purpose of this study to discover whether or not systematic differences existed between suburbs according to functional type as of 1960, and (if so) to delineate suburban profiles by reference to characteristics enumerated in the 1960 Censuses of Population and Housing. In short, it is our intention to retest one of the more neglected hypotheses advanced by Louis Wirth in his well-known essay, "Urbanism as a Way of Life":

> An industrial city will differ significantly in social respects from a commercial, mining, fishing, resort, university, and capital city. A one-industry city will present different sets of social characteristics from a multi-industry city, as will an industrially balanced from an unbalanced city, a suburb from a satellite, a residential suburb from an industrial suburb. . . .[5]

One of the new questions in the 1960 Census concerned the workplace of each employed person. Initially, we had hoped to make use of this item in order to make a precise identification of individual suburbs according to type. Unfortunately, the tabulation and publication of information on workplace makes use of such gross categories that it proved impossible to use these materials in the way that was originally contemplated. Workplaces are simply classified as lying inside or outside the worker's county of residence, and the only individual incorporated places that are recognized are those of 50,000 or more inhabitants—essentially the central cities of the Standard Metropolitan Statistical Areas and Urbanized Areas. In a few of these areas, however, workplace data can be used to characterize suburbs in a very rough fashion. In those few cases in which the central city is a separate county (e.g., San Francisco) or a quasi-county (e.g., St. Louis) it is possible to estimate the number of suburban commuters who work there. A person living in a New York suburb and working in the city itself, for example, will have to cross a county line, since the five boroughs making up the city are themselves separate counties. As a consequence, the proportion of a particular New York suburb's working population that is registered as "working in a county other than the county of residence" includes all those who commute to the central city together with those who travel to other employing centers in different counties. Thus the proportion working outside the county of residence serves as a rough index of the suburb's functional status, i.e., as an employing or a residential subcenter. A suburb with a high proportion of its employed population working outside the county is very probably a residential suburb. At the same time, a suburb with a very low proportion working in another county is quite likely to be an employing subcenter providing jobs for its own residents, if not for others as well. In any event, close inspection of the data for New York's suburbs indicated that this proportion would serve as a useful basis of classification. Let us examine the results.

The Suburbs of New York

In Table 1, 74 incorporated places of 10,000 or more inhabitants lying within the New York-Northeastern New Jersey Urbanized Area have been classified as belonging to one of three types of suburb. Places with less than 25 per cent of their employed populations working outside the county of residence are labeled "employing" suburbs. At the other extreme, places with 37.5 per cent or more workers commuting across a county line are characterized as "residential" suburbs; on average, a place in this category sends almost 50 per cent of its employed labor force into another county. Finally, a third "intermediate" or "mixed" category is recognized, wherein intercounty commuters make up 25 to 37 per cent of its resident working population. Recognition of this third category permits a more rigorous test of the hypothesis to the effect that there exist systematic differences between employing and residential suburbs; if such differences exist, the values registered for the intermediate type should fall somewhere between those found for the two polar types.[6] In fact, Table 1 shows that a number of systematic differences according to type do characterize the suburbs of New York.

Age and ethnic composition—Panel A in Table 1 shows that the three types of suburb differ in population composition. Employing suburbs contain larger proportions of foreign-born and nonwhite inhabitants. In particular, the proportion nonwhite in residential suburbs is notably lower than in the two

Table 1—Social and Economic Characteristics of Suburbs in the New York Urbanized Area, 1960

	TYPE OF SUBURB		
	Employing	Intermediate	Residential
A. Age and Ethnic Composition			
1. Percentage foreign-born	12.9	12.7	11.9
2. Percentage nonwhite	10.6	7.8	1.5
3. Percentage aged 65 or more	10.2	9.6	9.4
B. Fertility and Dependency			
4. Nonworker-worker ratio	1.27	1.33	1.41
5. Fertility ratio	391	401	376
6. Percentage with children under 6	26.0	27.6	25.9
C. Socioeconomic Status			
7. Percentage completed high school	40.9	42.9	50.6
8. Percentage in white-collar occupations	44.9	47.2	58.0
9. Median family income	$7,051	$7,337	$8,994
D. Population Growth, 1950–60			
10. Median rate of increase	5.7	17.5	32.1
11. Percentage of places losing population	24.0	25.0	8.0
12. Percentage migrant 1955–60	11.8	14.0	20.1
E. Housing Characteristics			
13. Percentage built between 1950 and 1960	16.8	20.8	24.4
14. Percentage owner-occupied units	50.3	55.0	67.7
15. Percentage one-family units	48.5	50.1	63.9
No. of suburbs	25	24	25

other types. Finally, the proportion of the population aged 65 or more tends to vary systematically from one suburban type to the next, although the differences tend to be rather small.[7]

Fertility and dependency—Panel B shows the nonworker-worker ratio for the three types of suburb; this is the ratio of the number of persons not in the labor force (including children under 14 years of age) to the number within the labor force. On average, it can be seen that residential suburbs have a heavier burden of dependency. This ratio is mainly a function of two factors—age composition and labor force participation. Suburbs with large numbers of dependent old and young persons can be expected to exhibit higher ratios, as can those in which labor force participation rates are lower. The second and third lines suggest that the variations in dependency between types of suburb are not simply the result of variations in levels of fertility. The fertility ratio (children under 5 years old per 1,000 women 15 to 49 years old) proves to be highest in the intermediate type, with lower values in the two polar types of suburb.[8] Similarly, the proportion of married couples with children under 6 years of age is highest in the intermediate type. It is interesting to note that these are the only two characteristics in which the values for the intermediate type do not fall between those for the two polar types of suburb.

Socioeconomic status—Perhaps the clearest differences between New York suburbs emerge when three measures of socioeconomic status are considered. Among persons aged 25 years and older, Panel C reveals that residential suburbs have clearly higher proportions who completed twelve or more years of education. Similarly, among members of the employed labor force, comparable differences between suburban types appear with respect to the proportions engaged in white-collar pursuits—those in professional, managerial, clerical, and sales occupations. Finally, systematic variations can be observed with respect to median family income. The relatively self-contained suburbs (employing subcenters) have the lowest average income, while residential suburbs register substantially higher income. These differences are clearly in accordance with earlier findings.[9]

Population growth—Still another series of differences between employing and residential suburbs that has been subjected to some prior research concerns population change. Two earlier studies have suggested that residential suburbs tended to grow faster than employing suburbs in the 'thirties and the 'forties.[10] Panel D indicates that these growth differentials persisted in the 'fifties, at least among the New York suburbs under examination. While employing suburbs were growing at a rate that averaged less than 6 per cent over the decade, residential suburbs increased by over 30 per cent in the same interval. The second line shows that less than one out of every ten residential suburbs lost numbers during the decade, while one out of every four registered population losses in the other two types. That these growth differentials were brought about mainly by variations in migration is suggested by the last line in Panel D, where it can be seen that one out of every five inhabitants of residential suburbs was an in-migrant, i.e., lived in a different county in 1955 and 1960. Intermediate and employing types of suburb had notably lower proportions migrant according to this measure.

Housing characteristics—The last set of characteristics examined here has to do with certain features of the housing stock found in different types of suburb.[11] In accordance with the growth differentials previously observed, it can be seen that the housing stock of residential suburbs is much newer than that of other types; almost one out of every four housing units in New York's residential suburbs is to be found in a structure built between 1950 and 1960. Similarly, occupancy by owners is much more frequent in residential suburbs, for over two out of every three occupied units is inhabited by the owner. In contrast, almost half the units found in New York's employing suburbs are occupied by renters. Finally, clear-cut differentials may be observed with respect to type of residential structure. Over six out of every ten housing units in the residential suburbs of New York are in "one-housing unit structures," i.e., single-family residences. This contrasts with the situation in employing and intermediate suburbs, where roughly half the dwelling units are found in multiple-family structures.

THE EMPLOYMENT-RESIDENCE RATIO

Unfortunately, the methods used in classifying New York's suburbs cannot be employed in other areas. In most cases, the central city is located in the same county as the suburbs surrounding it. As a consequence, these suburbs cannot be readily characterized as "employing" and "residential" in accordance with the census data on workplace. Even the detailed tabulations of workplace—wherein commuter trips to central cities of 50,000 and over will be separately identified—will not permit an exact classification of suburbs according to type, since work trips to places other than central cities will not be separately reported.

For these reasons, we have turned to another source of information as a means of classifying suburbs according to functional type. We have used the "employment-residence ratio" computed by Jones and Collver for all incorporated places of 10,000 or more inhabitants in 1950; as they indicate, "the employment-residence ratio was obtained by comparing the number of workers employed in the city in 1954 in manufacturing and trade with the number of employed residents reporting these same occupations."[12] Cities are differentiated, then, on the basis of the net daily movement of workers into and out of them. A place with a high ratio tends to have many more jobs than employed workers, and can be fairly characterized as an employing subcenter. On the other hand, a place with a low employment-residence ratio has more workers than jobs available locally, and can be aptly categorized as a residential subcenter.

In all, the 25 largest Urbanized Areas contain exactly 300 suburbs for which employment-residence ratios have been calculated. The list in Table 2, ordered by population size, shows the number of suburbs found in each of the 25 Urbanized Areas of more than 750,000 inhabitants in 1960.

Once again there is the problem of establishing "cutting

points." For present purposes, suburbs with employment-residence ratios of 101 or more were classified as "employing" subcenters. Those with ratios falling between 51 and 100 are termed "intermediate," and those with ratios of 50 or less are treated as "residential" suburbs.[13] As it happens, this procedure yields three groups of approximately equal size.

Table 2—Number of Suburbs in Each of 25 Urbanized Areas of More Than 750,000 Inhabitants, 1960

Urbanized Area	Population 1960	Number of Suburbs in Study
New York–Northeastern New Jersey	14,114,927	74
Los Angeles–Long Beach, Calif.	6,488,791	34
Chicago–Northwestern Indiana	5,959,213	30
Philadelphia, Pa.–N.J.	3,635,228	14
Detroit, Mich.	3,537,709	22
San Francisco–Oakland, Calif.	2,430,663	18
Boston, Mass.	2,413,236	16
Washington, D.C.–Md.–Va.	1,808,423	4
Pittsburgh, Pa.	1,804,400	22
Cleveland, Ohio	1,784,991	12
St. Louis, Mo.–Ill.	1,667,693	12
Baltimore, Md.	1,418,948	0
Minneapolis–St. Paul, Minn.	1,377,143	4
Milwaukee, Wis.	1,149,997	7
Houston, Texas	1,139,678	3
Buffalo, N.Y.	1,054,370	5
Cincinnati, Ohio–Ky.	993,568	4
Dallas, Texas	932,349	4
Kansas City, Mo.–Kans.	921,121	1
Seattle, Wash.	864,109	1
Miami, Fla.	852,705	4
New Orleans, La.	845,237	1
San Diego, Calif.	836,175	3
Denver, Colo.	803,624	2
Atlanta, Ga.	768,125	3

Table 3 shows the economic base of each suburb according to functional type. It will be seen that the employing suburbs are heavily specialized in manufacturing; in fact, if one adds together the first three categories—manufacturing, industrial, and diversified suburbs in which manufacturing predominates—one finds four out of every five employing suburbs represented. At the other extreme, residential suburbs are heavily specialized in the provision of retail trade and services. Over half these places are retail trade centers, and if one combines the last three categories—retail trade centers, diversified centers in which retail trade predominates, and service centers—one finds four out of every five of the residential suburbs so classified. As expected, the intermediate suburbs represent a greater mixture of places from the standpoint of their economic bases. These materials suggest that in working with subcenters classified ac-

Table 3—Economic Base of Suburb by Type

Economic Base	TYPE OF SUBURB		
	Employing	Intermediate	Residential
Percentage Mm (manufacturing)	70.6	33.3	2.0
Percentage M (industrial)	3.9	7.1	2.0
Percentage Mr (diversified, with manufacturing predominant)	7.8	16.2	13.1
Percentage S (service)	2.9	2.0	5.1
Percentage Rm (diversified, with retail trade predominant)	5.9	23.2	23.2
Percentage Rr (retail trade)	8.9	18.2	54.6
Total	100.0	100.0	100.0
Number of suburbs	102	99	99

cording to their employment-residence ratios we are dealing with more or less distinctive types of suburb which play dissimilar roles in the metropolitan economy.

SOCIAL AND ECONOMIC CHARACTERISTICS OF 300 SUBURBS

Table 4 gives summary profiles of 300 employing, intermediate, and residential suburbs, using the employment-residence ratios as the basis of the typological distinction. The characteristics shown include all those previously analyzed for the suburbs of New York.

Age and ethnic composition—As in the case of New York, suburbs generally appear to vary systematically with respect to certain compositional features. Employing suburbs contain not only higher proportions of foreign-born inhabitants, but they also contain larger percentages of nonwhites. The nonwhite representation in residential suburbs is again notably lower than in the other types. With respect to age composition, employing suburbs tend to have larger proportions of older inhabitants, but the other two types do not differ much in this respect.

Fertility and dependency—Similarly, residential and inter-mediate types of suburb are not clearly distinguished with respect to dependency, for their nonworker-worker ratios are identical. This ratio, seen in Panel B, is only slightly lower for employing suburbs. These findings represent a departure from the patterns exhibited by New York's suburbs, where a rather clear gradient was in evidence. Like New York's suburbs, how-ever, the larger sample reveals the highest fertility ratios in the intermediate type of suburb; employing and residential suburbs

Table 4—Social and Economic Characteristics of Suburbs in the 25 Largest Urbanized Areas, 1960

	TYPE OF SUBURB		
	Employing	Intermediate	Residential
A. Age and Ethnic Composition			
1. Percentage foreign-born	10.5	8.5	7.7
2. Percentage nonwhite	7.0	6.2	2.4
3. Percentage aged 65 or more	9.7	9.0	9.1
B. Fertility and Dependency			
4. Nonworker-worker ratio	1.41	1.44	1.44
5. Fertility ratio	421	437	422
6. Percentage with children under 6	27.8	29.2	28.2
C. Socioeconomic Status			
7. Percentage completed high school	43.2	48.2	55.8
8. Percentage in white-collar occupations	44.6	49.8	58.5
9. Median family income	$6,869	$7,510	$8,210
D. Population Growth, 1950–60			
10. Median rate of increase	6.0	18.1	26.9
11. Percentage of places losing population	30.4	24.2	16.2
12. Percentage migrant 1955–60	13.8	16.7	17.4
E. Housing Characteristics			
13. Percentage built between 1950 and 1960	24.1	29.4	31.6
14. Percentage owner-occupied units	57.7	63.1	71.4
15. Percentage one-family units	62.3	68.2	75.9
No. of suburbs	102	99	99

have child-woman ratios that are lower and virtually identical. Similarly, the proportions of married couples with children under six years of age are lower in the two polar types of suburb, with a higher proportion found in the suburbs of the intermediate type. Again, these findings reproduce the patterns observed when only the 74 New York suburbs were under scrutiny.

Socioeconomic status—The New York sample also proved to be typical with respect to differentials in socioeconomic status between suburbs of varying type. Panel C in Table 4 shows that the highest proportion completing high school is found in the residential suburbs. Similarly, the largest relative number of employed persons in white-collar occupations is found in this same type of suburb. Finally, income differentials are again very pronounced. A gap in excess of $1,300 dollars separates the median incomes of employing and residential suburbs, with the latter type clearly favored.

Population growth—We have already referred to evidence to the effect that the growth of residential suburbs outstripped that of employing suburbs during the 1930's and 1940's. During the 1950's, according to Panel D, this differential clearly persisted. While employing subcenters grew an average of only 6 per cent over the 1950–1960 decade, residential suburbs grew by almost 27 per cent. Again, suburbs of intermediate type registered intermediate gains. We also see that three out of every ten employing suburbs actually lost population during the decade, while only half as many residential suburbs registered losses during the same interval. Again, as in the case of the New York sample, residential suburbs were generally more likely to contain migrants, i.e, people who lived in different counties in 1955 and 1960.

Housing characteristics—The final array of characteristics examined here refers to housing in employing, intermediate, and residential suburbs. Panel E reveals higher proportions of new housing (built between 1950 and 1960) in residential suburbs; this finding, of course, is in accordance with the expectation formed on the basis of examining differentials in population growth. Another set of differences that was anticipated—largely on the basis of New York suburban experience—has to do with housing tenure. Panel E shows that dwelling units in residential suburbs are more likely to be occupied by owners than by renters. Finally, the three types of suburb differ systematically with respect to type of residential structure. While lower proportions of dwelling units are of the one-family style in employing and intermediate suburbs, fully three out of every four units are designed for single-family occupancy in residential suburbs. As in most of the preceding comparisons, then, the housing data for all 300 suburbs reflect the patterns observed in the more limited sample drawn from the environs of New York.

SUMMARY AND CONCLUSIONS

The massive shifts in population denoted by the concept of "suburbanization" have been thoroughly documented in demographic research.[14] Moreover, detailed case studies have reminded us of the diversity of suburbs in America.[15] As Riesman has observed, however, "we cannot link nation-wide data on changes in metropolitan areas with Whyte's descriptions of how Park Forest feels toward its pro tem inhabitants. This is the characteristic situation in sociology today—that research in the macrocosmic and in the microcosmic scarcely connect, scarcely inform each other."[16] This study represents an effort at portraying what is typical in contemporary suburbia while simultaneously giving attention to variations within the broad category "suburb."

We have followed the sociological tradition by identifying two major types of suburb—employing and residential. For purposes of analysis, however, we have recognized a third—an intermediate type. Some fifteen social and economic characteristics were then examined, first in a sample of 74 suburbs surrounding New York City and subsequently in a group of 300 suburbs found within the 25 largest Urbanized Areas.

The values observed for thirteen of these fifteen characteristics tended to increase or decrease systematically as one moved from one type of suburb to the next. In other words, the characteristics of the intermediate class of suburbs tended to fall somewhere between those of employing and residential suburbs. The exceptions to this pattern both involved characteristics reflecting suburban fertility—the child-woman ratio and the proportion of married couples with children under six years of age. Both of these measures turned out to be higher (in both samples) for intermediate suburbs than in employing or residential subcenters.

Perhaps the most clear-cut set of differences were those having to do with socioeconomic status. Measures of income, education, and occupational standing all showed the same results in both samples, i.e., the highest values were registered in the residential suburbs, somewhat lower values in the intermediate class, and the lowest values in the employing category. Other measures with a "status" connotation—proportions foreign-born and nonwhite, and proportions in owner-occupied and single-family dwelling units—showed similar patterns.

Finally, this study has demonstrated the continuation of a long-term trend with respect to population growth. Growth differentials favoring residential suburbs continued to characterize the 'fifties, just as they did the 'thirties and the 'forties. While it is undeniable that suburbs vary in many respects, it is equally clear that these variations are quite systematic and predictable.

NOTES

1. Coleman Woodbury, "Suburbanization and Suburbia," *American Journal of Public Health*, 45 (January, 1955), p. 2.

2. Graham R. Taylor, *Satellite Cities* (New York and London: D. Appleton and Co., 1915); Harlan Paul Douglass, *The Suburban Trend* (New York and London: The Century Co., 1925), and his "Suburbs," in *The Encyclopaedia of the Social Sciences* (New York: The Macmillan Co., 1934), Volume 14, pp. 433–35.

3. Chauncy D. Harris, "Suburbs," *American Journal of Sociology*, 49 (May, 1943), p. 6.

4. Leo F. Schnore, "The Functions of Metropolitan Suburbs," *American Journal of Sociology*, 61 (March, 1956), pp. 453–458, and his "The Growth of Metropolitan Suburbs," *American Sociological Review*, 22 (April, 1957), pp. 165–73.

5. Louis Wirth, "Urbanism as a Way of Life," *American Journal of Sociology*, 44 (July, 1938); reprinted in Paul K. Hatt and Albert J. Reiss, Jr. (editors), *Cities and Society* (Glencoe, Illinois: The Free Press, 1957), p. 49.

6. The "intermediate" type recognized in this paper should not be confused with the "balanced" type of suburb identified by Douglass, wherein jobs and workers are approximately equal in number.

7. The proportions nonwhite and aged 65 and over were taken from U.S. Bureau of the Census, *U.S. Census of Population: 1960, General Population Characteristics* (Washington, D.C.: U.S. Government Printing Office, 1961), Table 13 for each state. Unless otherwise indicated, the remaining characteristics were taken from U.S. Bureau of the Census, *U.S. Census of Population: 1960, General Social and Economic Characteristics* (Washington, D.C.: U.S. Government Printing Office, 1961), Tables 32 and 33 for each state. These two publications are Chapters "B" and "C" respectively, and will be so identified in subsequent references. Unless otherwise indicated, the values shown are unweighted means for the type of suburb in question.

8. The source of the fertility ratio was Chapter "B," Table 13. This measure is also commonly known as "the child-woman ratio."

9. Leo F. Schnore, "Satellites and Suburbs," *Social Forces*, 36 (December, 1957), pp. 121–27.

10. For growth rates between 1930 and 1940, see Harris, *op. cit.* Suburban growth between 1940 and 1950 is examined in Schnore, "The Growth of Metropolitan Suburbs," *op. cit.*, and in his "Components of Population Change in Large Metropolitan Suburbs," *American Sociological Review*, 23 (October, 1958), pp. 570–73. The growth rates for 1950–1960 were computed on the basis of data taken from U.S. Bureau of the Census, *U.S. Census of Population: 1960*, Volume I, *Characteristics of the Population*, Part A, "Number of Inhabitants." (Washington, D.C.: U.S. Government Printing Office, 1961), Table 8 for each state. The rates of growth were adjusted for annexations of territory and population between 1950 and 1960 by reference to Table 9. For the importance of this adjustment, see Leo F. Schnore, "Municipal Annexations and the Growth of Metropolitan Suburbs, 1950–60," *American Journal of Sociology*, 67 (January, 1962), pp. 406–17.

11. All of the housing data were taken from U.S. Bureau of the Census, *U.S. Census of Housing: 1960*, Volume I, *States and Small Areas* (Washington, D.C.: U.S. Government Printing Office, 1962), Table 1 for each state.

12. Victor Jones and Andrew Collver, "Economic Classification of Cities and Metropolitan Areas," in Orin F. Nolting and David S. Arnold (editors), *The Municipal Yearbook, 1959* (Chicago: The International City Managers' Association, 1959), p. 72.

13. Jones and Collver suggest that cities with ratios below 50 should be treated as "dormitory suburbs," and they point out that "all but three of these cities are located within SMA's and only four are manufacturing or industrial cities." *Ibid.*, p. 71.

14. See, for example, Amos H. Hawley, *The Changing Shape of Metropolitan America: Deconcentration Since 1920* (Glencoe, Illinois: The Free Press, 1956).

15. See, for example, William H. Whyte, Jr., "The Transients," in his *The Organization Man* (New York: Simon and Schuster, 1956), Part VII; and Bennett M. Berger, *Working-Class Suburb* (Berkeley and Los Angeles: University of California Press, 1960).

16. David Riesman, "The Suburban Dislocation," *Annals of the American Academy of Political and Social Science*, 314 (November, 1957), p. 125.

Chapter 10

Forms of Government
and Socioeconomic
Characteristics of Suburbs

THE TOPIC of metropolitan government has been widely discussed for a number of years, but there is a surprising dearth of information about forms of government employed by municipalities in metropolitan areas. We are aware, of course, of the great number of separate municipalities to be found in these areas and of the fact that they have increased rapidly over the years.[1] Indeed, it is the proliferation of incorporated places and other units of government that is thought to give rise to "the metropolitan problem." In spite of much concern with this problem among urban planners and administrators, a recent critique by Sayre and Polsby concluded:

> Knowledge about suburban politics is at best highly generalized, for the most part unabashedly impressionistic. There are quite obviously many different kinds of suburbs—old, new,

This study was supported by the research phase of the University of Wisconsin Urban Program, under the terms of a grant from the Ford Foundation.

homogeneous, heterogeneous, Republican, Democratic, residential, industrial, populous, sparsely settled, upper class, middle class, restricted, unrestricted, and others. Most current generalizations ignore or blur these variations.[2]

Why do we find so little documentation of contemporary suburban political forms? One hypothesis is that the sheer variety of suburbs makes the task overwhelmingly difficult. Wood has offered the following tentative explanation:

> By and large, no muckrakers have appeared on the scene to describe in chapter and verse the inner workings of suburban politics in the way that big city bosses and urban political-business alliances were detailed fifty years ago. This is not surprising; the number and variety of possible suburban political patterns make the documentation needed for sound generalizations an exceedingly formidable job. It is little wonder that we know most about our national, less about state, and least about local politics. The task of research expands geometrically as we go down the scale.[3]

Certainly the full diversity of suburban political patterns would be difficult to chart and analyze in any full and comprehensive fashion, but it is literally impossible to analyze any social or political phenomenon in its totality. It is probably the case study approach of many social scientists, which emphasizes the unique historical features of each city or political system, that has hindered the full development of comparative urban studies. It might be better to regard the great numbers of suburbs as an opportunity to gain general knowledge of the factors related to different political forms, since modern analytical techniques readily permit the handling of masses of data.

It is easy to classify cities according to form of government. Once this is done, other characteristics can be examined. The materials in Table 1, for example, are frequently cited. It is clear that the mayor-council form is most frequently found in the very largest and smallest cities. In contrast, the council-manager and commission plans are more often encountered in cities of intermediate size.[4] If one should ask about systematic variations in social and economic characteristics of suburbs with different forms of government, however, the literature yields little more than a scattering of speculative assertions that are entirely undocumented. Adrian, for example, has held that "the upper-middle-class suburbs which are the homes of metropolitan businessmen are characteristically administered by a

Table 1—Forms of City Government (U.S.), by Size[a]

Population[b]	% Commission	% Mayor-council	% Council-manager	No.
500,000 or more	0.0	94.1	5.9	17
250,000–500,000	21.8	39.1	39.1	23
100,000–250,000	20.6	42.6	36.8	68
50,000–100,000	19.7	34.1	46.2	132
25,000– 50,000	15.5	37.1	47.4	283
10,000– 25,000	14.6	45.6	39.8	800
5,000– 10,000	10.0	60.6	29.4	1,146
All cities	13.0	51.2	35.8	2,469

a. Adapted from Orin F. Nolting and David S. Arnold, eds., *The Municipal Year Book, 1958* (Chicago, 1958), p. 62.
b. Population classified according to size in 1950.

manager."[5] Even more typical is the kind of loose linkage between style of government and socioeconomic status postulated by Banfield and Grodzins:

> The independent suburban corporations, clustered around the central cities, exhibit a variety of social characteristics. There are fashionable communities inhabited by wealthy business and professional people who want and can easily pay for a high level of governmental services. Suburbs of this kind are generally very proud of their schools and of the businesslike and impartial way in which their affairs are managed. . . . There are middle-class suburbs in which, characteristically, the residents are anxious to have a high level of local governmental service but, somewhat inconsistently, are also anxious to keep taxes down, at least until their mortgages have been reduced.[6]

The vast and sprawling literature on metropolitan government includes only one study that offers an empirical examination of the association between political characteristics and socioeconomic attributes of suburbs. A case study of the Chicago metropolitan area by Liebman posed the following question: "Do cities or suburbs, distinguished on the basis of their economic functions . . . vary with respect to their political characteristics?"[7] It is the purpose of this paper to turn Liebman's question around, i.e., *to determine whether suburbs possessing different forms of government display measurable differences in social and economic characteristics.*

FORMS OF GOVERNMENT

The types of government recognized here are the three major forms employed by cities in the United States—*commission, mayor-council,* and *council-manager.* The problem of classifying these political forms along meaningful dimensions is a difficult one, and the following suggestions are necessarily tentative. The oldest form, of course, is the weak *mayor-council* system, under which the mayor possesses neither veto power over council legislation nor administrative power over city departments. The need for leadership in larger cities has strengthened the mayor's position in many cases, giving rise to the strong mayor-council forms. The various mayor-council forms remained the most popular mode of governmental organization in 1958, being found in over half of all U.S. cities having more than 5,000 inhabitants.

The *commission* form was created in 1900, and it spread rapidly to some 500 cities by 1918, but it has declined since that time. Under this form, three to seven persons serve as individual heads of separate administrative departments and act together as the policy-making body for the city. The use of the commission form declined to 320 cities by 1958. The *council-manager* form is the newest, originating in 1908 and spreading since then to 885 cities by 1958. Under this form, a hired professional manager is responsible to the council for administration of the city's affairs.

The commission and council-manager forms were both essentially reform governments, but the council-manager form has proved to be more successful than the commission form, and it has replaced the mayor-council arrangement in a great many cities. This is probably related to the degree of *administrative centralization* characteristic of the three different forms.

The commission form appears to be the least centralized of the three, since responsibility is divided among individual heads of departments, who apparently find it rather difficult to function collectively as a policy-making body. The weak mayor-council form is somewhat more centralized, since there is a council charged with appointing department heads, and responsibility can be fixed upon the council. The strong mayor-council form is still more centralized, and the council-manager form—under which the council functions much like a board of directors—is apparently the most centralized of all. The historical trend toward more centralized forms is probably due to the increased size and complexity of urban government. This may explain, at least partially, the decline of the weak mayor-council form, the failure of the decentralized reform government (the commission plan), and the success of the two strong forms: the council-manager system and the strong-mayor form, either with or without a chief administrative officer.[8]

Both the commission and council-manager forms may be conceived as "businesslike" replacements for the mayor-council form, which was attacked at the end of the nineteenth century for its corruption. But the commission form was like an early nineteenth-century business: both were attempts to reflect the image of a few men working together for common ends—the "one big happy family" myth. Company unions emerged from the same ideology. (Although this myth has been perpetuated by twentieth-century corporations trying to promote employee loyalty, *structural* changes that embody the myth have seldom been contemplated.) Ideally, the commission was to operate like a small corporation with each member of the "family" running his own department and getting together once a week to talk over common problems. Urban conflicts and the exigencies of administrative requirements proved this conception of the nature of city problems to be unrealistic, at least in its structural embodiment as the commission form. In contrast, the council-manager form is like a large twentieth-century corporation: the board of directors hires a plant manager, and there is no illusion of democracy, except through the distant intervention of the "stockholders" (the urban electorate), who get a chance to select members of the board at the annual meeting.

This version of democracy, of course, is a far cry from the Jeffersonian ideal of direct democracy with continual checks upon representatives.

Here we are emphasizing the structural changes taking place as responses to new problems, rather than as conscious shifts in ideology. The commission form and the council-manager form were both seen as efficient and businesslike replacements of earlier forms when they emerged at the turn of the century, but cities have changed to other forms without any drastic revisions in ideological rationale. Businesslike efficiency was then and still is highly valued today, no matter what the form of local government. We do not know which structure is most likely to achieve this goal. And what of other goals? Democratic ideology, involving equitable representation to various socioeconomic groups and geographic areas, has continued to receive emphasis in American politics. Perhaps the conflict between these two ideologies—efficiency and representation—could be traced in cities which have experienced serious disputes over forms of government. More comparative research into urban history is needed on such topics.[9]

Both the commission and manager forms imply that the city is essentially like a business, with few conflicts of interest, and therefore can function like an administrative machine. This view is sometimes challenged by organized labor, and for much the same reasons that legitimate unionism challenges the undisputed leadership of management in the corporation. The more the city government is seen by important and politically sensitive groups as the arena for the contesting of crucial and conflicting interests, the more a form of government (and election) which gives representation to more than one interest group is likely to be sought. Therefore, wherever labor unions (other than old-line, apolitical AFL unions) are strong, we may expect the prevalence of the mayor-council form, with election by wards on a partisan basis, which will give representation to minority and working-class areas, largely Democratic in orientation. The nonpartisan election will be more prevalent in the "businesslike" forms (commission and council-manager) than in the mayor-council form. Size of city is also a factor, since (other things equal) we may expect that unionism will be stronger in the larger cities; the mayor-council form, with partisan elections, should therefore be more prevalent in such cities. Regional location should also affect the form of government, since the absence of traditional forms in the newer cities of the West should promote the form that is thought to be most appropriate to modern conditions, i.e., the council-manager form.

To summarize, the various forms of government can be ranked in terms of their *degree of centralization* and related to the type of social and economic composition that we would expect to find in cities with those forms.[10] The commission form is likely to be found in older, less modernized cities, where (*1*) the city does not face the kinds of problems requiring more centralized governmental forms, or (*2*) it does not have the aggressive community leadership which can produce political change. Commission cities should be at one end of a continuum of city characteristics indicating growth and modernization. The more centralized mayor-council form is likely to be found (*1*) in larger cities or (*2*) in cities where class cleavages have become politically relevant. The mayor-council form is somewhat difficult to delimit precisely because it is still found in all types of cities, but it should be found between the commission and council-manager forms when social and economic characteristics are compared. The most centralized form of government—the council-manager system—should be found (*1*) in younger cities, (*2*) in cities facing problems requiring centralized leadership, or (*3*) in cities lacking a sustained challenge to twentieth-century business leadership.

Evidence for all these assertions is regrettably lacking, but at least some of them can be checked by means of census data and materials from the *Municipal Year Book*.

THE SUBURBS IN THE STUDY

For our purposes, we have assembled data on 300 suburbs lying within the twenty-five largest "Urbanized Areas."[11] The aggregate suburban population under study was 12,023,674 in

1960. Each unit in the study was an incorporated municipality having at least 10,000 inhabitants in 1940, and a series of some eighteen social and economic characteristics were assembled for each unit from various publications of the United States Bureau of the Census on population and housing in 1960. Table 2 provides some data on our sample in terms of the size and

Table 2—Forms of Suburban Government by Size and Regional Location

Size and Location	% Commission	% Mayor-council	% Council-manager	No.
Size of suburb, 1960[a]				
100,000 or more	12.5	37.5	50.0	16
50,000–100,000	13.8	41.4	44.8	58
25,000– 50,000	13.6	39.8	46.6	103
10,000– 25,000	13.8	61.0	25.2	123
Regional location				
Northeast	21.2	63.6	15.2	132
North Central	11.0	50.5	38.5	91
South	16.7	33.3	50.0	18
West	0.0	16.9	83.1	59
All suburbs	13.7	48.7	37.6	300

Form of government was taken from Orin F. Nolting and David S. Arnold, eds., *The Municipal Year Book, 1959* (Chicago, 1959), Table VI.
a. Population classified according to size in 1960.

regional location of the 300 suburbs. The council-manager form tends to predominate in the very largest suburbs, while the mayor-council arrangement is most prevalent in the smaller suburbs, occurring in over six out of every ten in the smallest-size class. The commission form, which has lost popularity over the years since World War I, is found in a minority of suburbs in each size class. Regionally, the suburbs in the Northeast are notable for the frequency of the mayor-council form. Even more noteworthy is the large number of councils and managers in the West, where more than eight of every ten suburbs are administered by managers and where the commission form is lacking altogether. These western suburbs are of more recent origin.

Suburbs with each of the three forms of government show distinctive age profiles. If one measures "age" by observing the census year in which the suburb first included 10,000 inhabitants, commission suburbs are 47.5 years old, on the average. This compares with 37.5 years for mayor-council suburbs, and 28.3 for council-manager suburbs. With respect to the suburban economic base, over seven out of every ten commission suburbs (70.7 per cent) and 62.3 per cent of mayor-council suburbs are predominantly manufacturing subcenters. In sharp contrast, two out of every three council-manager suburbs (67.3 per cent) are predominantly trade and service centers, conforming to the popular image of the "bedroom town" or "dormitory city."[12]

Before proceeding to a detailed enumeration of the social and economic characteristics of suburbs with different forms of government, it is desirable to indicate the association between form of government and form of elections. As Wood has re-

Table 3—Forms of Suburban Government by Form of Election

Form of Government	% Partisan	% Nonpartisan	No.
Commission	26.8	73.2	41
Mayor-council	56.9	43.1	146
Council-manager	15.9	84.1	113
All suburbs	37.3	62.7	300

Source: As in Table 2.

marked, "we know at least the extent to which nonpartisan elections prevail in the suburbs and the number of streamlined city-manager forms of government that have been established."[13] Actually, suburbs with both the council-manager form and the commission plan—products of the urban reform movement of the early part of the century—are likely to have nonpartisan elections. Table 3 shows that seven out of every ten commission suburbs and over eight out of every ten council-manager suburbs have nonpartisan elections. In contrast, well over half the mayor-council suburbs maintain partisan elections. The popularity of nonpartisanship in the suburbs, however, is evidenced by the fact that over six out of every ten suburbs in the total sample have adopted this mode of electing officials.

SOCIAL AND ECONOMIC CHARACTERISTICS

Table 4 shows the characteristics of the three types of suburbs. Unless otherwise noted, the values shown are unweighted means. Taken together, they provide convenient summary profiles.

Table 4—Social and Economic Characteristics of Suburbs by Form of Government

Characteristics	Commission	Mayor-council	Council-manager
Age and ethnic composition (%)			
Foreign-born	9.5	9.3	8.0
Nonwhite	8.7	5.1	4.3
Aged 65 years and over	10.3	9.2	8.9
Fertility and dependency			
Nonworker-worker ratio	1.42	1.43	1.43
Families with children under 6 years (%)	26.8	28.6	28.9
Cumulative fertility rate	1,477	1,542	1,556
Employment and socioeconomic status			
Married women in labor force (%)	28.6	29.2	30.3
Working 50–52 weeks in 1959 (%)	58.5	59.5	59.8
In white-collar occupations (%)	47.4	48.2	55.6
Completing high school (%)	42.1	45.6	56.0
Median family income, 1959	$6,816	$7,379	$7,977
Population growth and mobility (%)			
Median rate of change, 1950–60	−0.7	17.4	28.5
Suburbs losing population, 1950–60	53.7	20.5	15.8
Migrant, 1955–60	12.1	13.4	20.6
Moved since 1958	19.6	19.7	25.5
Housing (%)			
Housing units built since 1950	17.9	25.8	35.3
Dwelling units occupied by owner	56.9	64.7	65.7
Families living in one-family units	60.5	67.1	73.7

Sources: See note 14.

Age and Ethnic Composition—The three types of suburbs appear to differ systematically with respect to certain compositional features. Commission-plan suburbs contain not only higher proportions of foreign-born inhabitants, but also larger percentages of nonwhites.[14] The representation of minority populations is lowest in the suburbs with the council-manager form of government. With respect to age composition, commission suburbs also tend to have larger proportions of older persons. Both in age and ethnic composition, the values for suburbs with the mayor-council form are found to be intermediate between those of the commission and council-manager suburbs.

Fertility and Dependency—Table 4 also shows the nonworker-worker ratio for the three types of suburb; this is the ratio of the number of persons *not* in the labor force (including children under fourteen years of age) to the number within the labor force. It is clear that the three types are not distinguished from each other in terms of dependency, for their ratios are virtually identical. With respect to fertility, however, the suburbs reveal systematic differences according to type. Two measures are shown: (*1*) the proportion of families with children of preschool age, and (*2*) the cumulative fertility rate, i.e., the number of children ever born per 1,000 women 15 to 44 years old of all marital classes. Both measures reveal the highest values in the manager cities, intermediate values in the mayor-council suburbs, and the lowest values in the suburbs governed by commissions.

Employment and Socioeconomic Status—Equally clear differences appear when the three types of suburbs are compared with respect to various indicators of employment and socioeconomic status. Employment stability (the proportion working from 50 to 52 weeks in the year preceding the census) is found to be highest in council-manager suburbs, where higher proportions of married women are found in the labor force. Again, mayor-council suburbs occupy intermediate positions on both measures, with commission-governed suburbs ranking lowest on the average.

Even sharper differences are encountered when various indicators of socioeconomic status are examined. Manager suburbs reveal the highest proportion in white-collar occupations (professional, managerial, clerical, and sales positions). Similarly, the highest proportions completing high school among those aged twenty-five or older are found in these suburbs. Finally, median family income is highest in manager-adminis-

tered communities. In clear contrast, commission-governed suburbs rank lowest on each of these three measures, while suburbs
with the mayor-council form of government occupy an intermediate position.

Population Growth and Mobility—The three forms of
suburban government are associated with distinctive growth
patterns over the past decade. Table 4 shows that over half the
commission suburbs lost population between 1950 and 1960;
their median rate of change, as a consequence, was negative.
Mayor-council and council-manager communities, in contrast,
grew quite rapidly, with the largest increments occurring in
suburbs with the council-manager form of government.[15] In
addition to the fertility differences previously noted, the three
types of suburbs vary in the extent to which they have attracted migrants from other areas. The proportions "migrant"
—defined as those persons aged five years or over who have
lived in different counties in 1955 and 1960—are highest in the
council-manager suburbs, lower in mayor-council suburbs, and
lowest in commission suburbs. Moreover, exactly the same pattern is revealed in the statistics on residential mobility, where
the question relates to the proportions who have moved into
their current residences since 1958. As in the preceding comparisons, the striking feature of the data shown in Table 4 is
the consistency of the results.

Housing Characteristics—The final array of characteristics
examined here refers to selected aspects of the housing stocks
found in the three types of suburb. Table 4 reveals higher proportions of new housing in the council-manager suburbs, where
over one-third of all the dwelling units were built between 1950
and 1960. Roughly one out of every four units is new in the
mayor-council suburbs, and the comparable fraction is less than
one out of every five in the commission suburbs. This finding,
of course, is in accord with the expectations suggested by the
differentials in population growth. Another set of differences
has to do with housing tenure. Table 4 shows that although in
all suburbs the dwelling units are more likely to be occupied by
owners than by renters, the proportion is highest in council-
manager suburbs and lowest in commission suburbs. Finally, the

three types of suburbs differ systematically with respect to type of residential structure. Although only three out of every five dwellings in commission suburbs are of the one-family style, almost three out of every four are designed for single-family occupancy in council-manager suburbs. Again, as in almost every comparison in Table 4, suburbs with the mayor-council form of government occupy a position that is between those of the manager and commission suburbs.

CONCLUSIONS

"Politically, the suburbanite is becoming increasingly important. His numbers alone make him a political factor to be counted."[16] It would seem that because of sheer numbers the suburbs themselves also warrant attention and analysis. This paper has been predicated on the assumption that we might begin the long-neglected study of suburban politics by giving some attention to the variety of political forms manifested in suburban municipalities and to their social and economic characteristics.

We found a whole series of systematic differences between suburbs having the three principal forms of government—commission, mayor-council, and council-manager. Although these differences were not great in every case, they were remarkably consistent. In general, we found the popular image of the council-manager suburb verified; it does tend to be the natural habitat of the upper middle class. In addition, however, we found this type to be inhabited by a younger, more mobile, white population that is growing rapidly. The type that is least similar to the mayor-council suburb in terms of political structure—the commission suburb—we found to be least similar to it in social and economic characteristics. Commission suburbs tend to include persons of lowest socioeconomic status and to be occupied by a slightly older population and by more members of minority groups. We also found that over half the commission cities were losing population during the 1950–1960 decade. In one characteristic after another, we found mayor-council suburbs occupying a position intermediate between those with council-manager and commission forms of government.[17]

We must introduce a note of caution concerning the problem of characterizing suburbs in terms of *differences* rather than predominant characteristics. Clearly none of the suburbs under study is heavily nonwhite nor populated by an absolute majority of persons over 65 years of age. Therefore, we cannot explain the differences in political structure in terms of these compositional characteristics per se. The causal connections are not as clear as they might be if we had found, for example, that nine out of every ten commission cities had over 70 per cent in working-class occupations, while only one out of every ten council-manager suburbs had such a high proportion of workers. It would then be far easier to argue that there was a causal relationship present and to proceed to theorize about the connection between suburban occupational composition and political structure.

The kind of systematic tendencies actually found in the data argue for a different kind of connection between the social and economic composition of the suburb and its political structure. It is possible that there is a threshold effect in operation; thus if the white-collar population (with its typical characteristics, such as better education, higher income, single-family residence, and the like) constitutes a majority, then the political attitudes of this socioeconomic stratum will come to influence the political structure of the suburb, e.g., by favoring the nonpartisan and managerial forms. How these compositional features actually become effective through organizations and political parties must inevitably be examined by means of detailed case studies of the political histories of specific suburbs varying in these several dimensions.

Some of the implications of these patterned differences are obvious. The council-manager suburb, for example, tends to be in a more favorable position with respect to its tax base; not only does it have a white-collar population with higher average income, but it also tends to have a somewhat higher proportion of homeowners. Offsetting these advantages, of course, is the necessity for providing educational facilities for its younger, more fertile population. Other implications, however, are somewhat less obvious. To take an example from the political arena, we might consider the question of territorial annexation. Suburbs with different forms of government have had quite different kinds of experience in this area over the past intercensus decade. Only 28.1 per cent of mayor-council suburbs annexed territory between 1950 and 1960, and only a slightly higher proportion (31.7 per cent) of commission suburbs were able to add to their legal areas. In contrast, well over half the council-manager suburbs (54.0 per cent) were successful in extending their territorial limits.[18] Political *forms*, then, in conjunction with social and economic characteristics that accompany them, would seem to make a difference in certain phases of the political *process;* we find different outcomes consistent with the more centralized, modern character of the council-manager form.

Almost all of the foregoing discussion has been geared to a cross-sectional view of suburban government. We have examined various characteristics of three formal types of suburban government at a particular time. The pressing need would now seem to be for longitudinal analyses showing developments over time. Changes in form of government may be studied with relative ease.[19] In any case, the investigations should be broadly comparative in approach.

NOTES

1. Amos H. Hawley, "The Incorporation Trend in Metropolitan Areas, 1900–1950," *Journal of the American Institute of Planners,* 25 (Feb. 1959), 41–45.

2. Wallace S. Sayre and Nelson W. Polsby, "American Political Science and the Study of Urbanization," a paper prepared for the Committee on Urbanization, Social Science Research Council, July, 1961. See also Robert T. Daland, "Political Science and the Study of Urbanism," *American Political Science Review,* 51 (1957), 491–509.

3. Robert C. Wood, *Suburbia: Its People and Their Politics* (Boston, 1959), p. 177.

4. Generalizations concerning city size and form of government may be found in Charles R. Adrian, *Governing Urban America* (New York, 1955), ch. viii; Stuart A. Queen and David B. Carpenter, *The American*

City (New York, 1953), pp. 310–313; and Alvin Boskoff, *The Sociology of Urban Regions* (New York, 1962), pp. 230–233. The most sophisticated treatment of this subject came to our attention after this study was completed; see John H. Kessel, "Governmental Structure and Political Environment: A Statistical Note about American Cities," *American Political Science Review*, 66 (1962), 615–20. Kessel deals with city size, rate of population growth, ethnic composition, location, and economic base. Each of these variables enters into our analysis, but here we confine our attention to *suburbs* rather than all cities for which data are available.

5. *Op. cit.*, p. 206.

6. Edward C. Banfield and Morton Grodzins, *Government and Housing in Metropolitan Areas* (New York, 1958), pp. 18–19.

7. Charles S. Liebman, "Functional Differentiation and Political Characteristics of Suburbs," *American Journal of Sociology*, 66 (1961), 486.

8. The same view of the relative degree of administrative centralization produced by the different governmental forms is presented in Amos H. Hawley, "Community Power and Urban Renewal Success," *American Journal of Sociology*, 68 (1963), 427–428. An early statement justifying the commission form held that "the commission plan has drawn straight from American business experience its essential elements of success, discarding, so far as city government is concerned, the theory of strict separation of powers, since the main functions of cities are similar to those of business corporations." Cf. E. S. Bradford, *Commission Government in American Cities* (New York, 1912), p. 193. This view implies that the commission form is more centralized than the mayor-council form, since there is no division of powers among commissioners. This may not be the case, however, if the functioning of commissioners as heads of divisions actually overrides their functioning as representatives of the city as a whole. Recent research on corporate, military, and governmental bureaucracies suggests that generalized responsibilities tend to be superseded in practice by highly specific responsibilities.

9. Since World War II, school district reorganization has been a fertile field for the study of the conflict between the ideologies of representation and of efficiency. See Robert R. Alford, "School District Reorganization and Community Integration," *Harvard Educational Review*, 30 (1960), 350–71.

10. The relationship of political to social and economic characteristics of cities may be obscured if there are legal obstructions to a city changing its political form to one more appropriate to its social and economic character. In any large study of American cities, such factors as state regulations must be taken into account. For example, all 47 of Pennsylvania's third-class cities were required to use the commission form as of 1955. It is probable that the social and economic character of commission cities would be even more clearly different from the other types if these cities were not considered. Actually, the commission form is prominent in only three states: Pennsylvania, New Jersey, and Illinois (see Adrian, *op. cit.*, p. 194).

11. The "Urbanized Areas," with the number of suburbs they included given in parentheses, are: New York (74), Los Angeles (34), Chicago (30), Philadelphia (14), Detroit (22), San Francisco-Oakland

(18), Boston (16), Washington (4), Pittsburgh (22), Cleveland (12), St. Louis (12), Minneapolis-St. Paul (4), Milwaukee (7), Houston (3), Buffalo (5), Cincinnati (4), Dallas (4), Kansas City (1), Seattle (1), Miami (4), New Orleans (1), San Diego (3), Denver (2), and Atlanta (3). Baltimore, the twelfth largest area, contained no suburbs meeting the specifications of the study.

12. The suburban economic base was taken from Victor Jones and Andrew Collver, "Economic Classification of Cities and Metropolitan Areas," in Orin F. Nolting and David S. Arnold, eds., *The Municipal Year Book, 1959* (Chicago, 1959), Table VI.

13. *Op. cit.*, p. 176. An association between form of government and form of election is noted by Adrian, *op. cit.*, pp. 190, 204. For a general discussion, see Charles R. Adrian, "Some General Characteristics of Non-partisan Elections," *American Political Science Review*, 46 (1952), 766–76.

14. The proportions of nonwhite and aged 65 and over were taken from U.S. Bureau of the Census, *U.S. Census of Population: 1960, General Population Characteristics* (Washington, D.C., 1961), Table 13 for each state. Unless otherwise indicated, the remaining characteristics were taken from U.S. Bureau of the Census, *U.S. Census of Population: 1960, General Social and Economic Characteristics* (Washington, D.C., 1961), Tables 32 and 33 for each state. The growth rates for 1950–1960 were computed on the basis of data taken from *U.S. Census of Population: 1960*, Vol. I, *Characteristics of the Population* (Washington, D.C., 1961), Part A, "Number of Inhabitants," Table 8 for each state; the rates of growth were adjusted for annexations of territory and population between 1950 and 1960 by reference to Table 9. For the importance of this adjustment, see Leo F. Schnore, "Municipal Annexations and the Growth of Metropolitan Suburbs, 1950–1960," *American Journal of Sociology*, 67 (1962), 406–17. All the housing data were taken from U.S. Bureau of the Census, *U.S. Census of Housing: 1960*, Vol. I, *States and Small Areas* (Washington, D.C., 1962), Table 1 for each state.

15. As noted, population change over the decade was measured within 1950 boundaries in order to control for differences in the extent to which the three types of suburb were able to annex surrounding territory.

16. Robert H. Connery and Richard H. Leach, *The Federal Government and Metropolitan Areas* (Cambridge, Mass., 1960), p. 183.

17. It may be noted that most of these relationships between form of government and socioeconomic characteristics remain when partisan or nonpartisan suburbs are examined separately. Indeed, the ideal type of upper-middle-class suburb appears even more sharply delineated when only nonpartisan council-manager places are examined.

18. Annexation data were taken from *U.S. Census of Population: 1960*, Vol. I, *Characteristics of the Population*, Table 9 for each state.

19. See, for example, Edwin K. Stene and George K. Floro, *Abandonments of the Manager Plan: A Study of Four Small Cities* (Lawrence, Kan., 1953); and Arthur W. Bromage, *Manager Plan Abandonments* (rev. ed.; Chicago, 1949).

Part Four

The Socioeconomic Status
of Cities and Suburbs

THE ECOLOGIST'S INTEREST in suburbs is not confined to their functions and growth. Along with other sociologists, he is also interested in cities and suburbs as places of residence for people of widely differing social status. Suburbs, of course, are commonly supposed to be inhabited by populations ranking higher in socioeconomic status than the cities they surround. It happens, however, that this is a considerable overgeneralization, for it holds only for cities of a particular type—the older and larger cities. This is shown quite clearly in Chapter 11, which first appeared in the *American Sociological Review*, Volume 28 (February, 1963), pp. 76–85.

Chapter 12 is a direct follow-up to this study of cities and suburbs. It was originally published in *Demography*, Volume 1 (1964), pp. 164–76. In this chapter, the residential locations of detailed educational classes are examined. It is shown that there is a striking variety of patterns on view in American cities. In many instances, as expected, cities contain disproportionate numbers in the lower educational classes, while their suburbs are inhabited by persons at the top of the educational ladder.

In many other cases, however, cities are over–represented at the two extremes, with larger than the expected numbers of persons at the very bottom *and* the very top. Indeed, quite a large number of cities show a perfect reversal of the expected pattern. In other words, they are inhabited by people with more than average education, while their suburbs—supposedly "elite" areas—are filled with people having little or no formal schooling.

Chapter 13 pursues this subject still further. It was co-authored by J. John Palen and originally appeared in *Land Economics*, Volume 41 (February, 1965), pp. 87–91. It takes up the critical question of the effect of differences in color composition upon the direction of city-suburban status differences. This is important because, as we shall see in the next major section, whites and nonwhites are not randomly distributed as between cities and their surrounding suburbs. The two color groups are also different in terms of social class composition, having different amounts of education and income and having dissimilar occupational standing. This chapter also raises the issue of regional location, and shows that cities and suburbs in the South deviate considerably from the patterns observable throughout the rest of the country.

Chapter 11

The Socioeconomic Status
of Cities and Suburbs

STUDENTS OF URBANIZATION in the United States seem to take it as axiomatic that the socioeconomic status of "suburbia" is higher than that of the city. At least since the first statement of the Burgess zonal hypothesis in 1924, it has been generally assumed that such measures as income, education and occupational standing will ordinarily tend to exhibit an upward-sloping gradient with increasing distance away from the center of the urban agglomeration.[1] The Burgess scheme, taken in all its detail, has been subjected to considerable critical debate over the years. It has been attacked and defended with great vigor.[2] Despite the lack of consensus concerning the concentric-zonal model as an adequate description of cities in general, the existence of broad status differences in favor of American suburbs seems to be an accepted part of our thinking. Hauser has pro-

This study was supported by the research phase of the University of Wisconsin Urban Program, under the terms of a grant from the Ford Foundation. I am also grateful for assistance and technical facilities provided by the Social Systems Research Institute and the Numerical Analysis Laboratory, University of Wisconsin. The aid of four of my colleagues in the Institute—Arthur S. Goldberger, Verona Hofer, Roger F. Miller, and Norman B. Ryder—is especially appreciated.

vided a succinct account, and one to which most students of
the subject would probably subscribe:

> Residential land use patterns were a function of the geome-
> try of urban growth and the play of market forces. Since the
> city necessarily grew away from its point of origin, the newer
> residential areas were always farthest away from the center. . . .
>
> The histories of the inner and older areas of our cities have
> been, on the whole, remarkably uniform. Present inner and
> older areas were, at their origin, outlying suburbs containing
> the residences of the fashionably elite. With the continued
> growth of the city they became, more and more, inner zones,
> and followed similar patterns of changes in their residential oc-
> cupancy. They housed first the middle class, then working-
> men's families and finally, in many cases, they were turned over
> to rooming houses and slums. . . .
>
> Explosive urban and metropolitan growth, together with the
> play of market forces, determined both the patterns of land use
> and the distribution of population in space. Place of residence
> in metropolitan areas was determined by social and economic
> status, with the lower income groups living in the center of the
> city and the higher income groups toward the periphery. . . .
>
> Because city boundary lines have tended to remain relatively
> fixed while metropolitan clumpings of people and economic
> activities expanded, larger and larger proportions of the total
> central city land area have become inner and older zones of the
> entire metropolitan area and have been taken over by lower in-
> come groups; and increasing proportions of the higher income
> groups in the entire metropolitan area have become residents
> of suburbia.[3]

While this passage would not be accepted as a "universal" account, applicable to cities around the world,[4] it sums up the
prevalent view with respect to the development of current
differences in socioeconomic status between cities and suburbs
in the United States.

Even the most familiar notions, however, are deserving of
re-examination from time to time. In this instance, there are a
number of reasons for reopening the question. First, the results
of inquiries in other parts of the world, and in other historical
periods, might lead us to question some of our cherished gen-

eralizations.[5] Second, generalizations about American cities and suburbs tend to be based upon highly aggregated statistics for all "metropolitan areas" taken together, with contrasts between "central cities" and outlying "rings" emphasized; the hazard here is that the experience of the very largest metropolitan areas will unduly influence the results by sheer weight of numbers. Third, "suburbs" lacking the characteristics commonly attributed to them can be found in all parts of the United States. Many of them are quite low on all the common measures of socioeconomic status.[6] Moreover, even the most vigorous defenders of the Burgess hypothesis have seen fit to limit its scope rather sharply.[7] Finally, an exploratory study of income differentials between larger American cities and suburbs in 1950 has suggested that city-fringe income differentials are not so clearly and uniformly in favor of outlying areas as commonly supposed.[8]

UNITS, DATA AND PROCEDURES

The availability of new 1960 census materials permits some simple tests of the hypothesis that suburban fringe populations possess, on the average, higher socioeconomic status than the populations of central cities. Rather than using materials for metropolitan areas, where the rings frequently contain rural and agricultural populations, we have selected the "urbanized area" as the basic unit. The U.S. Bureau of the Census delineated 213 such areas in conjunction with the 1960 census. According to an official description:

> An urbanized area contains at least one city of 50,000 inhabitants or more in 1960, as well as the surrounding closely settled incorporated places and unincorporated areas. . . . *An urbanized area may be thought of as divided into the central city, or cities, and the remainder of the area, or the urban fringe.* . . .

Arrangements were made to include within the urbanized area those enumeration districts meeting specified criteria of population density as well as adjacent incorporated places. Since the urbanized area outside of incorporated places was defined in terms of enumeration districts, the boundaries of the urbanized area for the most part follow such features as roads, streets, railroads, streams, and other clearly defined lines which may be easily identified by census enumerators in the field and often do not conform to the boundaries of political units.[9]

Although the U.S. Bureau of the Census has carefully avoided using the term "suburb" in describing the outlying portion of the urbanized area, such a usage is somewhat preferable to calling this area the "urban fringe," for the latter term has been commonly employed to refer to an area of mixed rural and urban land use. With Duncan and Reiss, we prefer to conceive the outlying (noncentral city) portion of the urbanized area as consisting of *two* areal components—suburbs *and* the urban fringe—but we will use the term "suburb" as a matter of convenience.[10]

Our procedure was extremely simple. Comparisons of central cities and suburbs were possible in 200 urbanized areas.[11] We have tabulated the number of areas in which the values on certain socioeconomic status variables were higher in one or the other of these two areas—city or suburb. The three measures of socioeconomic status employed here were: (*1*) median family income, (*2*) the per cent of the population aged 25 years or over with four years of high school or more, and (*3*) the proportion of the total employed labor force in white-collar occupations. In short, we have used measures of income, education, and occupation—the three traditional variables employed in sociological analyses of stratification.

FINDINGS: CITY-SUBURBAN STATUS DIFFERENTIALS BY SIZE

Table 1 contains a comparison of the socioeconomic status of central cities and suburban fringes in areas categorized by population size. While none of the cities in the two largest size classes exceeds its suburbs in income, increasing proportions do so as one moves down the size range to the very smallest areas. The same general results are seen in the second column, where a measure of educational achievement is employed. Again, the

Table 1—City-Suburban Differentials in Socioeconomic Status, by Size of Urbanized Area, 1960

PER CENT OF URBANIZED AREAS WITH
SUBURBAN VALUES HIGHER IN:

Size of Urbanized Area, 1960	Median Family Income	Per Cent Completing High School	Per Cent White Collar	Number of Areas
1,000,000 and over	100.0	100.0	87.5	16
500,000–1,000,000	100.0	100.0	86.4	22
250,000–500,000	79.3	75.9	55.2	29
150,000–250,000	72.1	62.8	48.8	43
100,000–150,000	70.3	64.9	40.5	37
50,000–100,000	56.6	49.1	30.2	53
All areas	74.0	68.5	50.5	200

two largest size classes (38 areas) fail to show a single instance in which cities outstrip their suburbs. Moving down the full range of sizes, however, one finds that many small cities rank higher in educational status than their suburbs. Finally, the third column reveals the same general picture, although there are differences in detail. While there are a few very large central cities containing higher proportions of white-collar workers than their respective suburbs, they are not nearly so numerous—absolutely or relatively—as in the smaller size classes. In the smaller areas, in fact, clear majorities show higher values for central cities.

In sum, the popular view of city-suburban differentials in socioeconomic status is derived mainly from the experience of the larger areas. Since the averages for all areas taken together are inevitably weighted by the situation in the largest areas, they can be very misleading as a description of individual areas.[12] In smaller areas (those between 50,000 and 100,000), the city itself is more likely to contain populations that are—on the average—higher in status than those found in the suburban fringe. Whether one measures socioeconomic status by income, education, or occupation, the results are the same: there is a marked association between size and the direction of city-suburban differentials.

What are the factors that lie behind the differences that can be observed among size classes? One line of interpretation involves sheer *age of settlement*. Cities vary in age, and a well-known association exists between age and size; in the 213 urbanized areas of 1960, for example, the correlation between size of central city and age is +.478, and that between size of urbanized area and age is +.502.[13] Nevertheless the correlation is not very high, and it might be expected that areas of the same size, but differing in age, will differ in residential structure. But first let us examine the extent to which age itself is associated with city-suburban differentials in socioeconomic status.

FINDINGS: CITY-SUBURBAN STATUS DIFFERENTIALS BY AGE

We have measured the "ages" of these 200 urbanized areas by counting the number of decades that have passed since their central cities first contained 50,000 inhabitants. Table 2 shows the city-suburban comparisons on our three measures of socioeconomic status according to age. The first column reveals that suburban fringes consistently register higher median family incomes in the older areas; none of the 31 cities reaching a size of 50,000 in 1880 or earlier has a higher average income than its suburbs. In contrast, the newer urbanized areas tend consistently to show larger and larger proportions of central cities with higher incomes. When the measure of educational status is employed, as in the second column, the results are generally the same. The proportion of persons completing at least a high school education is consistently higher in the suburbs of older cities, while newer cities tend to show the opposite pattern. Similarly, the occupational measure suggests that age is clearly associated with city-suburban differentials in socioeconomic status. Examining the third column, we find that none of the 31 oldest cities exceeds its suburban fringe in the proportion of white-collar workers. At the other extreme, three out of every four of the newest cities contain higher proportions of white-collar workers than their adjacent suburbs.

As with size, then, we have found another series of marked associations between age and the direction of city-suburban differentials in socioeconomic status. The common conception —that higher status people live in the suburbs—tends to be true

Table 2—City-Suburban Differentials in Socioeconomic Status, by Age of Central City

PER CENT OF URBANIZED AREAS WITH
SUBURBAN VALUES HIGHER IN:

Census Year in Which Central City (or Cities) First Reached 50,000	Median Family Income	Per Cent Completing High School	Per Cent White Collar	Number of Areas
1800–1860	100.0	100.0	100.0	14
1870–1880	100.0	100.0	100.0	17
1890–1900	86.1	75.0	58.3	36
1910–1920	75.0	75.0	54.2	48
1930–1940	71.9	56.3	31.3	32
1950–1960	50.9	47.2	24.5	53
All areas	74.0	68.5	50.5	200

of the very oldest areas, but it is progressively less true of newer areas. In cities that have only reached substantial size (50,000 inhabitants) in recent decades, cities themselves contain populations that are higher in status than those in their own adjacent suburbs. Not only is the popular generalization concerning city-suburban status differentials inadequate as a description of all urbanized areas, but it is also directly contrary to the facts in the newest areas.

FURTHER ANALYSIS: A MULTIVARIATE APPROACH

The preceding comparisons of cities and their suburbs by socioeconomic status have demonstrated that higher status groups tend to occupy the periphery of *older* and *larger* urban areas. But age and size are themselves correlated. The next analytical problem became one of assessing the relative "weight" to be assigned to age and size as predictors of city-suburban differentials in socioeconomic status. In view of the marked correlation between the independent variables and the limited number of cases for analysis (200 urbanized areas), we were obliged to turn to partial correlation techniques.

Our procedure was again extremely simple. For each of the three separate measures of socioeconomic status for each urbanized area, we assigned arbitrary numerical values—a "0" if the central city was higher, and a "1" if the suburban fringe was higher.[14] We then computed zero-order and partial correlation coefficients between each of the three dependent variables (education, occupation, and income) and the independent variables. We then repeated the analysis using suburb-city ratios, i.e., dividing the suburb's value on each of the three measures by the city's respective value.

Besides age and size, however, we took care to add a third "independent" variable. *This variable was the percentage of the total urbanized area's 1960 population found within the central city or cities.* The rationale for its inclusion in this phase of the analysis was as follows: (*1*) The 200 urbanized areas under study differ considerably in this proportion, ranging from a low of 27.2 per cent in Wilkes-Barre, Pennsylvania, to a high of 99.7 per cent in Austin, Texas. (*2*) Inspection of the data for the 200 urbanized areas indicated that this proportion was negatively associated with all three of the dependent variables, the measures of socioeconomic status differentials, and with both of the independent variables whose predictive ability we wished to assess. In other words, urbanized areas with a high proportion of population in central cities tended to show higher city values on income, education, and occupation, and they also tended to be smaller and newer. (*3*) This proportion seemed to us a rough but useful measure of the extent to which a city has been successful in extending its official boundaries to keep up with the physical spread of urban development within its immediate vicinity. Some large cities are surrounded by "iron rings" of established incorporated suburbs or other political units which are extremely resistant to absorption by annexation, while other cities are free—whether by virtue of facilitating legal arrangements or by possession of powers of one kind or another—to annex outlying territory with relative ease.[15] In any event, we wished to eliminate the statistical effect of this "confounding variable," the extent to which the politically defined city is coextensive with the physically defined urbanized area. For ease of expression, we shall refer to this factor as the "annexation" variable throughout the balance of the discussion.

Table 3 shows the zero-order correlations between each of the six variables and every other variable included in the analy-

Table 3—Zero-Order Correlation Coefficients[a]

	INDEPENDENT VARIABLES			DEPENDENT VARIABLES		
	Size	Annexation	Age	Education	Occupation	Income
Size	—	−.2341	.5006	.1789	.1825	.1574
Annexation	−.2341	—	−.3457	−.2982	−.2733	−.2883
Age	.5006	−.3457	—	.3753	.4781	.3701
Education	.1975	−.3943	.4861	—	.6204	.7023
Occupation	.1730	−.4246	.4590	.9478	—	.5759
Income	.1730	−.3660	.4135	.8393	.8538	—

a. Above diagonal, correlations based on scoring cities and suburbs (0 and 1) as "dummy variables." Below diagonal, suburb-city ratios.

sis. The two bases of scoring cities and suburbs are shown above and below the diagonal. Except for the negative associations between the "annexation" factor and all the others, the coefficients are positive. Note the especially high correlations among the dependent variables when ratios are employed. The latter intercorrelations, although of interest, are of no immediate consequence for our analysis, since we wished to use these three variables as separate tests or assessments of the relative predictive ability of size and age, holding constant the confounding "annexation" factor.

The results of these three assessments are reported in Tables 4 and 5, summaries of the two partial correlation analyses. Besides the multiple and partial correlation coefficients, we show the *beta* coefficients—the partial regression coefficients in standard form—and t statistics. The three separate analyses of educational, occupational, and income differentials on two different bases yield highly similar results. Both tables show that the predictive ability of population size is substantially reduced when the other two variables—age and annexation—are taken into account. In fact, the signs of the coefficients are reversed in all three instances in both tables, shifting from positive in the zero-order correlations to negative in the partials, and falling below the level of statistical significance. By contrast, age continues to serve as a highly significant predictor of city-suburban differentials in socioeconomic status; when size and annexation are held constant, age continues to exert a large and measurable influence upon the direction of the differences between cities and suburbs.

Table 4a—Summary of First Partial Correlation Analysis, with Cities and Suburbs Scored as "Dummy Variables"

Dependent variable		Education	
Multiple correlation coefficient		.4012	
Independent variable	Size	Annexation	Age
Controlled variables	Annexation	Size	Size
	Age	Age	Annexation
Partial correlation coefficients	—.0263	—.1951	.2833
Beta coefficients	—.0277	—.1932	.3223
t statistics	—0.037	—2.785	4.136

Table 4b

Dependent variable		Occupation	
Multiple correlation coefficient		.4857	
Independent variable	Size	Annexation	Age
Controlled variables	Annexation	Size	Size
	Age	Age	Annexation
Partial correlation coefficients	—.0856	—.1375	.4164
Beta coefficients	—.0863	—.1287	.4768
t statistics	—1.202	—1.944	6.411

Table 4c

Dependent variable		Income	
Multiple correlation coefficient		.3943	
Independent variable	Size	Annexation	Age
Controlled variables	Annexation	Size	Size
	Age	Age	Annexation
Partial correlation coefficients	—.0494	—.1872	.2903
Beta coefficients	—.0523	—.1857	.3320
t statistics	—0.693	—2.668	4.246

CONCLUSIONS

Sheer age of settlement has emerged as the best predictor of the direction of city-suburban differences in socioeconomic status. Older urbanized areas tend strongly to possess peripheral populations of higher socioeconomic standing than found in the central cities themselves. In contrast, newer cities tend to contain populations ranking higher on education, occupation, and income than their respective suburbs. To some extent, these differences are also revealed when urbanized areas are classified by size, but control of the latter factor does not eliminate the apparent importance of age as a factor in residential structure.

What is it about sheer age of settlement that might account for the observed differences? The first thing the student of the American city might consider is the fact that the housing stock of older areas of occupance is obsolescent. These areas, concentrated near the center of the political city, are filled with older structures in such disrepair that enormous efforts have recently been directed toward slum clearance and renewal, and toward renovation of "blighted" areas which are fast becoming

Table 5a—Summary of Second Partial Correlation Analysis, with Suburban-City Ratios

Dependent variable		Education	
Multiple correlation coefficient		.5374	
Independent variable	Size	Annexation	Age
Controlled variables	Annexation	Size	Size
	Age	Age	Annexation
Partial correlation coefficients	—.0849	—.2818	.3986
Beta coefficients	—.0826	—.2627	.4366
t statistics	—1.192	—4.111	6.085

Table 5b

Dependent variable		Occupation	
Multiple correlation coefficient		.5366	
Independent variable	Size	Annexation	Age
Controlled variables	Annexation	Size	Size
	Age	Age	Annexation
Partial correlation coefficients	—.1036	—.3264	.3720
Beta coefficients	—.1010	—.3090	.4028
t statistics	—1.458	—4.834	5.610

Table 5c

Dependent variable		Income	
Multiple correlation coefficient		.4680	
Independent variable	Size	Annexation	Age
Controlled variables	Annexation	Size	Size
	Age	Age	Annexation
Partial correlation coefficients	—.0653	—.2653	.3217
Beta coefficients	—.0665	—.2580	.3576
t statistics	—0.916	—3.853	4.756

slums. These are the areas which have come to be occupied by groups at the bottom of the socioeconomic ladder—groups which have strictly limited housing choices. In the older urbanized areas, new additions to the available housing stock have tended over the years to be added at the physical margins of the built-up area. New housing developments, in other words, have been concentrated in outlying zones, where they have come to be occupied by those who can afford the costs of home ownership and the added transportation charges that go with peripheral residence.[16]

In newer urbanized areas, the housing stock of the central city itself is neither so old nor so run-down as to be unattractive to potential home-owners of the expanding "middle class." At the same time, the pressures exerted by the competition of alternative (nonresidential) land uses on inner zones now appear to be less intense in these newer cities than they were in older cities at comparable stages in the past; with the availability of the automobile and the truck, industrial and commercial land uses are less likely to be thrusting out inexorably from the heart of the city, and more likely to be "leap-frogging" the interior residential zones for new shopping centers and industrial parks at the outer periphery. As a consequence, central residential zones in newer cities may be less likely to undergo the "succession" or "sequent occupance" of progressively lower status groups experienced by neighborhoods in the older cities.

As for the older cities, a fascinating question is raised by these materials: *Have they evolved in a predictable direction?* Burgess conceived his zonal hypothesis as a "growth model," or a statement couched entirely in terms of process, and not as a static or cross-sectional representation of urban spatial structure. The very title of his original essay—"The Growth of the City"—indicated his intentions. In referring to the stylized map of Chicago that accompanied his original statement of the zonal hypothesis, Burgess remarked that "This chart represents an ideal construction of the tendencies of any town or city to expand radially from its central business district. . . .

This chart brings out clearly the main fact of expansion, namely, the tendency of each inner zone to extend its area by the invasion of the next outer zone."[17]

As to the location of the "elite," in fact, Burgess noted that "the present boundaries of the area of deterioration were not many years ago those of the zone now inhabited by independent wage-earners, and within the memories of thousands of Chicagoans contained the residences of the 'best families.' "[18] Or consider the testimony of Homer Hoyt. Two sets of maps showing "high-grade," "intermediate," and "low-grade" residential areas for Chicago in 1857, 1873, 1899, and 1930 reveal that the "high-grade" areas were very near the center in 1857 and that they shifted toward the periphery over the years.[19] But Chicago is only one case. Consider Heberle's account of developments in the American South:

> It seems to be characteristic for the older, smaller, cities in the South that the homes of the socially prominent families were to be found just outside the central—and only—business district. . . . As the city grew and as wealth increased, the "old" families tended to move towards the periphery. . . . The old homes are then converted into rooming houses and "tourist homes." This in itself is nothing peculiar to the South. However, it so happens that in the kind of city under consideration, the poorer people usually lived at the edge of town. This was particularly the case with Negroes. It happens, therefore, quite frequently that white people infiltrate into suburban areas occupied by Negroes, buying their property or cancelling their leases.[20]

In sum, we might outline a rough "evolutionary model" to describe the changes in older urban areas. With growth and expansion of the center, and with radical improvements in transportation and communication technology, the upper strata have shifted from central to peripheral residence, and the lower classes have increasingly taken up occupancy in the central areas abandoned by the elite. Despite mounting land values occasioned by the competition of alternative (nonresidential) land uses, the lower strata have been able to occupy valuable central land in tenements, subdivided dwellings originally intended for single families, and other high-density "slum" arrangements.

The evolutionary sequence roughly sketched here is far from complete. For one thing, it requires more attention to what Burgess called "the survival of an earlier use of a district." A case in point is the persistence of elite areas near the centers of many cities, a deviation from the general pattern to which we have already alluded. More generally, it requires elaboration of the role of "historical residues," such as the significance of a city's development in a particular transportation era. For example, casual observation suggests a whole series of differences between pre- and post-automobile cities in the United States—differences in street patterns, land uses, and residential densities. Unfortunately, precise historical data are rather difficult to obtain and to evaluate, and the problem of attributing current significance to "survivals" from an earlier epoch always remains.[21]

Nothing in the preceding account is intended to suggest that a fixed and immutable "final stage" has been achieved in older American cities. Concerning the future implications of current developments, Hauser has observed:

> The combination of urban renewal in the inner zones of central cities and blight and urban sprawl in the suburbs is tending to disrupt the pattern of population distribution which has placed the higher income groups farthest out from the center of the city. Should these trends continue, the residential land use pattern in metropolitan areas would be turned inside out, with the newer and more desirable areas located in the rebuilt inner city zones as well as in the most distant parts of suburbia.[22]

In conclusion, we must emphasize that our own efforts to reconstruct the past development of urban residential structure are speculative. They are based on a thin line of evidence derived from cross-sectional observations of broad status groups in cities of different age. One hesitates to assert on the basis of these materials that a determinate "evolutionary sequence" occurs with the maturation of urban areas. Longitudinal inferences cannot be readily derived from cross-sectional observations. Nothing presented here denies the existence of an historical series of outward shifts of higher status groups from the center to the periphery, but proof of such a sequence is not established in this study.

Further research must undertake just such historical reconstructions of the major shifts in location of socioeconomic strata in cities as they have grown and matured. The availability of census tract data for 30 years in a number of urban areas opens up one line of analytical possibilities. Certainly the finer observational grain afforded by tract analyses is preferable to the kind of gross city-suburban comparisons set out in this paper. Models for comparative research of this kind already exist in the literature.[23] Perhaps a more pressing need is that for models which will predict the future growth and structure of newer cities. It is already apparent that their development will differ in numerous respects from the patterns displayed by older cities. A revival of urban research effort, focussed on certain "classic" problems in ecological analysis, and using modern research techniques in a comparative framework, should yield rich returns in the way of understanding the growth and changing spatial structure of the American city.

NOTES

1. It will be recalled that the Burgess zones were originally described largely in terms of socioeconomic status. Thus outside the CBD and the "zone in transition" (containing "first-settlement immigrant colonies, rooming-house districts, and homelessmen areas") were Zone III, "The Zone of Independent Workingmen's Homes," Zone IV, "The Zone of Better Residences," and Zone V, "The Commuter's Zone." See Ernest W. Burgess, "The Growth of the City: An Introduction to a Research Project," *Publications of the American Sociological Society*, 18 (1924), pp. 85–97; reprinted in Robert E. Park, Ernest W. Burgess, and Roderick D. McKenzie, *The City*, Chicago: University of Chicago Press, 1925, pp. 47–62.

2. For criticisms, see Milla A. Alihan, *Social Ecology: A Critical Analysis*, New York: Columbia University Press, 1938; Maurice R. Davie, "The Pattern of Urban Growth," in George Peter Murdock, editor, *Studies in the Science of Society*, New Haven: Yale University Press,

1937, pp. 133–161; Walter Firey, *Land Use in Central Boston*, Cambridge: Harvard University Press, 1947. For a defense, see James A. Quinn, "The Burgess Zonal Hypothesis and Its Critics," *American Sociological Review*, 5 (April, 1940), pp. 210–18.

3. Philip M. Hauser, *Population Perspectives*, New Brunswick, New Jersey: Rutgers University Press, 1960, pp. 110–12. In subsequent sections, Hauser goes on to suggest some ways in which the future patterns of American cities may differ from the historical sequence described in the quotation.

4. Referring especially to a series of studies in Latin America, Gist has observed that there is "ample evidence that ecological theory based on the study of [North] American cities is not necessarily applicable to cities in other parts of the world." Noel P. Gist, "The Urban Community," in Joseph B. Gittler, editor, *Review of Sociology: Analysis of a Decade*, New York: John Wiley and Sons, Inc., 1957, p. 170.

5. With respect to the residential location of socioeconomic strata in "preindustrial" cities, Sjoberg reports as follows: "The preindustrial city's central area is notable also as the chief residence of the elite. . . . The disadvantaged members of the city fan out toward the periphery, with the very poorest and the outcastes living in the suburbs, the farthest removed from the center." He reports that archeological and historical evidence, together with accounts of the residential structure of contemporary cities in all major world regions, "all confirm the universality of this land use pattern in the non-industrial civilized world." See Gideon Sjoberg, *The Preindustrial City: Past and Present*, Glencoe, Ill.: The Free Press, 1960, pp. 97–98.

6. See Bennett M. Berger, *Working-Class Suburb*, Berkeley and Los Angeles: University of California Press, 1960. In addition to residential suburbs inhabited by blue-collar workers, there are many industrial satellites characterized by low income. See Leo F. Schnore, "Satellites and Suburbs," *Social Forces*, 36 (December, 1957), pp. 121–27.

7. See James A. Quinn, *Human Ecology*, New York: Prentice-Hall, Inc., 1950, Chapter VI.

8. Leo F. Schnore, "City-Suburban Income Differentials in Metropolitan Areas," *American Sociological Review*, 27 (April, 1962), pp. 252–55.

9. U.S. Bureau of the Census, *U.S. Census of Population: 1960*, Volume I, *Characteristics of the Population*, Part A, "Number of Inhabitants," Washington, D.C.: U.S. Government Printing Office, 1961, pp. xviii–xx; italics added. See also Richard A. Kurtz and Joanne B. Eicher, "Fringe and Suburb: A Confusion of Concepts," *Social Forces*, 37 (October, 1958), pp. 32–37.

10. Otis Dudley Duncan and Albert J. Reiss, Jr., *Social Characteristics of Urban and Rural Communities, 1950*, New York: John Wiley and Sons, Inc., 1956, Chapter 11; see especially footnote 3, p. 118.

11. The thirteen urbanized areas for which city-suburban comparisons could not be made include Meriden, Connecticut; Topeka, Kansas; Lewiston-Auburn, Maine; Raleigh, North Carolina; Lawton, Oklahoma; and the following eight areas in Texas: Amarillo, Beaumont, El Paso, Laredo, Lubbock, San Angelo, Tyler and Wichita Falls. All of the data were

taken from the U.S. Bureau of the Census, *General Social and Economic Characteristics*, "Advance Reports," Series PC(A3), Tables 32 and 33. Individual reports for states were issued between July 14, 1961 and April 27, 1962.

12. The following differences appeared between cities and suburbs in the 157 urbanized areas delineated in conjunction with the 1950 census:

	Cities	Suburbs
Median school years completed	9.9	11.1
Per cent in white-collar occupations	45.2	46.9
Median personal income (dollars)	2,249	2,499

Source: Duncan and Reiss, *op. cit.*, pp. 127–130; city-suburban differentials were also shown according to sex and color.

In 1960, the 213 urbanized areas showed the following aggregate differences:

	Cities	Suburbs
Median school years completed	10.7	12.0
Per cent in white-collar occupations	40.6	50.3
Median family income (dollars)	5,945	7,114

Source: "Advance Reports," Series PC(A3)-1, Table 100.

The status differentials again favor the suburbs. The 38 urbanized areas of 500,000 or more contained more than 70 per cent of the total population in urbanized areas (almost 96 million persons), and the above averages are heavily weighted by the experience of these large areas. The popular generalizations regarding city-suburban differences are accurate as descriptions of *individuals according to place of residence*, but they are misleading statements about *areas of habitation*.

13. The measure of "age" is the number of decades that have passed since the central city (or cities) first contained 50,000 inhabitants. Bogue and Harris reported a correlation of +.596 between age (as measured here) and size of 125 metropolitan areas in 1940; see Donald J. Bogue and Dorothy L. Harris, *Comparative Population and Urban Research via Multiple Regression and Covariance Analysis*, Oxford, Ohio and Chicago: Scripps Foundation for Research in Population Problems, Miami University, and Population Research and Training Center, University of Chicago, 1954, Appendix Table II, p. 75.

14. See Daniel B. Suits, "The Use of Dummy Variables in Regression Equations," *Journal of the American Statistical Association*, 52 (December, 1957), pp. 548–551; for an illustrative usage, see John B. Lansing and Dwight M. Blood, "A Cross-Section Analysis of Non-Business Air Travel," *Journal of the American Statistical Association*, 53 (December, 1958), pp. 923–47.

15. State laws are extremely variable in this respect. Texas statutes apparently grant the municipality the greatest freedom to annex nearby territory, and it is noteworthy that all of the Texas cities in this study expanded their limits between 1950 and 1960. Law is apparently not the only critical factor, however, for some cities are reputed to use their control over the water supply or vital municipal services as a means of coercing outlying populations into joining the city. As for the ability of

the measure used here to serve as a "proxy variable," representing annexation success, the following tabulation suggests that it is reasonably adequate:

Per Cent of Urbanized Area Population in City, 1960	Number of Urbanized Areas	Per Cent with Annexations by Central City, 1950–60
90.0 or more	39	89.7
80.0–89.9	36	83.3
70.0–79.9	33	78.8
60.0–69.9	36	75.0
50.0–59.9	29	72.4
Less than 50.0	27	55.6
All areas	200	77.0

16. We say that the more favored classes will ordinarily pre-empt the newer and more desirable housing areas, and that with the expansion of the built-up territory, these areas have been typically located at the periphery in American cities. We simply assume a high degree of locational freedom on the part of the wealthy, who may occupy practically any area, as compared with the lower classes, who are much more severely restricted with respect to residential choices. Thus the wealthy may live very near the center if they are willing to pay the high costs involved in competing with nonresidential land uses. Most American cities reveal such elite enclaves very near the downtown area; consider only Beacon Hill in Boston, as described by Firey, and Chicago's Gold Coast, shown in the original Burgess map as a deviant case. From one perspective, these areas represent "survivals" of an earlier pattern of land use, but there is nothing mysterious about the mechanism that produces them.

17. Burgess, "The Growth of the City," in *The City, op. cit.,* p. 50.

18. *Ibid.,* pp. 50–51.

19. Homer Hoyt, *The Structure and Growth of Residential Neighborhoods in American Cities,* Washington, D.C.: Federal Housing Administration, 1939, Figure 29, p. 83, and Figure 31, p. 166. This shift is described in detail in Homer Hoyt, *One Hundred Years of Land Values in Chicago,* Chicago: University of Chicago Press, 1933, Chapter VI.

20. Rudolf Heberle, "Social Consequences of the Industrialization of Southern Cities," *Social Forces,* 27 (October, 1948), pp. 34–35.

21. A suggestive treatment of the evolution of residential neighborhoods is contained in Edgar M. Hoover and Raymond Vernon, *Anatomy of a Metropolis,* Cambridge: Harvard University Press, 1959, pp. 190–207. See also Raymond Vernon, "The Economics and Finances of the Large Metropolis," *Daedalus,* 90 (Winter, 1961), pp. 31–47.

22. Hauser, *op. cit.,* p. 115.

23. Beverly Duncan, Georges Sabagh, and Maurice D. Van Arsdol, Jr., "Patterns of City Growth," *American Journal of Sociology,* 67 (January, 1962), pp. 418–29; Otis Dudley Duncan and Beverly Duncan, "Residential Distribution and Occupational Stratification," *American Journal of Sociology,* 60 (March, 1955), pp. 495–503; Otis Dudley Duncan and Stanley Lieberson, "Ethnic Segregation and Assimilation," *American*

Journal of Sociology, 64 (January, 1959), pp. 364–74; Stanley Lieberson, "Suburbs and Ethnic Residential Patterns," *American Journal of Sociology*, 67 (May, 1962), pp. 673–81. The only related topic that has received detailed historical treatment is the outward dispersion of various immigrant groups over the years; see Paul F. Cressey, "Population Succession in Chicago: 1898–1930," *American Journal of Sociology*, 44 (July, 1938), pp. 59–69; Richard G. Ford, "Population Succession in Chicago," *American Journal of Sociology*, 56 (September, 1950), pp. 156–160; and Stanley Lieberson, "The Impact of Residential Segregation on Ethnic Assimilation," *Social Forces*, 40 (October, 1961), pp. 52–57.

Chapter 12

Urban Structure
and Suburban Selectivity

Introduction

THE FOCUS of this chapter is a classic problem in ecological analysis, for it deals with variations in the residential distribution of socioeconomic strata in urban areas. A large part of the literature dealing with this topic treats it as a longitudinal problem, i.e., variations over time are stressed, as in the Burgess theory concerning "The Growth of the City."[1] This chapter, however, will be largely cross-sectional in approach and will stress variations from place to place at a given point in time, with only passing attention to historical trends.

The results reported here represent two extensions of the chapter entitled "The Socioeconomic Status of Cities and Suburbs," where it was shown that American "cities" and "suburbs" cannot be unequivocally characterized as "higher" or "lower" in socioeconomic status. The suburban population of *larger* Urbanized Areas are typically higher in average socioeconomic standing than the great cities they surround, but this situation tends to be reversed as one moves down the size scale. In the *small* Urbanized Area (between 50,000 and 100,000 in-

[222]

habitants), the city itself is—on the average—more likely to contain a population with higher socioeconomic standing than that of its own suburban fringe.[2]

But the study reported above had many limitations, not the least of which was its dependence upon (1) cross-sectional observations of (2) highly simplified measures of socioeconomic status for (3) whole populations without regard for age, sex, or color composition.[3] The data were taken from a series of "Advance Reports" from the 1960 Census of Population issued between July 1961 and April 1962. The current availability of more detailed census tabulations permits the removal of some of the more severe limitations upon the earlier exploratory study.[4]

The Measurement of Residence and Socioeconomic Status

While we have continued to work with the gross distinction between "city" and "suburbs," we have turned to a single indicator of socioeconomic status—the number of school years completed by the population aged 25 years or older. The earlier study simply involved a comparison of the proportions in cities and suburbs completing at least 12 years of schooling. Rather than continuing to work with this single value, however, we have examined the residential distributions of eight detailed educational classes.

Measuring the "suburban selectivity" of educational classes —The first basic question asked was, *What is the current residential distribution—city versus suburb—of each educational class?* The procedure is set out in Table 1, where data for males in the four largest metropolitan areas (SCA's and SMSA's) are shown in detail. The second-last column shows the proportion of each detailed educational class that resides in the city, and the last column shows a simple "index of suburbanization" which consists of (1) the proportion living in the city *for each educational class* in the metropolitan area in question divided by (2) the proportion living in the city *among all males 25 years of age or older* in the same area. The resulting ratios can

Table 1—Residential Distribution of Educational Groups in Four Metropolitan Areas, 1960

Males, 25 Years of Age or Older, by Years of School Completed	Number in SMSA or SCA	Number in City	Number in "Ring"	Per Cent in City[a]	Index of Suburbanization[b]
New York SCA	4,283,823	2,319,679	1,964,144	54.1	100
None	150,864	110,211	40,653	73.0	135
Grade: 1–4	201,047	126,994	74,053	63.1	117
Grade: 5–6	277,119	162,260	114,859	58.5	108
Grade: 7–8	1,009,038	575,609	433,429	57.0	105
High: 1–3	870,075	468,266	401,809	53.8	99
High: 4	851,210	433,729	417,481	50.9	94
College: 1–3	379,374	188,722	190,652	49.7	92
College: 4+	545,096	253,888	291,208	46.5	86
Chicago SCA	1,897,558	1,029,007	868,551	54.2	100
None	36,518	26,963	9,555	73.8	136
Grade: 1–4	99,114	68,796	30,318	69.4	128
Grade: 5–6	117,439	76,651	40,788	65.2	120
Grade: 7–8	455,124	269,211	185,913	59.2	109
High: 1–3	390,603	220,291	170,312	56.3	104
High: 4	402,146	192,772	209,374	47.9	88
College: 1–3	194,801	95,303	99,498	48.9	90
College: 4+	201,813	79,020	122,793	39.1	72
Philadelphia SMSA	1,199,583	565,652	633,931	47.1	100
None	26,714	18,238	8,476	68.2	148
Grade: 1–4	61,301	37,554	23,747	61.2	130
Grade: 5–6	94,840	53,525	41,315	56.4	120
Grade: 7–8	288,925	149,809	139,116	51.9	110
High: 1–3	263,492	132,900	130,592	50.4	107
High: 4	244,043	99,418	144,625	40.7	86
College: 1–3	89,414	33,395	56,019	37.3	79
College: 4+	130,854	40,813	90,041	31.2	66
Los Angeles SMSA	1,868,544	721,264	1,147,280	38.6	100
None	28,355	15,420	12,935	54.4	141
Grade: 1–4	61,745	28,380	33,365	46.0	119
Grade: 5–6	85,312	37,527	47,785	44.0	114
Grade: 7–8	318,880	118,302	200,578	37.1	96
High: 1–3	377,263	134,431	242,832	35.6	92
High: 4	468,183	172,726	295,457	36.9	96
College: 1–3	286,725	113,146	173,579	39.5	102
College: 4+	242,081	101,332	140,749	41.9	109

a. "Per cent in city" shows the proportion of a given educational class in the entire SMSA (or SCA) that resides in the central city.

b. The "index of suburbanization" is the above value for each educational class divided by the proportion for the total male population aged 25 and over.

be interpreted as variations around the hypothetical "expected value" of 100 which would obtain if each class exhibited exactly the same balance between city and suburbs.[5] Values above 100 indicate over-representation in the city and values below 100 indicate over-representation in the suburbs.

The last column of Table 1 shows some rather interesting

patterns. In the first three instances—New York, Chicago, and Philadelphia—the ratios descend regularly from a high value for those with no formal schooling to a low value for those who have completed four years of college or more. This is the precise pattern that one would expect on the basis of contemporary discussions of "the flight of the elite to suburbia," "the loss of city leadership," etc., and we can take it as the "expected" pattern. But observe the deviant pattern presented in the case of Los Angeles; here we find *persons at the top and at the bottom* of the educational ladder over-represented in the city itself.

THE "POLARIZATION" OF EDUCATIONAL CLASSES OVER TIME

Up to this point, we have been examining the residential distribution of socioeconomic strata cross-sectionally, as of 1960. A longitudinal examination of pre- versus post-war patterns can also be fruitful. (The 1940 census was the first to report detailed data on school years completed; prior censuses depended upon a question relating to simple literacy.)

Table 2—Indexes of Suburbanization for the Detroit Metropolitan Area, 1940–60

Males, 25 Years of Age or Older, by Years of School Completed	PER CENT IN CITY:			INDEX OF SUBURBANIZATION:			DIFFERENCES IN INDEX:		
	1940	1950	1960	1940	1950	1960	1940–1950	1950–1960	1940–1960
Detroit (total)	69.6	63.4	46.9	100.0	100.0	100.0			
None	76.5	73.7	69.3	109.9	116.2	147.7	6.3	31.5	37.8
Grade: 1–4	72.1	71.3	64.6	103.6	112.4	138.3	8.8	25.9	34.7
Grade: 5–6	71.5	69.3	59.3	102.7	109.3	126.4	6.6	17.1	23.7
Grade: 7–8	69.1	62.8	51.4	99.3	98.8	109.5	−0.5	10.7	10.2
High: 1–3	69.0	62.2	45.9	99.1	98.1	97.8	−1.0	−0.3	−1.3
High: 4	70.4	61.2	40.5	101.2	96.5	86.3	−4.7	−10.2	−14.9
College: 1–3	69.9	63.3	40.1	100.4	99.8	85.5	−0.6	−14.3	−14.9
College: 4+	69.0	59.2	34.9	99.1	93.3	74.4	−5.8	−18.9	−24.7

Here the basic question is, *Are the various educational classes becoming more or less like each other with respect to residence?* To put it another way, we want to know whether or

Table 3—Differences in Index of Suburbanization, Ten Largest Metropolitan Areas, 1940–60

Males, 25 Years of Age or Older, by Years of School Completed	NEW YORK			LOS ANGELES			CHICAGO			PHILADELPHIA			DETROIT		
	1940–1950	1950–1960	1940–1960	1940–1950	1950–1960	1940–1960	1940–1950	1950–1960	1940–1960	1940–1950	1950–1960	1940–1960	1940–1950	1950–1960	1940–1960
None	−11	11	0	11	16	27	1	22	23	5	17	22	6	32	38
Grade: 1–4	4	11	15	11	3	14	6	18	23	6	20	26	9	26	35
Grade: 5–6	7	6	13	9	2	11	5	15	20	7	10	17	7	17	24
Grade: 7–8	−1	4	3	−1	−3	−1	−1	8	8	−1	7	6	−1	11	10
High: 1–3	0	2	2	−3	0	−3	2	2	4	4	4	8	−1	0	−1
High: 4	2	−2	0	−5	−2	−7	−1	−9	−10	3	−8	−5	−5	−10	−15
College: 1–3	−5	−1	−6	−1	1	1	−2	−5	−7	3	−7	−4	−1	−14	−15
College: 4+	−3	−7	−10	3	5	8	−3	−14	−17	−5	−12	−17	−6	−19	−25

Males, 25 Years of Age or Older, by Years of School Completed	SAN FRANCISCO			BOSTON			PITTSBURGH			ST. LOUIS			WASHINGTON		
	1940–1950	1950–1960	1940–1960	1940–1950	1950–1960	1940–1960	1940–1950	1950–1960	1940–1960	1940–1950	1950–1960	1940–1960	1940–1950	1950–1960	1940–1960
None	24	38	62	−4	16	12	16	17	33	−3	23	20	17	40	57
Grade: 1–4	13	17	30	1	27	28	7	19	26	5	33	38	13	39	52
Grade: 5–6	10	14	24	4	18	22	6	8	14	7	21	28	15	29	44
Grade: 7–8	−3	11	8	−2	6	4	−4	5	1	0	10	10	7	15	22
High: 1–3	−5	3	−2	6	10	16	−2	6	4	0	3	3	0	10	10
High: 4	2	−12	−10	2	−2	0	−15	−11	−26	−7	−12	−19	−6	−11	−17
College: 1–3	−3	1	−2	−2	−10	−12	−1	−11	−12	−4	−9	−13	−11	−7	−18
College: 4+	−2	−2	−4	−57	−6	−63	−10	−19	−29	−6	−17	−23	−11	−10	−21

not "residential segregation by social class" has been mounting. Much of the scholarly and semipopular literature on the subject would have us believe that "polarization" has been on the increase, with the city increasingly given over to the disadvantaged (educationally and otherwise), and with the suburb more and more occupied by the well–to–do.[6]

Table 2 shows a clear instance of increasing "polarization," particularly during the 1950–60 decade when the over-all "suburbanization" of the Detroit population was proceeding somewhat more rapidly than in the preceding ten years. This trend toward increasing "polarization" can be inferred from the last panel, where the differences between the index values for the three census years are set out. The very last column suggests that the twenty-year interval was characterized by a distinctly patterned "sifting and sorting" of the various educational classes between the city of Detroit and its surrounding suburbs, with the sharpest "polarization" occurring in the 1950–60 decade.[7]

To what extent, however, is Detroit's experience typical? Table 3 shows the interdecade differences in index values for the ten largest metropolitan areas. In this group, Detroit is fairly typical. If one examines the last column in each panel (referring to the 1940–60 comparisons), only Washington duplicates Detroit's perfect pattern, with regularly descending values. Three areas (New York, Chicago, and San Francisco) each show one deviation from a perfect pattern, Pittsburgh and St. Louis each show two, and Philadelphia and Boston each show three deviations. Again, however, Los Angeles is clearly exceptional; the city itself has gained persons of both high and low educational standing, but with a greater relative gain registered at the bottom of the educational ladder.[8]

Cross–Sectional Variations in Suburban Selectivity

A more direct follow-up to "The Socioeconomic Status of Cities and Suburbs" confines attention to the Urbanized Area as of 1960. One reason for preferring the Urbanized Area over

Table 4—Examples of Six Patterns of Residential Distribution of Educational Classes Based on Indexes of Suburbanization for Selected Urbanized Areas, 1960

Pattern of residential distribution	Highest educational classes are over-represented in the city		Both highest and lowest educational classes are over-represented in the city	Lowest educational classes are over-represented in the city		Inter-mediate educational classes are over-represented in the city	No systematic variation
Pattern label:	"A"	"B"	"C"	"D"	"E"	"F"	"X"
Name of area used in example:	Tucson	Albuquerque	Los Angeles	Baltimore	New York	Miami	Memphis
School years completed:							
None	90	85	131	128	129	83	98
Grade: 1–4	93	81	113	124	119	137	101
Grade: 5–6	96	88	110	117	111	136	101
Grade: 7–8	99	93	99	104	107	115	101
High: 1–3	100	97	94	98	100	100	100
High: 4	101	103	97	86	91	89	99
College: 1–3	102	106	102	86	87	84	100
College: 4+	103	110	106	87	84	81	100
Number of areas represented by example shown:	14	10	70	23	67	4	12

the various "Metropolitan" units (SMSA's, SMA's, MD's) is that one can more adequately represent the "suburban" area as it is commonly conceived.[9]

Table 4 was developed for illustrative purposes only. It shows that *a number of rather distinctive patterns can be discerned* when one examines the residential distribution (city *versus* suburbs) of the detailed educational classes represented in the census data. Examination of 200 Urbanized Areas has revealed the existence of *six basic types of "suburban selectivity,"* together with the need for recognizing the fact that some areas show no patterned selectivity whatever. The concrete examples shown in Table 4 are the largest areas showing each pattern.

Type "A" (exemplified by Tucson) is perhaps the most interesting of all, since it represents a perfect reversal of the "expected" pattern previously mentioned. In other words, persons with no formal schooling or with very little education are *under–represented* in the city itself. Those who have completed high school, and those who have attended college, are slightly *over–represented* in the city. This means that the suburbs of Tucson, and those of 13 other areas like it, show a systematic selection of persons at the bottom—rather than at the top—of the educational ladder, which is *the exact reversal of the common image of suburbia.*

Type "B" (ten cases, of which Albuquerque is the largest) is very much like Type "A," though there is a minor but systematic tendency in the direction of a reversal at the lower end of the educational ladder.

Type "C" is one with which we are already acquainted; Los Angeles is the largest example. Persons at both extremes are over–represented in the city. While the earlier encounter with this pattern suggested that Los Angeles might be a "deviant" case, Table 4 shows that "C" *is actually the modal type,* for fully 70 out of 200 Urbanized Areas show this pattern.

Type "D" (exemplified by Baltimore) almost achieves the "expected" pattern, i.e., a systematic decline in index values as one reads down the column, but there is a slight reversal at the upper end of the educational ladder.

The "expected" pattern is here labelled "E," and it is illustrated by New York. The pattern consists of a series of continuously declining values, indicating that (1) the city is characterized by an over–concentration of persons with minimal education, and (2) the suburbs are populated by a larger than expected proportion of persons with higher educational standing.

Type "F" represents only four cases, of which Miami is the largest. It is basically like Type "E," but there is a lower than expected number of persons without formal education in the city itself.

Finally, Memphis (Type "X") exemplifies the fact that there are a dozen Urbanized Areas (out of the 200 under study) that cannot be classified as falling into one or another of the six basic types.[10]

Characteristics of Urbanized Areas and patterns of suburban selectivity—The discovery of these patterns was rewarding in its own right; variation from city to city is always to be expected and further evidence of differences between cities is always welcome. Evidence of systematic variation is even more welcome. The most welcome evidence of all consists of finding systematic co-variation.

Our subsequent effort was thus directed toward *discovering those general factors that might underlie the systematic variations observed in suburban selectivity*. The search involved examining certain broad characteristics of whole Urbanized Areas which may be fairly regarded as basic "structural" features—location, size, age, and rate of growth. Since the earlier work documented the common sense observation that the scope of the city's boundaries (and changes therein) will affect city–suburban comparisons, we have also looked into this factor as a source of variation in apparent suburban selectivity. More particularly, we have tried to deal with the "annexation factor," recognizing that political boundaries are not rigid and impermeable.[11]

Table 5 summarizes the results. (Because of limited numbers of cases, Types "A" and "B" are combined in Table 5, as are

Table 5—Patterns of Suburban Selectivity by Selected Characteristics of Urbanized Areas

Selected characteristics, Urbanized Areas, 1960	Highest educational classes are over-represented in the city	Both highest and lowest educational classes are over-represented in the city	Lowest educational classes are over-represented in the city	Inter-mediate educational classes are over-represented in the city	No systematic variation	Total number of areas (equals 100%)
Census division						
New England	...	30.0	60.0	...	10.0	20
Middle Atlantic	4.8	4.8	85.7	...	4.8	21
East North Central	4.8	33.3	54.8	2.4	4.8	42
West North Central	5.9	58.8	29.4	...	5.9	17
South Atlantic	17.7	47.1	23.5	5.9	5.9	34
East South Central	7.7	30.8	46.2	...	15.4	13
West South Central	34.8	26.1	34.8	...	4.4	23
Mountain	30.8	46.2	23.1	...	...	13
Pacific	5.9	41.2	41.2	5.9	5.9	17
Size of Urbanized Area						
1,000,000 or more	...	6.3	93.8	...	...	16
500,000–1,000,000	...	18.2	68.2	4.6	9.1	22
250,000–500,000	10.3	27.6	58.6	...	3.5	29
150,000–250,000	16.3	27.9	41.9	4.7	9.3	43
100,000–150,000	13.5	46.0	37.8	...	2.7	37
50,000–100,000	17.0	52.8	20.8	1.9	7.6	53
Census year in which central city or cities first reached 50,000						
1800–1860	...	7.1	92.9	...	...	14
1870–1880	...	11.8	82.4	...	5.9	17
1890–1900	2.8	25.0	61.1	...	11.1	36
1910–1920	8.3	35.4	50.0	...	6.3	48
1930–1940	12.5	53.1	25.0	3.1	6.3	32
1950–1960	28.3	45.3	17.0	5.7	3.8	53

Table 5 (continued)

Selected characteristics, Urbanized Areas, 1960	Highest educational classes are over-represented in the city	Both highest and lowest educational classes are over-represented in the city	Lowest educational classes are over-represented in the city	Intermediate educational classes are over-represented in the city	No systematic variation	Total number of areas (equals 100%)
Percent in housing units built since 1950						
40.0 or more	30.0	26.7	30.0	10.0	3.3	30
35.0–39.9	18.5	51.9	22.2	....	7.4	27
30.0–34.9	16.0	40.0	44.0	....	....	25
25.0–29.9	5.4	37.8	54.1	....	2.7	37
20.0–24.9	6.8	22.7	59.1	....	11.4	44
Less than 20.0	2.7	37.8	48.7	2.7	8.1	37
Percent of central city population in area annexed 1950–60						
30.0 or more	43.5	30.4	21.7	....	4.4	23
20.0–29.9	12.5	54.2	29.2	....	4.2	24
10.0–19.9	10.0	45.0	32.5	2.5	10.0	40
5.0– 9.9	9.1	45.5	36.4	4.5	4.5	22
0.1– 4.9	12.1	30.3	51.5	....	6.1	33
None	1.7	20.7	69.0	3.5	5.2	58
ALL AREAS IN STUDY	12.0	35.0	45.0	2.0	6.0	200

Types "D" and "E.") The table can be read most efficiently by concentrating attention upon the first and third columns.

The first panel indicates that there is considerable variation from one census division to another. A majority of areas in three divisions—New England, Middle Atlantic, and East North Central—show the expected pattern (represented in the third column). The Urbanized Areas showing the most radical departure from the expected pattern (see the first column) are concentrated in three divisions—in the South Atlantic, and (more especially) in the West South Central and the Mountain divisions. But the various divisions differ in many respects as far as the characteristics of their constituent cities and Urbanized Areas are concerned. Contrasted with the Mountain states, for example, cities in the Middle Atlantic division are larger, older, and growing more slowly, and they tend to be ringed by established suburbs (usually incorporated places) that are resistant to annexation. Hence, the remaining four panels in Table 5 take up these characteristics one by one—size, age, growth, and recent annexation history.

In all four instances, a definite association is to be seen, although the details differ from one variable to another. In the case of *size*, the larger the area the more likely the appearance of the "expected" pattern (col. 3). These are the results one would anticipate on the basis of the earlier work, where simpler city-suburban comparisons were made.

Similarly, *age* appears to be associated with the patterns under examination. The third panel shows that areas with "older" central cities are more likely to show the "expected" pattern. The first column shows that the "unexpected" patterns (Types "A" and "B") are most frequently found in the areas with the "newest" central cities, i.e., those which have only recently achieved a size of 50,000 or more inhabitants.[12]

The two remaining panels in Table 5 throw further light on the patterns under investigation. The fourth panel suggests that the rate of recent population *growth* is at least roughly associated with the type of suburban selectivity.[13] The first column indicates that rapidly growing Urbanized Areas are the most likely to exhibit the "unexpected" pattern, wherein

Table 6—Patterns of Suburban Selectivity by Selected Characteristics of Urbanized Areas, White Population Only

Selected characteristics, Urbanized Areas, 1960	Highest educational classes are over-represented in the city	Both highest and lowest educational classes are over-represented in the city	Lowest educational classes are over-represented in the city	Intermediate educational classes are over-represented in the city	No systematic variation	Total number of areas (equals 100%)
Census division						
New England	...	38.5	53.9	...	7.7	13
Middle Atlantic	...	5.6	94.4	...	...	18
East North Central	7.5	35.0	47.5	2.5	7.5	40
West North Central	...	50.0	35.7	...	14.3	14
South Atlantic	20.6	47.1	20.6	2.9	8.8	34
East South Central	15.4	30.8	46.2	7.7	...	13
West South Central	36.4	31.8	22.7	...	9.1	22
Mountain	50.0	20.0	20.0	10.0	...	10
Pacific	6.3	43.7	43.7	6.3	...	16
Size of Urbanized Area						
1,000,000 or more	...	12.5	87.5	...	...	16
500,000–1,000,000	...	27.3	59.1	9.1	4.6	22
250,000–500,000	6.9	27.6	58.6	...	6.9	29
150,000–250,000	15.0	37.5	35.0	5.0	7.5	40
100,000–150,000	20.6	41.2	32.4	...	5.9	34
50,000–100,000	28.2	46.2	15.4	2.6	7.7	39

Table 6 (continued)

Census year in which central city or cities first reached 50,000						
1800–1860		14.3	78.6		7.1	14
1870–1880		13.3	80.0		6.7	15
1890–1900		22.6	64.5		12.9	31
1910–1920	10.9	39.1	43.5	2.2	4.3	46
1930–1940	15.6	53.1	15.6	9.4	6.3	32
1950–1960	38.1	40.5	16.7	2.4	2.4	42
Percent in housing units built since 1950						
40.0 or more	33.3	33.3	20.0	10.0	3.3	30
35.0–39.9	29.2	41.7	25.0		4.2	24
30.0–34.9	18.2	31.8	50.0			22
25.0–29.9	2.9	40.0	51.4	2.9	2.9	35
20.0–24.9	6.8	29.6	50.0		13.6	44
Less than 20.0	4.0	36.0	48.0	4.0	8.0	25
Percent of central city population in area annexed 1950–60						
30.0 or more	43.5	30.4	17.4	4.4	4.4	23
20.0–29.9	23.8	52.4	23.8			21
10.0–19.9	13.5	40.5	32.4	2.7	10.8	37
5.0– 9.9	10.0	45.0	40.0		5.0	20
0.1– 4.9	10.0	33.3	43.3	3.3	10.0	30
None	2.0	22.5	67.4	4.1	4.1	49

higher status groups are seemingly over-represented in the central city. The proportions set out in the third column, however, do not show the same sort of regularity.

The last panel in Table 5 again suggests the importance of *annexation*. Seven out of every ten cities which have failed to annex nearby territory over the last intercensal decade show the "expected" pattern. Conversely, cities which have been very actively annexing surrounding territory over the past decade show the "unexpected" pattern.[14]

Color composition and suburban selectivity—There are a number of reasons for wanting to take account of variations in color composition. For one thing, Urbanized Areas in the United States vary considerably with respect to the proportion of nonwhites they contain. More important, the residential patterns of whites and nonwhites are known to be highly dissimilar. Finally, the two broad color groups exhibit substantial differences in terms of educational attainment.

Unfortunately, the absolute numbers of nonwhites are so small in some cities and Urbanized Areas that the Bureau of the Census does not report their educational characteristics. Nevertheless, it is possible to assemble data by color and city-suburban residence for 180 Urbanized Areas. Once this is done, a striking set of facts emerge:

1. The concentration of nonwhites in central cities is very marked.[15] Indeed, three out of every four Urbanized Areas have 80 per cent or more of their nonwhites residing within the central cities.

2. The patterns that have resulted from the "sifting and sorting" of educational classes between cities and suburbs— along lines that are quite clear for the total population—are *not* found among nonwhites when the latter are considered separately. Fully 45 per cent of the 180 areas cannot be classified at all, i.e., they must be coded as Type "X" for nonwhites.

3. The pattern of city-suburban segregation of educational classes observable in the white majority does *not* serve as a good predictor of the pattern among the nonwhite minority.[16] Striking as they are, none of these facts should be surprising.

They merely reflect the simultaneous operation of two well-known principles of residential segregation in urban America—color and socioeconomic status.

In any case, Table 6 has been prepared to show the associations between selected characteristics of Urbanized Areas and the patterns revealed by their *white* populations considered alone. The findings are basically the same as those seen in Table 5, and they will not be discussed in detail. While the same associations are revealed in both tables, however, they are displayed in somewhat sharper form when attention is confined to the white population. In other words, "control" of color seems to bring out even more clearly the operation of the second principle of residential segregation, *viz.*, socioeconomic status.

Perhaps the most intriguing possibility raised by all these materials is suggested by the data relating to two variables—size and "age" of urban areas.[17] The regularities exhibited suggest that cities evolve in a predictable direction, i.e., pattern "A" through pattern "E."[18]

FURTHER EXPLORATIONS

We should critically examine the validity of the many and often conflicting notions being advanced by social scientists and other commentators on the American urban scene. We are said to be creating "tens of thousands of modern economic ghettos. . . . We tend to keep out everyone not belonging to a single economic class . . . whether they be the walls of a low-cost housing project, of a Levittown or Sunny Acres, or the zoning walls of Darien, Connecticut, or Grosse Point, Michigan."[19] At the same time, we are told that "The *suburbs* or the *suburban zone* is becoming increasingly heterogeneous in economic function and in class, ethnic, and racial characteristics."[20] We need some reduction of the current and considerable confusion concerning urban and suburban America.

RULES FOR CLASSIFICATION

Objective—Our purpose was to distinguish various types based on "patterns" or "configurations" formed by the ratios previously described. Since judgment is necessarily involved, we tried to establish clear-cut criteria yielding high reliability; the rules for classification were few in number and turned out to be easy to follow, but they were general enough to handle all the cases that were encountered. The following instructions were used by three coders.

Procedures—(1) Examine the over-all pattern of ratios first, and then proceed to a detailed consideration. (2) Use letter designations for the seven types. (3) Use numerical subscripts to identify the number of deviations from a perfect pattern; if there are no deviations, the subscript will be a zero. (4) Do not "force" the ratios into a pattern, i.e., do not hesitate to use the "X," which designates no pattern whatsover.

General rules—(1) *The minimum and maximum values should be separated by at least three points;* if the spread is zero, one, or two, code the column as "X" (no pattern). (2) *Ignore "ties,"* i.e., two or more ratios of the same value in sequence. (3) *Admit no more than two deviations;* if three or more values would have to be changed, treat the case as unclassifiable ("X"). (4) If the ratios in a particular column could be regarded as forming either of two types, *classify the case as the type requiring the least number of deviations.* (5) Similarly, if the number of deviations is the same, *classify the case as the type requiring the least change in magnitude.* (6) *Any changes in magnitude should not exceed a total (for one or two deviations) of eight points;* if the deviations total nine or more points, classify the case as "X."

NOTES

1. Ernest W. Burgess, "The Growth of the City: An Introduction to a Research Project," *Publications of the American Sociological Society*, 18 (1924), pp. 85–97. The time perspective that one employs is most important. Many of the apparent anomalies in the urban literature are the result of different writers using different temporal reference points. The most common comparisons are between (*a*) "preindustrial" *versus* "industrial" cities, (*b*) cities of the nineteenth *versus* the twentieth century, and (*c*) pre- *versus* post-World War II. For examples of each, see (*a*) Gideon Sjoberg, *The Preindustrial City: Past and Present* (Glencoe, Ill.: The Free Press, 1960), chap. iv; (*b*) Sam B. Warner, Jr., *Streetcar Suburbs* (Cambridge, Mass.: Harvard University Press and the M.I.T. Press, 1962); (*c*) S. D. Clark, "The Suburban Community," in S. D. Clark (ed.), *Urbanism and the Changing Canadian Society* (Toronto: University of Toronto Press, 1961), pp. 20–38.

2. The same kind of variation was observed when areas were crudely classified according to the "age" of their central cities.

3. For the importance of distinguishing between the sexes, see Otis Dudley Duncan and Albert J. Reiss, Jr., *Social Characteristics of Urban and Rural Communities, 1950* (New York: John Wiley and Sons, Inc., 1956). As for color, see *ibid.* and Leo F. Schnore, "City-Suburban Income Differentials in Metropolitan Areas," *American Sociological Review*, 27 (April, 1962), pp. 252–55.

4. The earlier study used materials from the U.S. Bureau of the Census, *General Social and Economic Characteristics*, "Advance Reports," Series PC (A3), preprints of Tables 32 and 33. This study draws mainly upon *ibid.*, Chapter "C" (Final Report), Tables 73 and 77, together with similar materials from the 1940 and 1950 Censuses of Population.

5. It would probably be preferable to call the measure an "index of centralization," since higher values indicate over-representation in the urban core. While the method of calculation differs, the "index of suburbanization" employed here is formally analogous to the "index of occupational specialization" (also called the "residence specialization index") that was reported for various parts of the New York Metropolitan Region by Hoover and Vernon. As they explain it, "Each coefficient is a *percentage ratio* of the share of a job type in a specified county or municipality to the share of that job type in the Region as a whole; thus, coefficients greater than 100 show 'over-representation,' or positive 'specialization' in the job type in question, while coefficients below 100 show 'under-representation' or relative deficiency." Edgar M. Hoover and Raymond Vernon, *Anatomy of a Metropolis* (Cambridge, Mass.: Harvard University Press, 1959), p. 303. See Appendix L, "Calculation of Indices of Specialization and Work-Residence Separation," pp. 303–306.

6. For a detailed discussion, see Philip M. Hauser, *Population Per-*

spectives (New Brunswick, N.J.: Rutgers University Press, 1960), chap. 4, especially pp. 109–12.

7. Knowledge of the changing color composition of the Detroit area would lead to predicting this pattern; see Harry Sharp and Leo F. Schnore, "The Changing Color Composition of Metropolitan Areas," *Land Economics*, 38 (May, 1962), 169–83. It is regrettable that American data do not permit the kind of refined analysis of migrant streams set out in Sidney Goldstein, "Some Economic Consequences of Suburbanization in the Copenhagen Metropolitan Area," *American Journal of Sociology*, 68 (March, 1963), 551–64. Goldstein concludes that "the heavy flow of persons with high income to the suburbs, countered by an almost equally large flow of persons with low income to the city, means that the redistribution of population within the metropolitan area is producing an increasingly homogeneous population within the city proper, one composed largely of persons of low economic status" (p. 551).

8. The serious weakness of much of the research on this topic is that it has been strictly cross-sectional in design; as a consequence, it has not yielded longitudinal inferences. The studies that have been truly longitudinal have been case studies of individual areas.

9. In different studies "suburbs" refer to (*a*) the metropolitan "ring," (*b*) that portion of the Urbanized Area lying outside the central city or cities, or (*c*) those incorporated places of 10,000 or more inhabitants lying within the metropolitan ring. The second version (b) is used here, even though the more cumbersome "suburbs and urban fringe" might be preferable. See Duncan and Reiss, *op. cit.*, p. 118.

10. Since the classification of Urbanized Areas into these types necessarily involved judgment, a set of rules was developed and the coding was done independently and on a "blind" basis by three different people. These rules are set out in an appendix to this chapter.

11. In "The Socioeconomic Status of Cities and Suburbs," *op. cit.*, we employed a "proxy variable"—the per cent of the urbanized area population residing in the central city—to represent annexation success. We have now moved toward a direct measure of recent annexation activity, by measuring *the proportion of the central city's 1960 population residing in territory annexed between 1950 and 1960.* Though only "recent" annexation history is thus taken into account, the argument is less strained if one employs a direct rather than an indirect measure.

12. This finding was also anticipated on the basis of the earlier pilot study. See "The Socioeconomic Status of Cities and Suburbs," *op. cit.*, Table 2, *et passim.*

13. *The per cent of the Urbanized Area's housing units found in structures built in 1950 or later* is here treated as a rough index of population growth. The basic data came from the 1960 Census of Housing conducted concurrently with the 1960 Census of Population, as reported in U.S. Bureau of the Census, *County and City Data Book, 1962* (Washington, D.C.: U.S. Government Printing Office, 1962), Table 4, Item 250.

14. This may mean nothing more than that they have succeeded, more often than not, in annexing high status areas.

15. For further details, see Sharp and Schnore, *op. cit.*

16. The following cross-tabulation will illustrate this last point:

Nonwhite Pattern	A–B	C	D–E	F	X	Total number of areas
		White pattern				
A–B	7	9	8	2	2	28
C	4	13	8	0	1	26
D–E	0	7	10	1	1	19
F	1	5	19	1	0	26
X	14	29	30	1	7	81
Total number of areas	26	63	75	5	11	180

17. As for the "age" of cities, the present measure (number of decades that have passed since the city entered a particular size class) is not entirely satisfactory because it tends to confound size, age, and long-term rate of growth.

18. This elaboration of the Burgess hypothesis is developed in more detail in "The Socioeconomic Status of Cities and Suburbs," *op. cit.*, and in Leo F. Schnore, "On the Spatial Structure of Cities in the Two Americas," a paper prepared for the Committee on Urbanization, Social Science Research Council.

19. Ralph Lazarus, President of the Federated Department Stores, as quoted in the *New York Times,* October 17, 1962.

20. William M. Dobriner, *Class in Suburbia* (Englewood Cliffs, N.J.: Prentice-Hall, Inc., 1963), p. 27.

Chapter 13

Color Composition and City-Suburban Status Differences: A Replication and Extension

CHAPTER 11 demonstrated that city-suburban status differences in larger Urbanized Areas are just the opposite of those seen in smaller areas.[1] In the older and larger areas, we found, the suburbs had higher socioeconomic status than their central cities, but this was progressively less true of smaller areas. In small Urbanized Areas, the status of city residents tends to be higher than that of suburbanites. This research, however, was based

For a detailed report, see J. John Palen, *The Effect of Color Composition on City-Suburban Status Differentials*, unpublished M.S. thesis, Department of Sociology, University of Wisconsin, 1963, pp. v + 29. The study was supported by the research phase of the University of Wisconsin Urban Program, under the terms of a grant from the Ford Foundation.

upon a series of "Advance Reports" that did not break down population characteristics by color. It was therefore impossible to examine the possible effect that city-suburban differences in color composition might have had on city-suburban status differentials. This was unfortunate because nonwhites are heavily concentrated within the nation's large cities; rather few live in the "suburbs," however the latter may be defined.[2] There are also well-known differences between the major color groups in socioeconomic status. Since more complete data are now available, it is clearly desirable to re-examine city-suburban status differences while controlling for color.

In our replication of the earlier study, it was hypothesized that the *white* population would show city-suburban status differences similar to those found for the total population. It was expected that population size and age of city would still be rather important factors: the larger and older the urban area, we believed, the higher the socioeconomic status of the white suburban population in comparison to that of the central city. For the *nonwhite* population, we anticipated no clear-cut relationship between the size and the age of the urban area, on the one hand, and city-suburban status differentials, on the other, since suburban communities have been so successful in excluding nonwhite residents.

In the original study it was possible to make city-suburban comparisons in 200 of the 213 Urbanized Areas officially delineated in conjunction with the 1960 Census of Population and Housing. For the present study such comparisons could be made for 180 areas using the white population, and for only 131 areas using the nonwhite population.[3] In each of these cases, we have determined whether the city or the suburban area was higher in socioeconomic status, using three traditional variables (income, education, and occupation). Income was operationally defined as median *family* income. The educational measure was the per cent of the population aged twenty-five years or over with four years high school or more. The occupational measure was the per cent of the employed labor force engaged in white-collar occupations.

Table 1—City-Suburban Differentials in Socioeconomic Status by Size of Urbanized Area and Color[a]

Size of Urbanized Area, 1960	PER CENT OF URBANIZED AREAS WITH HIGHER SUBURBAN MEDIAN FAMILY INCOME			PER CENT OF URBANIZED AREAS WITH HIGHER SUBURBAN PER CENT COMPLETING HIGH SCHOOL			PER CENT OF URBANIZED AREAS WITH HIGHER SUBURBAN PER CENT IN WHITE-COLLAR OCCUPATIONS			NUMBER OF AREAS		
	Total	Nonwhite	White	Total	Nonwhite	White	Total	Nonwhite	White	Total	Nonwhite	White
1,000,000+	100.0	75.0	100.0	100.0	50.0	93.8	87.5	25.0	75.0	16	16	16
500,000–1,000,000	100.0	59.1	100.0	100.0	54.5	90.9	86.4	50.0	54.5	22	22	22
250,000–500,000	79.3	60.7	75.9	75.9	53.6	69.0	55.2	46.4	48.3	29	28	29
150,000–250,000	72.1	62.1	67.5	62.8	44.8	57.5	48.8	41.4	37.3	43	29	40
100,000–150,000	70.3	68.4	47.1	64.9	42.1	55.9	40.5	42.1	20.6	37	19	34
50,000–100,000	56.6	64.7	46.2	49.1	29.4	48.7	30.2	35.3	20.5	53	17	39
All Areas	74.0	64.1	67.2	68.5	46.6	64.4	50.5	41.2	37.8	200	131	180

a. Sources: U.S. Bureau of the Census, U.S. Census of Population: 1960, General Social and Economic Characteristics, Final Report PC (1), Chapter "C" for individual states, Washington: U.S. Government Printing Office, 1962, Tables 73, 74, 76, 77, and 78.

CITY-SUBURBAN STATUS DIFFERENTIALS
BY SIZE AND COLOR

An examination of Table 1 indicates that the *white* population shows the expected pattern of association between city size and the direction of socioeconomic differentials. The larger the size, the greater the per cent of Urbanized Areas having higher status suburbs than central cities. The income data, for example, show that in Urbanized Areas with over 500,000 inhabitants there are no cases in which the central cities surpass their suburbs in median family income, while over half the cities do so in the smaller areas (under 150,000 inhabitants). When occupation is used as the status measure, however, the suburban advantage in the larger Urbanized Areas is no longer as definite, and in the smaller areas the city plainly has the advantage. Thus, there is a clear association between size and the direction of city-suburban differentials in white socioeconomic status. Another point worth noting is that the various proportions shown for the white population are generally lower than the comparable figures for the total population. This can be attributed to the well-known concentration of nonwhites in the central city. Removing the low status nonwhites from the city figures tends to raise the white city population's status in relation to the white population of the suburbs.

The data for *nonwhites* are not nearly as clear-cut as those for whites. The figures in Table 1 for nonwhite income, education, and occupation show a weak pattern of relationship between size of urban area and status differentials. Moreover, the 16 Urbanized Areas of over a million are especially "deviant" cases. This is particularly true of the occupational data; in the largest size class only one out of every four areas has status differentials favoring the suburbs. This is despite the fact that the comparable income data favors the suburbs over the central city in three out of every four large areas. At best, there is a very weak association between city size and the direction of socioeconomic status differentials among nonwhites. Perhaps the most striking finding for nonwhites is that the results of

Table 2—City-Suburban Differentials in Socioeconomic Status by Age of City and Color[a]

Census Year in Which City (or Cities) First Reached 50,000 Inhabitants	PER CENT OF URBANIZED AREAS WITH HIGHER SUBURBAN MEDIAN FAMILY INCOME			PER CENT OF URBANIZED AREAS WITH HIGHER SUBURBAN PER CENT COMPLETING HIGH SCHOOL			PER CENT OF URBANIZED AREAS WITH HIGHER SUBURBAN PER CENT IN WHITE-COLLAR OCCUPATIONS			NUMBER OF AREAS		
	Total	Nonwhite	White	Total	Nonwhite	White	Total	Nonwhite	White	Total	Nonwhite	White
1800–1860	100.0	71.4	100.0	100.0	57.1	100.0	100.0	21.4	85.8	14	14	14
1870–1880	100.0	92.9	100.0	100.0	64.3	93.3	100.0	64.3	86.7	17	14	15
1890–1900	86.1	78.3	87.1	75.0	47.8	71.0	58.3	52.2	48.4	36	23	31
1910–1920	75.0	50.0	76.1	75.0	50.0	69.6	54.2	43.7	34.8	48	32	46
1930–1940	71.9	50.0	50.0	56.3	35.0	53.1	31.3	35.0	18.8	32	20	32
1950–1960	50.9	60.7	33.3	47.2	35.7	40.5	24.5	32.1	14.3	53	28	42
All Areas	74.0	64.1	67.2	68.5	46.6	64.4	50.5	41.2	37.8	200	131	180

a. Sources: Same as Table 1.

city-suburban status comparisons depend so very heavily upon the measure used.

City-Suburban Status Differentials by Age and Color

As in the earlier study, the "age" of the Urbanized Area was determined by counting the number of intercensal decades that have passed since the central city first reached a population of 50,000 persons. Looking at Table 2, the columns for the *white* population indicate that age of the central city and higher suburban socioeconomic status are positively associated. The older the city, the larger the proportion of suburbs holding the status advantage over the central city. For whites, the measure of occupational status again tends to favor the central city more than do the measures of income and education.

The *nonwhite* population fails to show any clear relationship between a city's age and the relative status of city-dwellers and suburbanites. When occupation is used as the measure of status, status differentials are associated with city age only if one ignores the very oldest group of cities, i.e., those which first reached 50,000 between 1800 and 1860, and one would hardly recommend such a procedure.

Regional Variations

What accounts for the highly dissimilar city-suburban status differentials found in the two color groups? The most obvious factor that might influence the above results is regional location, which was not taken into account in the earlier study. This is especially likely to be true in the case of the nonwhite population. We therefore re-examined city-suburban differences in status while "controlling" crudely for region. As anticipated, Southern and non-Southern cities were most unlike. For convenience we shall refer to these areas as being either in the "South" or in the "North and West".[4]

An examination of Table 3 indicates that the previously observed association between size and the direction of city-

Table 3—City-Suburban Differentials in Socioeconomic Status by Size of Urbanized Area, Color, and Region[a]

Region and Size of Urbanized Area, 1960	PER CENT OF URBANIZED AREAS WITH HIGHER SUBURBAN INCOME			PER CENT OF URBANIZED AREAS WITH HIGHER SUBURBAN EDUCATION			PER CENT OF URBANIZED AREAS WITH HIGHER SUBURBAN OCCUPATION		
	Total	Nonwhite	White	Total	Nonwhite	White	Total	Nonwhite	White
South									
500,000+	100.0	38.5	100.0	100.0	30.8	92.3	92.3	15.4	53.8
250,000–500,000	60.0	40.0	50.0	70.0	40.0	60.0	60.0	40.0	50.0
150,000–250,000	64.7	73.3	52.9	52.9	40.0	35.3	35.3	33.3	17.6
100,000–150,000	92.3	83.3	46.2	53.9	50.0	38.5	46.2	41.7	7.7
50,000–100,000	52.9	90.0	18.8	29.4	40.0	18.8	23.5	30.0	6.3
All Areas	72.9	65.0	52.2	58.6	40.0	46.4	48.6	31.7	24.6
North and West									
500,000+	100.0	80.0	100.0	100.0	64.0	92.0	84.0	52.0	68.0
250,000–500,000	89.5	72.2	89.5	79.0	61.1	73.7	52.6	50.0	42.1
150,000–250,000	76.9	50.0	78.3	69.2	50.0	73.9	57.7	52.2	52.2
100,000–150,000	58.3	42.9	47.6	70.8	28.6	66.7	37.5	42.9	28.6
50,000–100,000	58.3	29.6	65.2	58.3	14.3	69.6	33.3	42.9	30.4
All Areas	74.6	63.4	76.6	73.9	52.1	75.7	51.5	49.3	45.0

a. Sources: Same as Table 1.

suburban status differences continues to hold generally for the white population, regardless of region, although it is more marked in the South. In both broad regions, the larger Urbanized Areas have suburbs possessing higher socioeconomic levels than their central cities. The most striking regional differences for the white population occur in the smallest areas. The status differentials in the South overwhelmingly favor the city proper, while this does not occur in the North and West.

The nonwhite patterns were, as expected, considerably different for Southern and non-Southern cities. *The nonwhite population of Urbanized Areas in the North and West show a clear association between city size and city-suburban differentials in socioeconomic status.* Thus, nonwhites in these areas resemble the white population. *In contrast, Urbanized Areas in the South generally fail to show an association between size and city-suburban differentials in socioeconomic status.* In fact, the income data for Southern nonwhites in Table 3 show a perfect reversal of the pattern of association shown by the data for whites.

In Table 4, the white population again exhibits the expected association between age of the city and city-suburban status differentials in both *broad* regions. The nonwhite figures for income and education show a rough association between city age and the direction of city-suburban status differentials in the North and West, but no noticeable association was found in the South on any of the three measures.

Conclusions

Our first hypothesis—that the white population would show city-suburban status differentials similar to those of the total population—was confirmed by the data. Within the *white* population there was a definite and regular association between the age and size of the Urbanized Area, on the one hand, and the direction of city-suburban status differentials, on the other. The older and larger areas were much more likely to have high status suburban populations, while in the newer and

Table 4—City-Suburban Differentials in Socioeconomic Status by Age of City, Color, and Region[a]

Region and Census Year in Which City (or Cities) First Reached 50,000 Inhabitants	PER CENT OF URBANIZED AREAS WITH HIGHER SUBURBAN INCOME			PER CENT OF URBANIZED AREAS WITH HIGHER SUBURBAN EDUCATION			PER CENT OF URBANIZED AREAS WITH HIGHER SUBURBAN OCCUPATION		
	Total	Nonwhite	White	Total	Nonwhite	White	Total	Nonwhite	White
South									
1800–1880	100.0	60.0	100.0	100.0	40.0	100.0	100.0	0.0	80.0
1890–1900	100.0	75.0	100.0	87.5	37.5	62.5	87.5	50.0	50.0
1910–1920	70.6	58.8	70.6	70.6	47.1	58.8	64.7	29.4	29.4
1930–1940	76.5	60.0	47.1	47.1	33.3	41.2	23.5	40.0	11.8
1950–1960	60.9	86.7	18.2	39.1	40.0	22.7	30.4	26.7	9.1
All Areas	74.3	68.3	53.6	58.6	40.0	46.4	48.6	31.7	24.6
North and West									
1800–1880	100.0	87.0	100.0	100.0	65.2	93.8	100.0	52.2	87.5
1890–1900	82.1	80.0	82.6	71.4	53.3	73.9	50.0	53.3	47.8
1910–1920	77.4	40.0	79.3	77.4	53.3	75.9	48.4	60.0	37.9
1930–1940	66.7	20.0	53.3	66.7	40.0	66.7	40.0	20.0	26.7
1950–1960	43.3	30.8	50.0	53.3	30.8	60.0	20.0	38.5	20.0
All Areas	73.8	60.6	75.7	73.8	52.1	75.7	51.5	49.3	45.9

a. Sources: Same as Table 1.

smaller areas, the city itself was most likely to enjoy the status advantage.

The second hypothesis, to the effect that the *nonwhite* population would not show the same relationships, was only partially confirmed. It was discovered that there was another important factor in addition to city age and size. That factor was the regional location of the Urbanized Area. Looking at the nonwhite data, without respect to region, there is practically no relationship between size and age, on the other hand, and the direction of city-suburban variation, on the other. When region is controlled, however, such relationships do tend to appear in the North and West. City-suburban status differentials among nonwhites in the North and West are generally similar to those shown by the white population in both broad regions. In contrast, the nonwhite data for Southern areas do not reveal any clear and consistent set of associations between *either* (1) the age *or* (2) the size of the Urbanized Area and (3) the direction of city-suburban status differences.

Why does the Southern nonwhite population fail to show such consistent relationships? We can only speculate at this point. Some of the unusual features of the Southern nonwhite findings are probably due to the effects of housing segregation, which recent research shows to be increasing in that section of the country while decreasing in the North and West.[5] However, the most probable reason why the Southern nonwhites fail to show the usual city-suburban status differences is that in the South, as opposed to the North, the poorer and less advantaged nonwhite residents traditionally lived on the periphery of the city.[6] Although there are indications that this pattern is changing, there still exist many nonwhite areas at the *edges* of Southern cities, large and small, old and new. This "historical survival" of low status neighborhoods on the Southern city's periphery, as well as in its central core, may be confounding the pattern of city-suburban status differentials found in other populations. The Southern nonwhite population, in short, may be in a state of transition between the traditional residential pattern of the Old South, and the contemporary

American urban pattern seen in both white and nonwhite neighborhoods in the rest of the country.

NOTES

1. Leo F. Schnore, "The Socioeconomic Status of Cities and Suburbs," *American Sociological Review,* 28 (February, 1963), pp. 76–85.

2. See Leo F. Schnore and Harry Sharp, "Racial Changes in Metropolitan Areas, 1950–1960," *Social Forces,* 41 (March, 1963), pp. 247–253.

3. Nonwhite Urbanized Area or central city figures were not available in 20 cases. Since the *white* figures were obtained by subtracting the appropriate *nonwhite* figures from the *total* figures, the absence of nonwhite statistics made it impossible to determine the characteristics of the white population. The nonwhite sample was further reduced by excluding any Urbanized Area containing less than seventy "suburban" nonwhite residents. In every other respect, the study summarized here was an exact replication of the earlier research, including a multiple correlation analysis not reported here.

4. Urbanized Areas were assigned to regions according to the state location of their principal central cities. The "South" was identified according to traditional census practice, i.e., as consisting of the District of Columbia and the following states: Maryland, Delaware, West Virginia, Virginia, North Carolina, South Carolina, Kentucky, Tennessee, Georgia, Florida, Alabama, Mississippi, Arkansas, Louisiana, Oklahoma, and Texas. Among the 200 Urbanized Areas studied in Chapter 11, 70 were in the South and 130 were in the North and West. White population data were available for 69 of these areas in the South and for 111 in the North and West. Nonwhite population data are reported here for 60 of the Urbanized Areas in the South and for 71 in the North and West.

5. Karl E. Taeuber, "Negro Residential Segregation: Trends and Measurement," *Social Problems,* 12 (Summer, 1964), pp. 42–50.

6. Rudolf Heberle, "Social Consequences of the Industrialization of Southern Cities," *Social Forces,* 27 (October, 1948), pp. 29–37.

Part Five

The Changing Color Composition of Metropolitan Areas

CHAPTER 13 showed that variations in color composition are important in understanding city-suburban differences in socioeconomic status. Chapter 14 turns more directly to the topic of color composition as a subject for research in its own right. It was first published in *Land Economics*, Volume 38 (May, 1962), pp. 169–85, and it was co-authored by Harry Sharp. Focussing on the twelve largest metropolitan areas in the country, it shows thirty-year trends in the balance between two color groups, whites and nonwhites, in central cities and suburban rings. The remarkable increase in numbers and proportions of nonwhites in large central cities is fully documented.

Chapter 15 narrows the time span to a consideration of only the most recent intercensal decade, 1950–1960, but it expands the coverage to all metropolitan areas in the United States. Also co-authored by Harry Sharp, this chapter first appeared in *Social Forces*, Volume 41 (March, 1963), pp. 247–53. Once again, important regional differences are shown. Outside the South, over nine out of every ten metropolitan areas experienced sizeable relative gains in the number of nonwhites. In the South, however, over six out of every ten metropolitan areas had *lower* proportions nonwhite in 1960 than a decade earlier.

Chapter 16 narrows the focus to the nonwhite ghetto itself. It raises an important question concerning residential segregation: Is the ghetto, which is itself a manifestation of segregation according to color, also segregated along social class lines? In Northern and "border" cities, the socioeconomic status of nonwhite neighborhoods tends to rise regularly with increasing distance from the center of the city. This pattern, however, is not generally observed in Southern, Southwestern and Western cities, where an alternative configuration appears. Socioeconomic status tends to rise and then to decline with increasing distance from the central business district. Once again, then, important regional variations are observed; cities in all parts of the country do not manifest precisely the same patterns.

Chapter 14

The Changing Color
Composition of Metropolitan
Areas

SOME YEARS AGO, an economist and statistician described the current growth of the nonwhite population in our major metropolitan centers as "one of the outstanding sociological phenomena of our time."[1] Basing his analysis upon scattered statistics from various special censuses conducted during the 'fifties, he suggested that there was every reason to believe that the long-term trends observed earlier were continuing and that nonwhites were displacing whites in many large cities. The availability of 1960 census materials now permits an assessment of these claims. For technical reasons, including frequent annexations of territory by cities, we will be obliged to confine most of our attention to the very largest metropolitan communities in the United States.

Some of the results of this study were presented at the 1961 meetings of the Population Association of America. Completion of the study was supported by the research phase of the University of Wisconsin Urban Program, under the terms of a grant from the Ford Foundation.

If we examine the changing color composition of the Standard Metropolitan Statistical Areas (SMSA's), we find that 148 out of 211—or 70 percent—had increasing proportions nonwhite. Outside the South, this mounts to 90 percent, for 121 out of 134 non-Southern SMSA's showed nonwhite increases between 1950 and 1960. In the South (defined in terms of census divisions) the situation is clearly different, for only 27 out of 77 SMSA's—or 35 percent—experienced relative gains in numbers of nonwhites. Over six out of every ten Southern SMSA's had lower proportions nonwhite in 1960 than in 1950.

Up to this point we have been discussing the metropolitan area as a whole. What about the changing color composition of major metropolitan centers? When we turn to cities, rather than metropolitan areas, changes in city boundaries between 1950 and 1960 make it impossible for us to determine the

Per Cent Nonwhite		1960 1950 bound- aries	1960 1960 bound- aries
City	1950		
New York	9.8	14.7	a
Chicago	14.1	23.6	b
Los Angeles	10.7	16.8	b
Philadelphia	18.3	26.7	a
Detroit	16.4	29.2	a
Baltimore	23.8	35.0	a
Houston	21.1	26.0	23.2
Cleveland	16.3	28.9	a
Washington, D.C.	35.4	54.8	a
St. Louis	18.0	28.8	a
San Francisco	10.5	18.4	a
Milwaukee	3.6	10.5	8.8
Boston	5.3	9.8	a
Dallas	13.2	18.7	19.3
New Orleans	32.0	37.4	a
Pittsburgh	12.3	16.8	b
San Antonio	7.2	7.9	7.4
San Diego	5.5	8.5	7.8
Seattle	5.8	9.8	8.3
Buffalo	6.5	13.8	a
Cincinnati	15.6	22.0	21.8
Memphis	37.2	42.7	37.1
Denver	4.4	7.7	7.1
Atlanta	36.6	46.6	38.4
Minneapolis	1.6	3.2	a
Indianapolis	15.0	23.0	20.7

numbers of whites and nonwhites for most of the "central cities." For the very largest places, however, data compiled by the Population Studies Center, University of Pennsylvania, allow us to make comparisons for identical physical areas. The following list shows the proportions nonwhite in 1950 and 1960 for each of the fifty largest cities in the continental United States. Each of these cities contained at least 250,000 inhabitants in 1960 and they are listed in order of size. *Without exception, these fifty metropolitan centers, regardless of their regional location, show increases in the proportion nonwhite.* In some cases (e.g., Minneapolis, St. Paul, and El Paso), the increases are modest, with a difference of only one or two percentage points. In other instances, however, the changes are substantial; for example, Newark changed from 17.2 to 34.4 per cent nonwhite, and Washington's proportion nonwhite rose from 35.4 to 54.8 in 1960.[2]

Per Cent Nonwhite		1960 1950 bound- aries	1960 bound- aries
City	1950		
Kansas City	12.3	19.3	17.7
Columbus, O.	12.5	19.0	16.6
Phoenix	6.2	8.4	5.9
Newark	17.2	34.4	a
Louisville	15.7	21.4	18.0
Portland, Ore.	3.5	5.7	5.6
Oakland	14.5	26.4	b
Fort Worth	13.3	17.3	15.9
Long Beach	2.6	5.1	4.3
Birmingham	39.9	41.1	39.6
Oklahoma City	9.3	13.8	13.1
Rochester	2.4	7.6	b
Toledo	8.3	13.5	12.7
St. Paul	2.0	3.0	a
Norfolk	29.7	32.6	26.4
Omaha	6.7	10.0	8.7
Miami	16.3	22.6	b
Akron	8.7	13.1	b
El Paso	2.6	3.1	2.6
Jersey City	7.0	13.5	a
Tampa	22.0	29.0	16.9
Dayton	14.1	22.8	21.9
Tulsa	10.0	14.0	10.0
Wichita	5.0	11.7	8.3

a. No boundary changes between 1950 and 1960.
b. Minor boundary changes; annexations affected less than 0.5% of 1960 city population.

The 28 large cities which accomplished major annexations of territory during the decade tended to show lower proportions nonwhite within their official 1960 boundaries than they would have contained within their 1950 limits. Examining the last two columns in the list of large cities, we find that all but one city annexed territory that was predominantly occupied by whites. (Dallas is the only exception.)

It would be highly desirable, of course, to examine changes in the color composition of the smaller constituent parts of the whole metropolitan area but this must await detailed analysis of statistics for census tracts. In the meantime it is not even possible to deal with changes in all central cities and "rings"—the outlying parts of metropolitan areas—because of the large number of SMSA's affected by annexations. For this reason we are obliged to narrow our focus and to concentrate upon a limited number of areas. As the list of cities reveals, annexations by the very largest places were infrequent between 1950 and 1960. In fact, we were able to find a dozen areas in which annexation ceased to be a major factor by 1920. As a consequence, we can extend the temporal coverage by narrowing the scope of our analysis to the dozen largest SMSA's.

The Twelve Largest Metropolitan Areas

As of April, 1960, the twelve largest Standard Metropolitan Statistical Areas were, in order of size: New York, Los Angeles–Long Beach, Chicago, Philadelphia, Detroit, San Francisco–Oakland, Boston, Pittsburgh, St. Louis, Washington, Cleveland, and Baltimore. Each contained at least 1.7 million inhabitants, and the combined population of these communities numbered over forty-seven million, or slightly more than one-quarter of all persons living in the United States.[3] In Table 1 the aggregate population of the twelve largest SMSA's is shown as a percentage of the total population of the United States for each census year since 1930. As a group these SMSA's have claimed a progressively larger share of the population of the United States. The relative increase in size, however, was very modest. Though their outlying parts—

their larger population, there remains a relative loss registered in these central cities. In 1940 the central cities contained over 62 percent of the metropolitan people but by 1940 the outlying areas held almost their invariable as the cities. The proportion of the population of the United States who lived in these twelve central cities had fallen slightly but steadily

Table 1—Per Cent Distribution of the Combined Population of the Twelve Largest Standard Metropolitan Statistical Areas (1960), the Central Cities, and the Rings, by Race, for Total Population of the United States: 1930–1960

The Twelve Largest SMSA's, Central Cities, Rings, and Remainder of the United States	TOTAL POPULATION				Per Cent Distribution by Race: 1930–1960							
					WHITE				NONWHITE			
	1960	1950	1940	1930	1960	1950	1940	1930	1960	1950	1940	1930
Twelve Largest SMSA's (1960)	26.3	25.6	24.6	24.4	25.8	25.7	25.4	25.4	29.7	24.2	17.6	15.5
Central Cities	(13.2)	(15.7)	(16.5)	(16.8)	(11.6)	(15.2)	(16.7)	(17.3)	(24.7)	(20.2)	(14.5)	(12.5)
Rings	(13.1)	(9.9)	(8.1)	(7.6)	(14.2)	(10.5)	(8.7)	(8.1)	(5.0)	(4.0)	(3.1)	(3.0)
Remainder of United States	73.7	74.4	75.4	75.6	74.2	74.3	74.6	74.6	70.3	75.8	82.4	84.5
Total United States	100.0	100.0	100.0	100.0	100.0	100.0	100.0	100.0	100.0	100.0	100.0	100.0

Figure 1—Combined Population of the Twelve Largest Standard Metropolitan Statistical Areas (1960), the Central Cities, and the Rings, by Race, 1930–1960

Since 1910, while the population of these metropolitan areas has constantly increased, doubling in the central cities. In addition, although the white population is decreasingly more concentrated in the twelve largest SMSA's, the relative number of nonwhites in these rings (only 3 percent in 1930) has grown by just two percentage points in thirty years. It their "rings"—grew substantially, there was a relative loss registered in their central cities. In 1930 the central cities contained over twice as many people as the rings but by 1960 the outlying areas held almost as many people as the cities.

The proportion of whites in the United States who lived in these twelve central cities has fallen slightly but steadily

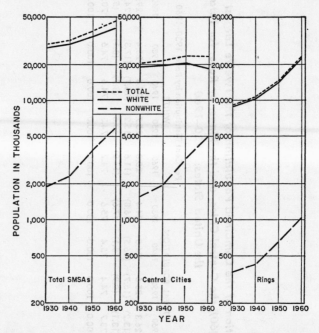

Figure 1—Combined Population of the Twelve Largest Standard Metropolitan Statistical Areas (1960), the Central Cities, and the Rings, by Race: 1930–1960

since 1930, while the proportion of nonwhites has consistently increased, doubling in the thirty-year interval. In addition, although the white population has become progressively more concentrated in the rings of the largest SMSA's, the relative number of nonwhites in these rings (only 3 percent in 1930) has grown by just two percentage points in thirty years. It may be noted also that the largest nonwhite percentage increase in the central cities occurred in the 'forties, while the losses in central city white population were most pronounced in the 'fifties.

The combined population of the twelve largest SMSA's, 1930 to 1960, has been plotted on semi-log charts in Figure 1. As may be seen, total population in these areas (the first panel of Figure 1) grew slowly in the 'thirties and then considerably faster in each of the last two decades. The nonwhite population in the twelve SMSA's was increasing much more rapidly than the white; in percentage terms the thirty-year growth rates of whites was 46.5 percent, while the comparable figure for nonwhites was 215.2 percent.

The combined central cities had only modest rates of growth during the 'thirties and 'forties and as a group they were slightly smaller in 1960 than they were ten years previously. The loss experienced by these cities in the 'fifties was due entirely to a drop in the white population; nonwhites in the center have shown a sizeable increase in numbers in each decade since 1930 although growing somewhat faster between 1940 and 1950 than more recently. It must be stressed here that we are not dealing with large percentage changes based on relatively small absolute numbers. Between 1950 and 1960, for example, these twelve central cities lost over two million whites while they were gaining 1.8 million nonwhites. At the same time the white and the nonwhite populations of the ring areas of the largest SMSA's have shown very sharp increases since 1930. Even so, the absolute number of nonwhites in the rings remains comparatively small.

INDIVIDUAL GROWTH PATTERNS

To this point we have considered these twelve areas in the aggregate. What has been the experience of the individual metropolitan area? In Figure 2 the size of the *total SMSA*, 1930–1960, is charted for each of the twelve metropolitan communities under consideration. The collective pattern described above is generally reproduced in each of the twelve areas taken individually. The total population increased slowly in 1930–40, then grew faster over the last two decades. The nonwhite populations are growing at rates which are from two to four times greater than those of the white populations.

The *central city* population for each of the twelve SMSA's is plotted in Figure 3. Again, almost all of the central cities individually have followed the general trend for the combined population. While the rates of nonwhite growth since 1930 have been very large indeed, those for central city whites remained remarkably stable between 1930 and 1950 and then became negative during the 'fifties. The only central area of the twelve which did not experience an absolute loss in number of whites between 1950 and 1960 was Los Angeles-Long Beach. And in this case the rate of growth of whites fell off during the last decade while that for nonwhites continued to rise at an

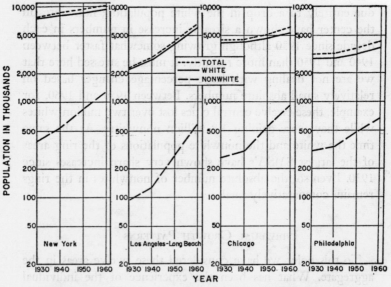

Figure 2a, b, and c—(above and on opposite page)
Population of the Twelve Largest Standard Statistical Areas (1960), by Race: 1930–1960

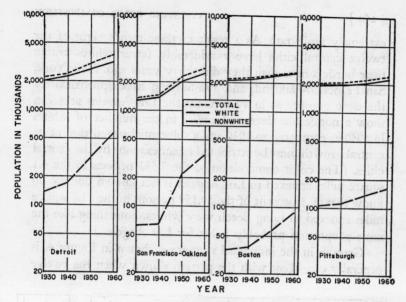

Figure 2b

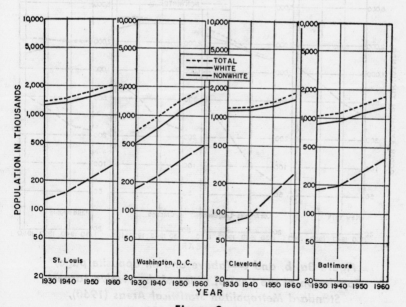

Figure 2c

extremely rapid rate. As a result of these trends eight of the twelve central cities have considerably fewer whites within their borders now than they did thirty years ago. New York, San Francisco-Oakland, and Washington have approximately the same number as in 1930. Only the Los Angeles area can show a noticeable absolute increase in the number of whites in 1960 as compared to 1930 and a substantial proportion of its central growth must be attributed to annexations by the central cities. (The color composition of the 7,557 persons in the 4.1 square miles annexed to Los Angeles is not known but we do know that 99.3 percent of the 59,159 persons in the 11.2 square miles annexed to Long Beach were whites. Something like the same proportion probably holds for Los Angeles.)[4]

Growth in the individual *ring* areas, shown in Figure 4, is generally consistent with the pattern shown when the twelve

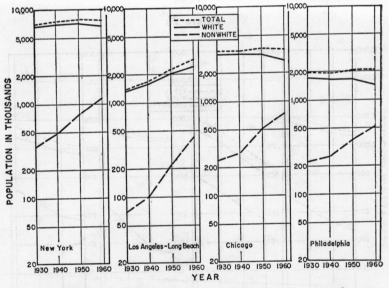

Figure 3a, b, and c—(above and on opposite page)
Population of the Central Cities of the Twelve Largest
Standard Metropolitan Statistical Areas (1960),
by Race: 1930–1960

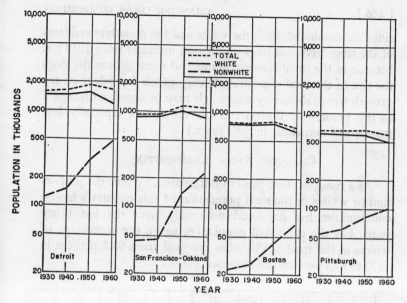

Figure 3b

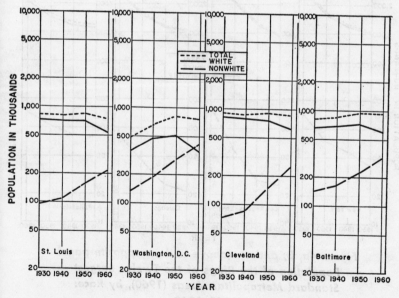

Figure 3c

rings are combined. Both the white and the nonwhite residents of the rings have had large population increases since 1930 but because of the small absolute number of nonwhites in the rings the size of the total population is very much dependent on the growth trends shown by whites. (It may be noted, with regard to this point, that Boston and Cleveland have especially low numbers of nonwhites in their rings.)

Changing Racial Composition

As a result of these growth differentials by race the proportion of whites in the total population of this country's largest communities has decreased noticeably over the last thirty years. For the combined population, again, the percentage of whites in the total SMSA's has dropped from 93.6 percent in 1930 to 87.1 percent in 1960. (See Table 2).

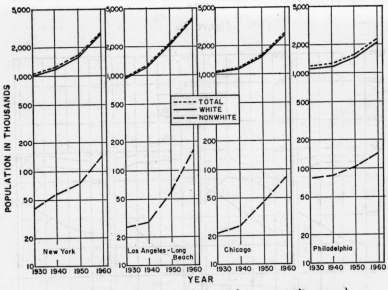

Figure 4a, b, and c—(above and on opposite page)
**Population of the Rings of the Twelve Largest
Standard Metropolitan Areas (1960), by Race:
1930–1960**

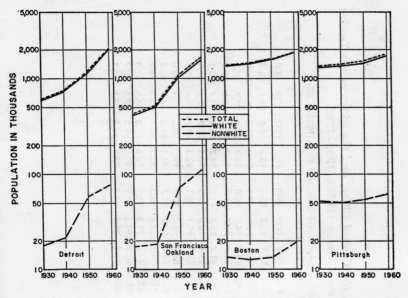

Figure 4b

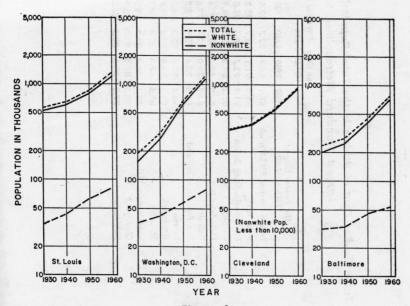

Figure 4c

Table 2—Per Cent of Whites in the Total Population, the Central Cities, and the Rings of the Twelve Largest Standard Metropolitan Statistical Areas (1960): 1930–1960

Per Cent of Whites in Total SMSA, Central Cities, and Rings: 1930–1960

The Twelve Largest SMA's (1960)	TOTAL SMSA				CENTRAL CITY				RING			
	1960	1950	1940	1930	1960	1950	1940	1930	1960	1950	1940	1930
Twelve Largest SMSA's: all	87.1	89.9	92.7	93.6	78.6	86.3	91.0	92.4	95.6	95.6	96.1	96.0
New York	88.0	91.1	93.9	95.2	85.3	90.2	93.6	95.1	95.2	95.5	95.4	96.2
Los Angeles-Long Beach	91.2	93.7	95.6	96.0	84.7	90.2	94.0	95.0	95.9	97.3	97.7	97.3
Chicago	85.2	89.3	92.3	94.1	76.4	85.9	91.7	92.9	96.9	97.1	97.8	98.0
Philadelphia	84.3	86.8	89.5	90.4	73.3	81.7	86.9	88.6	93.7	93.4	93.4	93.3
Detroit	84.9	88.0	92.7	93.6	70.8	83.6	90.7	92.2	96.2	95.0	97.1	97.1
San Francisco-Oakland	87.5	90.6	95.6	95.3	78.9	88.2	95.1	95.1	93.2	93.2	96.4	95.9
Boston	96.6	97.7	98.3	98.3	90.2	87.7	96.7	97.1	99.0	99.2	99.1	99.0
Pittsburgh	93.2	93.8	94.6	94.7	83.2	82.0	90.7	91.7	96.6	96.5	96.4	96.2
St. Louis	85.5	87.4	89.6	90.7	71.2	84.7	86.6	88.5	93.7	92.7	93.3	93.9
Washington, D.C.	75.1	76.6	76.2	75.0	45.2	64.6	71.5	72.7	93.6	91.3	86.3	81.0
Cleveland	85.5	89.5	93.0	93.9	71.1	83.7	90.3	91.9	99.2	99.2	99.1	98.9
Baltimore	77.8	80.6	82.5	83.2	65.0	76.2	80.6	82.3	93.1	89.8	88.1	86.2

Taking the twelve areas individually the proportion of whites has been declining since 1930 in all but one SMSA. The single exception is Washington, D.C.; about three-quarters of Washington's residents were white in each decennial census since 1930. Among these twelve areas the Washington SMSA had the highest proportion of nonwhite residents in 1930—as it does at the present time; Baltimore is now a close second, however.

The relative number of whites in every one of the twelve large *central cities* has decreased drastically over the last thirty years. This trend started slowly in the 'thirties, gained momentum in the 'forties, and became most pronounced during the 'fifties. The experience of one central city—Washington, D.C.—touches on the dramatic. In 1930 almost three-quarters of the inhabitants living in the city of Washington were white; currently, more than one-half of the residents of this city are nonwhite.

In contrast to the sharp drop in the proportion of whites in the central cities the most common pattern in the *rings* is one of near stability in racial composition. Thus, despite the rapid absolute growth of the ring area and despite the fact that the nonwhite rate of growth in the ring often is superior to that of the whites, the proportion of whites in eight of the twelve SMSA rings changed by less than three percentage points between 1930 and 1960. In Washington, D.C., and in Baltimore, the relative number of whites in the ring *increased* substantially during these thirty years.

The relationships discussed above become clearer when the data in Table 3 are examined. This table shows the ring population as a percentage of each SMSA. The first panel shows that every one of the twelve largest metropolitan communities has undergone a considerable amount of "decentralization" over the last thirty years. And for every one, again, this process has been gaining momentum since 1930, each decade showing a larger shift to the ring than the one before it. At the present time, only in New York, Chicago, and Baltimore does the population of the central city still exceed that of the ring. Moreover, the build-up of whites in the rings is of striking

Table 3—Per Cent of Population in the Rings of the Twelve Largest Standard Metropolitan Statistical Areas (1960) by Race: 1930–1960

Per Cent of Population in Rings, by Race: 1930–1960

The Twelve Largest Standard Metropolitan Statistical Areas (1960)	TOTAL POPULATION				WHITE				NONWHITE			
	1960	1950	1940	1930	1960	1950	1940	1930	1960	1950	1940	1930
Twelve Largest SMSA's: all	50.0	38.5	33.0	31.2	54.9	40.9	34.2	32.1	17.0	16.7	17.8	19.3
New York	27.2	17.4	14.4	13.1	29.5	18.3	14.6	13.2	10.9	8.8	10.8	10.5
Los Angeles–Long Beach	58.1	49.1	42.8	40.7	61.1	51.0	43.7	41.3	27.3	21.0	22.3	27.1
Chicago	42.9	30.1	25.7	24.1	48.8	32.7	26.9	25.1	9.0	8.1	8.2	8.2
Philadelphia	53.9	43.6	39.6	37.8	59.9	46.9	41.4	39.0	21.6	21.7	25.0	26.4
Detroit	55.6	38.7	31.7	28.0	63.0	41.8	33.2	29.0	14.1	16.1	12.7	12.8
San Francisco–Oakland	60.2	48.2	35.9	31.9	64.1	49.6	36.2	32.0	33.0	34.8	28.8	28.4
Boston	73.1	66.8	65.1	64.0	74.9	67.8	65.7	64.4	22.4	24.2	33.3	37.5
Pittsburgh	74.9	69.4	67.7	66.9	77.6	71.4	69.1	67.9	37.9	39.5	47.7	48.4
St. Louis	63.6	50.2	44.3	40.7	69.7	53.2	46.1	42.2	27.7	28.9	28.3	26.6
Washington, D.C.	61.8	45.2	31.7	27.8	77.0	53.8	35.9	30.0	16.0	16.9	18.3	21.1
Cleveland	51.2	37.6	30.7	27.6	59.5	41.6	32.7	29.1	2.8	3.0	3.8	4.8
Baltimore	45.6	32.4	24.6	22.4	54.6	36.1	26.3	23.2	14.3	17.1	16.7	18.3

magnitude and is consistent within each community. In 1930 the proportion of white residents of these SMSA's who were in the rings exceeded fifty percent for only Boston and Pittsburgh. At the present time a clear majority of the white population in ten of the twelve SMSA's is found in the ring. Chicago and New York are the exceptions and for these cities it is quite probable that the SMSA definition employed in 1960 excludes a substantial population that might otherwise be considered as living in "ring" areas.[5]

In stark contrast to the distributional patterns shown by whites, the nonwhites are *not* increasingly found in the rings. Only the San Francisco-Oakland SMSA provides a major exception to this generalization. Six of the twelve large communities show almost no change over the thirty-year period in the proportion of all nonwhites who are found in the ring. And in five of the twelve, nonwhites are actually less likely to live in the ring today than they were in 1930.

The above discussion has shown that, while some individual variations occur, the twelve largest SMSA's in this country have been following essentially the same general patterns of population growth and distribution. These patterns were at least evident in the 1930–40 decade (and probably earlier) and have become most pronounced during the last ten years. The SMSA as a whole has been increasing in size but only because the ring area is growing very fast. With the exception of Los Angeles and Long Beach, the central cities grew quite slowly if at all between 1930 and 1960. Eleven out of twelve central areas suffered absolute losses during the last decade.

Since 1930 the nonwhite population has expanded rapidly in every one of the large central cities; correspondingly, the central city white population has remained relatively stable or has substantially declined. This process of racial turn-over reached a peak of intensity between 1950 and 1960. The population decline of our largest cities would have been much more pronounced if increased numbers of nonwhites had not partially compensated for the loss of the white population. As we have noted, the flow to the rings was even greater over the last ten years than earlier. But this "decentralization" movement seems to involve a distinct color line. While the cities are becoming more and more nonwhite the rings maintain an amazingly high and constant proportion of white residents; without exception, from 93 to 99 percent of the population in the rings of our twelve largest metropolitan communities are white and this situation is basically unchanged since 1930.

DETROIT: A CASE STUDY

We may now turn to Detroit, a rather "typical" large community, and follow in more detail the population changes which have been occurring within various parts of this SMSA since 1930. For purposes of this analysis, the entire three-county Detroit SMSA has been divided into a series of seven contiguous, semi-circular zones drawn from the very heart of the central business district of the city of Detroit. As may be seen in Figure 5, the central city has been partitioned into four distance zones, the building blocks of which were census tracts. Detroit has two enclaves, Hamtramck and Highland Park, separate incorporated municipalities which are defined here as part of the "central city." Within the city four zones have been established on the basis of distance. The "ring" of the Detroit SMSA consists of three zones. The first ring zone borders directly on the central city and is commonly thought of as "suburban" Detroit. The second zone is the tier of townships bordering on the first zone. The outlying zone encompasses the remainder of the three-county area; this last zone is from twenty to forty-five miles from the center of the community.

The Detroit SMSA has followed very closely the general pattern of population growth described earlier. The total SMSA had a small population increase in the 'thirties and added about 25 percent to its population in each of the two following decades. (The metropolitan community's rate of growth has been slightly greater than that of the State of Michigan throughout the 1930–1960 period.)

The central city itself (here defined as including the two enclaves) enjoyed a modest increase in population in the

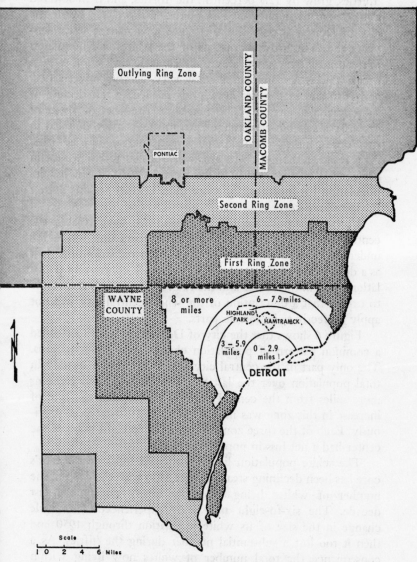

Figure 5—The Detroit Standard Metropolitan Statistical Area

'thirties, grew by 12.5 percent in the 'forties, and then suffered a 10.2 percent population loss in the 'fifties. As a result the city of Detroit is only slightly larger now than it was thirty years ago. The growth patterns of the whites and nonwhites in the central city, however, are in diametric opposition to each other. The white population grew very slowly between 1930 and 1950 and in the last decade experienced a net decline of substantial proportions. The nonwhite residents of the city grew by a sizeable percentage even in the 'thirties, doubled in the 'forties, and experienced a 60 percent increase in the 'fifties. As a result, although there are over 300,000 *fewer* whites in the central city now than there were in 1930, the nonwhite population has increased by more than 370,000 persons during the last thirty years.

Up to this point in the discussion we have treated the central city as though it were a homogeneous unit which has undergone a certain pattern of population redistribution. Just as a description of the total SMSA will mask contrasting population flows in the center and the ring, however, it is reasonable to expect that a description of the whole central city will not apply perfectly to its various parts.

Figure 6 shows that the city of Detroit has not experienced a common pattern of population change throughout its area. The only part of the central city which has grown steadily in total population over the last thirty years is located eight or more miles from the central business district and the rate of increase in this zone was much smaller in 1950–60 than previously. Each of the three zones located within eight miles of the center had a net loss in population in the 'fifties.

The white population living within six miles of the city's core has been declining steadily since 1930 with the drop in the number of whites being especially severe during the last decade. The six-to-eight mile zone experienced very little change in the size of its white population through 1950 and then it too lost a substantial number during the 'fifties. As a consequence the total number of whites now living within eight miles of the Detroit central business district is only one-half of the corresponding number in 1930. This loss represents a net decline of two-thirds of a million whites in thirty years.

Only in the outer area of the central city has the white population steadily increased since 1930. This zone's gain was sizeable in the 'forties, a period when the interior zones of Detroit were losing white residents. During the last decade the white population in the outer zone continued to grow but at a much reduced rate.

The trends of the nonwhite population within the four central city distance zones reveal three distinct patterns. Nonwhites were increasing in the innermost zone until 1950 and then experienced a net population loss. The decline of this group, however, was less substantial than that of the whites. The two middle zones have consistently added nonwhites to their populations throughout the last thirty years with the greatest growth occurring in the zone located six to eight miles from the center. Combined, the two middle zones have increased their nonwhite population by more than 700 per cent

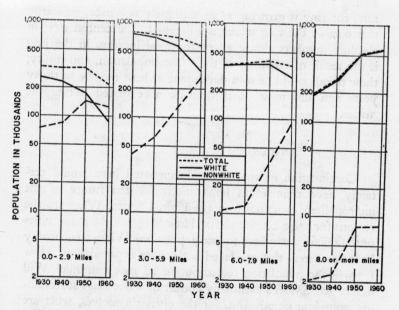

Figure 6—Population of the Central City and Its Enclaves in the Detroit Standard Metropolitan Statistical Area, by Distance of Residence from the Center and Race: 1930–1960

since 1930; during the same time span the white population of these two zones has declined by almost one-half.

During the last thirty years the fastest growth within the ring occurred in the zone directly adjacent to the central city while the zone which is most distant from Detroit has shown the slowest rate of increase. It is interesting to note that nonwhite growth in the innermost ring zone was much less during the 'fifties than was true in the remainder of the ring. This pattern corresponds to the very modest nonwhite increase over the last decade in the outermost zone of the central city.

At the present time the population dynamics of the Detroit SMSA could be summarized as follows: both whites and nonwhites are leaving the very core of the central city; the white population is failing to maintain its numbers in the middle sections of the city while the nonwhite residents are accumulating there very rapidly; the outer zone of the central city is adding to its white population although at a much reduced rate; the ring is growing at an extremely fast pace, especially that part of the ring which is adjacent to the central city; in absolute numbers almost all of the total increase in the ring is the result of additions to the white population; and finally, these trends could be seen developing at least twenty to thirty years ago and most of them were accentuated during the 'fifties.

ANALYSIS

Continuation of the trends documented here would certainly have tremendous implications for the future of the metropolitan community in the United States. What are the reasons for these massive shifts? How long will the major cities of the country continue to lose population? Will we eventually have core areas that are faced with acute depopulation? How far will the population redistribution by race continue? Will our largest SMSA's eventually consist of white rings surrounding nonwhite cities? And, for the cities themselves, what are the implications of these major changes in population composition? Let us consider a few of these questions.

The question of causation is most difficult of all. Among the reasons why the central city is losing its white population are the following: whites in the city are older and thus have somewhat higher death rates; more importantly, undeveloped land in the city is in very short supply for the building of new homes; those dwellings that are available for occupancy in the city often are not as attractive to young families as are comparably priced homes in the suburbs; and, for at least a certain number of whites, fears of various kinds—physical violence, loss of property values, etc.—begin to operate when nonwhites become neighbors.

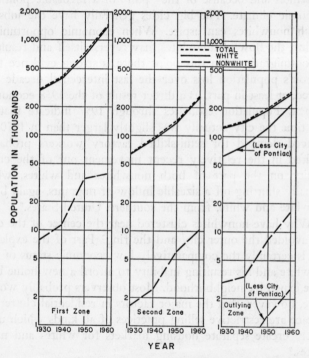

Figure 7—Population of the Ring of the Detroit Standard Metropolitan Statistical Area, by Distance of Residence from the Center and Race: 1930–1960

The ring population is increasing at a tremendous rate not only because of movements into them but also because suburban areas have a high proportion of young couples who are producing children at a very rapid pace. Additional factors which have contributed to the accumulation of population in the ring are: the greater ability of families to pay the costs of transportation; the decentralization of industrial and commercial enterprises; and the construction of vast suburban housing tracts and massive expressways which lead into the heart of the city.

Nonwhites are increasingly represented in the larger cities both because of the higher birth rates possessed by central city nonwhites and because of the "pull" of a favorable political-economic climate. The big cities generally have the jobs to which nonwhites can aspire. When economic opportunities decline, the flow of nonwhites may reverse itself and result in net outmigration. On this point there is strong evidence that Detroit's population loss over the last intercensal decade occurred, at least in part, as a direct result of the 1958 economic setback. Population estimates through 1957 indicate that at that time the city actually was slightly larger than in 1950. A reduced demand for semi-skilled factory workers probably resulted in the relatively recent movement out of the community on the part of both nonwhites and whites, while virtually shutting off a sizeable inflow of migrants, again both nonwhite and white, from the southern United States.[6]

Why have nonwhites clustered near the center of the city and avoided the outer city and the ring? Part of the explanation is certainly the comparatively low economic status of the nonwhite and his resulting inability to afford a new home in a more expensive neighborhood. Most observers probably would agree, however, that the major factors in residential clustering by race are restrictive selling practices of all kinds which ultimately create separate housing markets for whites and nonwhites.[7]

Do major cities face eventual depopulation? Many of this nation's largest cities are now in the midst of large-scale urban renewal programs. Like other material facilities, cities wear out and must be rebuilt. Perhaps the rebuilding has been too long delayed and the fruits of this delay are now apparent. A certain amount of the population decline suffered by the largest cities since World War II may be due to the temporary or permanent removal of land from residential use. The construction of expressways, the demolition of blighted areas, and similar activities conceivably have forced many families away from the core area. That this factor cannot be the entire explanation for the decline of the inner city is obvious to anyone who drives through the heart of a major metropolis. At the present time, if a statistical illustration is needed, about one out of four dwelling units within three miles of Detroit's center is vacant; the comparable proportion for the remainder of the city is approximately one vacancy in every twenty dwellings.

This analysis has shown that the twelve largest SMSA's have experienced very similar population shifts between the central city and the ring over the last thirty years. It is probable, also, that the more detailed trends apparent within the city of Detroit are present in most of the other large cities under discussion. For a variety of reasons the central cities, particularly their innermost cores, are falling short of compensating for the residents they are losing to the suburbs. Some observers have claimed that new public housing and other redevelopments in the inner city have begun to slow the general suburban drift and may eventually reverse it.[8] While this may occur in the future, the available data for large cities do not yet provide much support for this contention.

NOTES

1. Paul F. Coe, "The Nonwhite Population Surge to our Cities," *Land Economics*, 35 (August, 1959), 195. Data for the 1940–50 intercensal decade are provided in Paul F. Coe, "Nonwhite Population Increases in Metropolitan Areas," *Journal of the American Statistical Association*, 50 (June, 1955), 283–308.

2. Ann Ratner Miller and Bension Varon, *Population in 1960 of Areas Annexed to Large Cities of the United States between 1950 and 1960 by Age, Sex, and Color* (Philadelphia, Pennsylvania: University of Pennsylvania Population Studies Center, November 1961), Tables 1 and 1a. The role of boundary changes is discussed in Leo F. Schnore, "Mu-

nicipal Annexations and the Growth of Metropolitan Suburbs, 1950–60," *American Journal of Sociology,* 67 (January, 1962), 406–417.

3. The territory included in each SMSA as of 1960 was matched in each earlier census year. The "ring" area, as is customary, includes all of the incorporated and unincorporated territory lying beyond the boundary of the central city but within the metropolitan area. Color is categorized, following current official procedures, as "white" and "nonwhite." The 1930 census classified Mexicans as nonwhite while subsequent censuses placed these persons in the white category. In this study the 1930 figures have been corrected by reclassifying Mexicans as white so that the data are comparable for each decade.

4. See Miller and Varon, *op. cit.*

5. The use of "Standard Consolidated Areas" for New York and Chicago undoubtedly would show different results. These areas, larger than the SMSA's, were delineated for New York and Northeastern New Jersey and for Chicago and Northwestern Indiana.

6. These annual population estimates were prepared by the Detroit Area Study, University of Michigan.

7. See Beverly Duncan and Philip M. Hauser, *Housing a Metropolis —Chicago* (Glencoe, Illinois: Free Press, 1959), and Otis Dudley Duncan and Beverly Duncan, *The Negro Population of Chicago: A Study of Residential Succession* (Chicago: University of Chicago Press, 1957).

8. Using housing and school data for New York City, A. F. Parrott has argued that "The Flight to the Suburbs Slackens," in *Proceedings of the Social Statistics Section, American Statistical Association, 1960* (Washington, D.C.: American Statistical Association, 1960), pp. 152–58.

Chapter 15

Racial Changes in Metropolitan Areas, 1950–1960

Introduction

RECENT HISTORICAL EVENTS have focussed increasing attention on various aspects of "the race issue" in the United States. In this context, the sheer number and physical distribution of non-whites are matters of fundamental significance. Long-term trends include the flows of both white and nonwhite migrants out of the rural South into cities of all regions of the United States. These movements became numerically noteworthy during World War I and are continuing to provide important migratory streams. It is the purpose of the present chapter to document some basic shifts in the color composition of metro-politan areas in various regions of the country—shifts that have become dramatically evident in the past decade.

Color Composition of Large Cities

In Chapter 14, we discussed the tremendous increase in the proportion of nonwhite residents of the 12 largest cities of the

This study was supported by the research phase of the University of Wisconsin Urban Program, under the terms of a grant from the Ford Foundation.

United States.[1] Our concern now is an investigation of the extent to which this finding may also apply to somewhat smaller metropolitan centers. The problem of changing political boundaries through annexation becomes of considerable importance, however, when attention is directed to smaller sized units. For this reason, the data presented in Table 1 for the 50 largest cities in the continental United States account for annexation by holding area constant as of 1950. That is, the figures for each city have been adjusted so that the areal base is identical in both census years.[2]

For each of the 50 largest cities, Table 1 shows the per-

Table 1—Nonwhite Population as a Per Cent of Total Population, 1950 and 1960, and Per Cent Change in White and Nonwhite Population, 1950–1960, 50 Largest Cities in Continental United States

Region and City	PER CENT NONWHITE		PER CENT CHANGE, 1950–1960	
	1950	1960	White	Nonwhite
Northeast				
New York	9.8	14.7	—6.7	47.2
Philadelphia	18.3	26.7	—13.3	41.2
Boston	5.3	9.8	—17.1	59.9
Pittsburgh	12.3	16.8	—15.3	22.3
Buffalo	6.5	13.8	—15.3	94.7
Newark	17.2	34.4	—26.8	84.2
Rochester	2.4	7.6	—9.3	208.8
Jersey City	7.0	13.5	—14.1	77.8
North Central				
Chicago	14.1	23.6	—12.8	64.4
Detroit	16.4	29.2	—23.5	60.4
Cleveland	16.3	28.9	—18.6	69.3
St. Louis	18.0	28.8	—24.0	39.9
Milwaukee[a]	3.6	10.5	—10.1	185.5
Cincinnati[a]	15.6	22.0	—9.4	39.4
Minneapolis	1.6	3.2	—9.0	84.2
Indianapolis[a]	15.0	23.0	—9.1	53.9
Kansas City[a]	12.3	19.3	—12.7	49.9
Columbus, O.[a]	12.5	19.0	—2.4	58.8
Toledo[a]	8.3	13.5	—7.1	59.4
St. Paul	2.0	3.0	—0.3	49.8
Omaha[a]	6.7	10.0	0.4	54.7
Akron	8.7	13.1	0.7	58.7
Dayton[a]	14.1	22.8	—15.4	52.7
Wichita[a]	5.0	11.7	—5.4	138.8

Table continued

Table 1 (continued)

Region and City	PER CENT NONWHITE 1950	PER CENT NONWHITE 1960	PER CENT CHANGE, 1950–1960 White	PER CENT CHANGE, 1950–1960 Nonwhite
South				
Baltimore	23.8	35.0	−15.6	45.3
Houston[a]	21.1	26.0	8.1	42.1
Washington, D.C.	35.4	54.8	−33.3	47.3
Dallas[a]	13.2	18.7	4.9	59.2
New Orleans	32.0	37.4	1.2	28.6
San Antonio[a]	7.2	7.9	8.9	20.0
Memphis[a]	37.2	42.7	−1.2	24.1
Atlanta[a]	36.6	46.6	−19.6	21.2
Louisville[a]	15.7	21.4	−17.1	21.6
Fort Worth[a]	13.1	17.3	2.4	40.0
Birmingham[a]	39.9	41.1	−1.5	3.8
Oklahoma City[a]	9.3	13.8	−0.9	54.9
Norfolk[a]	29.7	32.6	−2.3	11.8
Miami	16.3	22.6	8.2	62.2
El Paso[a]	2.6	3.1	5.8	91.8
Tampa[a]	22.0	29.0	−1.7	42.1
Tulsa	10.0	14.0	−16.1	22.0
West				
Los Angeles	10.7	16.8	17.2	97.2
San Francisco	10.5	18.4	−12.9	66.8
San Diego[a]	5.5	8.5	46.9	135.1
Seattle[a]	5.8	9.8	−3.5	69.5
Denver[a]	4.4	7.7	5.8	91.8
Phoenix[a]	6.2	8.4	−2.3	34.6
Portland, Ore.[a]	3.5	5.7	−5.4	57.6
Oakland	14.5	26.4	−17.7	73.9
Long Beach[a]	2.6	5.1	10.7	121.7

a. Extensive annexations occurred during the 1950–1960 decade; data refer to populations within the 1950 boundaries at both dates.

centage nonwhite, 1950 and 1960, and the per cent change during this decade for whites and nonwhites. These cities are grouped by region and ordered by size within regions. All of the cities listed in Table 1 evidenced higher proportions nonwhite in 1960 than ten years earlier. The larger cities in all regions of the United States, therefore, are undergoing similar patterns of change in the color composition of their residents.

There is no readily apparent trend by city size within region in the changing proportion of nonwhites. We cannot say from these data, for example, that beyond a population of 250,000 the size of a city is likely to be related to changes in the relative number of nonwhites.

Although all of the country's largest cities had a greater representation of nonwhites in 1960 than in 1950, the reason for this shifting distribution by color varies from place to place. In this respect, regional differences become apparent. In each of the Northeastern cities, and in all but two of the 16 cities in the North Central region, the changing balance between color groups was accentuated by absolute losses in number of whites and substantial gains in number of nonwhites. The outward flow of whites and the in-migration of nonwhites to these cities represents a sharpening of a trend which has been developing for some years.[3]

In 13 of the 50 cities, both whites and nonwhites increased in absolute numbers. In these cases, then, the rise in proportion nonwhite reflects a more rapid increase for this group as compared to whites. Cities where both whites and nonwhites grew in number are clustered in the South and the West. It should be pointed out, however, that the majority of the large cities in the South and the West also experienced a net loss of whites while their nonwhite populations were increasing.

Variations by Region and Size for Metropolitan Areas

The larger cities of the continental United States generally are following a common pattern with regard to changes in racial composition. This statement appears to be valid even when annexation and other boundary changes are not allowed to confuse the discussion. To this point, however, we have considered only the largest cities without regard to the suburban areas around them. Now let us turn to a consideration of the entire metropolitan community, city and suburb combined, by an analysis of the racial changes which have occurred recently in the "Standard Metropolitan Statistical Areas" (SMSA's) of the United States.[4]

Table 2 presents a summary of changes in the nonwhite

Table 2—Summary of Changes in Proportions Nonwhite, 1950–1960, with Metropolitan Areas Classified by Region and by Size in 1950

PROPORTIONS NONWHITE:

Region and Size in 1950	Higher	Same or Lower	Total
Northeast: all	38	0	38
500,000 or more	14	0	14
250,000–499,999	11	0	11
Under 250,000	13	0	13
North Central: all	54	5	59
500,000 or more	11	0	11
250,000–499,999	10	0	10
Under 250,000	33	5	38
South: all	27	50	77
500,000 or more	7	2	9
250,000–499,999	5	7	12
Under 250,000	15	41	56
West: all	23	6	29
500,000 or more	6	0	6
250,000–499,999	4	4	8
Under 250,000	13	2	15
Total	142	61	203

proportion of the population in each SMSA, 1950–1960. The metropolitan communities are classified by region and by size within region. Seven out of every ten SMSA's in the United States had a higher percentage nonwhite population in 1960 than in 1950. Thus, metropolitan communities resemble the largest cities in the pronounced tendency for the nonwhite segment of their population to become proportionately larger in recent years.

Striking changes in the racial composition of metropolitan areas have occurred in accordance with regional location. In the Northeastern census region (comprising the New England and Middle Atlantic divisions) every one of the 38 metropolitan areas registered higher proportions nonwhite in 1960 than in 1950. The size of communities in the Northeast obviously cannot be a factor, for all communities in this region changed in the same direction.

In the North Central region of the United States, the nonwhite population of all SMSA's of 250,000 or more inhabitants in 1950 also grew at a faster rate than the white population. In the smaller metropolitan areas of this region, however, a few communities (5 out of 38) did not follow this trend. Thus, in the North Central census region, there is a slight indication that smaller SMSA's are more likely to have experienced a different racial growth pattern than have the larger areas. Nonetheless, in 87 percent of the North Central metropolitan areas of less than 250,000 in 1950, the proportion of the nonwhite population was greater in 1960 than in 1950.

In the West (defined as the Mountain and Pacific census divisions), the relative size of the nonwhite population in all of the largest SMSA's increased during the 'fifties. Western metropolitan areas of less than 500,000 population did not uniformly follow this pattern: four out of the eight medium-sized areas showed increases, while 13 out of 15 Western areas of less than 250,000 were so classified.

The experience of the South stands in sharp contrast to that of the other regions of the United States. In the Northeast, North Central, and West from 79 to 100 percent of all SMSA's were experiencing a faster growth rate of nonwhites than of whites between 1950 and 1960; over six out of every ten southern metropolitan areas showed *lower* proportions of nonwhites in 1960 than ten years previously. A clear majority of the large urban communities in the South, then, have become progressively more "white" during the last decade, while just the reverse is true for nonsouthern regions of the continental United States.

A similar *pattern* of change in color composition according to population size is found throughout three of the four census regions of this country. The slight tendency for size to be directly related to the relative growth of the nonwhite population was noted for the North Central and West; this relationship is pronounced in the South. Seven of the nine southern SMSA's with over 500,000 population in 1950 had higher proportions nonwhite in 1960 than in 1950. Only 42 percent of the medium-sized southern communities, and but 27 percent of these metropolitan areas in the South with less than 250,000 residents can be so classified.

In the largest metropolitan areas of the United States, then, the nonwhite population is increasing in relative size. This statement applies to all communities of 500,000 or more outside the South, and to all but two of nine large southern areas. The medium and small SMSA's also are following this pattern of change, with the exception of those in the South. Residents of southern metropolitan areas of less than 500,000 population in 1950 are more likely to be "white" in 1960 than ten years earlier. This probability statement is not valid for other regions of the continental United States.

ANALYSIS OF "DEVIANT CASES"

These contrasts are sufficiently important to merit closer examination. In an attempt to gain insight into these relationships, we have examined some of the "deviant cases"—i.e., the Southern areas showing relative gains, and the Northern and Western areas showing lower proportions nonwhite. The four exceptions within the North Central region are in border locations. Nonwhite declines were registered in Springfield and St. Joseph, Missouri, in Topeka, Kansas, and in Evansville, Indiana; part of the Evansville SMSA, it should be observed, lies in Kentucky. In the West, the exceptions are Phoenix and Tucson, Arizona; Honolulu, Hawaii; and San Jose and Santa Barbara, California. Honolulu and the two Arizona areas, of course, are resort-and-retirement centers that have experienced white in-migration on a massive scale in recent years. The two California SMSA's have grown very rapidly in response to the development of educational facilities; both contain centers that are part of the University of California system, and white students and staff have increased enormously over the past decade.

Exceptions to the southern pattern of decreasing proportions nonwhite in SMSA's are most likely to have occurred in those communities which have a relatively small rural component. These data are shown in Table 3. About seven out of

Table 3—Summary of Changes in Proportions Nonwhite, 1950–1960, by Per Cent of Population in Rural Areas, 1960, for SMSA's in the South

Per cent in rural areas, 1960	Higher	Same or Lower	Total
		PROPORTIONS NONWHITE	
Less than 10.0	13	6	19
10.0–19.9	8	17	25
20.0–29.9	4	13	17
30.0 or more	2	14	16
Total	27	50	77

every ten SMSA's in the South with less than 10 per cent of the population in rural areas had relatively more nonwhites in 1960 than in 1950; the comparable proportion for southern SMSA's with 30 per cent or more rural population was slightly greater than one out of every ten. This finding is consistent with the tendency for the largest metropolitan communities in the South to show gains for nonwhites. In gross regional terms, then, the southern whites are increasing in numbers relative to nonwhites in the smaller and more rural SMSA's of the South. The larger and heavier urban southern metropolitan areas, in contrast, are showing much the same pattern of growth as is found in other regions of the United States.

An examination of each of the 27 "exceptions" to the pattern followed by the majority of southern SMSA's (i.e., a gain in proportions white) reveals important subregional variations. Most of the so-called deviant communities are in the Southwest (the West South Central division, in census terms). They include Fort Smith, Arkansas; all three SMSA's (Oklahoma City, Tulsa, and Lawton) in Oklahoma; and 13 of the 20 SMSA's in Texas. Among the others which do not follow the general regional pattern, three are part of "Megalopolis," representing the southern-most extension of the heavily urbanized Northeastern seaboard—Washington, Baltimore, and Wilmington, Delaware;[5] two others are located in border states—Huntington, West Virginia and Louisville, Kentucky; and still another (Miami, Florida) is a resort-and-retirement center not ordinarily regarded as part of the traditional South.

In fact, only three SMSA's in the "Deep South" showed larger proportions nonwhite in 1960 than in 1950; they were New Orleans, Gadsden and Tuscaloosa.

AREAS LOSING ABSOLUTE NUMBERS

For the most part, metropolitan areas in the South are growing at moderate to high rates, and are gaining both whites and nonwhites. In a majority of cases, the growth of the white population has outstripped that of the nonwhites; as a consequence, 48 out of 77 Southern SMSA's have lower proportions nonwhite in 1960 than they had in 1950.

There are four cases, however, in which absolute population losses have been registered by one or both color groups. In two areas—Texarkana, Texas-Arkansas; and Wheeling, West Virginia-Ohio—both whites and nonwhites registered absolute losses between 1950 and 1960. In two other cases—Charleston, West Virginia; and Asheville, North Carolina—white gains were large enough to compensate for nonwhite losses. The 1950–60 rates of change for these four SMSA's were as follows:

| | PER CENT CHANGE: | | |
Area	White	Nonwhite	Total
Texarkana	—2.1	—6.1	—3.1
Wheeling	—2.9	—9.5	—3.0
Charleston	+6.5	—7.2	+5.5
Asheville	+6.2	—7.3	+4.6

Absolute losses in one or both color groups occurred in six metropolitan areas outside the census South. In one of these —St. Joseph in the border state of Missouri—both whites and nonwhites declined in absolute numbers. In five other cases, all in the Northeast, the white population declined absolutely while nonwhites increased. Four of these latter areas are located in the coal-mining regions of Pennsylvania—Altoona, Johnstown, Scranton, and Wilkes-Barre-Hazleton. The remaining case is perhaps the most dramatic of all: Jersey City, New Jersey lost almost 55,000 whites while gaining over 18,000 nonwhites. Rates of change between 1950 and 1960 for these six non-Southern SMSA's were as follows:

| | PER CENT CHANGE: | | |
Area	White	Nonwhite	Total
St. Joseph	—6.1	—17.7	—6.5
Altoona	—1.7	+10.7	—1.6
Johnstown	—3.8	+13.9	—3.6
Scranton	—9.0	+21.5	—8.9
Wilkes-Barre–Hazleton	—11.6	+32.6	—11.5
Jersey City	—8.8	+75.9	—5.7

Without exception, the long-term trend in the communities discussed above has been in the direction of population decline. Most of these SMSA's are economically depressed; it is therefore not surprising to find them deviating from the patterns found in growing areas.

RACIAL CHANGE AND SUBURBANIZATION

One frequently offered explanation of metropolitan suburbanization relates to the changing racial composition of the central city. It is argued that cities undergoing the most rapid increases in nonwhites are being quickly abandoned by whites. This hypothesis, of course, is ordinarily presented as an explanation for the movement of individual families. It is possible to test it, however, for the 50 largest central cities and the metropolitan areas in which they are located.

As a measure of the rapidity of suburbanization, we employed the algebraic difference between the 1950 and 1960 percentages of the total metropolitan population living in the suburban "rings," i.e., the portions of the Standard Metropolitan Statistical Areas lying outside the central cities.[6] Two measures of racial change were used: (a) the percentage-point difference in the proportion nonwhite, 1950 and 1960, and (b) the percentage increase in nonwhite population, 1950–1960. The rank order correlation coefficients were found to be —.04 and —.05 respectively, indicating a lack of relationship between racial change and rapidity of suburbanization. Cities undergoing varying degrees of racial change during the last decade seem to have suburbanized at comparable rates.

NEGRO SUBURBS

Metropolitan "rings" are overwhelmingly populated by whites. In fact, there is historical evidence that the outlying portions of some of the larger metropolitan areas are getting "whiter" with the passage of time.[7] In other words, the proportion nonwhite in the suburban ring often is declining rather than increasing. The Negro suburb generally is rare and numerically small. The nonwhite *rate* of growth in the suburbs may be substantial as a result of an extremely modest base. The white rate of growth in the suburbs approximates that of the nonwhite, although the absolute number of whites involved is many times greater. Thus, we can claim that the drift to the suburbs has been a selective process from the standpoint of color.

Yet it must be observed that some suburbs exist to which nonwhites have moved in substantial numbers. These "Negro suburbs" can be found in all sections of the country. The list of 24 places in Table 4 includes all those suburbs of the 50 largest cities in which nonwhites represented at least 20 per cent of the population in 1960. In all but four cases, the proportion nonwhite rose during the 'fifties; three of the four exceptions are located in the Deep South: Gretna, Louisiana; and Bessemer and Fairfield, Alabama. It will be recalled that a majority of the metropolitan areas in the South experienced relative losses in nonwhites between 1950 and 1960.

The only case in the remainder of the United States where the nonwhite percentage of the population declined over the last decade is that of Inkster, Michigan. Inkster is a highly segregated community which experienced a tremendous influx of whites in the 'fifties. The older portion of this Detroit suburb had relatively little undeveloped residential land by 1950 and was heavily Negro. The newer segment of Inkster had room to grow and the growth was in larger proportion "white."

Table 4—Incorporated Places of 10,000 or More Inhabitants Having 20 Per Cent or More Nonwhites in 1960 and Lying Within the Metropolitan Rings of the 50 Largest Cities

		PER CENT NONWHITE	
Central City	Suburb	1950	1960
New York	Hempstead, N.Y.	8.9	22.4
"	Plainfield, N.J.	13.6	21.9
"	Orange, N.J.	17.9	23.3
"	East Orange, N.J.	11.5	25.1
"	Montclair, N.J.	20.7	24.1
"	Englewood, N.J.	18.2	27.3
Philadelphia	Chester, Pa.	21.0	33.4
"	Camden, N.J.	14.1	23.8
"	Burlington, N.J.	16.3	21.7
Pittsburgh	Aliquippa, Pa.	16.0	21.0
"	Clairton, Pa.	17.4	21.9
"	Braddock, Pa.	16.3	23.6
Detroit	Highland Park, Mich.	8.6	21.4
"	River Rouge, Mich.	31.9	32.4
"	Ecorse, Mich.	32.6	33.3
"	Inkster, Mich.	53.7	34.7
St. Louis	East St. Louis, Ill.	33.5	44.6
Birmingham	Bessemer, Ala.	60.7	57.5
"	Fairfield, Ala.	60.1	52.5
New Orleans	Gretna, La.	28.8	25.5
Norfolk	South Norfolk, Va.	23.0	26.3
Los Angeles	Compton, Calif.	4.8	40.1
San Francisco	Berkeley, Calif.	15.4	26.2
"	Richmond, Calif.	14.3	22.0

In general, then, an examination of individual suburbs tends to confirm the patterns discovered earlier when the entire metropolitan area was subjected to study. Again, regional differences are very pronounced, with the South deviating sharply from the patterns observed in the rest of the country.

SUMMARY

All of the largest cities of the United States showed marked increases in proportion nonwhite between 1950 and 1960. Without exception, every city of 250,000 or more inhabitants showed the same trend in racial composition.

In gross regional terms, over six out of every ten southern SMSA's exhibited lower proportions nonwhite in 1960 than in 1950. Outside the South, over nine out of every ten metropolitan areas contained higher proportions nonwhite in 1960 than a decade earlier.

Nevertheless, it must be pointed out that the rate of nonwhite increase was unrelated to the speed of suburbanization during the past decade. Finally, it is possible to identify a group of "Negro suburbs" in all parts of the country. Again, the regional factor is pronounced in its effect, for those suburbs outside the South are showing rapid gains in proportions nonwhite, whereas southern suburbs are tending to lose nonwhites.

NOTES

1. Harry Sharp and Leo F. Schnore, "The Changing Color Composition of Metropolitan Areas," *Land Economics*, Vol. 38 (May 1962), pp. 169–185.

2. The data for 1960 populations within 1950 city boundaries were taken from Ann Ratner Miller and Bension Varon, *Population in 1960 of Areas Annexed to Large Cities of the United States Between 1950 and 1960 by Age, Sex, and Color* (Philadelphia: University of Pennsylvania Population Studies Center, November 1961), Tables 1 and 1a.

3. Shifts between 1940 and 1950 are analyzed in Donald J. Bogue, *Components of Population Change, 1940–50* (Oxford, Ohio: Scripps Foundation for Research in Population Problems, Miami University, 1957). Thirty-year trends in the cities and rings of the twelve largest metropolitan areas are shown in Sharp and Schnore, *op. cit.*

4. In New England, we used "county-equivalent metropolitan areas" in place of Standard Metropolitan Statistical Areas. This was the procedure used in Donald J. Bogue, *Population Growth in Standard Metropolitan Areas, 1900–1950* (Washington, D.C.: Housing and Home Finance Agency, 1953); see p. 7 and Appendix Table 2.

5. See Jean Gottmann, *Megalopolis* (New York: Twentieth Century Fund, 1961), especially pp. 17–22.

6. After reviewing the properties of a number of alternative measures, Bogue and Harris concluded that this is "the best index for measuring the speed of suburbanization." See Donald J. Bogue and Dorothy L. Harris, *Comparative Population and Urban Research via Multiple Regression and Covariance Analysis* (Oxford, Ohio and Chicago: Scripps Foundation for Research in Population Problems, Miami University, and Population Research and Training Center, University of Chicago, 1954), p. 45.

7. Sharp and Schnore, *op. cit.*

Chapter 16

Social Class Segregation
Among Nonwhites
in Metropolitan Centers

A RATHER CLEAR-CUT SEGREGATION of color groups is a "fact of life" within large cities in all parts of the United States. Whites and nonwhites are residentially segregated from each other.[1] We also know that urban populations are residentially segregated according to social class. The wealthy do not ordinarily live side by side with the poor in the community at large. In part, of course, the residential segregation of *color* groups is a *class* phenomenon. Despite recent advances in income, for example, most Negroes simply cannot afford life in "suburbia," no matter how much they might like to move out of the crowded ghettoes of the metropolitan centers.

These facts lead to some interesting questions: (*1*) Does residential segregation according to social class exist *within* color groups? (*2*) More particularly, are the social classes segregated within the nonwhite ghetto? In other words, does the force of color segregation today operate to oblige nonwhites of widely different social status to live "side by side"?

Such questions have been raised repeatedly by social scientists; studies have been carried out again and again, in the North and in the South, in small towns and in large cities. For example, small southern towns in the 'thirties were usually characterized by social scientists as so rigidly segregated according to color that class segregation could not be expressed. Speaking of one such town she had studied, the anthropologist Hortense Powdermaker referred to the area "Across the tracks, where side by side live the respectable and the disreputable, the moderately well-to-do and the very poor, the pious and the unsaved, the college graduates and the illiterates . . . all thrown together because all are Negroes."[2] Given the sweeping social changes since that time, in the South and elsewhere, it may be worth our while to consider some of these questions again.

RESIDENTIAL SEGREGATION BY SOCIAL CLASS
WITHIN THE NONWHITE GHETTO

The framework for this study was supplied some forty years ago by a group of sociologists working at the University of Chicago. One of these men—Professor Ernest W. Burgess—set out an account of urban community development that came to be known as the concentric–zonal hypothesis. His hypothesis represented an attempt to describe some consequences of growth and radial expansion for changing land uses, residential and nonresidential, and his stylized map of Chicago has been frequently reproduced, appearing again and again in social science textbooks.

For our purposes, the most interesting portion of the Burgess hypothesis concerns the changing residential distribution of "social classes." Stated most succinctly, his idea was that growth of the city core and extension of the urban periphery set off "waves of succession." New groups of in-migrants, low in income, education, and occupational standing, settled in and around the central business district; as these groups worked their way *up* in the social class structure, they worked their way *out* toward the periphery, only to be "succeeded" by other more recent arrivals. As long as this process continued, then, one would expect to find people with higher income, education, and occupational standing living farther out from the

center. As one examines a map of the city, and moves his eye
from the center toward the edge in any direction, progressively
higher status groups should be found.[3]

Does the Burgess pattern appear within subcommunities?
Sometimes it does. One of the earliest uses of census statistics
in *testing* the Burgess hypothesis was made by one of his students at the University of Chicago, and it happens to have been
concerned with the Negro ghetto. In a doctoral dissertation on
The Negro Family in Chicago, the late E. Franklin Frazier examined 1920 census statistics and other materials for the "Black
Belt" that stretched southward from the Loop.[4] Some years
later, and in another book dealing with the American Negro,
Frazier summed up his earlier findings on Chicago in this way:

> The expansion of the Negro community was similar, on the
> whole, to that of other racial and cultural groups. The Negroes
> had gained a foothold in and near the center of the city and as
> the city expanded, the segregation of the Negro population was
> part of the general process of segregation of different racial,
> economic, and cultural groups. Moreover, as the Negro com-
> munity moved southward [toward the edge of Chicago] there
> was a process of selection and segregation of various elements
> in the Negro community on the basis of occupation, intelli-
> gence, and ambition. . . . It was possible to measure the process
> of selection and segregation in the Negro community in 1920
> by dividing the community into zones coinciding more or less
> with the expansion of the city as a whole.[5]

Tables and maps prepared by Frazier suggest a rather regular
progression upward in various measures of socioeconomic
status with increasing distance from the Loop.[6]

One might ask, however, whether or not this pattern has
been observed within Chicago's "Black Belt" *since* 1920. It has.
Subsequent studies, using somewhat different methods, have
confirmed the fact that it has persisted in a general way as the
"Black Belt" has expanded. Two of these studies are reported
in *Black Metropolis*, by St. Clair Drake and Horace R. Cayton,
and in *The Negro Population of Chicago*, by Otis Dudley
Duncan and Beverly Duncan, and they make use of 1930 and
1950 census materials respectively.[7]

A more critical question, however, concerns the extent to which we can generalize about this matter in American cities other than Chicago. Frazier himself examined this question in later years, setting out some brief accounts, mostly impressionistic, of color *and* class segregation in northern and southern cities in the 'twenties, 'thirties, and 'forties.[8] A more solidly-based inquiry, confined to ten large cities, and looking at a number of other ethnic minority groups as well as Negroes, was published more recently by Lieberson. In this study, Lieberson examined long-term trends, as revealed in census statistics, up to and including 1950.[9]

But what is the situation in nonwhite ghettoes *today?* As we all know, the 'fifties comprised a decade of remarkable changes in relations between whites and nonwhites in all parts of the country. Moreover, Lieberson and Frazier and others have shown us that such patterns as can be observed with census statistics do not "hold still" for us; equally important, they have shown that there are variations from one city to another at any one point in time.

METHODS AND LIMITATIONS OF THIS STUDY

Unfortunately, not many cities can be subjected to a comparable mode of analysis with published census tract statistics. Census tract statistics have distinct limitations for this type of study. Census tracts, of course, are small areas into which large cities and adjacent areas have been divided for statistical purposes. They vary in size and shape; they are not easily arranged into neat distance zones. Although census tract publications give considerable detail on such matters as income, education, and occupation, there are inevitable problems stemming from nonresponse, deliberate distortion, etc. The use of self-enumeration, sampling, and electronic computer processing in the 1960 census did not solve all these problems. In some of the very areas we are considering—nonwhite ghettoes—the mobility of the population, lower-than-average levels of literacy, and technical problems involved in field enumeration and mechanical allocation of nonresponse combined to yield new diffi-

Table 1—Per Cent with Family Income of $7,000 or More in 1959, by Distance from Central Business District, Nonwhite Families, 24 Selected Cities, 1960

	NORTH								SOUTHWEST		WEST		
Miles	New York	Chicago	Detroit	Philadelphia	Cleveland	Indianapolis	Newark	Buffalo	Dallas	Houston	San Francisco	Oakland	Los Angeles
0–1	9.3	12.2	3.3	8.2	11.8	11.4	13.5	7.9	5.5	4.2	29.6	14.3	14.8
1–2			6.7	12.4	10.8	15.2	17.5	12.5		8.2	23.6	15.2	
2–3	12.8	11.8	10.7	15.4	19.1	16.1	33.8	22.1	7.9	19.6	32.8	26.3	19.3
3–4	13.6	16.2	15.7	26.1	29.3	25.9	37.4	32.3	5.5	7.2	26.7	27.3	21.8
4–5	18.8	20.4	21.2	26.2	36.0	46.0			5.0	8.6	40.8	31.0	29.8
5–6	18.8	27.9	23.7	29.8	46.1					10.8	50.5	37.8	34.3
6–7	22.5	26.8	27.3	37.5								27.2	35.6
7–8	15.0	27.7	30.8										24.1
8–9	11.3	41.2											16.3
9–10	....	50.4											29.5
10–11	25.6	45.6											
11–12	40.0	54.6											
12–13	46.9												

	BORDER						SOUTH				
Miles	Washington	St. Louis	Kansas City	Baltimore	Cincinnati	Louisville	Atlanta	Richmond	New Orleans	Birmingham	Memphis
0–1	12.6	1.8	4.1	7.0	4.7	4.0	5.1	4.0	5.5	2.3	1.9
1–2	19.1	4.1	7.9	11.2	9.6	8.3	8.0	10.9	6.5	8.2	4.2
2–3	24.4	9.4	17.4	21.2	18.1	12.7	10.6	10.4	10.3	10.5	5.4
3–4	35.1	15.7	17.3	27.5	29.1	16.1	14.9	10.4	8.7	8.0	8.0
4–5	41.0	21.4	28.7							7.0	6.7
5–6	28.0									8.2	4.0

culties. There is published evidence of such problems having arisen in certain parts of Chicago's "Black Belt," for example.[10] This fact makes comparisons with earlier studies of Chicago less than perfectly precise, and it gives us another reason for wanting to look at more than just one large city.

In any case, we have examined 1960 census tract statistics in the areas of heaviest nonwhite concentration within a number of large metropolitan centers. We selected only those tracts (1) which contained at least 400 nonwhites and (2) which were contiguous to the main areas of nonwhite concentration, i.e., the major ghettoes. We then eliminated those tracts with unusual population characteristics, such as those containing large institutional populations.[11] Finally, we tabulated the data —for nonwhites only—by combining tracts within radial distance zones, based on a one–mile interval, and (except in New York City) centered on the heart of each central business district.[12] The results are presented in the form of averages for the nonwhite populations of the various distance zones.

The three measures of socioeconomic status used in this study comprise a familiar set—income, education, and occupation. *Income* here means family income rather than individual income. *Education* refers to the number of school years completed by persons aged 25 years and over. Only the *occupation* of employed males aged 14 and over was considered. The three tables shown in this chapter report simple proportions for each zone of each named metropolitan center. As noted, these proportions are averages for each distance zone, and each of them conceals a certain amount of intra–zonal variation, i.e., there are differences from tract to tract within each zone. Moreover, each of the three measures comes from sample statistics, rather than "complete–count" data, and this fact introduces another element of variability.

FINDINGS

The entries in Table 1 show the percentage of all nonwhite families in each zone reporting an aggregate income of $7,000 or more in the calendar year preceding the 1960 census. Simi-

Table 2—Per Cent Completing High School, by Distance from Central Business District, Nonwhite Population Aged 25 and Over, 24 Selected Cities, 1960

| | NORTH | | | | | | | | SOUTHWEST | | WEST | | |
Miles	New York	Chicago	Detroit	Philadelphia	Cleveland	Indianapolis	Newark	Buffalo	Dallas	Houston	San Francisco	Oakland	Los Angeles
0–1	37.0	17.1	12.5	12.4	16.9	14.2	16.4	16.2	23.6	22.3	29.7	21.6	28.6
1–2			15.0	16.4	16.3	20.9	21.1	17.7		28.7	39.0	26.7	
2–3	27.2	16.9	16.4	21.1	26.2	26.0	32.0	26.5	25.4	45.1	45.6	32.9	37.1
3–4	24.9	22.1	23.2	35.6	35.0	32.2	42.3	36.7	25.5	21.8	34.5	38.8	37.8
4–5	30.0	21.7	30.5	30.6	39.1	52.2			19.7	21.3	51.8	48.0	44.7
5–6	26.7	28.2	34.1	35.1	46.9					22.8	50.4	50.6	52.3
6–7	32.1	30.0	35.2	47.8								36.1	52.7
7–8	25.2	33.1	38.2										38.7
8–9	23.5	41.1											30.0
9–10	....	52.5											37.7
10–11	34.3	48.6											
11–12	45.9	50.5											
12–13	51.4												

| | BORDER | | | | | | SOUTH | | | | |
Miles	Washington	St. Louis	Kansas City	Baltimore	Cincinnati	Louisville	Atlanta	Richmond	New Orleans	Birmingham	Memphis
0–1	18.1	11.5	16.8	8.4	6.1	12.6	10.4	16.8	11.2	11.5	11.0
1–2	25.7	11.0	23.5	12.9	11.9	17.7	20.1	17.3	13.5	21.5	13.1
2–3	27.6	16.6	33.1	22.1	26.8	32.2	29.3	22.2	17.7	23.4	14.9
3–4	42.3	25.5	38.2	32.0	38.3	32.4	29.2	17.9	15.0	18.4	16.7
4–5	50.7	32.5	46.2							19.0	17.3
5–6	35.8									19.6	14.0

[300]

larly, the entries in Table 2 show for each zone the percentage of all nonwhite persons aged 25 or over who reported that they had completed 12 or more years of formal schooling. Finally, Table 3 shows for each zone the percentage of all employed nonwhite males aged 14 or over who reported that they worked in occupations classified by the census as (a) professional, (b) owners, managers, and officials, (c) clerical, or (d) sales. In sociological parlance, these are "white-collar" as opposed to "blue-collar" occupations.

The various metropolitan centers have been grouped according to the broader regions in which they are located. It will be seen immediately that these are *not* the "regions" traditionally recognized in census publications over the years. Note that a "border" region is designated in the tables. The "border" cities are those which have been repeatedly identified as "way stations" in the literature dealing with the northward migration of southern Negroes over the years, or as cities "caught between North and South" as far as social and cultural influences are concerned.[13] The four main quadrants of each table have been arranged in a way that permits a quick grasp of the major findings. In each column of figures—zonal percentages for each named metropolitan center—the highest percentages have been italicized.

As expected, the Burgess pattern was found to be quite general as far as Northern metropolitan centers were concerned. The upper-left quadrant in each table shows that the highest value occurs in the outermost zone in 22 out of 24 instances. In general, there is an upward-sloping gradient with increasing distance from the center. If we ignore minor deviations, it is safe to say that the nonwhite ghettoes in large northern cities still tend to display the pattern observed earlier in considering Chicago. That is, *as distance increases from the center of the city, the socioeconomic status of nonwhite neighborhoods goes up. Nonwhite family income is higher, nonwhite educational levels mount, and the relative number of nonwhite males in "white-collar" employment increases.*

Some of the deviations just characterized as "minor" are quite interesting, e.g., the obvious tendency in a number of

Table 3—Per Cent Employed in White-collar Occupations, by Distance from Central Business District, Employed Nonwhite Males Aged 14 and Over, 24 Selected Cities, 1960

NORTH

Miles	New York	Chicago	Detroit	Philadelphia	Cleveland	Indianapolis	Newark	Buffalo
0–1	35.0	11.2	7.6	13.2	10.1	6.4	11.0	6.6
1–2	24.1	11.8	9.7	12.4	8.0	9.4	9.6	6.0
2–3	21.8	15.1	8.9	14.5	13.4	13.9	14.9	11.5
3–4	24.3	13.1	10.8	23.5	16.2	15.1	26.1	25.0
4–5	18.3	16.2	14.6	24.8	20.5	32.0		
5–6	21.5	16.7	15.4	23.5	25.5			
6–7	17.4	17.0	18.6	32.8				
7–8	16.5	22.2	18.6					
8–9	....	33.0						
9–10	22.2	30.2						
10–11	27.0	33.2						
11–12	32.4							

BORDER

Miles	Washington	St. Louis	Kansas City	Baltimore	Louisville	Cincinnati
0–1	16.2	11.5	7.8	11.7	6.9	6.7
1–2	18.7	8.4	10.5	11.1	7.6	9.6
2–3	19.6	11.7	15.1	13.5	14.5	18.7
3–4	32.1	17.4	18.2	21.8	17.3	19.5
4–5	39.4	17.7	23.0			
5–6	28.7					

SOUTH

Miles	Atlanta	Richmond	New Orleans	Birmingham	Memphis
0–1	6.2	9.9	8.5	5.7	7.7
1–2	10.3	13.5	11.7	11.3	9.2
2–3	15.9	14.4	12.8	11.5	9.1
3–4	20.2	11.5	11.9	8.5	11.2
4–5				6.7	11.7
5–6				9.5	5.4

SOUTHWEST / WEST

Miles	Dallas	Houston	San Francisco	Oakland	Los Angeles
0–1	8.6	7.3	33.0	14.4	21.7
1–2	12.3	12.4	26.3	13.7	26.5
2–3	10.3	22.2	26.6	18.8	22.6
3–4	7.7	9.4	19.9	20.1	27.9
4–5		8.9	34.3	29.2	30.4
5–6		10.6	26.8	31.3	29.2
6–7				17.5	17.9
7–8					12.0
8–9					17.3

cities for the first or innermost zone to exhibit higher values than the next. Some of these departures from a "perfect" pattern are apparently attributable to urban renewal programs focussed on the "blighted cores" in and around central business districts. In other cases, deviations stem from the fact that nonwhites other than Negroes are included in the study.

The exception to be stressed in this group of eight Northern cities concerns the case of New York City. Tables 2 and 3 suggest a rather marked departure from a perfect pattern. When graphed, the data on education and occupation approximate a U-shaped pattern rather than an upward-sloping gradient with distance from the center. This is mainly attributable to the fact that tracts throughout the entire city were classified according to distance from a *single* point—the midpoint of the southern border of Central Park in Manhattan. Actually, substantial concentrations of nonwhites are now found in four of the five boroughs of the city of New York—not just in Harlem and the Lower East Side of Manhattan, as in the past.[14]

If we turn now to the data for the "border" cities—represented in the lower–left quadrant—we see the Burgess pattern manifested again. In five out of the six cities, the highest values appear in the outermost distance zones. Again, there is generally an upward-sloping gradient. Washington, D.C. is a clear-cut exception, showing three out of three deviations from the pattern found in the other five border cities. In general, however, *nonwhite ghettoes in large border cities tend to resemble those in cities of the North, insofar as internal "class segregation" is concerned.*

As for Washington itself, the widely noted influx of nonwhites into the city, especially since World War II, is apparently the main cause of the deviation from a perfect zonal pattern. Nonwhites have spread from "traditional Negro neighborhoods" into formerly white neighborhoods throughout much of the city. The changes that have occurred there do not represent a steady progression away from the center and toward the periphery in only one or two directions, as in most other Northern and border cities.

When we turn to the large cities of the South, where most

nonwhites are Negroes, quite a different pattern appears. Examination of the lower-right quadrants in the three tables reveals that four out of five cities display a certain consistency: *moving away from the center of the city, nonwhite areas show a rise in socioeconomic status, followed by a decline.*

Atlanta constitutes a clear–cut exception; the values are highest in the outermost zone in two out of three instances, and in the case of education (Table 2) the difference between the third and the fourth zone is trivial. In short, Atlanta resembles the northern and border cities in the study more than it resembles the other four southern cities.

There is no ready explanation for *either* (*1*) the "southern pattern," or lack of pattern, revealed in these four cities *or* (*2*) Atlanta's departure from the regional configuration. In any case, the writer is not sufficiently familiar with southern cities to hazard any *ad hoc* "explanations" of the differences. An examination of the literature dealing with nonwhite areas in southern cities, supplemented by conversations with knowledgeable people from the South, has produced quite a long list of factors that *may* explain the similarities and the differences. Most of these seem to involve "history" over the short or long run; they include such factors as changing patterns of migration and residential mobility on the part of both whites and nonwhites, the impact of urban renewal and slum clearance, and the location of Negro colleges and universities.

Up to this point, we have talked only about "southern" *versus* "northern" patterns of class segregation within nonwhite subcommunities, noting that "border" cities tend to resemble cities in the North. We should probably be surprised if clear–cut differences *didn't* exist between North and South. But some of the dangers attending easy and casual "explanations" of such materials as these are suggested by the remaining quadrant in the tables.

The upper–right quadrant shows data for five metropolitan centers. The first two are in the "Southwest"—Dallas and Houston. In both cases, the patterns of class segregation within nonwhite areas are clearly more similar to comparable areas in Southern cities than to Northern nonwhite ghettoes. Perhaps this will come as no surprise to those who are familiar with these two cities, but the results do tend to contradict assertions to the effect that developments of the 'forties and 'fifties had made both Dallas and Houston much less "Southern" and more "Northern" and/or "Western."

As for the metropolitan centers of the Far West, the same upper–right quadrant gives a summary characterization of Los Angeles and the San Francisco–Oakland "Bay Area." Superficially, they would appear to resemble the southwestern and southern cities as far as class segregation within major nonwhite areas is concerned. Actually, the data are not unequivocal. In the case of Los Angeles, there are a number of problems of interpretation because of the many peculiarities in the legal city limits. A long series of annexations of territory, and the persistence of enclaves like Beverly Hills, would make an analysis of city tracts alone very difficult, and the results wouldn't be very meaningful. But ignoring the city's legal boundaries, as in this study, requires the use of many odd–shaped census tracts.[15] In the Bay Area, we have given separate consideration to San Francisco and Oakland. In any case, the situation can be summed up very briefly: (1) San Francisco reveals the "northern" pattern in only one out of three instances. (2) Oakland's three "deviations" from the same pattern seem almost entirely due to the influence of the University of California at Berkeley, Oakland's "neighbor." The Berkeley ghetto is included in the data for Oakland, and even though tracts with large numbers of students were eliminated, the impact of the university's presence is still quite evident.

One last point: the "nonwhite areas" in metropolitan centers of the Far West are not at all like the "Negro ghettoes" in some other parts of the country. The same thing can be said for Dallas and Houston. For one thing, ethnic minority groups other than Negroes are present in large numbers. In Dallas and Houston, there are substantial numbers of Mexican–Americans, most of whom are white according to census terminology; the areas most heavily occupied by persons of Mexican descent in these two cities happen to overlap the nonwhite areas of concentration rather considerably. The same thing can be said for

Los Angeles, with the added qualification that nonwhite persons of Oriental descent are also present in large numbers; this complicates the question of "class segregation" considerably. Finally, all these groups are well represented in the San Francisco–Oakland Bay Area. This caveat is inserted to prevent possible misunderstandings concerning the implications of the observed patterns in these five cities.

CONCLUSIONS

We found a pattern of class segregation *within* a number of nonwhite areas that is very familiar to all students of the American city; it can be summed up as "The higher up the social ladder, the farther out you live." Perhaps even more important, however, is the fact that we found variations. The *regional* variations stressed in this chapter are perhaps the most interesting of all the differences from city to city so evident in the data presented here.

A number of scholars have diligently pursued the quite diverse historical forces that lie behind these gross differences in pattern, forces which deserve continuing attention in research on the American city. There is no quick and easy substitute for detailed historical study—and in as much "depth" as our data permit. It is hoped that the comparative materials presented here will provide a framework within which detailed historical studies of individual cities will become more meaningful.[16]

NOTES

1. See Karl E. Taeuber, "Negro Residential Segregation: Trends and Measurement," *Social Problems,* 12 (Summer, 1964), pp. 42–50.

2. Hortense Powdermaker, *After Freedom* (New York: Viking Press, 1939), p. 13.

3. Ernest W. Burgess, "The Growth of the City: An Introduction to a Research Project," *Publications of the American Sociological Society,* 18 (1924), pp. 85–97; reprinted in Robert E. Park, Ernest W. Burgess, and Roderick D. McKenzie, *The City* (Chicago: University of Chicago Press, 1925), pp. 47–62.

4. E. Franklin Frazier, *The Negro Family in Chicago* (Chicago: University of Chicago Press, 1932).

5. E. Franklin Frazier, *The Negro in the United States* (New York: Macmillan, 1949), pp. 257–58.

6. Some of these materials have been reproduced in a posthumously published essay; see E. Franklin Frazier, "The Negro Family in Chicago," in Ernest W. Burgess and Donald J. Bogue (editors), *Contributions to Urban Sociology* (Chicago: University of Chicago Press, 1964), especially Table 1, p. 407.

7. St. Clair Drake and Horace R. Cayton, *Black Metropolis: A Study of Negro Life in a Northern City* (New York: Harcourt, Brace and Co., 1945); Otis Dudley Duncan and Beverly Duncan, *The Negro Population of Chicago: A Study of Residential Succession* (Chicago: University of Chicago Press, 1957), especially pp. 278–98.

8. Frazier, *The Negro in the United States, op. cit.*, Chapter XI, "Urban Negro Communities," pp. 229–72.

9. Stanley Lieberson, *Ethnic Patterns in American Cities* (New York: Free Press of Glencoe, 1963).

10. See U.S. Bureau of the Census, *U.S. Censuses of Population and Housing: 1960, Census Tracts*, Final Report PHC (1)–26 (Washington: U.S. Government Printing Office, 1962), Appendix Table A, "Per cent of persons in sample and percent of persons with sample information, for census tracts in Chicago city: 1960," pp. 675–78. Chicago was the only city for which such a tabulation was published. The extent of the under-reporting of sample information can be seen in some of the "Black Belt" tracts:

Census tract number:	Per cent of persons with sample information:
357	55.4
368	63.8
369	59.6
372	51.4
516	65.0
573	66.2
574	68.4
579	61.2
880	61.8
898	63.1

11. Tracts eliminated included those with majorities of the nonwhite population living in group quarters—people living in "rooming houses, college dormitories, military barracks, or institutions." *Ibid.*, p. 3.

12. Census tracts identified as part of the "central business district" in each city are listed in U.S. Bureau of the Census, *U.S. Census of Business:* Volume VII, *Central Business District Report*, Summary Report BC58-CBD 98, Revised (Washington: U.S. Government Printing Office, 1961), Appendix 3.

13. Frazier, *The Negro in the United States, op. cit.* See also T. J. Woofter, Jr. (editor), *Negro Problems in Cities* (Garden City, N.Y.: Doubleday, Doran and Co., 1928); Charles S. Johnson, *Patterns of Negro*

Segregation (New York: Harper and Brothers, 1943); Robert C. Weaver, *The Negro Ghetto* (New York: Harcourt, Brace and Co., 1948).

14. Oscar Handlin, *The Newcomers: Negroes and Puerto Ricans in a Changing Metropolis* (Cambridge, Mass.: Harvard University Press, 1959).

15. For a detailed study of this area, see Dorothy Slade Williams, *Ecology of Negro Communities in Los Angeles County: 1940–1959* (unpublished doctoral dissertation, Department of Sociology, University of Southern California, 1961). Williams examined data for 1940 and 1950 and found that "Educational attainment of communities showed no progressive rate of increase or decrease with greater distance from the city center outward." *Ibid.*, p. 148.

16. See Williams, *ibid.*, and Karl E. Taeuber and Alma F. Taeuber, "The Negro as an Immigrant Group: Recent Trends in Racial and Ethnic Segregation in Chicago," *American Journal of Sociology,* 69 (January, 1964), pp. 383–94. For comparative data, see Karl E. Taeuber and Alma F. Taeuber, *Negroes in Cities: Residential Segregation and Neighborhood Change* (Chicago: Aldine Press, 1965), Chapter VIII, "Race and Residential Differentiation."

Part Six

Studies in Urban Circulation

CHAPTER 17 first appeared in *Traffic Quarterly*, Volume 16 (October, 1962), pp. 488–98. Like all of the empirical chapters preceding it, Chapter 17 is based on census materials. It sets out to account for the variation among cities in the extent to which public transportation is utilized in commuting to work. The explanatory variables employed comprise a familiar set of ecological factors: the population size, density, and age of urban areas. An attempt is made to predict from these simple factors the proportion of the working population using public means of transportation. The "prediction," of course, is of the conditional form, *viz.*, if A, then B. The chapter provides a kind of contextual background or framework of understanding for planners and others interested in particular places.

Chapter 18, which is a very brief attempt at moderately long-range forecasting, continues the emphasis upon rather gross variables. It first appeared in Donald J. Bogue (editor), *Applications of Demography; The Population Situation in the United States in 1975* (Oxford, Ohio and Chicago: Scripps Foundation for Research in Population Problems, Miami University and Population Research and Training Center, University of Chicago, 1957), pp. 73–5. It is an example of the kind of "prediction" *about* the future which ecologists and demographers hope to be able to make in the future. In some respects, it consists of a longitudinal extrapolation of some scattered cross–sectional observations. By examining the differences between places of different size as of a particular point in time, it is possible to form some idea of how growing places will change as they increase in size. Such an extrapolation is hazardous, of course, but it is often our only recourse in the absence of adequate historical records.

But predictions of any consequence require more than the grossness of the statements exemplified in Chapters 17 and 18. To be of any use to a planner, for example, a finer grain is required. Thus, Chapter 19 turns to the study of a single urban area. It first appeared in *Social Forces*, Volume 32 (May, 1954), pp. 336–43, and it is the only "case study" in the entire volume. Although it is the earliest of the essays reprinted here, it points the way to a future line of ecological work far more clearly than any of the others, not so much in substance as in basic materials. Rather than census materials, it makes use of "origin-destination" survey data. This kind of material frees the ecologist and the demographer from the subject-matter limits of the census schedule. More importantly, it focusses attention on what people *do*, in addition to who they *are*. It approximates a "time budget" of human activities which, if extended, would yield rich information of the kind only available to the omnipotent observer of urban behavior in the hovering helicopter.

The final essay, Chapter 20, is therefore more programmatic. It first appeared in the *Journal of the American Statistical Association*, Volume 55 (March, 1960), pp. 8–22, and it contrasts three sources of data on commuting that are amenable to ecological–demographic analysis. Beyond this, it provides a rough paradigm for the consideration of such problems as that of the appropriate unit of analysis and that of cross-sectional versus longitudinal study design. We might look forward to the day when repeated surveys of the sort represented by origin–destination studies will provide more detail on the unfolding histories of urban areas. In the end, of course, we are all writing history.

Chapter 17

The Use of Public
Transportation in Urban Areas

MUCH HAS BEEN WRITTEN about the transportation crisis facing our largest cities. Federal involvement on a massive scale is imminent. The American metropolis has been portrayed as increasingly choked, or strangled, by automobile traffic, and the related problems are seen as complex and ramified—e.g., the decline of the central business district, the inadequacy of parking facilities, and the impending demise of public transportation.[1] Literally millions of dollars have been spent in simply accumulating the data necessary to establish the dimensions of the problem, with hundreds of traffic studies initiated since World War II. The existence of real problems has been well documented by this research. Moreover, the studies already accomplished have demonstrated the intimate interconnections between the transportation system and patterns of land use,[2] so that the attention of planners is increasingly focused on questions of movement and circulation.

It has been noted, however, that the cities that have been

This study was supported by the research phase of the University of Wisconsin Urban Program under the terms of a grant from the Ford Foundation.

studied most closely may constitute a highly selected sample of all urban areas. By and large, studies are only initiated in a locality where the traffic situation has seriously deteriorated. It is only when the traffic problem becomes pressing enough to merit widespread attention, for example, that expensive and time-consuming origin-and-destination (O-D) surveys are considered. For this reason, much of what we think we know about the urban transportation problem may be exaggerated or distorted by simple reason of bias in the sample of cities studied.

It is for this reason that the new 1960 census data on workplace and method of travel are particularly welcome at this time. Although confined to a 25 per cent sample of persons enumerated, and although limited to work-trips, this new body of information provides data on the full range of urban communities to be found in the nation as a whole, and it opens up a host of new research possibilities.

Of all the questions that can be asked of these new materials, our initial concern is with the factors that make for variations in the use of mass transit, or public transportation. Other investigators have been obliged to deal with this question with more limited bodies of data. Working with a sample of 33 cities, Smith has asked: "Do cities vary in the extent to which they rely on these systems of [mass] transportation in their daily ebb and flow of traffic? If they do vary, why is it that in some cities people more typically take the bus or subway to work or to shop, while in others they drive their own cars?"[3]

Census data are particularly appropriate for answering such inquiries because of the sheer number of cities and the great variety of community characteristics that can be examined. One need only think of the following considerations:

> As against management records, which are practically confined to larger enterprises, census data have the advantage of covering every type of industry and occupation, including those in which establishments are small and typically characterized by owner operation. Unlike O-D studies, which have been conducted only in urban areas, the census covers the nation and encompasses areas of every type—metropolitan and

nonmetropolitan, urban, suburban, fringe, village, and open country. . . . The new census data on method of travel to work are also promising from a research standpoint. For one thing, it will be possible to test the common-sense observation to the effect that the use of public transportation increases with population size and density, and that such methods of travel are infrequently used in "post-automobile cities," i.e., those in which the major part of growth and development has occurred since 1920.[4]

The basic question, then, is how to account for variability in one aspect of urban transportation—the commuter's dependence upon public facilities for mass transit.

THE DATA

The 25 per cent sample (self-enumeration) questionnaire used in the 1960 census of population and housing contained the following queries:[5]

If this person worked last week, answer questions P28 and P29.

P28. *What city and county did he work in last week?*
If he worked in more than one city or county, give place where he worked most last week.
a. City or town.....................................
b. If city or town—*Did he work inside the city limits?*
                                          Yes □
                                          No □
c. County................State......................

P29. *How did he get to work last week?*
(Check one box for principal means used last week)

Railroad ...... □	Taxicab ..... □	Walk only. □
Subway or	Private auto	Worked at
elevated..... □	or car pool. □	home..... □
Bus or		
streetcar .... □	Other means—Write in:	

....

Those who checked railroad, subway or elevated, and bus or streetcar were treated as users of public transportation. The proportions of such users have now been reported for selected units in a series of "Advance Reports" of the 1960 census.[6] Extreme variability is evident. While no workers commute by public transportation in Midland, Texas, 61.0 percent of the employed persons in New York City travel to work by mass transit.

In this chapter we will be concerned with the use of public transportation in the central cities of the 213 "urbanized areas," those densely settled conurbations within which the urban transportation problem is ordinarily regarded as most severe. Subsequent analyses will be able to extend the coverage to smaller places, and to relate the use of public transportation to such characteristics of individual workers as age, sex, color, occupation, and income. At the moment, however, we will confine our attention to characteristics of cities, *per se*, and to those areas over which the greatest concern has been expressed.

HYPOTHESES

As we have indicated, we are interested in certain gross characteristics of cities themselves—characteristics that might be expected to influence the resident populations of cities in their travel behavior. This line of analysis is taken not only because of the immediate availability of appropriate data for cities, but also because of a conviction that it represents a viable alternative to an individualistic approach wherein characteristics of persons are examined in relation to travel patterns. The rationale is as follows: "Stated most simply, [this approach] rests upon the assumption that *transportation* systems are properties of *socioeconomic* systems. A corollary premise asserts that the nature of the socioeconomic system will shape the essential features of the transportation system. . . ."[7]

But what characteristics of cities should be examined? Certainly a great number of features may be regarded as relevant, ranging from whether or not mass transit facilities are publicly owned to such geographic features as topography and land forms. Out of the great welter of potentially relevant characteristics of cities, we have selected three for immediate analysis: (*1*) the size of the city, (*2*) its population density, and (*3*) its age. The significance of each of these variable city characteristics can be briefly sketched.

(1) *City size*—Size is of potentially great import because it determines the limits of the *market* for public transportation. It is quite unlikely that a very small place will have extensive facilities simply because there is not much demand for the service. A large population, on the other hand, is far more likely to represent a large demand for public transportation services. The contrast between a city like Midland, Texas (with a population of 62,625) and New York City (with 7,783,314 inhabitants) is too obvious to ignore.

(2) *Population density*—Quite apart from size, sheer density of habitation might be expected to play a role in affecting the availability and use of public transportation. Real *economy* of operation appears to require that certain minimal densities obtain. A widely dispersed population—large as it might be—would be very expensive to serve, while *per capita* costs might be considerably reduced in serving a densely settled area.[8]

(3) *Age*—In addition to size and density, age of settlement is a potentially important factor. Cities of different age grew up in radically different technological eras. More particularly, older cities in the United States experienced their major period of growth and development prior to the widespread ownership and use of automobiles dating from the 1920's. It might be expected that such cities would be better equipped with public transportation facilities, having been obliged to install and maintain mass transit systems before the turn of the century. Newer, post-automobile cities, on the other hand, might be expected to be less well equipped from the standpoint of mass transit equipment.

FACTORS: SIZE, DENSITY, AND AGE

Table 1 shows that the use of public transportation is clearly associated with city size. In the very largest cities (those with more than one million inhabitants) fully one-third of the employed persons use public transportation. At the other extreme, less than one out of every ten workers uses mass transit facilities in commuting in the two smallest size classes.

Table 1—Use of Public Transportation by City Size, 1960

PER CENT OF EMPLOYED PERSONS IN CENTRAL
CITY (OR CITIES) USING PUBLIC TRANSPORTATION
TO WORK

Size of Central City, 1960	0.0–9.9 Per Cent	10.0–19.9 Per Cent	20.0–29.9 Per Cent	30.0 Per Cent or More	N	Average (Unweighted Mean for Size Class)
1,000,000 or more	0	1	1	4	6	33.5
500,000–1,000,000	1	4	6	5	16	24.8
250,000–500,000	5	18	4	0	27	15.2
150,000–250,000	10	17	4	1	32	13.2
100,000–150,000	17	17	0	0	34	9.9
50.000–100,000	63	29	6	0	98	9.0
	96	86	21	10	213	12.5

Table 2 reveals that population density is similarly related to the use of public transportation. The association is positive in form, i.e., the higher the density, the greater the use of mass transit. In cities with the most dense patterns of settlement (between 7,000 and 10,000 persons per square mile) almost one out of every three workers travels to work by railroad, subway, elevated, bus, or streetcar. In contrast, less than seven out of every hundred workers use these means of transportation in cities with density ratios under 2,000.

Table 2—Use of Public Transportation by City Density, 1960

PER CENT OF EMPLOYED PERSONS IN CENTRAL
CITY (OR CITIES) USING PUBLIC TRANSPORTATION
TO WORK

Central City Density, 1960	0.0–9.9 Per Cent	10.0–19.9 Per Cent	20.0–29.9 Per Cent	30.0 Per Cent or More	N	Average (Unweighted Mean for Density Class)
7,000–10,000	1	3	6	8	18	28.4
6.000–7,000	5	9	2	0	16	13.5
5,000–6,000	15	11	2	1	29	11.3
4,000–5,000	14	15	0	0	29	10.2
3,000–4,000	22	20	2	1	45	11.2
2,000–3,000	24	13	1	0	38	8.7
Under 2,000	13	6	0	0	19	6.9
	96	86	21	10	213	12.5

Finally, Table 3 suggests that the age of the city may be a significant factor in determining the relative importance of public transportation. When cities are classified according to the length of time that has passed since they achieved considerable size (50,000 inhabitants), the differences according to age emerge sharply and clearly. One out of every three workers in the very oldest cities commutes by means of mass transit. At the other extreme, only about one out of 20 employed persons in the newest cities makes use of public transportation.

Table 3—Use of Public Transportation by Age of City, 1960

PER CENT OF EMPLOYED PERSONS IN CENTRAL
CITY (OR CITIES) USING PUBLIC TRANSPORTATION
TO WORK

Census Year in Which Central City (or Cities) First Exceeded 50,000 Inhabitants	0.0– 9.9 Per Cent	10.0– 19.9 Per Cent	20.0– 29.9 Per Cent	30.0 Per Cent or More	N	Average (Unweighted Mean for Age Group)
1800–1850	0	1	3	4	8	34.3
1860	0	2	1	3	6	27.7
1870	0	0	4	3	7	26.7
1880	2	6	2	0	10	15.0
1890	3	11	6	0	20	16.1
1900	2	13	1	0	16	13.9
1910	10	14	1	0	25	11.5
1920	10	14	1	0	25	12.2
1930	14	11	1	0	26	10.3
1940	6	3	0	0	9	7.5
1950	22	6	1	0	29	7.8
1960	27	5	0	0	32	5.4
	96	86	21	10	213	12.5

In summary, all three city characteristics—size, density, and age—appear to be associated with the use of mass transportation. A difficulty emerges, however, when one attempts to interpret the meaning of these associations. The problem arises from the fact that all three characteristics are themselves intercorrelated. That is, older cities tend to be larger and more densely settled than newer cities. These intercorrelations are not perfect, but they are substantial, as shown in Table 4. The problem then becomes one of assessing the relative weight to be assigned to each of the three variables in explaining variations in the use of public transportation.

In view of the situation just described, it is highly desirable to measure the effects of each of the three independent variables (size, density, and age) with the others held constant. We have therefore employed a multiple-regression analysis, the main results of which are shown in Table 5. It will be seen in the upper panel (devoted to first-order correlations) that successive control of the variables reduces the extent of association in every case. It is also noteworthy, however, that the extent of the reduction is least in the case of age. Similarly, the lower panel (where second-order correlations are shown) reveals that age more successfully survives the control of other variables than either size or density, both of which are substantially reduced in predictive power.

Table 4—Zero-order Correlation Coefficients, Selected Variables

	City Size	City Density	Age of City	Per Cent Using Public Transportation
City size	1.0000	.5506	.4779	.5680
City density		1.0000	.6459	.6718
Age of city			1.0000	.7516
Percent using public transportation				1.0000

A MULTI-VARIATE APPROACH

One last question that can now be answered concerns the extent to which the three independent variables—in combination—are capable of predicting the dependent variable, the proportion of employed persons using public transportation. As it turns out, the multiple correlation (R) has a value of .8032 when corrected for 210 degrees of freedom. The resulting coefficient of determination (R^2) is .6452, indicating that almost two-thirds of the variance has been successfully accounted for in terms of the three independent variables.

We have demonstrated that three characteristics of cities—their size, density, and age—exert a measurable influence upon the use of public transportation by their inhabitants. Moreover, we have shown that one of these characteristics—sheer age—is especially powerful in the explanation of the variations from one city to another. These results could hardly be labelled as surprising, yet it is gratifying to find a common-sense proposition so clearly verified.

The significance of age is widely recognized, as witnessed by the following passage:

> Historically, public transportation and rail commuter travel developed in our older metropolitan areas before the general use of the automobile. In these areas increased use of private automobiles has put financial strain on mass transit and rail commuter facilities. Some of our newer metropolitan areas have come to rely predominantly or almost exclusively on the private automobile supplemented by bus systems.[9]

But these are historical observations from the vantage point of the 'sixties, and one would hardly hazard an extrapolation from the past and predict that the use of mass transportation will increase as cities age. In fact, most students of the subject foresee the opposite trend—increased use of the private automobile.

Table 5—Summary of Partial Correlation Analysis

A. First-order Partial Correlations

Independent variable	Size	Density	Size	Age	Density	Age
Controlled variable	Density	Size	Age	Size	Age	Density
Partial correlation coefficient	.3204	.5226	.3604	.6641	.3701	.5617
t[a]	4.913	8.904	5.612	12.900	5.787	9.863

B. Second-order Partial Correlations

Independent variable	Size	Density	Age
Controlled variables	Density Age	Size Age	Size Density
Partial correlation coefficient	.2619	.2759	.5381
t[a]	3.932	4.160	9.251

a. t > 3.291, p < .001.

The problems facing public transportation are many, but one that is rather frequently overlooked arises out of two simple considerations: homes and workplaces are becoming less compactly arranged, and more decentralized or diffused over a greater area. With continuation of these well-established trends:

> Simple geometric reasoning points to an increasing amount of lateral movement, in complicated cross-currents of commuter streams. The direct implication is a *longer*—not shorter—average trip to work. Moreover, a more diffuse pattern of workplaces will also further reduce the chances for economical operation of mass transit facilities, so that the private automobile will probably become even *more* important except for commuting to certain central workplaces.[10]

Older cities face one range of problems, but newer cities are in quite a different situation, chiefly by virtue of their dissimilar patterns of land use. As Bello has observed,

> The new home-to-work pattern seems to be beyond any solution based on mass transit. The subway was ideal for moving people between high-density housing and high-density work places. The commuter railroad took over to move people to the same work areas from low-density housing. But there seems no way to provide an efficient mass-transit system that can move people from low-density housing to factories—and even offices—spotted over the countryside.[11]

Massive involvement on the part of government is apparently no panacea:

> Some states show signs of getting into the problem, for instance, by providing help in meeting the capital needs of the mass transit facilities and by enacting measures to encourage local tax abatement for such facilities. It is not farfetched to suppose that the Federal government will eventually get into mass transit as well . . . as an inexorable consequence of its present involvement in the financing and planning of the nation's highway system. One way or another, there will be efforts to redress the balance between mass transit and the automobile. But the results promise to be slow in coming and fragmentary in their application. In fact, before such results materialize, the most pressing transportation problem inside some metropolitan areas may have changed in character. Instead of wondering how to haul people to and from the central business district with comfort and dispatch, our prime question may

well be how to move people from the dispersed homes in one suburb to the dispersed plants in another.[12]

What stance should the urban planner adopt in the face of such gloomy forecasts? Is there, to use Coleman Woodbury's apt phrase, a "glacial inevitability" about the massive trends that we have been discussing? Is there no control—no leverage —to be exercised? Our response to such questions must be sharply qualified. Certainly, the kinds of data reviewed here should promote a healthy respect for the *limits* of planning; variables like size, age, and (to a large extent) density are not within immediate range of control. They are simply not manipulatable. At the same time, we are probably too conscious of other kinds of limitations—limitations which inhibit the exercise of imagination. To take only one example, the prospects for public transportation might appear in an entirely new guise if we would abandon the idea of mass transit—whether privately or publicly owned—as a profit-making enterprise.

Finally, we would only add a plea for more research. Certainly, the availability of the new census materials should encourage a fresh look at the factors which encourage and discourage the use of public transportation on the part of the individual. Planners and others interested in the subject would do well to explore the analytical possibilities presented by this unprecedented body of information on workplace and method of travel. As Woodbury has observed, "Many persons are inclined to classify mass transit services and their many problems as examples of the pathologies of urban life. One does not have to agree with this view to argue that these services and their role in the circulation systems of urban areas of differing size, density, and economic character merit thorough study."[13]

NOTES

1. The most comprehensive treatment is to be found in Wilfred Owen, *The Metropolitan Transportation Problem*, The Brookings Institution, Washington, D.C., 1956.

2. Robert B. Mitchell and Chester Rapkin, *Urban Traffic: A Function of Land Use*, Columbia University Press, New York, 1954. An entire

issue of the *Journal of the American Institute of Planners* (May, 1959) was given over to "Land Use and Traffic Models."

3. Joel Smith, *Some Social Aspects of Mass Transit in Selected American Cities*, Institute for Community Development and Services, Michigan State University, East Lansing, 1959, p. 4.

4. Leo F. Schnore, "Three Sources of Data on Commuting: Problems and Possibilities," *Journal of the American Statistical Association, 55* (March, 1960), pp. 16 and 18.

5. U.S. Bureau of the Census, *U.S. Censuses of Population and Housing, 1960: Principal Data-Collection Forms and Procedures*, U.S. Government Printing Office, Washington, D.C., 1961, p. 41.

6. This series, PC (A3), consisted of 52 reports, one each for the United States, each of the 50 states, and the District of Columbia, and were issued between July 14, 1961, and April 27, 1962. They contain the first data issued on the subject of method of travel.

7. Leo F. Schnore, "Transportation Systems, Socioeconomic Systems, and the Individual," *Transportation Design Considerations*, National Academy of Sciences–National Research Council, Washington, D.C., May, 1961, p. 202. O-D data suggest that greater use of public transportation is found among nonwhites, employed females, and those of lower socioeconomic status. These characteristics can only be directly examined when the Bureau of the Census releases a special report on the public-use sample.

8. Density ratios were taken from U.S. Bureau of the Census, *U.S. Census of Population: 1960*, Volume I. *Characteristics of the Population*, Part A, "Number of Inhabitants," U.S. Government Printing Office, Washington, D.C., 1961, Table 22.

9. Research and Policy Committee, Committee for Economic Development, *Guiding Metropolitan Growth*, Committee for Economic Development, New York, July 1960, p. 22. Norton has supplied a brief sketch of the major transportation eras in the following passage: "About 1830 the horse-drawn omnibus opened the era of mass transportation by public carrier within cities. The horse-drawn street railway car came somewhat later, to be followed by suburban railways in the 1850's and 1860's. In the 1880's and 1890's the cable car, elevated railway, and electric surface streetcars were developed. Finally, at the turn of the century, subways were built, marking the high point of the development of mass transportation by railway. At the same time the infant auto industry appeared on the scene." C. McKim Norton, "Metropolitan Transportation," in Gerald Breese and Dorothy E. Whitman (editors), *An Approach to Urban Planning*, Princeton University Press, Princeton, New Jersey, 1953, p. 78.

10. Leo F. Schnore, "The Journey to Work in 1975," in Donald J. Bogue (editor), *Applications of Demography; The Population Situation in the U.S. in 1975*, Scripps Foundation for Research in Population Problems, Miami University, and Population Research and Training Center, University of Chicago, Oxford, Ohio, and Chicago, 1957, p. 74.

11. Francis Bello, "The City and the Car," in The Editors of *Fortune* (editors), *The Exploding Metropolis*, Doubleday and Co., Garden City, New York, 1958, pp. 55–56. Only 13 of the 213 urbanized areas

show higher rates of public transportation usage in the suburban fringes than in the central cities.

12. Raymond Vernon, "The Economics and Finances of the Large Metropolis," *Daedalus*, 90 (Winter, 1961), pp. 43–44.

13. Coleman Woodbury, *A Framework for Urban Studies: An Analysis of Urban-Metropolitan Development and Research Needs*, Highway Research Board, National Academy of Sciences—National Research Council, Washington, D.C., October 1959, p. 23.

Chapter 18

The Journey to Work

in 1975

Scope and Limitations

THIS DISCUSSION of the journey to work in 1975 will be confined to the metropolitan areas of the United States. These are the very areas in which commuting poses a problem—whether viewed from the standpoint of the entire community or the individual worker—and it seems clear that an increasing proportion of our national population will be living and working in a metropolitan context.

Even with this limitation, however, it is no easy matter to forecast the future, for we have very limited data on commuting in the past and at the present time. Our decennial census—although long used as a model by other nations—was the last in the Western world to collect data on the place of work of employed members of the labor force. In the absence of appropriate data on commuting itself, we have to be content with projections of certain other trends and developments that presumably have an important bearing upon the journey to work.

CURRENT TRENDS IN COMMUTING

Before making an assessment of future prospects, let us identify the trends in commuting that are apparent today. Despite the lack of precise data with which to document these statements, certain tendencies seem almost undeniable. First of all, increasing urbanization and "metropolitanization" of the labor force means that increasing numbers of workers are involved in daily commuting.

Within metropolitan areas, moreover, two additional trends seem obvious: (1) the average distance of the journey to work is increasing; and (2) progressively higher proportions of work-trips are made by private automobile.

These two aspects of commuting—the length of the work-trip and the method of travel utilized—are primarily functions of (a) the spacing of both homes and workplaces, and (b) the available routes and carriers that connect these two sites. It appears, then, that future patterns of commuting can be more intelligently assessed if we consider whether or not current trends in the spatial arrangements of homes and workplaces will continue in the same direction, and if we examine the probable effects of changes in the routes and carriers that serve to link places of employment and residence.

THE FUTURE DISTRIBUTION OF HOMES AND WORKPLACES

Homes—The current trend, of course, is toward a more diffuse pattern of residential development within metropolitan areas, especially marked by the spread of single-family dwellings into formerly open country. It has been evident for some time that suburban living is no longer the sole prerogative of the economically favored segment of our population. Despite certain counter-pressures toward "re-centralization"—such as the construction of more multiple-family units in central cities —there is no strong evidence that the outward thrust of residential population will cease in the near future.

Workplaces—Although the center will continue to be a

major area of employment, it seems reasonable to expect that the current decentralization of workplaces will also continue for some time. As in the past, it will probably be a selective decentralization, with not all types of enterprise participating in the movement. However, the simple application of already existing technology will free more industries from central location. Increased use of the motor truck will release many industrial establishments from locations near the existing rail network; automation will further reduce the need for location at points of maximum accessibility to large pools of labor; atomic energy may even permit further scatter away from present power grids.

Not only will industry continue to decentralize, but more and more retail and service establishments will be obliged to follow both industry and residential population as they shift outward. Moreover, as these "tertiary" activities provide employment for an expanding proportion of the labor force, their dispersed location becomes increasingly important as a factor in commuting.

In the light of these forecasts for continued decentralization of both homes and workplaces, it might seem that the average length of future work-trips would be reduced. However, such a view assumes that workplaces and workers decentralize together. There is no evidence that this is yet the case. On the contrary, the decentralization that has already occurred in metropolitan areas has been notably uncoordinated, with workplaces and homes developing in different sectors.

Should this situation continue—and there is ample reason to believe that it will—simple geometric reasoning points to an increasing amount of lateral movement, in complicated cross-currents of commuter streams. The direct implication is a *longer*—not shorter—average trip to work. Moreover, a more diffuse pattern of workplaces will also further reduce the chances for economical operation of mass transit facilities, so that the private automobile will probably become even *more* important except for commuting to certain central workplaces.

FUTURE ROUTES AND CARRIERS

Routes—Routes have obvious implications for the distribution of homes and workplaces, and thus indirectly affect commuting patterns. New construction of roads and streets—including the current federal program—will undoubtedly permit even further dispersal of homes and workplaces. Assuming the same amount of commuting time, these improved and extended channels of surface movement will probably permit work–trips of even greater length. However, we need not assume that commuting time will remain the same. Historically speaking, much of the time gained in the shortening of the individual's workday has already been spent in increased travel time, and this seems likely to continue in the future.

Carriers—Surface routes, of course, are not the only routes. More and more central cities are devoting attention to mass transit as a means of alleviating traffic congestion. But underground and overhead transit lines are tremendously expensive; in fact, the barriers to further use of mass transportation seem to be *economic*, and not technical, with respect to both construction and operation. Subways and elevated lines can be installed only at enormous costs. Even in those areas where they already exist, the fact that work–trips are so heavily concentrated within a few hours makes for difficulties; facilities that are over-crowded during the rush-hours are under-used during the remainder of the day. Mass transit simply cannot provide the flexibility offered by the automobile.

Transportation specialists have come to essentially similiar conclusions regarding commuting by helicopter, i.e., that the problems are mainly economic, and not technological. The consensus seems to be that it is technically feasible but probably well beyond the means of most workers during the immediately foreseeable future. Thus for all but a minority, existing surface carriers will probably provide the means of movement to and from work in 1975.

The Future of Commuting

The first post-war decade evidently witnessed a delayed reaction to the widespread use of the automobile that began in the 'twenties. The removal of depression and wartime restrictions on the construction of residences, routes, and workplaces obviously initiated a massive readjustment to a radically new scale of distance—itself created by the automobile. Although it involves enormous costs, this readjustment will probably continue until 1975 and well beyond, if past experience provides any guide to the future.

The future of commuting can probably best be read in the light of current trends already well-established in residential, industrial, and commercial location. If our assumption of increased lateral movement with further decentralization is correct, the continuation of current trends would clearly imply *even longer work-trips, most of them by private automobile,* until some new locational equilibrium is reached.

Of course, systematic planning would permit the emergence of more or less self-contained "satellite cities"—with homes within easy access of workplaces, so that commuting time and distance would be reduced and more people could walk to work. As yet, however, there has been little disposition on the part of American business, industry, or government to undertake the comprehensive planning required. The reason may lie in the fact that the immediate costs of commuting—in time, money, and energy—are borne by the individual worker, and in the fact that the monetary costs are well hidden in the family budget.

However, the absence of adequate data also inhibits sound planning. Cities are now obliged to depend upon "origin-and-destination" sample surveys and other extremely expensive methods in order to gain some understanding of present traffic patterns. In view of this fact, the commuting question on the 1960 census should receive considerable attention. Although there are many technical problems to be solved, this innovation in our census promises data of unprecedented scope. With more factual information in hand, we would stand a better chance of solving many of the crucial practical problems now facing metropolitan areas throughout the country; and we would also be in a better position to forecast future patterns of commuting with some assurance.

Chapter 19

The Separation of Home
and Work: A Problem
for Human Ecology

THE DAILY JOURNEY to work is receiving increased attention in discussions of the urban community. Seen in historical perspective, the separation of place of work from place of residence is a relatively recent phenomenon and has been closely associated with the course of industrialization. Liepmann has suggested that these recurrent daily movements between home and work *supplement* migration and enhance the stability of community structure by contributing to the flexibility of industrial–economic organization. This contribution is most important in effecting adjustments to the changes that occur with the expansion and decline of particular industries, the short–distance relocation of factories, and seasonal fluctuations.[1] It has even been suggested that the daily journey to work might be tending to *supersede* migration as a means of

The study reported here was carried out while the author had a research fellowship in the Metropolitan Community Seminar, Social Science Research Project, University of Michigan.

[330]

adjustment to change, since the lengthening commuting radius of the automobile has reduced the amount of migration necessary within local areas.[2]

The separation of home and work, however, is not without its dysfunctional features. Some attention has been directed toward the possibility of severe physiological and psychological strain upon individual employees who must travel long distances to work. In addition, there have been numerous discussions of the problems of cities themselves, increasingly threatened with a drastic shrinkage of their tax bases. The problems of financing municipal services may be expected to multiply with a continuation of the trend toward decentralization. In addition to the costs of daily movement to the family budgets of modern workers, the costs of elaborate transportation systems to the municipality must be considered. In particular, the initial capital costs of underground and overhead systems in the largest cities are enormous. Added to these, however, are operating expenses, many of which elude exact calculation. Still another increasing cost to the city is that represented by the loss of revenue, arising out of traffic congestion for component business units. A significant proportion of this congestion is brought about by the work trips of persons finding employment within the local area.

The traffic problem has persuaded planners and other interested officials to participate in such efforts as the federal program of origin-and-destination traffic studies. These surveys, jointly supported by federal, state, and municipal funds, have been carried out in a large number of cities, and represent a valuable new source of urban data.[3] With the inception of such studies a large body of by-product material has become available for analysis by social scientists and a fund of research knowledge is being rapidly accumulated.[4]

THE PRINCIPLE OF LEAST EFFORT

In the course of two examinations of the residential locations of industrial employees, it has been asserted that their distribution is the consequence of the operation of an underlying "principle of least effort."[5] An application of this hypothesis to account for the residential distribution of industrial workers was first attempted by Carroll, whose principal argument is "that employees of industrial plants seek to minimize the distance between home and work, and that the aggregate choices of large numbers of employees will tend to produce the observed pattern."[6] More recently, the staff of the Industrial Areas Study, University of North Carolina, has subscribed to this explanatory device.[7]

The weight of Carroll's argument rests upon the observation of a gradient pattern of worker residences by distance from the workplace. "The central thesis of this paper," he says, "is that industrial workers will seek to minimize distance from home to work. This generalization was based on data showing that the number of employees resident in each successive mile zone from the plant site beyond the first few miles diminished as distance was increased."[8] Some attention is given by Carroll to factors other than the possible motives of the industrial employees studied. Some interesting hypotheses pertaining to the possible influence upon residential distribution patterns of such variables as type of industry, wage level, and size of city are presented. In the main, however, these are conceived only as limiting conditions to the operation of the "fundamental principle" of least effort. In Carroll's words:

> It will be sufficient to indicate that, while many factors are involved in the selection of homes and places of work, the persistence of the desire to minimize the distance separating workplace from home acting through each individual worker may be the single element which can create pattern out of the aggregate choices of large numbers of workers. It is, of course, obvious that these choices are differentially limited for each individual worker so that only in large aggregates can patterns begin to appear.[9]

Thus, the cause of the observed gradient distribution is to be found in a single dominating desire experienced by individual workers. It might be argued, however, that should an individual have at his disposal time and money in quantities sufficient to relieve him, to some extent, from the ordinary restrictions imposed by transport costs, he might locate his residence almost anywhere, and for any of a variety of motives. The latter might include, in fact, a desire to maximize the distance between home and work. The least-effort hypothesis appears to confuse motivation with its external limiting conditions.

Even if the foregoing consideration is omitted, however, the least–effort hypothesis remains subject to serious question on logical grounds. If the tendency to minimize effort is assumed to be *constant* throughout the population, it appears that the hypothesis offers a plausible explanation of the *concentration* of residences near work sites, but fails to account for the equally obvious *scatter* away from those sites. This assumption of a constant desire to minimize effort meets still another difficulty if an explanation of change over time is attempted. Given this constant, the antecedent factors responsible for any change must be sought in the external conditions which limit the "basic desire" to minimize effort, for this desire is not conceived as a variable. Thus an explanation, in these terms, of the decentralization movement would appear to require an assumption to the effect that the desire to minimize effort has been on the wane in recent years.

These observations suggest that the factors considered by Carroll as comprising only limitations upon the operation of the least-effort principle may be those worthy of more serious study in their own right. Toward this end, certain findings taken from a study of Flint, Michigan will be presented here.[10]

FINDINGS

The Distance Between Home and Work—The fact that the distribution of worker residences assumes a gradient pattern with respect to distance might have been anticipated on the basis of Carroll's research. The upper panel of Table 1 shows that, in the case of all six plants, the great majority of workers live within six miles of their place of employment. The computation of ratios of workers to resident population,[11] however,

Table 1—Per Cent Distribution and Ratio of Workers to Resident Population of Employees of Principal Industrial Installations in Flint, Michigan, by Distance, 1950

DISTANCE ZONES (IN MILES)	A	B	C	D	E	F	Total
			Industrial Installation				
			Per Cent Distribution				
0–6	80.4	85.2	85.9	84.4	77.5	97.2	83.4
6–12	7.6	5.3	6.0	6.6	9.9	1.3	6.6
12–18	4.6	4.7	5.8	7.0	5.0	0.9	4.9
18–30	5.4	4.2	1.9	1.6	3.8	0.6	3.8
30+	2.0	0.6	0.4	0.4	3.8	....	1.3
Total	100.0	100.0	100.0	100.0	100.0	100.0	100.0
		Number of Workers per 1,000 Resident Population					
0–6	90.2	62.2	36.5	27.3	21.8	13.1	251.1
6–12	63.7	29.1	19.0	16.1	10.8	1.3	140.0
12–18	35.2	23.8	17.2	15.6	10.4	0.9	103.1
18–30	2.7	1.4	0.4	0.2	0.5	a	5.2
30+	0.1	a	a	a	0.1	a	1.9
N	24,700	16,100	9,360	7,130	5,710	2,970	65,970

a. Less than 0.05.

shows that *each plant draws workers from each of the five distance zones in accordance with the number of persons it employs.* The gradient pattern of these ratios in strict accordance with size of plant employment could not be readily deduced from prior suggestions to the effect that the average distance between home and work varies directly with the size of plant employment.[12]

The ratio for the largest plant (A) is seen to decline steadily with distance, reaching a plateau at approximately 18 miles and beyond. The ratios for the remaining plants, however, begin to level off at the second zone, with the decline remaining in strict accordance with the size of plant employment. It is interesting to note that the only one of the smaller plants exerting any pulling power over the area in the last distance zone (plant E) is the newest of the major industrial sites in the Flint area. The tendency for newer and more rapidly expanding industrial installations to draw workers from a wider area has been noted by other investigators.[13]

Thus the size of the plant employment and the length of

time that it has been located at a given site appear to be variables of more than passing interest to one who would explain the residential distribution of industrial employees. Even if viewed as conditions to the operation of some more basic tendency, their importance should not be overlooked.

The Distribution of Workers by Workshift—The fact that the origin-and-destination data used here contain information on the time of arrival at work allows an examination of the spatial distribution of employees working on different shifts.

Table 2—Per Cent Distribution of Employees of Principal Industrial Installations in Flint, Michigan, by Shift, by Distance, 1950

Workshift	0–6	6–12	12–18	18–30	30+	Total
		DISTANCE ZONE (IN MILES)				
First	57.3	50.7	46.3	37.8	22.9	54.5
Second	38.4	45.1	49.4	56.5	68.5	41.1
Third	4.3	4.2	4.3	5.7	8.6	4.4
Total	100.0	100.0	100.0	100.0	100.0	100.0
N	38,530	4,276	3,466	2,457	722	49,451[a]

a. The total number of cases is less than the total in Table 1 because no data were available regarding the workshift of employees who must be assumed to walk to work.

Table 2 summarizes the results of this study. As may be seen, *the proportions of workers on the first (day) shift decline regularly with distance, while the proportions of those employed on the two remaining shifts increase as distance increases.*[14] Again, the least–effort hypothesis suggests nothing in the way of an explanation, for it assumes that the desire to minimize effort is a constant, that is, an attribute of all workers. Certain other possibilities, given no recognition in the development of the least-effort hypothesis, might be considered here.

First of all, it should be remembered that more recently employed workers, those with the least accumulated seniority, are most often assigned to the afternoon and evening shifts. These are the employees hired periodically in response to fluctuations in demand, and represent "marginal workers," a concept widely used in labor force analysis. The relationship found here between workshift and distance suggests the hypothesis that *the "marginal labor force" may also be physically marginal to a given industrial community.*[15]

From the standpoint of the individual worker, residential location some distance from a center might be advantageous in two ways. For one thing, alternative sources of employment in nearby cities are more accessible. Secondly, a mode of adjustment to fluctuation in labor demand is made possible—a way of life promising more security than can be gained through industrial employment alone. Here we refer to the pattern of part–time agriculture discussed in detail by Firey.[16]

Firey identifies a trend toward what can be described as an urbanization of the originally rural population and a ruralization of the urbanites participating in the outward drift from the city. It is his judgment that Genesee County (of which Flint is the center) is one of those counties in Michigan within which the farm population has most fully taken to urban wage employment, while at the same time its decentralizing urban population has begun the practice of extensive gardening and part-time farming in the area surrounding the city. "Thus gardening or part–time farming," he concludes, "has in a certain sense become a way of life for a large proportion of the people in Genesee County. This is particularly true of the zone which immediately surrounds Flint and the radial bands which extend along the paved highways leading outward from the city . . . [for] within this star-like area part-time farming or gardening is the predominant pattern."[17] Whether or not for the same reasons, this pattern has long been established in the continental countries, where great numbers of workers alternate between agricultural and industrial employment during the course of the year.[18] Its emergence in this country is not surprising, since our urban communities have tended to become increasingly market–oriented and, thus, increasingly subject to fluctuations in supply, demand, and employment opportunities.

Proportionately greater difficulty in securing off-season employment is encountered where the units of production are highly specialized or where the occupational specialization of the workers is great. An increase in the size of the production unit may also be expected to result in further difficulties should a temporary shutdown become necessary, since great numbers of workers are released at one time and in one place. The automobile industry, which forms the basis of Flint's economy, serves as an excellent example of this situation. The industry as a whole employs thousands and is, moreover, highly concentrated geographically. "The results," according to one observer, "are aggravated by the sensitive inter-linkages among units, which necessitate that the closing of one unit be followed by the closing of others. Thus, a cessation of activities in the automobile industry throws such large numbers out of work that it is impossible for the community to absorb them in other types of employment . . ."[19]

Perhaps it is this difficulty of finding other full-time employment in nearby industries that encourages the widespread part-time farming by shop workers observed by Firey. Given a location on one of the major arteries leading to the city, a factory worker is within relatively easy access of industrial employment, yet has ample land on which to raise garden crops in sufficient quantity to supplement purchased foodstuffs. Such a practice would be encouraged if he should be employed on either the late afternoon or evening workshift in the plant, for he would then be able to utilize the daylight hours in work on the land. It is even conceivable that great numbers of these workers prefer work on the later shifts, especially during the planting and harvesting seasons when the daylight hours can be used to greater advantage. It should also be remembered that the factories represent a significant source of extra income to persons whose principal occupation is farming and who maintain their rural residence. At any rate, the observed relationship between distance from workplace and the time of work may have as one consequence the stimulation of the pattern of part-time agriculturism discussed here, and it is within this broader community context that the findings might be interpreted.

Ride Sharing and the Ability to Pay Costs of Transportation—Still another matter we might consider is the ability of workers to pay the costs of transportation to and from work.

Table 3 shows that *as distance increases up to approximately 30 miles, the proportion of cars in which only one person is travelling to work declines, while the proportions in which there are two, three, and four or more persons increase. The mean number of passengers per car also increases with distance up to this "breaking point."*[20] One possible explanation for the reversal of the observed tendency in the last distance zone may be found in the widely scattered distribution, at this extreme distance, of those who must regularly travel to the city for employment. Since the area surrounding the central city increases as the square of the radial distance from it, workers are presumably more scattered at this extreme distance, and thus find it more difficult to make ride-sharing arrangements with others.

Table 3—Per Cent Distribution of Cars Travelling to Principal Industrial Installations on Work Trips in Flint, Michigan, by Number of Persons in Car, by Distance, 1950

Number of Persons in Car	DISTANCE ZONE (IN MILES)					
	0–6	6–12	12–18	18–30	30+	Total
One	79.6	62.8	55.3	44.9	61.7	75.0
Two	15.2	24.4	24.7	23.9	16.4	17.0
Three	3.1	7.8	10.2	11.0	6.6	4.3
Four+	2.1	5.0	9.8	20.2	15.3	3.7
Total	100.0	100.0	100.0	100.0	100.0	100.0
Mean	1.29	1.58	1.79	2.24	1.90	1.35
N	18,315	2,038	1,505	812	274	22,944

When considered in an *a priori* manner, ride-sharing might be expected to increase with distance, for such a practice is an effective method of distributing the high costs of automobile transportation.[21] The significance of this practice may be realized when it is remembered that the ability to pay transport costs to and from centers of activity appears to be one of the most critical selective factors in the centrifugal shift of our decentralizing urban population. It might be suggested here that *many family units which otherwise could not participate in the decentralization movement may be able to do so by virtue of such arrangements as ride-sharing. Such a minimization of transport costs, together with the added security obtained by part-time agricultural activities, may account for the presence in these peripheral areas of large numbers of families whose general economic status would otherwise not permit such location.* These are the persons whose scattered residential distribution remains inexplicable when the least–effort hypothesis is utilized.

CONCLUSIONS AND IMPLICATIONS

We have indicated in the foregoing sections certain apparent limitations upon the use of the least–effort hypothesis in this problem area. These limitations, for the most part, appear to be a consequence of the form in which that hypothesis is stated. The postulation of a constant attribute as a fundamental causal factor meets resistance when variation is encountered. The remaining space will be devoted to the consideration of an alternative hypothesis of an intentionally different form.

From one theoretical point of view, the daily journey to work may serve as one of the most easily perceived data in the observation of community organization. As treated by one student of human ecology, the regular ebb and flow of community activity is viewed as itself expressive of community structure. According to Hawley:

> Recurrent movements, as the name indicates, comprise all those movements that are routine and repetitive. They might also be called functional, for it is by this type of movement that the functioning of the community is carried on. . . . Each [of these movements] is an integral part in an established organization and is therefore essential to the maintenance of that organization. Recurrent movements involve no break with the past, no disruption of an established order. They are the means by which an existing equilibrium is maintained.[22]

The increasing *spatial* differentiation of the modern community, of which the separation of home and work is one aspect, might also be considered as reflecting an increasing *functional* differentiation. Such an interpretation assumes, of course, that space presents at least one measurable dimension of community structure. This assumption is, in fact, given formal expression by Hawley when he suggests that "the distribution of the elements of [the physical] structure [of the city] form a pattern of land uses which presumably is expressive of the interdependence among the various activities comprised by the city."[23]

In this spatial pattern, the functional units[24] occupying different sites may be thought of as possessing different locational requirements. One requirement common to all units, of course, is *space itself*, or room in which to operate. But units may differ in the amount of space required. Because space is limited, particularly at the center of an area, those requiring the greatest amounts of space might be expected to locate away from that center. At the same time, any location involves cost to the occupant by virtue of his occupancy. Costs being highest at the center, the units least able to maintain occupancy of sites at the center may be expected to be found at or near the periphery.[25] This cost, however, is not the only one exacted from a unit.

One other key characteristic of any site is the degree of *accessibility* to other units it may have. Units may have quite specifically defined needs for accessibility to other units, and this may be taken as another locational requirement. Just as with space, moreover, this need is fulfilled only at a cost to the unit involved.[26] The cost, in this case, is experienced as the cost of transportation, for either the movement of the members of the unit from the site to another place or for the movement of goods and services to the site occupied.

Two assumptions regarding these costs underlie this discussion. The first is that rent, or the cost of occupancy of a site, *declines with distance* from an activity center. The most frequently observed decline is at a somewhat greater than proportional rate. Secondly, transport costs are assumed to *increase with distance*, at an approximately proportional rate, although significantly modified by the method of transport utilized. If it is then assumed that costs of location represent the sum of these costs, the following hypothesis suggests itself:

The maximum distance from significant centers of activity at which a unit tends to locate is fixed at that point beyond which further savings in rent are insufficient to cover the added costs of transportation to these centers.

It is, perhaps, in the interaction of these two broadly conceived "cost" factors that an explanation of the residential distributions of employees may be found. Units obviously differ in their ability to pay both of these costs, and the family unit is no exception. First of all, the work site may be taken to represent one of the most significant "centers of activity" for the family unit of the employee. Exchanges between the family unit and the production unit at the work site—in the form of the physical movement of the worker—are frequent, so that a certain degree of access is an important requirement. Within this broad range, then, it might be expected that the cost-paying ability of the family unit becomes significant. The area in which any given unit may be able to afford location may also be fairly broad. In the aggregate, however, the area open to families of a given cost-paying ability may be distributed about the relevant centers of activity in such a manner that the gradient pattern of residential distribution becomes readily observable. Since the ability to pay costs of transport and occupancy are conceived as *variables* in this formulation, no difficulty is encountered in the fact of scatter. Indeed, such a gradient distribution would be expected to follow.

It is in the light of this hypothesis that the characteristics of the population participating in the outward drift from the city may be reasonably interpreted. Available census data indicate that the ability to pay transport costs may well be a selective factor in residential decentralization, for peripheral areas of metropolitan districts are found to be occupied by families of higher than average socioeconomic status.[27] In addition to costs of transport, of course, other financial considerations are involved in peripheral location. The entire range of family purchases may be expected to be somewhat more costly in the outlying areas, at least until sufficient densities of population make possible greater economies in the provision of goods and services. These remarks are not intended to imply that the economic aspect of location is the only one that can be identified, or that these costs are somehow the only factors operative. Nor are space and time granted some kind of deterministic role with reference to the location of units of the community. Emphasis is placed upon spatial and temporal relations in this approach for the simple reason that the patterns and processes in which we are interested occur in a space–time context.

In addition to static descriptions of community structure, ecological theory attempts to provide some information upon the processes of change in that structure. The general approach sketched here might also prove useful in an attack upon the problem of change in community organization. The hypothesis suggested above might be utilized in accounting for changes observed in the patterns of population distribution. That important changes have occurred is well known. Although changes in costs of occupancy should not be overlooked, the long–range trend toward residential decentralization can be viewed, in this context, as a consequence of a long–range decline in transportation costs. As such, this interpretation represents a formal statement of the frequent impressionistic observation to the effect that the automobile has "released" population from the immediate confines of the city. At any rate, some attention should be directed toward the development of hypotheses suitable to the description of change, in addition to those which offer only plausible accounts for observations relating to a given point in time, as in the case of the least–effort hypothesis.

With respect to the distribution of other centers of activity significant to the functioning of the family, it has been found that many are located at a lesser average distance than that between home and workplace.[28] The location of these units could also be approached through the use of hypotheses of this general order. Retail shopping centers, for example, might tend to locate at a relatively low average distance from their supporting populations (made up of family units, in the main) by virtue of the necessity for frequent contacts with those populations. The latter need may well be one of the key locational requirements of such units, and the concomitant costs could be treated from the point of view outlined here as those deriving from the necessity for a high degree of accessibility to other units. The study of the location of industrial activities and other work sites might also be approached in this manner. Treatment of the location of *all* units comprising the community would be necessary in a complete description of communal land uses.

In any event, the approach outlined here—although far from entirely satisfactory—might be productive of more general information than would one in which a single observed relationship is given priority out of proportion to its apparent significance. This discussion is intended primarily to indicate that another approach of apparently equal feasibility is possible. The fact that the least–effort hypothesis has happened to dominate the little research already carried out in this problem area should not deter the presentation of alternative modes of explanation.

NOTES

1. Kate K. Liepmann, *The Journey to Work* (New York: Oxford University Press, 1944), pp. 10–19.

2. Amos H. Hawley, *Human Ecology* (New York: The Ronald Press, 1950), p. 337.

3. The survey method is described in some detail in J. F. Harbes, "Urban Origin-and-Destination Traffic Surveys," *Traffic Engineering*, 15 (1945), pp. 296–299; and J. T. Lynch, "Traffic Planning Studies in American Cities," *Public Roads*, 24 (1945), pp. 161–78.

4. A review of available studies using these and other data has been carried out by Donald L. Foley; see his "Urban Daytime Population: A Field for Demographic-Ecological Analysis," *Social Forces*, 32 (1954), pp. 323–30.

5. This hypothesis is given its most detailed elaboration in George K. Zipf, *Human Behavior and the Principle of Least Effort* (Cambridge: Addison-Wesley Press, 1949). A summary exposition may be found in "The Hypothesis of the 'Minimum Equation' as a Unifying Social Principle," *American Sociological Review*, 12 (1947), pp. 627–50.

6. J. Douglas Carroll, Jr., *Home-Work Relationships of Industrial Employees* (unpublished doctoral dissertation, Harvard University, 1950), p. 21. Certain of Carroll's research findings are summarized in "Some Aspects of Home-Work Relations of Industrial Workers," *Land Economics*, 25 (1949), pp. 414–22, and in "The Relation of Homes to Work

Places and the Spatial Pattern of Cities," *Social Forces,* 30 (1952), pp. 271–82.

7. Residential Distribution Patterns of the Workers of Manufacturing Installations and Daytime-Nighttime Differentials in Proportional Distribution of the Total Population of Selected Domestic Urban Areas: Flint, Michigan (unpublished pilot study, Industrial Areas Study, Institute for Research in Social Science, University of North Carolina, 1952), pp. 501–502.

8. *Home-Work Relationships of Industrial Employees,* p. 130.

9. *Ibid.,* p. 24.

10. The data presented below were gathered in the origin-and-destination traffic study carried out in Flint. The author is indebted to the Michigan State Highway Department for the use of these materials. The time of the traffic survey, the summer of 1950, permitted some use of these data in combination with statistics from the decennial census. Flint, a single-industry city, had a population just in excess of 163,000 in 1950. The study reported here was confined to the 66,000 employees of the six Flint plants of the General Motors Corporation: (A) Buick Motor, (B) Chevrolet Motor, (C) Fisher Body, (D) A. C. Sparkplug–Dort Highway, (E) Chevrolet Assembly, and (F) A. C. Sparkplug—Industrial Avenue. Reference will be made to these plants by these letter designations.

11. This ratio, shown in the lower panel of Table 1, is a rough measure of the "pulling power" of each of the plants. A more adequate measure would be one expressing the ratio of workers to the resident population 15–65 years of age. Such a ratio would contain a denominator more closely representative of the actual numbers of potential workers. Unfortunately, the data necessary for the computation of such a ratio for the areal units treated here were not available.

12. Liepmann, *op. cit.*

13. "It is in fact," according to Liepmann, "a common experience that new and expanding works have high proportions of their employees coming from considerable distances, as against more local recruitment by old-established firms." *Ibid.,* p. 15.

14. This same relationship between distance and workshift was found for each of the six individual plants studied, although data for the latter are not presented in this report.

15. Estimates of manufacturing employment in Flint have been made for 1950, which has been identified as an extremely stable year when the magnitude of fluctuation in employment from month to month was at a minimum. These figures approximate the employment of the six General Motors plants under study. Manufacturing employment rose from 63,300 in May to a high of 67,400 in September, and then fell off to 66,400 by November. The difference of 4,100 between the high (September) and low (May) figures provides an estimate of the size of Flint's marginal labor force during this period. (These estimates were abstracted from the Monthly Estimate of the Labor Force prepared by the Flint Office of the Michigan Unemployment Compensation Commission, and appear in the appropriate issues of the *Labor Market Letter* published by that office.)

16. Walter Firey, *Social Aspects to Land Use Planning in the Coun-*

try-City Fringe: The Case of Flint, Michigan (East Lansing: Michigan State Agricultural Experiment Station, Special Bulletin 339, 1946). Although Firey's study was also limited to Flint, a similar pattern has been found in many other areas. See, for example, Nathan L. Whetten and R. F. Field, *Studies of Suburbanization in Connecticut, 2, Norwich: An Industrial Part–time Farming Area* (Storrs: Connecticut State Agricultural Experiment Station Bulletin 226, 1938).

17. *Op. cit.*, pp. 16–17. Statistics revealing the number and size of farm units within the county offer a measure of corroboratory evidence. As farms have increased in number there has occurred a concomitant decrease in their size.

18. Liepmann, *op. cit.*, p. 17.

19. Hawley, *op. cit.*, p. 312.

20. Although not shown in Table 3, the same relationship between distance and the number of persons in the car was found for each of the six individual plants studied.

21. It has been estimated that each mile added to the daily journey to work adds an additional $25.00 to the annual cost of work transportation alone. Richard Dewey, "Peripheral Expansion in Milwaukee County," *American Journal of Sociology*, 54 (1948), p. 121.

22. *Op. cit.*, pp. 326–27. The material upon which the following discussion is based was drawn from a seminar at the University of Michigan conducted by Hawley.

23. *Ibid.*, p. 382.

24. "Functional unit" is used here in a very general sense. It may be tentatively defined as "an organization of activities dependent upon still other activities." In other words, it is the unit referent of which the interdependent community is composed.

25. The usual explanation of this pattern attributes these cost differentials to competitive bidding for sites. The limited quantity of space at the center plays a large role in such an interpretation. See, for example, Edgar M. Hoover, *The Location of Economic Activity* (New York: McGraw-Hill Book Co., Inc., 1948), p. 92.

26. Here, especially, "cost" must not be taken solely in a monetary sense, for costs in time and energy are equally relevant. The term is here conceived in a generic sense, subsuming all of these conceptions.

27. Outlying areas of metropolitan districts have been found to contain significantly greater proportions of persons with the following characteristics: one or more years of college education; self-employed; females not in the labor force; professionals and proprietors, managers and officials. Census of Housing data provide interesting supplementary evidence. Among other differences, the outlying areas have been found to contain higher proportions of one-family, owner–occupied homes, of larger and more recent construction.

28. Trips to 20 other activities have been found to be shorter than work trips. See Donald L. Foley, "The Use of Local Facilities in a Metropolis," *American Journal of Sociology*, 56 (1950), pp. 238–46. See also Carroll, *Home-Work Relationships of Industrial Employees*, pp. 71–4 and 86, where it is noted that "trips to work are short, but shopping, school, and church trips are shorter."

Chapter 20

Three Sources of Data

on Commuting:

Problems and Possibilities

THIS PAPER discusses some methodological problems and research possibilities in the use of three sources of mass data on commuting. If one may judge from the number of recent publications, this is a subject of increasing interest to demographers, ecologists, economists, civil defense authorities, labor market analysts, and planners.

The occasion for this review is the decision of the U.S. Bureau of the Census to collect 1960 data on place of work, the topic most frequently requested by the public in recent years. The United States census—long used as a model by other

This review was originally developed as a working memorandum for a committee of the Population Association of America, comprising Beverly Duncan (University of Chicago), Albert J. Mayer (Wayne State University), and the author. Henry D. Sheldon and Gordon F. Sutton (U.S. Bureau of the Census) served ably as the Bureau's representatives to the committee. Although it has benefited from the group's discussion, the paper expresses the author's opinion and does not necessarily reflect the views of the committee, the Association, or the Bureau.

nations—is one of the few in the Western world that had never previously collected information on the places of work of employed members of the labor force as part of its full–scale operations. (This subject has had a place on the Current Population Survey, but not in the regular decennial enumeration.) However, the 1960 population census finally followed long–established European precedent and added such a question. Another query was directed to the method of transportation used in the work-trip, with both commuting questions appearing on the sample self-enumeration schedule. Automobile ownership was included in the section devoted to housing facilities.

In addition to the sample data from the population census, two other bodies of information are considered here; these are "origin-and-destination" traffic studies, and management records. Although not designed explicitly or exclusively to gather commuting data, they both yield unique items of information appropriate to "secondary analysis." As with the use of any by–product materials, there are obvious disadvantages involved in working with information gathered for different purposes. These purposes—which may have only a tangential relationship with those of the researcher—determine the form of the data. Since the researcher ordinarily has no control over the scope of the coverage, the construction of the instrument, the questions asked, and the coding of the answers, the results are often made available in a form that is inappropriate to his conceptual framework or his practical needs. However, there is a clear advantage, for the use of previously gathered mass data omits the most expensive, time–consuming, and frequently most frustrating phase of research—the period in which data are actually collected. A further advantage of the two non-census sources considered here lies in the fact that most of the data are in readily usable form, with much of the material already on IBM cards. Aside from these general considerations, it will become evident that each of the three main sources of mass data on commuting has certain peculiarities of its own that gives it advantages and disadvantages relative to other sources.

Our purpose here is to compare the three sources of mass data in terms of their utility in different types of research on commuting patterns, particularly within the metropolitan areas of the United States. By and large, emphasis will be placed upon studies that focus upon areally-delineated aggregates; this emphasis reflects the author's research interests and experience. However, some attention will also be given to the uses of these materials in studying the commuting behavior of individuals and whole categories of employees. For the most part, however, the units of analysis to be discussed will be areal segments rather than individual persons or classes (e.g., income or occupational groups).

LAND USE AND MOVEMENT BETWEEN AREAS

Among the really crucial functional prerequisites of modern urban communities are *movement systems*—facilities providing for the physical movement of objects (whether commodities, waste, fuel, power, or people). Certain of these technological systems ordinarily lie beyond the purview of social scientists, e.g., the networks of pipe that supply fuel and water, and that carry away waste products of every description. More narrowly defined, however, transportation and communication systems have been technological items of traditional interest. (Perhaps the greatest theoretical attention has been focused upon transportation by the ecologists, who have come to be preoccupied with spatial distributions of population and land use, as well as their determinants and consequences.)

The modern urban community, of course, is characterized by a complex division of labor, and some writers have pointed out that this complicated network of human relationships is mirrored in the pattern of land uses that obtains. Once this assumption is made, it is possible to view the urban community as a kind of patchwork of specialized parts, easily represented in a map of land uses. These parts are further assumed to be integrated, directly or indirectly, by movement systems. Although we will ignore the detailed processes by which this elaborate fragmentation of land uses came into being in the modern era, it will be worth our while briefly to sketch the main features of the relationship between land use and movement, and more specifically, between land use and commuting. To quote Foley:

> In the contemporary large American city a mosaic of functional areas has evolved seemingly as an inevitable counterpart of the broader fact of economic specialization. Ecologists term this process segregation. So long as a city is characterized by specialization and, specifically, by segregation, we can expect that communication and movement among these divergent functional areas will be necessary if that city is to function as an integrated community. . . . The development of efficient communication devices, particularly the telephone and postal service, has made it possible for much daily activity to be handled without movement of persons. Nevertheless . . . a vast amount of daily travel is necessary . . . [The] movement of persons in the course of carrying out day-to-day activities provides a dynamic mechanism by which the city's various functional areas are linked.[1]

With this background, it is possible to construct a highly simplified but nonetheless useful model of the urban area in its spatial aspect. For the sake of our discussion, we can subdivide the total area into *three* broad types of land—*industrial, commercial,* and *residential.* From the standpoint of commuting to work, the first two types (industrial and commercial) reduce to one, for they are essentially *attracting* areas—i.e., daily streams of commuters flow into them. In contrast, residential areas are *dispersing* areas—reservoirs of manpower, containing the dwelling places of those who staff the enterprises located in other parts of the community. The community, then, can be viewed as containing only *two* types of area—*employing* and *residential*—and workers flow between these areas in visible, measurable streams. This simple conception is obviously related to the distinction made by Liepmann, who identified two fundamental and complementary ways in which to view the journey to work: (*1*) as "conflux at the workplace," by focussing on employing areas, and (*2*) as "dispersal from the dwelling place," by focussing on residential areas.[2] This is not to ignore the significantly different traffic generating characteristics of different types of land use; detailed studies require more precise classifications of land use, such as those discussed in Mitchell and Rapkin.[3]

If we grant some face validity to this simplified model of the daily functioning of the urban community, what do we need to know empirically about the movement of commuters between these two foci—home and work? For even a rudimentary description we appear to require the following: (1) some indication of the *orientation* of these streams, or the direction in which they tend to flow (e.g., centripetal, centrifugal, and lateral); (2) some idea of the *size* of these variously oriented streams, or the sheer number of workers involved; and (3) the functional *composition* of these streams (e.g., the occupational make-up of these aggregates). As we shall see, these are hardly the only questions to be answered, but they provide a logical starting point. What are the uses to which the three sources of mass data can be put in attempts to answer such queries? Moreover, what other questions can be answered by the use of these materials?

TRAFFIC STUDIES

Traffic data comprise the first and perhaps most obvious source of information. In particular, "origin-and-destination" traffic studies appear to be useful. Roughly 150 such studies have been carried out in metropolitan and other urban areas of the United States since 1944, when a standard methodology was developed under federal sponsorship.

The basic design of the "O-D" study is extremely simple. A "cordon line" is arbitrarily drawn around the urban area to be studied. Since it is ordinarily drawn well beyond the legal boundaries of the city, it usually encompasses nearby suburbs, satellites, and densely-settled fringe areas as well. Once this line is established, two separate interview surveys are conducted—the so-called "external" and "internal" surveys.

The External Survey—For inter-area vehicular movements, roadside interviews are conducted on all major highways leading into the study area, with interview stations established at points intersecting the cordon line. Occupants of vehicles passing into, through, and out of the study area are questioned with regard to the origins and destinations—and the purposes —of their trips. (The question on "trip purpose" permits the identification of commuters to work.) The number of occupants of the vehicle is noted, and questions are also asked regarding intermediate stops within the study area, and regarding the place at which the vehicle is usually garaged (typically the home address of the driver in the case of private automobiles).

The Internal Survey—Within the territory arbitrarily defined by the cordon line, an area-probability sample of households is drawn, and home interviews are conducted. The basic goal is to gain a complete description—including origin, destination, purpose, time of arrival and departure—of every vehicular trip made by every person in the household during the preceding day. (Recent surveys have also sought comparable data for those who walk to work.) In addition to the trip data, a limited number of census-type characteristics are listed for each person and household.

We can summarize the most relevant content of the O-D data very briefly. The following items are available from the *internal* (household) survey: the age, sex, race, and occupational status of each trip-maker; for each trip on the sample day, the place of residence, place of trip origin, and place of destination (all coded in terms of blocks, wards, or tracts, and traffic zones); the time of origin and time of destination; the trip purpose and mode of travel utilized; the activity in which the person was engaged just prior to the trip in question; the number of persons in the automobile, if this was the mode of travel utilized; and the number of automobiles operated by the household.

From the *external* (vehicle) survey, the following data are available: the type of vehicle and the number of persons in it; the place where the vehicle is owned or ordinarily garaged, and the place of origin (all coded in terms of external urban places, townships, counties, or states); the place(s) of any intermediate stop(s) within the study area, and the place of ultimate destination (coded the same as internal locations if within the study area); the trip purpose and the purpose(s) of any intermediate stop(s); the route of entrance to or exit from the study area; and the time at which the cordon line was crossed. (In the present discussion, we will largely confine our attention to the internal survey data from the home interviews.)

Table 1—Per Cent Distribution of Employees of Six Principal Industrial Installations in Flint, Michigan, by Workshift and Distance between Residence and Workplace, 1950[a, b]

| | DISTANCE (IN MILES) | | | | | |
Workshift	0–6	6–12	12–18	18–30	30 or More	Total
First	57.3	50.7	46.3	37.8	22.9	54.5
Second	38.4	45.1	49.4	56.5	68.5	41.1
Third	4.3	4.2	4.3	5.7	8.6	4.4
Total	100.0	100.0	100.0	100.0	100.0	100.0
Number of workers	38530	4276	3466	2457	722	49451

a. The same general relationship between distance and workshift was found for each of the General Motors plants in the study.

b. Source: Leo F. Schnore, "The Separation of Home and Work: A Problem for Human Ecology," *Social Forces*, Vol. 32 (May, 1954), Table 2, p. 339. Reproduced by permission of the publisher.

Table 1 illustrates one use of these O-D materials. Since times were recorded in both internal and external surveys, it was possible to identify Flint auto workers according to workshift, and the detailed areal codes permitted their assignment to home–to–work distance zones. The proportions of workers on the first (day) shift decline regularly with distance, while the proportions of those employed on the two remaining shifts increase as distance increases. The managerial practice is to assign more recently employed workers, who have the least seniority, to the afternoon and evening shifts. This means that employees hired periodically in response to fluctuations in demand—or "marginal workers"—are found in disproportionately large numbers at greater distances. Thus, the findings summarized in Table 1 suggest that the "marginal labor force" may also be physically marginal to a given industrial community. In the terms used previously, these materials were viewed from the standpoint of "conflux at the workplace."

There is nothing in the nature of the data, however, to prevent the complementary view from being employed, i.e., "dispersal from the dwelling place." More important, the two views can be used simultaneously, in order to measure the size, direction, and composition of the streams flowing between the various functional parts of the total community area. Another advantage derives from the fact that work-trips can be compared with other types of movements, or "trip purposes." This permits the investigator to place commuting in a broader context of functional movements, for trips to work can be compared with the two next most frequent trip purposes— (1) "social–recreational" and (2) "shopping" and "business" trips—as well as others.

Two other studies drawn from the Flint O-D materials deserve mention here, in that they are not confined to commuting *per se*. Sharp conducted an intensive investigation of the composition of the population in Flint's central business district during the course of a normal day. Commuters to work, of course, represent only part of the day–time population of the central business district, and their hour–by–hour composition shows a number of interesting contrasts with shoppers, those transacting business, seeking recreation, etc. This study provides a new insight into the functioning of the "heart" of the urban area.[4]

Batten used the same basic materials in a more extensive study of Flint, examining the exchanges between the city and its hinterland, in the aggregate and according to specific purposes. It has been frequently suggested that commuter flows provide an especially good operational definition of the true functional boundaries of the community—in contrast with its formal, legal boundaries. (Such a conception, in fact, underlies the "metropolitan" units developed by the Bureau of the Budget and other federal agencies.) Batten's study is particularly interesting in that it provides a rather precise measure of the areal scope of Flint's "pulling power" by identifying its primary zones of interchange; retail trade zones as well as labor market areas are clearly specified.[5]

The study of the commuting behavior of individuals and nonareal aggregates is perhaps more severely limited by the nature of these traffic data, although the length and direction of the work-trip and the method of travel can be analyzed. The main limitation stems from the brief list of personal characteristics gathered, even in the internal survey based on home interviews. Thus O-D data seem most amenable to treatment within some kind of areal framework. The individual commuter can be more effectively studied with another type of mass data, the second to be considered here.

MANAGEMENT RECORDS

A second major source of data on commuting is represented by the employee records assembled and maintained by private business and industry. In the ordinary day–to–day operation of any sizable modern enterprise, a large number of items of information are recorded and kept on file, many of which are relevant for research purposes. Although somewhat less accessible than other sources, these data seem to be particularly appropriate to the study of the individual commuter, and they have been employed in a few investigations.

The following items of information on individual employees are usually available from the management records of the larger commercial and industrial establishments: age, sex, race, detailed occupational title, educational background, income, place of residence, marital status, number of children and other dependents, and date hired (length of service). There is, of course, considerable variation from plant to plant, but this list is probably representative of the great majority of larger enterprises. Many of these items are reported by the applicant at the time of his initial employment. A few of them are stable, in the sense that they need be recorded only once (e.g., sex and date of birth). The majority of items, however, are clearly subject to change during the period of the individual's employment—the more obvious examples include marital status, number of children, occupation, income, and place of residence. But the very fact that these are literally "variables" over a period of time leads to a special advantage for this type of material—the possibility of conducting longitudinal studies by means of continuous or closely-spaced observations.

Two examples of the types of investigation permitted by these data follow. Table 2 shows the distribution of workers according to commuting distance over a period of three decades. There is a notable stability to be observed over most of the period, with the exception of one interval during which the plant underwent rapid expansion, when its average commuting radius lengthened markedly by virtue of the attraction of workers from distant areas.

Table 2—Approximate Commuting Distances of Employees at Plant "X" in Upstate New York, 1921–1951

Distance between Residence and Workplace (Miles)	Date:							
	1921	1925	1930	1935	1940	1944[a]	1946	1951
	Per Cent Distribution							
0– 4.9	85.0	86.8	81.6	80.7	83.6	60.3	65.8	65.0
5–14.9	9.3	9.2	12.3	15.9	12.3	7.9	12.2	13.0
15–19.9	3.5	2.5	3.7	2.2	2.5	13.8	9.9	10.0
20 and over	2.2	1.5	2.4	1.2	1.6	18.0	12.1	12.0
Total	100.0	100.0	100.0	100.0	100.0	100.0	100.0	100.0

a. Employment at the plant more than doubled between 1940 and 1944.
Source: Unpublished company records cited by Leonard P. Adams and Thomas W. Mackesey, Commuting Patterns of Industrial Workers (Ithaca: Cornell University Housing Research Center, 1955), Table IV, p. 15. Reproduced by permission of the authors.

Still another type of investigation that can be effectively carried out with management data is represented in Table 3. In this instance, there can be seen a clear, positive association between income (hourly wage rate at time of hiring) and commuting distance. More important from a methodological standpoint, however, is the possibility of studying changes over time in these variables, i.e., the relationship between increases in the individual's income and changes in the length of his work-trip. This is the type of investigation that represents the truly "dynamic" possibilities of management data. A closely related item that is of special interest is the worker's seniority, or tenure status. It has been suggested that (other things equal) employees with higher seniority tend to live nearer the workplace, while those of shorter tenure live at greater average distance. Many of the latter probably represent former farm operators who are in the process of taking up full–time urban and industrial employment, but who are yet to be fully absorbed into the nonagricultural sector of the economy. Without a firm foothold in the urban economy, many of them appear to be maintaining their old farm residences, carrying on some part–time farming, and commuting considerable distances to work in the shops.[6]

Although we have said that these data recommend themselves to the study of individual commuters, there are other uses for these materials. Given the appropriate circumstances, a comparative study conducted over a period of time could

Table 3—Percentage Distribution of Sample of Newly Hired Factory Workers, by Beginning Hourly Wage Rate and Distance between Residence and Workplace, Franklin County, Ohio, 1940, 1943, 1947, and 1950

Year and Hourly Wage Rate	Number of Workers	Under 4 Miles	4 to 10 Miles	10 Miles or Over	Total
1940					
Below 40¢	113	78.7	19.5	1.8	100.0
40–59¢	138	76.1	16.7	7.2	100.0
60¢ or above	60	50.0	45.0	5.0	100.0
1943					
Below 60¢	1,227	63.4	30.9	5.7	100.0
60–79¢	3,594	26.3	61.0	12.7	100.0
80–99¢	380	22.9	53.2	22.9	100.0
100¢ or above	171	15.2	59.1	25.7	100.0
1947					
Below 80¢	532	73.5	19.7	6.8	100.0
80– 99¢	810	60.1	32.9	7.0	100.0
100–119¢	228	34.6	55.3	10.1	100.0
120¢ or above	110	19.1	56.4	24.5	100.0
1950					
Below 100¢	409	65.5	26.4	8.1	100.0
100–119¢	624	51.0	39.1	9.9	100.0
120–139¢	173	27.2	61.8	11.0	100.0
140¢ or above	105	18.1	54.3	27.6	100.0

Herbert S. Parnes, A Study in the Dynamics of Local Labor Force Expansion (Columbus: The Ohio State University Research Foundation, 1951), p. 176. Reproduced by permission of the publisher.

test at least one hypothesis drawn from Liepmann's work, *viz.*, that (1) communities dominated by expanding industries draw upon an extremely wide labor market, attracting commuters from great distances, while (2) those dependent upon older, established, and more stable industries have a much narrower commuting radius, drawing upon an essentially "local" labor market. Management data might also be particularly useful in observing seasonal shifts between industrial and agricultural activities. This is a firmly entrenched pattern in many European nations, and it has been observed in a number of industrial areas in the United States.

At any rate, the fact that modern management is required to maintain a continuous "inventory" of the work force appears to open up a number of intriguing possibilities for truly dynamic studies of the relationship between place of work and place of residence. In particular, it is possible to relate changes that are likely to take place at both ends of the work–trip. As an example, it seems entirely feasible to study two kinds of mobility with these data; the relationship between occupational and residential mobility could be determined with a fair degree of precision from management records, at least for those whose job changes entail no shift in employer. At the moment, we know relatively little concerning the extent to which these two forms of mobility are linked, and a large part of our ignorance must be attributed to the lack of appropriate data.

Finally, if we assume that the investigator has access to the material, through the cooperation of management, the inclusion of other items of information opens up a whole range of additional research opportunities. A great number of writers have commented upon the presumed stress and strain involved in long–distance commuting. In this context, Liepmann and others have suggested that the length of the work-trip is causally related to the incidence of absenteeism and even illness. Management records on absenteeism and days lost due to illness would provide convenient measures, and—when combined with the basic data on commuting—would permit a test of this hypothesis with other relevant variables (age, etc.) controlled. Questionnaire surveys conducted at the plant, of course, might also be employed to investigate such subjects as methods of travel, ride–sharing, home ownership, part–time farming, attitudes toward commuting, etc.

CENSUS DATA

The great advantage of the U.S. census statistics lies in the sheer scope of their coverage. This is despite the fact that tabulation plans for the 1960 commuting data tend to limit most analyses to the study of "dispersal from the dwelling area." Data for areas as small as census tracts are shown in the tracted portions of SMSA's when the latter are viewed as residential areas; regarded from the standpoint of "conflux at the workplace," some data are shown for counties and the central cities of SMSA's.

As against management records, which are practically confined to larger enterprises, census data have the advantage of covering every type of industry and occupation, including those in which establishments are small and typically characterized by owner operation. Unlike O-D studies, which have been conducted only in urban areas, the census covers the nation and encompasses areas of every type—metropolitan and nonmetropolitan, urban, suburban, fringe, village, and open country. (However, relatively little information on commuting will be made available for nonmetropolitan counties.)

Despite many potential advantages, there are severe limitations on the use of census materials on commuting. For many tabulations, the areal categories in which the workplace data are presented are rather gross. As noted, whole counties and central cities of SMSA's are the smallest areal units recognized in certain series. We can probably anticipate some of the same difficulties that have been experienced with census migration data coded and tabulated in these terms. Moreover, reporting error is apparently a problem of even greater magnitude than in the migration statistics; many people simply do not know the name of the county in which they work, and they are often unaware of whether or not their workplace lies within city limits. (In the light of these facts, it must be conceded that gross areal units like counties are probably justified, because tabulations for smaller areal units would probably contain many more reporting errors. Size of the areal unit and extent of reporting error appear to be inversely related.)

The Bureau of the Census has already experimented extensively with the question on the place of work; some results have been shown in a report from the Current Population Survey. The data were presented in county terms, i.e., the number of employed persons working in the county of residence, in another county, or in another state. Table 4 illustrates the type of results obtained. It can be seen that major industry groups vary considerably in the extent to which their workers engage in intercounty commuting. Agriculture, forestry, and fisheries have understandably low proportions, as do personal services and retail trade. (The latter two categories contain high proportions of female workers, who tend to travel shorter distances to work.) At the other extreme are (1) mining, (2) wholesale trade, and (3) transportation, communication and other public utilities, in which high proportions of employees

Table 4—County of Work and County of Residence, for Workers at Work in the Week Ending September 11, 1954, by Major Industry Group, United States

| Major Industry Group | PER CENT DISTRIBUTION BY COUNTY OF WORK | | |
	Same as County of Residence	Other County or Counties	Same County and Other County or Counties
Agriculture, forestry and fisheries	96.0	2.6	1.4
Mining	70.4	22.2	7.5
Construction	81.1	15.4	3.5
Manufacturing	82.3	16.5	1.2
Transportation, communication, and other public utilities	74.4	15.9	9.7
Wholesale trade	76.5	13.8	9.7
Retail trade	91.0	7.2	1.8
Finance, insurance, and real estate	80.1	15.7	4.2
Business and repair services	87.5	9.8	2.8
Personal services	93.3	5.9	0.8
Entertainment and recreation services	85.7	11.0	3.3
Professional and related services	90.2	8.7	1.1
Public administration	82.9	14.9	2.2
Total	85.9	11.5	2.6

U.S. Bureau of the Census, "County of Work and County of Residence: September 1954," Current Population Reports, Series P-20, No. 60, August 17, 1955, Table 1, p. 3.

cross county and even state lines in the course of their journeys to work. These last two groups, of course, contain large numbers of drivers and deliverymen, the nature of whose jobs occasion long trips.

Another use of these same county-based materials would permit additional information where coding and tabulation follow the schemes previously utilized in some presentations of census migration statistics. Using a Standard Metropolitan Statistical Area (SMSA) as an example, work-trips can be classified (with respect to place of residence) as follows:

1. Same local area (city or county)
2. Other portion of same SMSA
3. Contiguous country outside SMSA
4. Noncontiguous county outside SMSA

The resulting information permits a rough approximation of the distance travelled by individual workers, and can be cross-classified against various personal characteristics. The kind of results to be expected are illustrated on an areal basis by sample data for New York City from the 1954 Current Population Survey cited in Table 4. (These percentages add to slightly more than 100 because workers employed in two or more different counties are counted more than once.)

Live and work in same borough of New York City	61.5%
Live and work in different boroughs of New York City	34.5%
Work elsewhere in New York SMA	4.8%
Work outside New York SMA	0.7%

As we have already noted, at least the central city is distinguished from the outlying "ring" in each SMSA, so that the size, direction, and composition of major commuting streams may be analyzed comparatively. The broad scope of census coverage should permit the testing of such hypotheses as the following: Work-trips in smaller metropolitan areas are mainly oriented to the center, i.e., commuters flow into central workplaces, and out toward peripheral residences. Special tabulations in selected areas might reveal that centrally-ori-

ented movements are relatively less frequent in larger metropolitan areas, where there seem to be significantly heavier
streams of lateral movement between peripheral residential
areas and outlying employing places. In addition to permitting
such studies of the relationship between population size and
commuting movements, the scope of census coverage might
also permit assessment of the importance of physical site
features (e.g., coastal cities versus those situated on level
plains), and of the urban economic base (e.g., industrial versus
trade centers).

The new census data on method of travel to work are also
promising from a research standpoint. For one thing, it is possible to test the common-sense observation to the effect that the
use of public transportation increases with population size and
density, and that such methods of travel are infrequently used
in "post-automobile cities," i.e., those in which the major part
of growth and development has occurred since 1920. (See
Chapter 17.) In addition, different classes of area can be distinguished, and methods of travel identified; Table 5 shows a
type of tabulation that can best be constructed by means of
census data on methods of travel.

Table 5—Plant Location and Method of Travel to Work, 36 Selected Plants, 1942–1943

| Location[a] | Number of Plants | UNWEIGHTED AVERAGE PERCENTAGE OF WORKERS | | |
		Auto and Truck	Bus and Streetcar	Walk
Urban	15	60.6	27.1	7.5
Suburban	14	72.1	17.0	7.2
Rural	7	77.7	17.1	4.7

a. No definitions of urban, suburban, and rural given.
Theodore M. Matson, *War Worker Transportation* (New York: Institute of Traffic
Engineers, 1943), p. 32. Reproduced by permission of the publisher.

One of the major practical uses of census data on workplaces will be the provision of a means of evaluating the delineations of SMSA's. Up to this time, reliance has been necessarily placed upon the availability of local data on commuting,
the existence of which is fortuitous. The only generally avail-

able information is that derivable from records of the Bureau of Employment Security, and these are limited with respect to industrial coverage. Census statistics will afford a precise, albeit *post factum*, assessment of the validity of each area's official delineation. Still another benefit to be derived from the new census statistics is the provision of "benchmark" data for comparison with subsequent censuses. Considerable interest attaches to the question of trends in commuting, but efforts up to this point have had to rely on scattered information and outright speculation, in the absence of reliable standardized data. (See Chapter 18.)

In the foregoing discussion, emphasis has been placed upon the uses of census data in research focussed on areal aggregates. But these materials will have many other uses; the study of individual commuters may be greatly enhanced by the availability of these data. It goes without saying that the great number of personal characteristics regularly gathered in the census include many of the basic variables that the researcher must have. Prior studies based on a variety of sources have shown widely divergent commuting patterns as between age grades, occupational and industry groups, income classes, racial groups, and between the sexes. Both the length of the work-trip and the method of travel have been shown to vary according to these social and economic characteristics, but the research literature reveals numerous contradictions. Although lacking the inherent dynamism to be found in management records, census data should yield invaluable results, particularly in view of the fact that the large number of cases available will permit the application of rigorous control by cross-classification. We should learn a great deal about "the commuter" himself from these new materials.

CONCLUSIONS

A brief comparative evaluation of these three sources of commuting data is in order. We can summarize the main features of the three sets of data for the two main types of study discussed here.

TYPE OF STUDY

Source of Data	Studies of Aggregate Commuting Flows between Areas	Studies of Individual Commuters and Nonareal Aggregates
Traffic Studies	Superior, permitting both points of view (conflux at workplace and dispersal from dwelling area); also permits land use to be related to movement; permits cross-sectional study of other types of movement	Limited by virtue of the cross-sectional character of the data and the few personal characteristics enumerated within study areas
Management Records	Limited to conflux at the workplace, though useful for certain longitudinal investigations that are impossible with the other two sources	Superior, possessing great advantages for longitudinal studies of many relevant personal characteristics; readily supplemented by other items of information (e.g., absenteeism)
Census Data	Potentially superior, though mainly confined to dispersal from the dwelling area; main advantage lies in coverage of many types of area and wide variety of industries; chief limitations derive from practical limits on publication detail	Superior, chiefly due to the wide range of personal characteristics enumerated, although limited to cross-sectional inquiries and subject to practical limitations with respect to published detail

From both the aggregate and individual standpoints, the greatest general potential appears to lie in the census materials, but the practical limits on coding and tabulation detail will probably not permit their maximum utilization. In fact, the limitations appear to be so serious for many important research purposes that we might better turn our attention to the other two sources of commuting data considered here—origin–and–destination traffic studies and management records.

If one is content with a static "snapshot" view—analogous to that provided by census data—then O–D traffic data appear to offer a great deal. Their outstanding advantages derive from the fact that more than simply work-trips can be examined, and that commuting can be viewed from two complementary perspectives—conflux at the workplace and dispersal from the dwelling place. One can observe a large part of the urban and metropolitan area, and one can link aggregate flows to the land uses that generate them. Depending upon the date at which the survey is taken, these traffic data can be combined in various ways with census data. However, if one is interested in the individual as the unit of analysis, these data have more restricted utility. This limitation is mainly due to the limited number of personal characteristics gathered in the survey, but it is also a result of the fact that these items are typically confined to the "internal" phase of the survey.

As we have tried to indicate, the great virtue of management records lies in the possibility of longitudinal studies, e.g., relating residential and occupational mobility. Although this potential has yet to be realized, it appears certain that the study of individual commuters would have a more appropriate starting point with these data than with the other two sources, especially if it would be feasible to add items of information. They seem to offer less to any researcher inclined to use areal units of analysis, because they are limited to the view identified here as "conflux at the workplace."

It should be evident that this evaluation would be far different if undertaken from other points of view, for the criteria would necessarily shift. However, it is hoped that this discussion will serve to suggest further uses of traffic data and management records; their value as sources of data can only be accurately judged after we have accumulated further experience with them in actual empirical studies, whether focussed upon areas or individual workers. These data are not widely used at the present time for purposes of scientific research, and it might be worth some effort to give them more careful consideration as sources of information on commuting, at least as a supplement to national census statistics.

NOTES

1. Donald L. Foley, "Urban Daytime Population: A Field for Demographic-Ecological Analysis," *Social Forces,* 32 (May, 1954), pp. 323–24.

2. Kate K. Liepmann, *The Journey to Work: Its Significance for Industrial and Community Life,* New York and London: Oxford University Press, 1944.

3. Robert B. Mitchell and Chester Rapkin, *Urban Traffic: A Function of Land Use*, New York: Columbia University Press, 1954.

4. Harry P. Sharp, *The Non-Residential Population of the Central Business District of Flint, Michigan*, Ann Arbor: University of Michigan, Social Science Research Project, 1954; see also his article on "The Non-Residential Population of the Central Business District," *Land Economics*, 31 (November, 1955), pp. 378–81.

5. Thelma F. Batten, *Flint and Michigan: A Study in Interdependence*, Ann Arbor: University of Michigan, Social Science Research Project, 1955.

6. See Leo F. Schnore, "The Separation of Home and Work: A Problem for Human Ecology," *Social Forces*, 32 (May, 1954), pp. 336–43.

Name Index

Subject Index